Voices from Srebrenica

Voices from Srebrenica

*Survivor Narratives
of the Bosnian Genocide*

Ann Petrila *and*
Hasan Hasanović

Foreword by Emir Suljagić

McFarland & Company, Inc., Publishers
Jefferson, North Carolina

Library of Congress Cataloguing-in-Publication Data

Names: Petrila, Ann, 1956– author. | Hasanović, Hasan, 1975– author. | Suljagić, Emir, writer of foreword.
Title: Voices from Srebrenica : survivor narratives of the Bosnian Genocide / Ann Petrila and Hasan Hasanović ; foreword by Emir Suljagić.
Other titles: Survivor narratives of the Bosnian Genocide
Description: Jefferson, North Carolina : McFarland & Company, Inc., Publishers, 2021 | Includes bibliographical references and index.
Identifiers: LCCN 2020040781 | ISBN 9781476683348 (paperback : acid free paper) ∞
ISBN 9781476641645 (ebook)
Subjects: LCSH: Yugoslav War, 1991–1995—Atrocities—Bosnia and Herzegovina—Srebrenica. | Yugoslav War, 1991–1995—Personal narratives, Bosnian. | Genocide survivors—Bosnia and Herzegovina—Srebrenica. | Genocide—Bosnia and Herzegovina—Srebrenica. | Muslims—Persecutions—Bosnia and Herzegovina—Srebrenica. | Srebrenica (Bosnia and Herzegovina)—History—20th century.
Classification: LCC DR1313.32.S68 P48 2020 | DDC 949.703—dc23
LC record available at https://lccn.loc.gov/2020040781

British Library cataloguing data are available

ISBN (print) 978-1-4766-8334-8
ISBN (ebook) 978-1-4766-4164-5

© 2021 Ann Petrila and Hasan Hasanović. All rights reserved

No part of this book may be reproduced or transmitted in any form or by any means, electronic or mechanical, including photocopying or recording, or by any information storage and retrieval system, without permission in writing from the publisher.

Front cover image Pilica Cultural Center execution site (photograph Kristian Skei)

Printed in the United States of America

McFarland & Company, Inc., Publishers
Box 611, Jefferson, North Carolina 28640
www.mcfarlandpub.com

To those who survived
the Srebrenica genocide
and to those who did not

"We must always take sides. Neutrality helps the oppressor, never the victim. Silence encourages the tormentor, never the tormented."
—Auschwitz survivor Elie Wiesel

Table of Contents

Acknowledgments	ix
Acronyms	1
Definitions	2
People and Places	5
Maps	12
Timeline	15
Foreword by Emir Suljagić	17
Preface by Ann Petrila	19
Introduction	27

Part I. Narratives

1. Execution Site Survivors — 36
   Ahmo Hasić 36
   Hakija Huseinović 44
   Mevludin Orić 50
   Nedžad Avdić 62

2. Death March Survivors — 81
   Dr. Fatima Dautbašić-Klempić 81
   Hasan Sejfo Hasanović 90
   Hasan Aziz Hasanović 103
   Haso Hasanović 113
   Ramiz Nukić 119

3. UN Base Survivor — 125
   Nesib Mandžić 125

4. Mothers of Srebrenica — 132
   Hajra Ćatić 132
   Nura Mustafić 143
   Saliha Osmanović 150

5. Human Rights Activists — 157
   Žarko Korač 159
   Staša Zajović 165
   Sonja Biserko 172
   Nataša Kandić 177

Table of Contents

Part II. Aftermath

6. Response — 184
    Mass Graves 184
    International Criminal Tribunal for the Former Yugoslavia (ICTY) 185
    The International Commission on Missing Persons (ICMP) 186
    Women's Associations 188
    The Srebrenica-Potočari Memorial Center and Cemetery 189

7. Ramifications — 193
    Psychological Responses to War and Genocide 193
    Treatment of Psychological Issues 199
    Sexual Violence 199

8. The Responsibility of the International Community — 203
    Failure to Protect 203
    Dayton Peace Agreement 209
    Failure to Deliver Justice 211

9. Lessons Learned — 214
    Nationalism 214
    Hate Groups 215
    Genocide: Theory and Prevention 216

Conclusion: Moving Forward — 220

Chapter Notes — 223

Bibliography — 227

Index — 239

Acknowledgments

We could not have written this book without the help and support of so many magnificent people in our lives. We thank all of you. To our families for their patience while we focused on this book for a very long time: Ben, Ellen, John, Amy, Jim, and Judy Petrila; Nermina, Dženita, Omer, and Sabra Hasanović. Many of them also gave generously of their time in reading draft after draft of chapters, along with Emily Gamm, Monica Green and especially Cat Galley. Thank you to our student assistants who were invaluable in helping with research and countless other tasks: Claire Marrow, Kelly Reeves and Kylie Bovenzi. To Dean James Herbert Williams and Dean Amanda Moore McBride for their ongoing support and encouragement. And to Dr. Emir Suljagić and Hasan Nuhanović. To those who housed us and fed us in Bosnia: Anesa and her parents in Srebrenica, Raza and Šefko at Hotel Kovači in Sarajevo, and Hasan's mother in Lukavac. Thank you to Kristian Skeie for the generous use of his photographs and to Michael Bowers for drawing original maps for us to use. To Duška Jurišić for connecting us with the human rights advocates in Serbia, Amir Kulaglić for explaining REKOM in a way that we understood, and Jimmye Warren for unraveling the mysteries of joint criminal enterprise. Šefik Suljić our friend and driver who took care of us in innumerable ways. To Sladjana Todorovic who has been a support every step of the way. To Layla Milholen, managing editor at McFarland, for her wisdom, patience and most of all for caring about these stories and the people who lived through this genocide. And to our friends, many thanks for encouraging us and waiting for us to reappear—you know who you are.

Most importantly, we must express our gratitude to those who courageously agreed to be interviewed for this book, for their stories to be heard so that justice might be better served.

Acronyms

APC: Armored personnel carrier
BiH: Bosnia and Herzegovina
BSA: Bosnian Serb Army
CANBAT: Canadian Battalion
DUTCHBAT: Dutch Battalion
EU: European Union
HR: High Representative
ICC: International Criminal Court
ICJ: International Court of Justice
ICMP: International Commission on Missing Persons
ICTY: International Criminal Tribunal for the former Yugoslavia
IFOR: Implementation Force, NATO, and Russia
JNA: Yugoslav People's Army
MSF: Médicins Sans Frontières (Doctors Without Borders)
NATO: North Atlantic Treaty Organization
NGO: Nongovernmental organization
OHR: Office of the High Representative
OSCE: Organization for Security and Cooperation in Europe
RECOM/REKOM: Regional Commission
RS: Republika Srpska
UN: United Nations
UNDP: United Nations Development Program
UNESCO: United Nations Educational, Scientific and Cultural Organization
UNHCR: United Nations High Commissioner for Refugees
UNPF: United Nations Peacekeeping Force
UNPROFOR: United Nations Protection Force
USAID: United States Agency for International Development
WIB: Women in Black

Definitions

Bosniak
Bosnian Muslims.

Bosnian Army
Armed forces of Bosnia and Herzegovina, official military force of the BiH state.

Bosnian Serb Army (BSA)
Paramilitary established by Bosnian Serb rebels, controlled by Radovan Karadžić and Ratko Mladić.

Canadian Battalion
UN Peacekeepers who arrived in Srebrenica on April 18, 1993.

Chetniks
Originally a term for a Serbian nationalistic guerrilla force formed in Serbia during World War II. Became a term used to describe Serb forces in Bosnia during the 1990s war.

Column
Single-file line of moving people.

Dayton Peace Agreement
Officially called *The General Framework Agreement for Peace in Bosnia and Herzegovina*, this is the agreement that officially ended the war. It is also known as Dayton, the Dayton Agreement, the Dayton Accords and the Dayton Peace Accords.

Death March
Sixty-mile (100 kilometer) walk through the forest from Srebrenica to Tuzla made by approximately 12,000 men and boys attempting to escape the genocide in July 1995.

Dutch Battalion
UN Peacekeepers who arrived in Srebrenica at the end of January 1994 to replace the Canadian Peacekeepers.

Enclave
Territory that is completely surrounded by the territory of one other state or parastate.

European Union
International organization comprised of 27 European countries which governs common economic, social, and security policies.

Genocide
Specific acts committed with intent to destroy, in whole or in part, a national, ethnic, racial or religious group.

High Representative (HR)
Oversees the Office of the High Representative (OHR). Appointed by the UN Security Council, is from the international community.

Implementation Force (IFOR)
NATO-led multinational force in Bosnia with a one-year mandate starting on December 20, 1995.

International Commission on Missing Persons (ICMP)
Organization that works with governments, civil society organizations, justice institutions, international organizations and others throughout the world to address the issue of people who have gone missing as a result of armed conflict, human rights abuses, disasters, organized crime, irregular migration and other causes.

International Criminal Tribunal for the former Yugoslavia (ICTY)
United Nations court of law that dealt with war crimes that took place during the 1990s Balkan conflicts. Its mandate lasted from 1993 to 2017.

JNA
Yugoslav People's Army. Military of Yugoslavia from 1945 to 1992. In Bosnia, taken over by the Bosnian Serbs and became the Bosnian Serb Army (BSA).

Médecins Sans Frontières—Doctors Without Borders
International, independent medical humanitarian organization that provides medical assistance to people affected by conflict, epidemics, disasters, or exclusion from healthcare.

Municipality
A region similar to a county.

Non-Governmental Organization (NGO)
Nonprofit organization that operates independently of any government, typically one whose purpose is to address a social or political issue.

North Atlantic Treaty Organization (NATO)
Created in 1949 by the United States, Canada, and several Western European nations to provide collective security against the Soviet Union.

Office of the High Representative (OHR)
Created under the Dayton Peace Agreement, OHR is an ad hoc international institution responsible for overseeing the implementation of civilian aspects of the Peace Agreement.

Organization for Security and Cooperation in Europe (OSCE)
World's largest regional security organization, with 57 participating states in North America, Europe and Asia. Works for stability, peace and democracy.

Peace March
Annual walk retracing the footsteps of men and boys from the Death March. Starts in Nezuk and ends in Potočari at the Genocide Memorial. Thousands participate every year. It is part of the annual July 11 Commemoration at the Memorial.

Playground massacre
April 12, 1993, on the playground of the Srebrenica primary school, 74 people were

killed and 100 wounded by the BSA. All were civilians and most were teenagers and children.

Rome Statute
 The international treaty which created the International Criminal Court (ICC) and defined war crimes, crimes against humanity, genocide, and aggression.

Safe Area
 UN designated area that should be free from any armed attack or any other hostile act and have unimpeded delivery of humanitarian assistance. There were six designated UN Safe Areas in Bosnia: Bihać, Goražde, Sarajevo, Srebrenica, Tuzla and Žepa.

Tuzla Gate massacre
 On May 25, 1995, annual Youth Day in Tito's Yugoslavia, the BSA launched an artillery attack against the town of Tuzla. The attack left 71 dead and 240 wounded, many of them children and teenagers who were outdoors in the city.

United Nations High Commission for Refugees (UNHCR)
 Organization that works to protect and assist refugees around the world.

United Nations Peacekeeping Force (UNPROFOR)
 Initially established in Croatia to ensure demilitarization of designated areas. Mandate was later extended to Bosnia and Herzegovina to support delivery of humanitarian relief, monitor no-fly zones and Safe Areas.

United Nations Protection Force (UNPROFOR)
 United Nations Peacekeeping Force in Bosnia and Herzegovina.

United States Agency for International Development (USAID)
 Humanitarian and disaster relief organization.

Yugoslav People's Army
 Also known as the JNA. Military of Yugoslavia from 1945 to 1992. In Bosnia, taken over by the Bosnian Serbs and became the Bosnian Serb Army (BSA).

People and Places

*Indicates people who were interviewed for this book.

People

Avdić, Nedžad *
One of two survivors from the Petkovci Dam execution site. Was a protected witness at the ICTY.

Biserko, Sonja *
Founder and president of the Helsinki Committee for Human Rights in Serbia. She has been a senior fellow in the United States Institute of Peace as well as part of many other organizations around the globe. She has received numerous international awards and was one of the 1,000 Women for Peace nominated for the Nobel Peace Prize.

Ćatić, Hajra *
Mother who survived the genocide. Instrumental in development of the first Women's Association and the Genocide Memorial. Her son Nino was an amateur radio operator and his broadcast was the last communication out of Srebrenica as it was falling. He is still missing.

Ćatić, Nino
Hajra's son, amateur radio operator who sent the famous last broadcast from Srebrenica. He is still missing.

Dautbašić-Klempić, M.D., Fatima*
Genocide survivor. Just one year out of medical school when she became one of six doctors serving 50,000 people in the hospital in war-torn Srebrenica.

Hasanović, Hasan Aziz *
Coauthor of this book. Director of Research at the Srebrenica-Potočari Genocide Memorial. Death March survivor.

Hasanović, Hasan Sejfo *
Death March survivor. Famous footage of him carrying his dead brother into the free territory.

Hasanović, Haso *
Death March survivor. Witnessed executions at Kravica. Was a protected witness at the ICTY.

Hasić, Ahmo *
Branjevo Farm execution site survivor. Was a protected witness at the ICTY. Was in his 80s and lived abroad when we interviewed him. Now deceased.

Huseinović, Hakija *

One of two survivors from the Kravica Warehouse execution site. Was a protected witness at the ICTY.

Husić, Sabiha*

Director of Medica Zenica, an organization that promotes justice and support services for survivors of sexualized wartime violence in Bosnia and Herzegovina. In 2014, she received the Woman of the World Award in New York from the women's rights organization Women for Women.

Izetbegović, Alija

Elected president of Bosnia and Herzegovina in 1990.

Kandić, Nataša *

Serbian human rights activist and founder/executive director of the Humanitarian Law Center, Belgrade, Serbia. Located and turned over an important video of Bosnian Serb paramilitary Scorpions executing six Bosnian Muslim prisoners. Nominated in 2018 for the Nobel Peace Prize by two members of the U.S. Congress.

Karadžić, Radovan

Bosnian Serb politician, trained as a psychiatrist, served as the first president of RS from 1992 to 1996. Fugitive for 12 years hiding in plain sight working as an alternative medicine practitioner in Belgrade. Convicted by the ICTY of genocide in Srebrenica, war crimes, and crimes against humanity, on March 24, 2016.

Karremans, Thomas

Commander of Dutchbat troops in Srebrenica at the time of the genocide.

Korač, Žarko *

Longtime member of the Serbian Parliament. He is a Serbian psychologist and politician who was deputy prime minister in the Government of Serbia between 2001 and 2004, and was briefly acting prime minister after Prime Minister Zoran Djindjić was assassinated in 2003.

Mandžić, Nesib *

Genocide survivor. School director in Srebrenica, chosen to represent the Bosnian Muslims as a negotiator with Ratko Mladić. Famous footage of these meetings from July 11 to 12, 1995, in Hotel Fontana in Bratunac.

Milošević, Slobodan

Yugoslav and Serbian politician who served as the president of Serbia from 1989 to 1997, and president of the Federal Republic of Yugoslavia from 1997 to 2000. Charged by the ICTY with 10 counts of crimes against humanity in Croatia, 27 counts of war crimes and crimes against humanity in Bosnia, as well as genocide and complicity in genocide. Also charged with war crimes in Kosovo. Died in his prison cell on March 11, 2006. First sitting head of state to be charged with war crimes.

Mladić, Ratko

Bosnian Serb military leader who commanded the Bosnian Serb Army during the Bosnian War. Fugitive for 16 years until found in Serbian village of Lazarevo 60 miles (100 kilometers) northeast of Belgrade. Convicted by the ICTY of genocide in Srebrenica, war crimes and crimes against humanity on November 22, 2017.

Morillon, Philippe
Commander of United Nations Protection Force (UNPROFOR) in Bosnia from 1992 to 1993.

Mustafić, Nura *
Mother who survived the genocide. Her husband and all three sons were killed. One son is still missing.

Nuhanović, Hasan
Genocide survivor, former UN interpreter, author of two books, a human rights activist, and a researcher.

Nukić, Ramiz *
Death March survivor. Kamenice Hill massacre occurred on a hill above his home. He has returned there and spends his days looking for human remains which he turns over to the ICMP.

Omanović, Ćamila
Genocide survivor. Negotiator with Mladić, tried to hang herself in the Battery Factory. ICTY witness. Later worked for the Memorial as an accountant.

Orić, Mevludin *
One of three survivors from the Orahovac execution site.

Orić, Naser
Commander of the Srebrenica defense from April 1992 to March 1995.

Osmanović, Saliha *
Mother who survived the genocide. Her husband, Ramo, and both sons were killed. Ramo is famous because he was filmed by the BSA when he was forced to call his son down from the Death March to surrender. She has testified several times, including against Mladić at the ICTY where she refused to be a protected witness.

Zajović, Staša *
Co-founder and coordinator, Women in Black, Serbia. A feminist peace activist, she has been the initiator, organizer, and active participant in all antiwar actions, peace marches and other Women in Black street actions since 1991. She has received numerous international awards. In 2005, she was nominated for the Nobel Peace Prize as part of the 1,000 Women for Peace campaign.

Places

Batković Concentration Camp
Located in Bijeljina, Bosnia 59 miles (95 kilometers) northwest of Srebrenica. First concentration camp in the Bosnian War. Run by Bosnian Serb authorities from April 1992 to January 1996. Prisoners were predominantly Bosnian Muslims, deprived of food and water, and tortured.

Battery Factory
Former state-owned factory in Potočari which became the site of the main UN base.

Belgrade
   Capital of Serbia.

Bihać
   Town on the banks of river Una in northwest Bosnia, 180 miles (290 kilometers) from the capital, Sarajevo. Proclaimed a UN Safe Area in May 1993.

Bijeljina
   Town in northeast Bosnia, located 53 miles (85 kilometers) from Srebrenica.

Branjevo
   Execution site. Village that contained an ex-military pig farm. Located 52 miles (84 kilometers) northwest of Srebrenica.

Bratunac
   Town located 6 miles (10 kilometers) from Srebrenica.

Bravo Base
   A small UN base on the outskirts of Srebrenica, located in a former embroidery plant. Occupied by the Canadian Peacekeepers followed by the Dutch.

Buljim
   Hill situated approximately 6 miles (10 kilometers) west of Srebrenica where the Death March started.

Burnice
   Village 15 miles (25 kilometers) north of Srebrenica in the municipality of Bratunac.

Charlie Base
   Main Dutch UN base located in the former Battery Factory in Potočari, about a mile (1.6 kilometers) from Srebrenica.

Drina River
   River in eastern Bosnia that is the natural border between Bosnia and Serbia.

Dubrave
   Village in the municipality of Živinice which housed the airport and a UN base during the war. Became a UNHCR site for refugees coming from Srebrenica. Also the name of the airport. Located nine miles (15 kilometers) from Tuzla.

Federation of BiH
   One of two political entities that compose Bosnia and Herzegovina, populated primarily by Bosnian Croats and Bosniaks. It has its own capital, government, president, parliament, police and education departments. The other entity is the Republika Srpska.

Foča
   Town and municipality approximately 88 miles (142 kilometers) south of Srebrenica. Site of a notorious rape camp where Muslim women were systematically raped during the war. This camp was run by the BSA, Bosnian Serb authorities, and the RS police.

Goražde
   Town designated as a UN Safe Area in May 1993 approximately 60 miles (96 kilometers) from Srebrenica.

Hotel Fontana
   Located in Bratunac, the site of three meetings with Ratko Mladić on the evenings of July 11 and 12, 1995.

Jadar River
Small river in eastern Bosnia that runs through municipalities of Srebrenica, Bratunac and Milići.

Kamenice Hill
Hill above the home of Ramiz Nukić, site of the July 13 ambush. Last place that many people on the Death March saw members of their family. Approximately 12 miles (20 kilometers) west of Srebrenica.

Kladanj
Town and municipality located approximately 46 miles (75 kilometers) west of Srebrenica.

Konjević Polje
Village located 15 miles (25 kilometers) west of Srebrenica. Important intersection that was cut off by the BSA starting July 13, 1995, to force those on the Death March to surrender.

Kozluk
Execution site and mass grave site which is now a trash dump. A village located 42 miles (68 kilometers) west of Srebrenica.

Kravica Warehouse
Agricultural warehouse that became a major execution site beginning July 13, 1995. Located in Kravica village, 14 miles (23 kilometers) west of Srebrenica.

Lolići
One of many small villages that people crossed through after surrendering on the Death March. Located 15 miles (25 kilometers) west of Srebrenica.

Milići
Town located 29 miles (47 kilometers) west of Srebrenica.

Nezuk
Village where survivors of the Death March came out of the woods. It was defended by Bosnian forces and remained a free territory throughout the war. It is located 22 miles (37 kilometers) from Tuzla.

Nova Kasaba
Small town between Konjević Polje and Milići where people surrendered. Currently a soccer field, the only place where people were killed or buried in 1995 that has any type of memorialization. It is 22 miles (35 kilometers) west of Srebrenica.

Orahovac
Execution site that is now a corn field next to a railway bridge, 39 miles (64 kilometers) west of Srebrenica.

Petkovci Dam
Execution site. It is a dam for a nearby aluminum factory and is located 39 miles (63 kilometers) northwest of Srebrenica.

Petkovci School
School where prisoners were held before their executions and some were killed there. It is currently a public elementary school located 39 miles (63 kilometers) northwest of Srebrenica.

Pilica Cultural Center
Execution site located 52 miles (85 kilometers) from Srebrenica.

Potočari
Village halfway between Bratunac and town of Srebrenica, 3.7 miles (6 kilometers) from Srebrenica. Site of the old Battery Factory, the main UN base and the Srebrenica Memorial Center.

Republika Srpska (RS)
One of the two entities that compose Bosnia and Herzegovina, populated primarily by Bosnian Serbs. It has its own capital, government, president, parliament, police and education departments. The other entity is the Federation of Bosnia and Herzegovina.

Sandići meadow
Approximately 2,000 men and boys from the Death March surrendered and were taken to this meadow which is 14 miles (24 kilometers) west of Srebrenica. It is very close to the Kravica Warehouse execution site and also close Ramiz Nukić's home. The majority of prisoners were taken to Kravica Warehouse and killed.

Sarajevo
Capital of Bosnia.

Srebrenica
Municipality and town in eastern Bosnia. Under siege by the BSA from 1992 to 1995. Became home to approximately 50,000 refugees from eastern Bosnia from 1992 to 1993. In early 1993, the UNHCR evacuated 10,000 refugees to Tuzla. From 1993, 40,000 refugees lived in Srebrenica until it fell to the BSA on July 11, 1995.

Sućeska
Area in Srebrenica municipality comprised of many villages. Eight miles (13 kilometers) southwest of Srebrenica.

Šušnjari
Village in Srebrenica municipality, located beneath Buljim, the hill where the Death March began. Six miles (10 kilometers) west of Srebrenica.

Tuzla
City 65 miles (105 kilometers) from Srebrenica. It remained a free territory, and was a multi-ethnic city throughout the war, which it still is today. The goal of those on the Death March was to reach Tuzla.

Udrč Mountain
Those on the Death March had to climb this mountain, the highest in the region at 3,400 feet (1,040 meters). From the top they could see the free territory of Tuzla. It is 24 miles (40 kilometers) from Srebrenica.

Vukovar
City in eastern Croatia, devastated by Serb paramilitary units and the JNA at the beginning of the Croatian war in November 1991.

Zagreb
Capital of Croatia.

Žepa
Village that became a UN Safe Area, 43 miles (70 kilometers) from Srebrenica.

Živinice
Town and municipality 10 miles (16 kilometers) from Tuzla. Dubrave airport is located there.

Zvornik
Town and municipality 31 miles (50 kilometers) from Srebrenica.

Maps

The former Yugoslavia (Michael Bowers).

Bosnia and Herzegovina today (Michael Bowers).

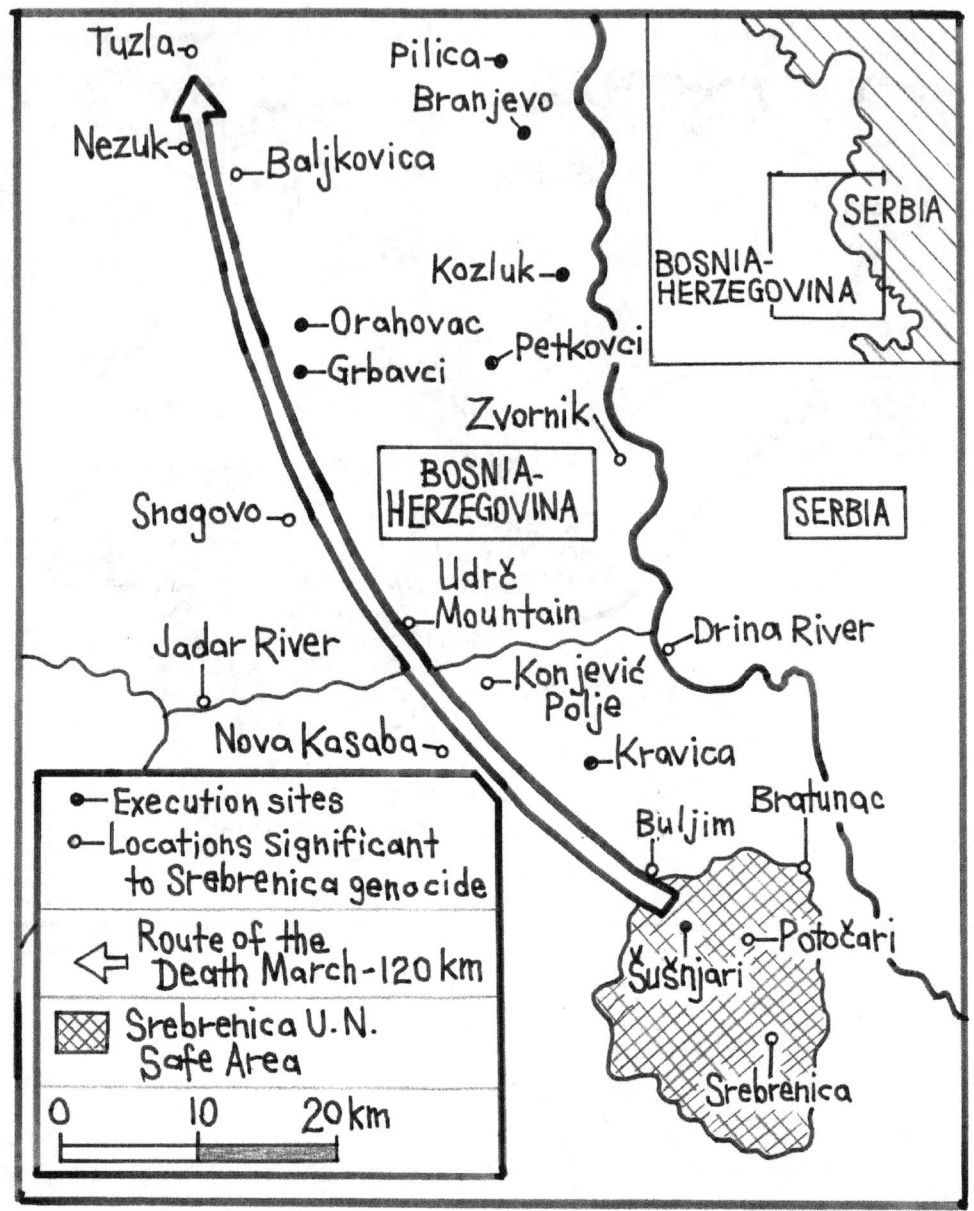

Srebrenica Death March and execution sites, 1995 (Michael Bowers).

Timeline

Bosnia and Herzegovina Timeline

Bosnia was part of the Roman Empire

Slavs began settling the region during the 7th century

Bosnia was first mentioned in the mid–10th century

1200: Independent state of the Kingdom of Bosnia

1463: Ottoman Empire conquered Bosnia

1906: Birth of the "Greater Serbia" ideology

1908: Austro-Hungarian Empire annexed Bosnia and Herzegovina

June 28, 1914: A Bosnian Serb nationalist, Gavrilo Princip, assassinated Austrian Archduke Franz Ferdinand and his wife, Sophie, in Sarajevo, precipitating World War I

1918: The Kingdom of the Serbs, Croats, and Slovenes was formed as a result of World War I, renamed Yugoslavia in 1923

1941–1945: Bosnia and Herzegovina occupied by Nazi Germany

1945: Liberated by partisans under Josip Broz Tito. Part of Socialist Federal Republic of Yugoslavia along with Slovenia, Croatia, Macedonia, Montenegro, and Serbia with two Autonomous Provinces, Vojvodina and Kosovo

May 4, 1980: Tito died without a succession plan

1990–1991: Following the collapse of the Soviet Union, Yugoslavia started to disintegrate; Slovenia and Croatia declared independence

January 9, 1992: Bosnian Serbs declared their own parastate within Bosnia, the Republika Srpska

March 1, 1992: Bosnia and Herzegovina gained independence

April 1992: Serb forces launched full-scale war in Bosnia and Herzegovina supported by Slobodan Milošević's regime from Belgrade, Serbia

Ethnic cleansing and occupation of eastern Bosnia began

April 12, 1993: Srebrenica playground massacre

April 16, 1993: UN Security Council declared Srebrenica a UN Safe Area

April 18, 1993: Canadian battalion of the UN arrived in Srebrenica

January 1994: Dutch battalion of the UN replaced Canadians

1995 Genocide

March: Radovan Karadžić issued Directive 7 which set the stage for genocide

July 6–10: Attacks on Srebrenica intensified, civilians began fleeing

July 11: Srebrenica fell to Bosnian Serb forces. Thousands of civilians fled to the main Dutch UN base in Potočari. Majority of men and boys headed through the woods toward the free territory of Tuzla, an event known as the Death March

July 12 and 13: In Potočari, women and children were deported while men and boys were separated and subsequently killed

July 13–16: Bosnian Serb Army hunted those in the woods capturing thousands and taking them to detention centers. They were subsequently taken to execution sites where they were massacred and hidden in mass graves. Ultimately over 8,000 were killed

July 16: After six days and nights, over 60 miles (100 kilometers), survivors of the Death March began to arrive in the free territory of Nezuk near Tuzla

August–September: Bosnian Serb Army and the Republika Srpska Government relocated human remains from primary mass graves to secondary and tertiary mass graves in an attempt to cover up the genocide

December 14: Dayton Peace Agreement signed ending the war in Bosnia and Herzegovina

Foreword
by Emir Suljagić

Voices from Srebrenica by Ann Petrila and Hasan Hasanović tells the story of the Srebrenica genocide through the personal accounts of fourteen genocide survivors and five human rights activists. Through individual narratives, this work forges an authentic personal connection between the reader and those with first-hand experience of the violence which took place in Srebrenica. These personal connections are the best way to ensure that "never forget" and "never again" become more than just catchphrases; that the flame of remembrance and prevention is kindled in the hearts of all those who come into contact with these harrowing stories of trauma and resilience.

This book is the product of more than five years of extensive research and interviews. The history of the war in former Yugoslavia, the facts of the Srebrenica genocide, and the judicial processes which took place in the aftermath of these tragedies have been meticulously scrutinized for accuracy. Furthermore, the work provides salient insights into the effects of the Dayton Accords on the post-war governmental structure in Bosnia and Herzegovina, as well as the social and psychological ramifications of not only the violence itself, but the culture of denial which has risen in its wake. These are not merely historical topics, only relevant to the study of a particular region; rather, given the dangers posed by the rise of nationalism and extremist right-wing ideology worldwide, they are topics of immediate and pressing importance in our present time, and around the world.

Voices from Srebrenica makes an invaluable contribution to the academic study of the Srebrenica genocide, genocide more generally, and the processes of reconstruction and reconciliation in post-genocide societies. Engaging and easily accessible, this work will also be of interest to wide segments of the general public who wish to learn more about the events which took place in Srebrenica through the personal accounts of genocide survivors.

The publication of this research in English could not come at a more critical moment. The judicially established, factual narrative of the Srebrenica genocide is currently under siege—not just from politically motivated revisionist forces in Republika Srpska and regionally, but from genocide deniers around the globe. Last year, the Swedish Academy awarded the world's most prestigious literary accolade, the Nobel Prize in Literature, to the Austrian writer and avowed genocide denier Peter Handke. Such an eminent endorsement from the highest echelons of Western intellectual society can only embolden the lesser-known actors seeking to obscure the truth of the Srebrenica genocide to further their own political or academic careers. This deceitful element of revisionist historians has also highlighted the efficacy of the personal narrative as a means of communicating history, as is evidenced by the proliferation of literature written by and about war criminals in recent years. In a world where the perpetrators of genocide have no shortage of platforms from which to tell their distorted versions of events, works like this one, which give voice to the victims of genocide, are even more imperative.

As the director of the Srebrenica Memorial Center, and a survivor of the genocide, I can only say that this is the book I have been awaiting for a long time. It gives the voice back to survivors, to the brave men and women who witnessed an attempt to destroy all of us, to destroy a nation. It takes them out of silence and anonymity and shares their stories, experiences and wisdom. And it shows that what they have to share does not belong only to us, who survived, but also to those who are not yet even born. There is a lesson for humanity in what we survived.

Emir Suljagić is the director of the Srebrenica-Potočari Genocide Memorial Center and a survivor of the 1995 Srebrenica genocide. For two years he was the only Bosnian journalist covering the ICTY trials in The Hague. He has served as the Minister of Education of Sarajevo Canton and Deputy to the Minister of Defense of Bosnia and Herzegovina. He has authored numerous books and articles about the Srebrenica genocide and is a professor of international relations at the International University of Sarajevo.

Preface
by Ann Petrila

On Thursday, July 13, 1995, I was listening to the radio while driving to the University of Denver where I was teaching a class at the Graduate School of Social Work. Linda Wertheimer, host of NPR's *All Things Considered*, was leading a discussion about reports that were beginning to come out of Bosnia focusing on the fall of Srebrenica and the fate of thousands of men and boys who were missing.[1] It was not yet clear what was happening but I knew from the reports that it could not be good. As the world would soon learn, the genocidal killing of Muslim civilians who had been expelled from the UN Safe Area of Srebrenica had already started by the time of this broadcast. Ten years later, I had the opportunity to go to Bosnia to do some work for the university. It was supposed to be a one-time trip.

And so begins the story of this book, which is coauthored by the two us, Ann Petrila and Hasan Hasanović. Given the nature of this topic and the intensity of the personal stories which make up the bulk of this book, it did not seem appropriate for the narrative to be one of a neutral voice. The stories of the survivors are told in their own words. The narrative portion of the book is in my voice. When the voice is "I," it refers to me. "We" or "us" refers to both authors together.

In 2009, the first time that I went to Srebrenica and Potočari, I was with Bosnian friends who had never been there before. We were looking for the Genocide Memorial, which is located in Potočari, but we had trouble finding it. There were no signs showing the way and we eventually had to stop and ask for directions in a town that I now know is called Bratunac. Once we finally found the Memorial, we were greeted by a young Bosnian man who had recently started working there as a curator and interpreter. He was getting ready to speak in English to a group of visitors and he invited us to join them. We sat down in an outdoor mosque in the cemetery and started to listen. The curator began with an overview of regional history, followed by an account of the genocide which had taken place there in July 1995, and concluded by telling us his own story. As I listened to him recount the deaths of his father and his twin brother and his own struggle for survival during the 1995 genocide, I found myself breathless and hardly able to move. The curator's name was Hasan Hasanović, and his personal story was so powerful that I knew it would have a lasting impact on me. He led us through the exhibits in the Memorial Room in the old Battery Factory and showed us a documentary film featuring other survivors of the genocide. We had so many questions and he answered all of them. After we left, I couldn't stop thinking about Srebrenica and knew that I needed to return to learn more. Hearing Hasan's story forever changed the way that I thought about responsibility for addressing human rights violations and social injustices.

The next time I went to Potočari was a year later with the first group of graduate students that I took to Bosnia. (The country at the heart of this book is officially named "Bosnia and Herzegovina" or BiH.[2] It is typically referred to as simply "Bosnia" which is what we have chosen to do in this book.) When we got to Potočari, Hasan was once again our teacher. He told us even more of his own story and showed us additional parts of the Memorial which I had not seen during my first visit. I remember asking him if there was a library there where I could do some research. The answer was no. I asked him if he could recommend a good book on the Srebrenica genocide. He suggested a few books but told me that what I was looking for had not yet been written in English.

I stayed with my students for a few hours at the Memorial that day before we headed back to Sarajevo. On our way out of Potočari, we took a short drive through the town of Srebrenica, a little over a mile away, which I had not done before. As our bus slowly made its way through the narrow streets and up the hills, the group sat in stunned silence taking in the devastation that could still be seen everywhere in town. There were crumbling walls where buildings used to be, virtually every standing building was still riddled with holes from sniper bullets, grenades and other heavy artillery. There were very few people on the streets.

Once out of town and on our way back to Sarajevo, I marveled at the beauty of the countryside, despite the skeletal remains of burned out villages all around me. There was such destruction in those villages that it seemed doubtful that anyone would ever return. Now I understand why people never returned, even once they were able. Back then, I didn't know that the rolling hills and vast fields were execution sites, that the forests and mountain ridges were the former hiding places of those who had attempted to escape almost inevitable slaughter. I didn't know that the schools we passed were also execution sites and that the football fields had been mass graves. I only saw what was beautiful back then. And while I can never know all that was lost in those hills and rivers, since the story does not belong to me, I can no longer just enjoy the beautiful countryside anywhere in Bosnia, knowing the true horror of what happened there.

Every summer after that I brought my students to the Memorial to hear the story of Srebrenica from Hasan, who was becoming my friend. The year before the 20th anniversary of the genocide, I had been coming to Bosnia for almost 10 years and had been bringing U.S. graduate students each summer for over half of that time. Hasan and I worked closely together each summer and I knew his story well, as did my students, due to his generosity of time and spirit when they studied the Srebrenica genocide as part of their summer program. That summer brought an opportunity to do something I hadn't done before.

Hasan invited me to accompany him on the annual July 13 visit to the main execution sites organized by the members of the Women and Mother's Associations. These organizations are comprised of women whose male children and other relatives were killed in the Srebrenica genocide. The goal of this annual visit is for the women to memorialize the execution sites and to honor their loved ones who were killed there. This is not an easy task given that the sites lie in the Bosnian Serb part of Bosnia, the Republika Srpska (RS), where genocide denial is rampant. Because of the culture of denial, the six main execution sites are not marked in any way. It is possible to drive past them and have no awareness that thousands of men and boys were killed there. Two of these sites were schools when the massacres took place and they are still functioning schools today. In these schools, the curriculum teaches students that the genocide in Srebrenica never took place. If you ask any of the local people living nearby about the events that took place there in 1995, they will similarly deny that the accounts of genocide are true.

Most of the men and boys who were killed in the Srebrenica genocide were rounded up and taken to one of these main execution sites. On that July 13, three buses full of women drove back and forth along the country roads outside of Srebrenica and it seemed to me that we were backtracking. Hasan explained that we were visiting these sites in the order in which the executions were carried out during those few days in July 1995. I wondered aloud how people who were interested in learning more about the Srebrenica genocide would be able to know that these buildings and fields were execution sites. It seemed next to impossible that anyone without the advantage of my present group would be able to locate the majority of these sites. Hasan agreed with me. It was a shame that the history and location of these sites was so difficult to find.

When we went inside Petkovci school, a young, soft-spoken man stood on the stairs with Hasan at his side, sometimes holding on to him as he spoke to the women gathered before him. This was Nedžad Avdić, speaking in public about his experiences for the first time. Gathered before him were women whose husbands, sons, brothers, fathers and other loved ones had been held, tortured and killed at that school or at the nearby dam that we visited next. Against the backdrop of the women's sobs and despite his own tears and trembling voice, Nedžad told the story of what happened in this school, a place which contains no memorialization of the slaughter that occurred there. While he was telling this story, with his voice alternatingly getting stronger and then shakier, I began to think that his story, along with those of the other handful of men and boys who survived these execution sites, needed to be documented. The stories needed to be told by those who had survived these harrowing experiences, if it was their wish to do so; and they

The Petkovci School detention site (photograph by Kristian Skeie, July 9, 2018).

needed to be told in a way which would allow them to be preserved and to reach a wide audience. Of the more than one thousand men and boys killed at Petkovci school and the aluminum factory dam nearby, only two survived: Nedžad, who was 17 years old at the time, and the man who saved him.

Why should we write a book about this atrocity that happened 25 years ago? Why should anyone be interested in a small country that is hard to get to, that many people don't know anything about, and where people have names that are hard to pronounce and even harder to remember? Why should we be concerned about these people, many of whom practice a religion that is now often vilified in the media and by politicians both in the U.S. and across Europe?

We should care for many reasons about these peaceful people who refuse to allow hate into their hearts, even after their families have been slaughtered. We need to honor and learn from those who were hunted and left for dead at execution sites, and from those who survived other atrocities. This genocide happened in Europe less than 50 years after the Holocaust which was supposed to be the ultimate "never again." This happened to innocent civilians in plain sight of the international community and under the protection of the UN. And it is still happening today in many parts of the world, again to people whose names might be difficult to pronounce, whose skin might be a different color, and who perhaps practice a religion that is not understood by those with resources and power.

It is for Nedžad and all the others that we wrote this book. Some may say it is naive to think that preserving these narratives may help stop any genocidal madness in the future, but as I have learned from the Bosnians, we must always keep trying.

The difficulty in locating and visiting the execution sites, the lack of memorialization and documentation of the genocide in an accessible format, as well as the culture of denial, led us to conclude that this horrific chapter in European history could easily be lost if we fail to preserve the first-hand accounts of those who survived.

The true strength of the book lies in the narratives told directly by the survivors and others who were reluctant participants in the roles they had to play during July of 1995. Our interviewees agreed to talk to us because they wanted to share their first-hand experiences, in their own words, with the world. They knew Hasan and trusted him, and by extension they then trusted me. Some of our interviewees, including some who were protected witnesses at the International Criminal Tribunal for the former Yugoslavia (ICTY),[3] still live in their original villages, surrounded by those who deny that the genocide ever took place. In some cases, survivors of genocide live side by side with perpetrators. Other survivors are still waiting for their husbands or sons to be found. They all share a common fear that their experiences of genocide will never be fully understood, documented or believed. It is for this reason that they have decided to share their stories.

Only ten people survived the mass executions, and only some of these were in a position to be interviewed afterward. We expanded the scope of our initial project, in which we had only planned to interview those survivors. We realized that the overarching narrative would be greatly enhanced by the inclusion of more perspectives and more experiences. In addition, several prominent politicians and human rights activists in Serbia met with us at length to share the perspectives of those in Serbia who, from the beginning, attempted to make the truth about Srebrenica public and to address the issue of genocide denial.

Between March 2015 and September 2019, we interviewed 18 people. We interviewed three people twice for a total of 21 interviews. We interviewed four execution site survivors, one from each site where someone survived. There were two sites where nobody survived. We also interviewed five Death March survivors, one UN base survivor, three mothers who lost their families, and four human rights activists from Belgrade, Serbia, and one from Zenica, Bosnia. Interviews were done in person with two exceptions. Ahmo Hasić's first interview was conducted via Skype because he was living out of the country at the time and the interview with Sabiha Husić in Zenica was done by phone.

We asked each participant to choose where they wanted to meet with us. We talked with people at cafes, restaurants, coffee bars, parks, and in their homes, where they welcomed us with coffee and food as is the cultural custom in Bosnia. I will never forget driving a considerable distance into the countryside to reach the home of Saliha Osmanović. Upon our arrival, she apologized profusely to us, saying that she hadn't had time to cook, and could "only" offer us cookies, juice, nuts, soup, stuffed pies, chicken, coffee and several desserts.

Interviews were conducted in English or Bosnian, depending on the preference of the interviewee. When the interviews were conducted in Bosnian, Hasan interpreted throughout the conversation. All interviews were recorded. We transcribed each interview, sending them back and forth to each other for correction and clarification many times. All interviewees gave their permission for us to include their narratives in this book. Some survivors had testified at the ICTY where they were given protected witness status. Understandably, they initially asked to remain anonymous. To our surprise, however, each one later decided that they wanted us to use their real identity in the book, because they felt it was important for their stories to be told using their own names.

For the sake of combatting genocide denial, it was also important to us to provide the judicially proven facts about what happened in Srebrenica. Hasan painstakingly researched these specifics, in addition to corroborating the details provided by the survivors about the days before, during, and after the genocide. It would be impossible to tell the entire story of Srebrenica, in all its complexity, in the course of this one volume. For this reason, we have provided additional resources for those who wish to learn more about this genocide and its historical context.

When interviewing survivors, we asked them to tell us as much about their life as they felt comfortable discussing. We were interested in their childhood, what they thought they wanted to do when they grew up, and other experiences prior to the war. We wanted to give everyone the chance to tell us things about themselves not connected to the war if they chose to do so. These incredible individuals are so much more than their wartime trauma. Many of our interviewees found it difficult, however, to talk about anything other than the part of their life that began with the war. When I asked Hasan about this, he suggested a couple of possible explanations for the widespread unwillingness or inability to talk about life before the war. For people who now live with such terrible memories, he said it can often be painful to remember a time when life was good. He gave the example of one of his friends who can no longer listen to the folk music he used to enjoy, because the memories it evokes of happier times are too painful. Another reason Hasan suggested that people may be hesitant to talk about their earlier life is because they believe that others are only interested in the war-related part of them. When Hasan started working on his first book, even he didn't think that any other part of his story would be of interest to the outside world.

Some of our interviewees are professors and some had to leave school after third grade to work in the family fields. Their narratives sometimes reflect their different levels of education. Some told their stories in very few words and others described events in such vivid terms that we sometimes felt like we were there with them at the sites of execution. Regardless of style, these war-related events define everyone in some way. As Hasan says, "it's important to always remember that anyone and everyone here has some sort of story to tell, even if they don't tell it. We are all survivors."

For the people in Srebrenica, victory comes from being alive, and from moving forward. The goal of the genocide was the total destruction of its Muslim population. While the perpetrators succeeded in killing thousands of people, they did not succeed in killing everyone, and those whom they forcibly deported from their homes have in some cases returned. Furthermore, the perpetrators of genocide in July 1995 came nowhere near to destroying Bosnian culture. Taking part in this book seemed very important to all of the survivors we encountered, as their contributions attest to these facts.

At times it was difficult for people to tell their stories, sometimes only mildly so, other times so much so that people had to walk outside to take a break. We frequently checked with each person throughout the interviews in order to determine how they were doing, and offering to stop the interview at any time. Every person wanted to tell their story even when it was very painful for them to do so. I struggled with the idea of asking people to tell these tender, at times excruciating stories. Some people said they wished they had told their story sooner. Others said they hoped that their voice would sound strong when it was heard. They each said that their story was not the worst, that someone else had a more difficult situation. There was an ongoing tension between the desire to have their stories preserved for others to read and the traumatic nature of reliving the details. Is it retraumatizing to tell such a story? Sometimes. Can it be part of healing? Sometimes. Who gets to decide? The person with the story to tell.

This issue was described by Eli M. Rosenbaum who worked for the U.S. Department of Justice, investigating and prosecuting cases against Nazi perpetrators from 1979 until 2010.

> Securing survivor testimony could be particularly wrenching. Rosenbaum remembers his "hardest experience" as a trip to Israel to interview survivor witnesses. "Almost all ... have a point at which they're going to fall apart—usually when talking about members of their family" he says, and he would always regret causing them pain. But when he asked if they wished to continue, they would all say, "Yes, justice is important."[4]

The people who agreed to be part of this book would like justice to be better served.

As hard as it might be to understand, another consistent part of the interviews was laughter. Every survivor said something funny and laughed. Is that part of the resilience that is so much a part of each survivor? Is this ability to laugh part of their ongoing survival? Whether directed at the current absurdities of the political situation in Bosnia or at the horror of what happened, that capacity for laughter was present in everyone we interviewed. People sometimes switched abruptly from crying to laughing; the ability to do so made it possible for them to continue telling their story, and I believe makes it possible for them to continue to survive. As Saliha, who started laughing during her interview, put it, "I can't bury myself alive. I have to live."

We asked each of the survivors why they think they survived the genocide. The answers were consistent. Each person said *Sudbina* and *Bog*—Destiny and God. These words were not absent from a single story. They were embedded in each explanation of survival. Additionally, several people said that they think they survived so that they could tell the story of what happened; so that they could speak for the dead, and ensure the truth was known.

The scope of this book is broad in one sense. In addition to the stories of the survivors, we have provided historical context as well as information related to the role of the international community and the psychological consequences of this war and genocide. Tracking down and verifying factual information about events, numbers killed and who was responsible was challenging. The Memorial Center is just beginning to do this type of analysis on its own. At this point in time, 25 years since the genocide in Srebrenica, scientifically researched books about this historical event remain relatively few. There are several reasons for this. It took many years for the war crimes trials to begin and for the information about the verdicts to be made accessible to the general public. There are several different politically motivated narratives about what happened in July 1995, and many writers have had to fear scrutiny and even repercussions for coming to what others may consider the wrong conclusions. Some information is available in English, but other information is available only in Bosnian. We were able to track down some sources only because of Hasan's detailed knowledge of this genocide, his understanding of the culture, and his knowledge of both Bosnian and English.

There are many parts of this genocide that defy the capacities of this book for in-depth description, factual representation, and analysis. Contextual information which is necessary for a full understanding of this genocide includes Slobodan Milošević's rise to power, decision making within the structure of UN, the UN mandate, the specific plans and strategies of the Bosnian Serb Army, and the ICTY proceedings and verdicts. We attempted to provide enough information for our readers to understand the basic subject and context of the genocide. It is our belief that the best understanding of what happened in Srebrenica is gained from the stories of survivors.

In the individual stories, there is sometimes conflicting information about numbers of dead or wounded, or specific days when certain events happened. Given the trauma and chaos of war, survivors' estimates of the dead that they saw, for example, may vary. Whenever possible, we have used verified sources to report these specific facts. If no such verification was available, we have indicated this.

We have kept as true to people's own words as possible. The only changes that we made were for clarity. Any errors that might be present are our own.

We did not go into detail about other significant areas of conflict in the former Yugoslavia. The greatest impact of this war was felt in Srebrenica and Sarajevo, the capital of Bosnia. Sarajevo was surrounded and under siege by the Bosnian Serb Army for 1,425 days, the longest siege of any capital city in the history of modern warfare.[5] More than 10,000 residents, primarily civilians, died as a result of shelling or other aspects of the blockade. An estimated 1,600 children are included in that number.[6] The siege of Sarajevo is well-documented in a film entitled, *Scream for Me Sarajevo*.[7]

The complicated story of this genocide is made more so by the fact that many people in Bosnia have similar names. Many have the same first, last or complete name. This does not necessary mean that they are related to each other although this is often possible as there are many family connections within the country. There are two people in this book with the same name, Hasan Hasanović. In order to distinguish between them in their chapters, we refer to each using their father's name as their middle name which is customary in certain situations in Bosnia. The coauthor of this book is Hasan Aziz Hasanović and the other survivor is Hasan Sejfo Hasanović. In this book there is also Haso Hasanović. We encourage our readers to refer to the list of people that we have provided in the preliminary section of the book in order to minimize confusion.

There are a few additional points of clarification.

The official name of the court which held the trials for this war is "The International Criminal Tribunal for the former Yugoslavia," known as the ICTY. Throughout this book people also refer to this court as The Hague and the Tribunal.

The official name of the Memorial in Potočari is "The Srebrenica-Potočari Memorial and Cemetery for the Victims of the 1995 Genocide." In this book it is also referred to as Potočari, the Memorial Center or Centre, the Cemetery, the Memorial, and the Genocide Memorial.

"The General Framework Agreement for Peace in Bosnia and Herzegovina" is the agreement that officially ended the war. It is also referred to as Dayton, the Dayton Agreement, the Dayton Peace Agreement, the Dayton Accords and the Dayton Peace Accords.

Throughout time, history has been written by those with the most power. Typically, that is who gets to control the narratives and the interpretations of events. In this book, however, that power belongs to the survivors. It is from them that we have the most to learn.

Introduction

Bosnia and Herzegovina (BiH), commonly referred to as Bosnia, is a country in southeastern Europe, bordering Croatia, Serbia, and Montenegro. Much of the terrain is hilly and mountainous, with dense forests and a small Adriatic coastline that runs for 12 miles (20 kilometers).[1] Approximately the size of West Virginia, Bosnia is a country full of contrasts. The picturesque landscape boasts turquoise rivers, deep blue skies, and rolling hills, as well as, unfortunately, the blown-out remains of wartime carnage and an estimated 80,000 uncleared landmines.[2]

Present-day Bosnia reflects the influence of several empires that controlled the country for centuries. The empires of the Romans and Byzantines, Ottomans, and Austro-Hungarians left their marks on both religion and culture. One of the legacies of these empires is that the country was divided into three groups, along religious lines. Those who converted to Catholicism under Roman Empire became known as Bosnian Croats; Converts to Orthodox Christianity under the rule of the Orthodox Byzantine Empire became known as Bosnian Serbs; Those who converted to Islam under the Ottoman Turks became known as Bosnian Muslims or Bosniaks.

With origins as southern Slavs, people who inhabit present-day Bosnia are typically fair-skinned, eastern Europeans. They identify as three different ethnic groups and ethnicity is defined differently in the former Yugoslavia than in many places. There is one language spoken with three names: Bosnian, Serbian and Croatian. There are regional differences with dialects and accents which cross ethnic lines. In the past, all children were taught both the Cyrillic and Latin alphabets but now Cyrillic is used primarily in the Bosnian Serb part of the country, the Republika Srpska (RS). Sometimes peoples' ethnicities can be distinguished by their first or last names, but not always. In Bosnia, ethnicity and religion are equivalent. A person may identify as Croat or Catholic and it means the same thing. The same goes for Serbs, who also describe themselves as Orthodox; and the Bosniaks who are Muslim. Religion is as much a demarcation of national identity as belief. As one writer, describing this phenomenon in Croatia, puts it:

> Viewing "religion" in this way—as national self-identity, not a practice of faith—helps explain a lot about life, culture and religion…. It also explains why religions that profess to be about peace and love can be seen as the driving force for warfare…. In Croatia, as in Bosnia and Serbia, being Catholic is more of a "nationality" than a religion.[3]

How did this all begin?

A Brief History of Yugoslavia and Bosnia[4]

Following the era of Roman and Byzantine occupation, the Ottoman Empire ruled the territory from the 15th century until the Austro-Hungarians occupied the region in the late 1800s. In 1914, Archduke Ferdinand, heir to the Austro-Hungarian throne, and his wife Sophie were assassinated in Sarajevo by a Bosnian Serb nationalist named Gavrilo Princip. The event is considered the spark that ignited World War I. Princip was, and still is, considered a terrorist by some and a hero by others.

In 1918, following the end of the First World War, Bosnia was annexed into the newly formed Kingdom of Serbs, Croats, and Slovenes. The name was later changed to the Kingdom of Yugoslavia in 1929.

When German armies invaded in 1941, they encountered a strong resistance led by Josip Broz Tito, commander of the Yugoslav Communist Partisans. Throughout World War II, the Partisans were the leaders of the anti–Nazi resistance and ultimately kept Yugoslavia independent from the Soviet Union and out from behind the Iron Curtain.[5]

After World War II, Bosnia became one of six constituent republics in the Socialist Federal Republic of Yugoslavia. Under the leadership of Josip Broz Tito, nationalist ideologies were disavowed in Yugoslavia, and replaced by the popular slogan of brotherhood and unity. Yugoslavia consisted of six republics: Bosnia and Herzegovina, Croatia, Macedonia, Montenegro, Serbia, and Slovenia. Serbia contained two Socialist Autonomous Provinces: Vojvodina and Kosovo. Of the six republics, Bosnia was the most ethnically integrated. Intermarriage was common in cities and larger towns.

Those who lived in Yugoslavia during Tito's time often remember those days with fondness. Everyone had a job and housing, companies provided accommodation on the coast for employees to go on vacation, a Yugoslav passport was strong and people had the freedom and means to travel.

Hasan describes life in Srebrenica during Tito's time and before the 1990s war. Everyone was employed, often in the mines or government factories such as the car battery factory in the village of Potočari. Nearly every miner and factory worker had an apartment, car, and summer cottage. By the 1990s, most households had a TV, VCR, and washing machine, as well as other modern appliances. Movie theaters and supermarkets were well stocked and heavily frequented, and local people had plenty of opportunities for leisure and recreation. By most accounts, the standard of living in Srebrenica and throughout Yugoslavia was comparable to that of the U.S. and Western Europe.

Post-Tito Bosnia

Tito died in 1980. With no clear successor, the dissolution of Yugoslavia began. Expressions of nationalism, which had been heavily restricted under Tito's governance, quickly began to resurface. Latent nationalist sentiments and historical grievances were exploited by a new generation of politicians in their rise to power. In Serbia, Slobodan Milošević, then president of the Socialist Party of Serbia (SPS), used state-controlled television to enflame nationalistic fervor. His hate-based propaganda was primarily directed against the Bosnian Muslims.

A struggle for control of Yugoslavia had begun. Back in 1974, Tito had instituted a new constitution that decentralized the country by granting a greater degree of self-governance to the republics and provinces, including individual presidents and more autonomous constitutional powers.[6] Milošević's goal was to rewrite the constitution and again centralize the country by consolidating governmental power in the Serbian capital of Belgrade. This plan was naturally unacceptable to the other Yugoslav republics. The

Slovenes and Croats were the first to voice their dissent, culminating in a division that led to the breakup of the Communist Party of Yugoslavia.

In 1990, when the first democratic parliamentary elections were held, nationalist parties won in every republic. These parties won on the platform of promoting individual ethnic identities at the exclusion of all others. The republics began declaring independence, beginning with Slovenia and Croatia. Each declaration was met with armed aggression from the Yugoslav People's Army which had been taken over by Milošević. At that time, it was the fourth largest army in the world, all of which came under his control. Through his massive propaganda campaign, hate speech and unbridled nationalism, Milošević successfully mobilized Serbs to dehumanize non–Serbs and to eventually destroy them.

The war varied in intensity in each republic, largely in accordance to its ethnic diversity. Those republics with a dominant ethnic group and a clear majority experienced shorter wars. Bosnia was the most multi-ethnic republic in Yugoslavia, consisting of roughly 44 percent Muslims, 31 percent Serbs, and 17 percent Croats. This ethnic mix and lack of a clear majority contributed to the length and ferocity of Bosnia's fight for independence.

Bosnia declared its sovereignty in October 1991, followed by its independence from the former Yugoslavia in March 1992. Although this move was soon recognized by the international community, the government in Belgrade and the Serb minority in Bosnia refused to acknowledge its legitimacy. Having recently declared themselves a parastate within Bosnia that would come to be known as Republika Srpska, Bosnian Serb rebels mobilized an illegal campaign to join the political project of Greater Serbia.

With a monopoly over the resources of the Yugoslav People's Army, the Milošević regime sponsored the formation of what would come to be known as the Bosnian Serb Army (BSA). Together with police forces and paramilitary units from Serbia and Montenegro, the BSA embarked on a campaign of ethnic cleansing in order to create an ethnically pure Serb parastate. Croatia's involvement in this campaign was complicated. Initially, both the Croatian and Serbian presidents had planned to divide Bosnia between themselves. At times Croatia fought with the Bosniaks against the BSA and at other times they fought against the Bosniaks.

The war raged throughout Bosnia. The capital city of Sarajevo was surrounded and put under siege by the Bosnian Serb Army for 1,425 days, the longest siege of any capital city in the history of modern warfare.[7] More than 10,000 residents of Sarajevo, primarily civilians, died as a result of shelling and other ramifications of the siege. This number includes an estimated 1,600 children.[8]

Srebrenica and Eastern Bosnia

Eastern Bosnia was another main target of the Bosnian Serbs throughout the war. The survivors whose stories are in this book all lived in that part of the country. They are all Muslims. Under horrific circumstances they each made their way to Srebrenica in 1992 as their towns and villages were being ethnically cleansed by the BSA and paramilitary units from Serbia. During that time at the beginning of the war, 10,000 civilians in eastern Bosniap were killed, countless women were raped and more than 150,000 civilians were expelled from their homes. Many people fled to three enclaves: Srebrenica, Žepa, and Goražde

The small town of Srebrenica eventually became home to approximately 50,000 people who had fled their residences in nearby towns and villages. During the siege of Srebrenica, which began in 1992, people lived in overcrowded and inhumane conditions. Dozens of people were often forced to cohabit a single small house or apartment, while others had to live on the streets, fully exposed to the violence and elements. Shelling from the BSA occurred often, sometimes daily. The narratives of the survivors in this book give detailed descriptions of what life was like in Srebrenica under siege. In April 1993, the UN Security Council declared Srebrenica an official Safe Area, which meant that UN battalions would be stationed there under a peacekeeping mandate which included the distribution of humanitarian supplies and observation of the conflict. First to arrive was a Canadian battalion (Canbat), which was later replaced by a series of Dutch battalions (Dutchbat). These international forces established the main UN base in the Battery Factory in the village of Potočari, just outside of Srebrenica.

Despite having been declared a UN Safe area, people in Srebrenica continued to live under brutal conditions, without food, water, medical equipment, electricity, or adequate housing. These conditions, combined with the unrelenting attacks by the Bosnian Serbs, continued to make life unbearable for about 50,000 civilians.

The situation continued to deteriorate and in July of 1995 the BSA attacked and captured Srebrenica. Over 25,000 women, children, and elderly fled to the UN base in hopes of being protected. They were later forcibly deported from in and around the base. A separate group of over 12,000 Bosniak men and boys escaped into the forest hoping to reach the free territory of Tuzla. Some men chose to go to the UN base in Potočari rather than through the forest. These were primarily men who trusted the UN or were unable to make the 60-mile trek through the woods, a horrific journey that would later be known as the Death March.

Between July 11 and 22, all of the men who had fled to Potočari and more than a half of the men who had taken to the forest, approximately 8,000 in total, were systematically executed by the BSA. The majority of these men were rounded up and taken to six main execution sites. Only 10 men survived the executions. These killings became the single largest massacre to take place on the European continent since World War II. In an effort to hide their crimes, the BSA buried the bodies in a series of mass graves throughout that part of eastern Bosnia. Despite Srebrenica's status as a UN Safe Area, neither members of Dutchbat nor the international community acted to protect the civilian occupants.

Within a week of murdering 8,000 men and boys in the vicinity of Srebrenica, the BSA carried out a mortar attack on a crowded food market in Sarajevo. Thirty-seven civilians were killed in this bloody attack, while ninety more were seriously injured.[9] News of this attack combined with surfacing details of the Srebrenica massacre compounded mounting pressure on the international community to put an end to the war.

Combined with targeted NATO airstrikes, a U.S.–led diplomatic initiative began to push for a peaceful solution to the war, resulting in the signing of the "The General Framework Agreement for Peace in Bosnia and Herzegovina" in December 1995. This agreement ended the war, and laid the foundation for the post-war governmental structure of Bosnia.

The Dayton Agreement, as it is commonly called, divided Bosnia into two entities and one district. The Federation of BiH, the first of these entities, comprises 51 percent of the country's territory and is primarily inhabited by Bosniaks and Bosnian Croats. The second entity, Republika Srpska, is comprised of 49 percent of the country's territory and is predominately populated by Bosnian Serbs. Brčko is a multi-ethnic, and self-governed district. While the Dayton Agreement was successful in bringing about an end to war, it institutionalized the ethnic divisions in Bosnian society within the official state structure. This problematic factor exacerbates the numerous obstacles on the road to reconciliation in Bosnia. The Dayton Agreement also established the Office of the High Representative for Bosnia and Herzegovina to oversee the implementation of the civilian aspects of the agreement.

The governmental structure of Bosnia has been called the most complicated government on earth.[10] It is a parliamentary republic that is governed by a tripartite presidency, consisting of one Croat, one Bosniak, and one Serb representative. In addition to three presidents active simultaneously at the federal level, each of the two entities has its own president.[11]

Over time, the crimes committed in Srebrenica were determined to be genocide by the International Criminal Tribunal for the former Yugoslavia (ICTY) in The Hague. These verdicts were later confirmed by the International Court of Justice (ICJ). Very few mass atrocities in history have received the official designation of genocide. There are many reasons for this. In order for genocide to be determined, a specific set of criteria must be present.

It is often a surprise when people learn that the Nazi perpetrators of the Holocaust were not found guilty of genocide at the Nuremberg trials. Nazi leaders were indicted and convicted of crimes against humanity, but there was not an emphasis on the Jewish identity of the victims. The crime of genocide, which is predicated on the intent to destroy an identity group, did not yet officially exist.[12]

This would change thanks to the tireless efforts of a Jewish lawyer from Poland named Rapheal Lemkin. Lemkin, who had lost 49 family members in Nazi concentration camps and fled to the United States when the German Army invaded Poland, spent decades of his life advocating for recognition of mass political murder as a distinct crime under international law.[13]

He coined the term *genocide* in 1944, defining it as "the destruction of a nation or an ethnic group."[14] He had no official position or job title, but he spent years lobbying members of the UN to adopt his new term as a distinct legal classification. After years of relentless advocacy, he was finally successful. In December 1948, the United Nations adopted the Convention on the Prevention and Punishment of the Crime of Genocide, often called the Genocide Convention, which classified genocide as a crime under international law.

Lemkin toiled tirelessly for this cause and ultimately it cost him his health and everything that he owned. Despite his enormous contribution to the protection of human rights and international law, he is almost unknown to the general public.

> By the early 1950s, Lemkin faded from the public view, increasingly tired and frail, worn down by his exertions. (He quipped that he suffered from genociditis.) By the mid-1950s, he was a broken man, embittered by the evident and growing indifference of the world around him to the significance of his achievement. Even during the height of his work at the U.N., he was virtually penniless, enduring the indignities of an indigent academic, whose minor celebrity did not pay the rent.[15]

In 1998, the Rome Statute established a permanent International Criminal Court (ICC) with jurisdiction over the most important international crimes, including genocide. Supported by more than 120 countries, the Rome Statute was enacted in July 2002. It represents the international community's determination to fight impunity for mass crimes: war crimes, crimes against humanity, genocide and aggression. It determined that no statute of limitations would apply to any of these crimes. The Rome Statute provides definitions necessary to understand the Srebrenica genocide and other crimes prosecuted by the ICTY, the Tribunal established to try crimes committed in Yugoslavia.[16]

The United States is not a state party to the Rome Statute, even though it was involved in negotiations while the ICC was being created. In 1998, only seven countries voted against the Rome Statute: the United States, China, Iraq, Israel, Libya, Qatar, and Yemen.[17] U.S. President Bill Clinton signed the Rome Statute in 2000 but did not submit the treaty to the Senate for ratification. In 2002, President George W. Bush effectively unsigned the treaty, sending a message to the secretary-general of the United Nations that the U.S. no longer intended to ratify the treaty and that it "did not have any obligations toward it."[18]

Despite the rulings of two international courts that genocide took place in Srebrenica, genocide denial persists throughout Serb-dominated territories of former Yugoslavia. Particularly in the RS, this pervasive culture of denial is the root of many of the challenges faced by post-war Bosnia.

Bosnia Today

The current population of Bosnia is estimated at 3.28 million people. The most populous city is the capital, Sarajevo, which is home to around 343,000 people. This is followed by Banja Luka, the RS capital, which has around 150,000 inhabitants, and then by the city of Tuzla, which is home to three salt lakes and about 110,000 people. Other notable cities in Bosnia include Zenica, Bijeljina, and Mostar.

As previously discussed, ethnic and religious identities are largely interchangeable in Bosnia. This is demonstrated by the following statistics, found in the CIA World Fact Book[19]:

Ethnic groups (self-identified):
Bosniak 50.1%, Serb 30.8%, Croat 15.4%, other 2.7%, not declared/no answer 1%

Religions: (self-identified)
Muslim 50.7%, Orthodox 30.7%, Roman Catholic 15.2%, atheist 0.8%, agnostic 0.3%, other 1.2%, undeclared/no answer 1.1%[20]

There are several religious and ethnic groups that are not officially recognized in the Bosnian constitution, and are generally subsumed under the ethnic and religious category of "other" in demographic statistics. The Jewish population of Bosnia, for instance, has played a very important role in the country's history and culture despite its lack of constitutional representation. There are an estimated 500–1,000 Jews living in Bosnia, accounting for around 0.012 percent of the total population and living primarily in Sarajevo, where they enjoy peaceful relations with other religious communities.[21]

The first Jews to arrive in Bosnia were Sephardic refugees who fled to Sarajevo in 1492 to escape the Spanish and Portuguese Inquisitions. An influx of Ashkenazi Jews subsequently arrived in the country during the 1800s, resulting in a unique intermixture of Ashkenazi and Sephardic cultures.[22] This diverse Jewish community continued to thrive in Bosnia until the outbreak of the Second World War. The Jewish population of Sarajevo, which had numbered around 15,000 before the war, was nearly destroyed when approximately 10,000 Bosnian Jews were murdered during the Holocaust.[23]

Introduction

The small number of Jews who returned to Sarajevo after World War II were not targeted by violence during the breakup of Yugoslavia. In fact, the Jewish community played a critical role in providing medical care and supplies to those in need, and helped to evacuate thousands of residents from Sarajevo during the siege.[24]

The impact of Jewish culture is still felt in Sarajevo today, where a number of notable historical sites bear testament to their important place in Bosnian history. The Old Sephardic Cemetery, dating back to 1439, sits on a hill above the city and has more than 3,850 tombstones. It is on the list of places being considered to receive designation as a UNESCO Cultural Heritage Site.[25]

The Old Synagogue is another prominent testament to the cultural contributions of Sarajevo's Jewish community. Today this facility functions as a Jewish museum, which houses a replica of one of the most famous and valuable books in the world, the Sarajevo Haggadah. The origins of this book are unknown, however, it dates back to the 14th century. Its survival can be attributed to the diligent efforts of individuals to preserve and hide the book in every subsequent war which has come to Bosnia. The stories of the people who hid this book are remarkable, and stand as shining examples of the true multi-ethnic nature of Bosnia, where different groups of people work together in order to preserve one another's cultures.[26]

The 1992–1995 war resulted in over 100,000 casualties, most of which were Muslim civilians. Just like the Holocaust 50 years before, the violence in former Yugoslavia in the 1990s was intended to destroy a specific group of people, their history, religion, and culture. Despite the abhorrent scale of the violence and devastation, the campaign to annihilate the Muslims of Bosnia was not successful. Bosniak culture is alive and well in the country today, and the survivors of this horrific violence are determined to share their experiences with the world, even when it is extremely painful to do so. Each person believes that part of the reason they survived was to be able to share their story. Through their pain and resilience, they hope that they can offer the world a valuable lesson on the dire consequences of radical hatred and collective inaction. Their stories are a reminder that we must commit ourselves with grave sincerity each time we vow "never again."

> Listening to survivors' stories is not about sympathy. They are about growing awareness of the reality of another's suffering. The outcome, in every case, is to enable us to gain respect for the other, as human beings, and as survivors of persecution, or exclusion, or difficulties of body or mind.[27]

PART I
Narratives

Chapter 1

Execution Site Survivors

Ahmo Hasić

In a town in eastern Bosnia, we finally found the house. While the man who we hoped to interview wasn't there, many family members were waiting for us. A young man was prepared to help us with the computer connection necessary for the scheduled Skype interview with his grandfather, Ahmo Hasić. It took a bit of time to get the connection. In the meantime, several children sat on the couch near us, staring and listening to everything that was going on. I wondered how much they knew of the story we were about to hear and what it might be like for them to be in the room during our interview. We seemed to take up the entire house, so it wasn't possible to have this conversation out of their hearing range and nobody seemed inclined to have them move.

Once the connection was made, Ahmo appeared on the screen, an elderly man with wonderfully prominent eyebrows. Like so many older people that are part of this story, his face is wise and his face is sad, reflecting the life experiences of his 78 years. He was ready for us, having clearly dressed up for our meeting in a striped V-neck sweater and a button-down shirt.

After introductions, he started talking even before we could ask him our first question. He didn't want to say where he lives now. He let us know that he was from a village outside of the town of Srebrenica and then he quickly jumped to 1992. There was no chance to talk with him about any other time in his life. In fact, that opportunity never presented itself at all during our conversation. I was hoping to learn more about this interesting man but his sole intention was to discuss the war years and he did so with such intensity that I wondered if he is ever able to let himself talk about anything else. When we heard his story, it's no wonder that he told it in such an intense way. It is one of the most complicated series of events that we heard during any of our interviews. His words came out deliberately with a resigned force of someone who couldn't change anything that had happened in the past.

> The question is why any of this happened because we didn't do anything wrong to anybody.

For Ahmo, it began in the area where he was living in 1992. Airplanes started flying over the villages dropping bombs. Ahmo said that they came from Serbia.

> My daughter-in-law was killed by bombs that were dropped in the area of Osat[1] from the planes. They came from the direction of Serbia and forced us all to flee from our homes and to head towards Srebrenica.

Ahmo stayed there for two and a half years.

> When I was in Srebrenica they were attacking from all sides all the time. Once they came from the Sase mine[2] through a tunnel and they fired at the hospital, other buildings and people. Then they left.
> When they attacked Srebrenica in 1995 they came from the direction of Zeleni Jadar.[3] They kept shooting at Srebrenica from the hills of Zvijezda,[4] Čauš[5] and from all other sides. When they were shelling the town, civilians were dying, children, women, the elderly.

When Srebrenica fell on Tuesday, July 11, most of men and boys set off through the forest. Ahmo decided to go to the UN base in Potočari. He was 60 years old at the time and made this decision because of his age. He described himself as an elderly man and walking through the woods would have been too difficult. He also expected that he would be safe at the base.

> I didn't do anything wrong to anybody. As a normal person, you couldn't have imagined what would happen. How could you presume that such horrible things could happen?

It all turned out so differently than he had assumed it would.

> When we came to Potočari the factories were full of people. Not everybody was able to fit inside so people were on the road.

Ahmo ended up spending the next three days and two nights outside the base in Potočari.

> That first night they were shelling the area near civilians to scare people and to make sure that people stayed there.
> On the 12th of July, which was a Wednesday, Ratko Mladić arrived and they brought a small truck of bread. They started throwing bread to people in the crowd and I grabbed some. Mladić was there and they were filming the whole thing to show to the world how gracious they were. When they started killing people later they were not filming it.
> Afterwards that day, when the dark started falling people started to scream outside of the UN base. When the screams started the whole crowd of people moved in a stampede. Then again, we could hear another scream from the distance and people started moving again in the same way.
> Two men who were separated were taken away to a nearby place where we could hear them beating them and they were screaming and moaning.
> Sometimes we could hear shooting and sometimes it would stop. These screams were strong and loud then they would stop all of a sudden. This is what happened. That night a lot of men and boys were taken away.
> When Mladić took over Srebrenica he said that they had conquered Srebrenica and his soldiers could do whatever they wanted. One could tell later that this was the case because they did what they wanted. Nobody stopped them. They were taking men and boys away and killing them. Some men were slain and their skulls were thrown in a stream.
> The next day it was Thursday and people were rushing onto the buses and trucks wanting to escape from the hell. There was a woman shouting out loud, "do not go, genocide is happening." She went to negotiate with Mladić in Bratunac and she understood that a massive killing will happen. This is why she was shouting out loud. I do not know her. I asked for her name in Tuzla and I heard that she survived. Nobody was able to tell me her name.

This woman was Ćamila Omanović from Srebrenica. She accompanied Ibro Nuhanović[6] and Nesib Mandžić to a "negotiation" meeting with Mladić in Bratunac on July 12, 1995. Afterward, Ćamila tried to hang herself in the UN base in Potočari. Some boys found her and alerted the Dutch Peacekeepers, who cut her down. She survived and eventually returned to her home in Srebrenica where she took a job as a bookkeeper at the Memorial.[7] She testified at the ICTY in The Hague and later died of a stroke.

> I was separated in Potočari with all the men and boys and then taken to Vuk Karadžić school[8] in Bratunac. When we arrived they immediately started killing all day and night. I spent two nights in Bratunac. They kept changing crews of soldiers while killing men and boys.
> Once the killing stopped they told us we would all go to Tuzla. We went outside and there were seven buses. We were on the buses and we came to Konjević Polje where there was fighting. They were shooting at the men and boys who were trying to get to Tuzla[9] and they were taking prisoners.

The bus took them on a circuitous route through Serbia and they ended up in Pilica.

> One of the men died on the bus. They pulled him out of the bus to the outside. Those who pulled him outside, one of them tried to run away but they killed him. It was dark once we got to Pilica and they took us to Pilica school. They brought us to Pilica at night so we wouldn't be sure where they had brought us.
> I was in the Pilica school for two nights. They kept constantly taking people outside and killing them. People were screaming outside. When you wanted to go to the toilet they would be in the corridor, waiting to beat people as they passed through to go to the toilet. When the prisoners came back they would beat them again. After that many prisoners wouldn't dare to ask to go to the toilet. People were peeing on the ground inside. People were peeing everywhere and trying to capture it as they were peeing to drink it as water.

In addition to describing how thirsty everybody was, Ahmo also talked about hunger. They hadn't had food for four days. One of the soldiers brought a piece of bread which he crumbled into small pieces and threw at the prisoners. The soldiers said that they didn't have enough food for themselves, so why should they give anything to the prisoners?

After two nights and two days, the soldiers asked the prisoners if they wanted to go to Sarajevo. They said that anyone who had the bus fare could go and that the bus fare was 20 Deutsche Marks. Some of the men had some money and gave it to the soldiers.

> Those who gave money got out of the school and on to a bus and they went away. They took them to Branjevo and killed them. It was just a trick to take money from them before they killed them.
> The buses came back to the school so quickly and they said that even those without money could go to Tuzla. This was another trick. They brought two bedding sheets and they made two prisoners tie the other prisoners and they started taking people out.
> They tied us up saying that we were going to Tuzla. We knew we were not going to Tuzla. It was suspicious. Why did they have to tie me up if I was going to Tuzla?

As they were taken out of the school and down the stairs, they saw one man dead on the stairs and another underneath on the pavement, blood running from his head. They saw two buses waiting for them across the square, and they boarded. Two soldiers also got on the bus and they were taken to Branjevo where the soldiers started shouting and the buses stopped.

> Soldiers surrounded the bus, the door opened, and they started swearing and cursing at all of us. They said that our president doesn't want us, that Alija Izetbegović doesn't want us.

Ahmo thought that this was the end of his life. He started counting the seconds until he would be killed.

> We were tied up, hungry, fearful, sleepy and half dead. They emptied half the bus. I was in the other half of the bus and I looked to see where they were taking people.

Ahmo saw the people being taken off the bus and herded toward a pile of those who were already dead.

> Then the shooting started.

The soldiers then returned to the bus, swearing and continuing to beat people. It was Ahmo's turn to get off the bus. The soldiers asked the men if they wanted to make the orthodox sign of the cross to pray so that their lives could be spared. Two men said yes but Ahmo knew that nobody would be spared.

> One man told the soldiers that he would give them 7,000 Deutsche Marks to spare his life. When the soldier told him to turn over the money, the man said he would write to his cousin to have him send the money. It was a trick. They wouldn't spare people, not a single person. If he would have had the money they would still have killed him. It didn't matter.

Ahmo describes another man, who had his hands tied, begging for water.

> He told the soldiers that once they gave him water then they could kill him. But it didn't matter because they still didn't care.

The prisoners were then taken to Branjevo, the place that would be their execution site.

> They took us to the piles where dead people were lying in rows. We went through the rows and beyond this pile, then they lined us up in a row and they shouted, "Turn your back." We did it. Then the shooting started and everybody fell. I fell too.

At this point in our interview, the Call to Prayer could be heard from the mosque near the house where we were sitting. Ahmo continued to talk to us from far away on the computer screen.

> Allah saved me. He left me to live to tell the story [of] what happened to all of us. I wasn't shot. Six or seven rows of prisoners were brought after us. Then the bullets were flying everywhere, the ground and the dust and the rocks were hitting my back. But the bullets didn't hit me. I saw them kill all of those people from the rows of prisoners. I saw them kill them all and then they went to have a rest in the shade.

At that point, Ahmo was still on the ground and started trying to untie himself, which wasn't easy since his neighbor was on top of him. The soldiers then started asking if anybody was alive. One or two men answered that they were alive at which point the soldiers came and shot them in the back of the head. The soldiers then went again to rest in the shade.

> I looked and they were gone, having a rest. I managed to untie myself and was thinking that it was maybe two and a half or three hours until the dark came. I was looking where to sneak out, to the forest. There was no place, just a small forest nearby, maybe 100 square meters, a small forest to the left.

Ahmo heard someone close to him moving so he said that if anyone else was alive they should make a run for it. He managed to untie himself and got to his feet, stumbling over dead bodies as he made his way to some bushes. Two more men stumbled into the bushes and then two more crawled over the bodies and also got into the bushes. There were five of them alive at that point, waiting for the darkness to come.

Ahmo overheard the soldiers bragging about what they had just done.

> They were speaking literally saying, "We committed genocide." The soldiers said, "We committed genocide like in 1941." I could hear them speaking. That is exactly what they said and I heard them.

Those who had been hiding in the bushes started walking through the forest. There was moonlight, so it was possible to see a bit but Ahmo was unable to keep up with the others. They were younger than him and they did not wait for him. He was suddenly alone but knew that he had to keep walking if he was going to escape.

> I was walking the whole night. Sometimes I would sit, sometimes I would run. I would lose my mind, sometimes I would get my mind back. I was wandering the whole night. I didn't know where I was going.

When daylight came, Ahmo realized that he had walked in one big circle. He had gone the wrong direction, toward the Drina river rather than to the west. He was almost back to where he started and was trying to decide which direction to go when he heard the sounds of machinery. He realized that they were working on a mass grave. They were burying people very close to where they had been killed. He started walking again and came to an asphalt road which was close to a small forest. He saw Red Cross vehicles pass but he didn't stop them for fear that they might have come from Serbia. He then looked more closely at the road and saw a lot of blood.

> I realized they were bringing the dead people in trucks down the road. They were bringing them to that field and they were even killing more people there. I was crossing that road, then the truck came. I looked at it. The truck was loaded with dead people. When the truck went by me the driver said to the person beside him, "There is the guy who ran away yesterday, that is him."

Ahmo continued walking down the road and he heard the truck slam on its breaks. He just kept walking. The truck stopped about thirty meters from him and he still kept walking.

> I didn't want to go off the road. There were houses on the sides of the road. I reached the bridge where there is a traffic sign which says Pilica. The driver was walking toward me and he looked at me at that bridge where the sign is. He must have thought that I was a Serb so he just walked back towards the truck. Because I made the decision not to run he probably thought I was Serb and he had just mixed faces up. Once the driver left I went under that bridge and started walking in the right direction, the way I had planned to go before.

He encountered some people along the way and walked with them through the woods for several days.

> We crossed two big hills then we turned ourselves in. We gave ourselves up again. In a village near Zvornik. We were put on a bus and taken to Karakaj.[10]
>
> In Karakaj they took us to a military building to turn us in but we were told to go in a different direction. We were put into a small truck full of prisoners and everyone but me was tied up. They gave me a canister of water and said I should give it to people if they are thirsty.
>
> The truck took us to the Batković concentration camp prison in Bijeljina, and there were some people from Srebrenica there. The Red Cross was there so we hoped that meant that we would stay alive. The Red Cross registered all of the prisoners and we were each given a blanket to use on the ground where we slept on pallets.
>
> While I was at Branjevo they didn't ask any questions, they just killed people. In the concentration camp, they were asking questions, interrogating people. I didn't tell them what I saw in Branjevo, I couldn't. They would kill me if I told them. So, for five months they didn't know what I had seen. I was there for five months until the 24th of December when we were exchanged.

Ahmo explained his survival in the same way as so many others in this story.

> It's God, Allah. They were killing so many people, it was impossible to survive. Probably there are two angels everyone has. I am the only one who was separated in Potočari who survived. The only one. There were elderly people, very old people, as old as 80. Children as young as 14. That's the genocide. Of my family seven males were killed. Elderly people, one was 65 and one was 70. They were killed and I saw it.

He later heard that the four men with whom he had escaped Branjevo were taken to Zvornik and killed, making him the only survivor of the Branjevo execution site.

In 2006, these four men, including 16-year-old Almir Halilović, became the subject of a documentary by Refik Hodžić entitled *Statement 710399*. Along with Almir, Fuad Djozić, Sakib Kiverić, and Emin Mustafić escaped from Branjevo and were later arrested by military police. They were taken to the Standard Barracks, which was a former factory, in Zvornik where they were interrogated. They were executed at a later date. Using statements signed and dated on July 23, 1995, Refik Hodžić attempted to discover the fate of the four men but, in spite of exhaustive research and investigation, was unable to do so.[11]

Ahmo says that he will never be able to get rid of the thoughts and images from that time in his life.

> It's all the time in my mind. Even at night the images emerge when I am imagining what happened. As if we were some animals being brought to be killed. Some of the people responsible for the genocide have been freed of all charges and let go from The Hague. They walk out free but the people that were killed in Srebrenica will never come back from the dead. Is that justice?

Ahmo was clearly tired by this point so we thanked him and said our goodbyes. At the time, we didn't know that we would meet Ahmo again, and that the next time would be in person.

The following summer, we were having dinner at Šefik Suljić's home, eating outside in his yard, a space that includes a magical garden. He had cooked a lamb and served us tomatoes, peppers, other vegetables, cantaloupe and watermelon that he had grown. Šefik mentioned that Ahmo was visiting his daughter who lived nearby and he asked if we would like to meet Ahmo. We were most excited to meet him and Šefik went and picked him up.

Ahmo joined us at the table, sitting next to me at the end of a picnic bench. His hands were shaking with some sort of tremor and I was struck by how thin his body was and how his skin was almost translucent. His gaunt face came alive when he smiled. Around the table were a lot of people including several children. As Ahmo started talking, the children appeared to be listening to every word. Just like the first time we met him via Skype, there were children listening. This made me uncomfortable but it was not mine to decide who listened and who did not.

Ahmo filled in many details of his story and also talked with us about some memories he had from his childhood. He was a child during World War II. He was the middle child of three.

> There were no windows in any of the houses, just newspaper on the windows because of the war. I used to poke holes in the newspaper to see out. But I never saw anything interesting, just snow and fields.
>
> I started school at age 14 because of WWII. I went through four grades in school. After that there were no other options. Schools hadn't been rebuilt from the war and my school only had four grades.

When asked what he had wanted to be when he grew up, he said that he didn't think about much of anything, until he started thinking about girls.

In our first conversation with Ahmo, he was solely focused on events of 1992–1995. When he joined us the following summer, he had more to say about his life before as well as after the war.

> Before the war I was an independent contractor building houses and barns in the villages. I went to Serb villages asking them not to join Serbia in the war that they knew was coming. We needed to stick together against a greater Serbia. They initially agreed but later changed their minds. In April 1992 I heard General Živanović[12] on the radio giving orders to capture Muslim villages. That's how I knew war was coming.

Ahmo had two sons and three daughters. Both of his sons were killed in 1995 and both have been identified. One complete skeleton was found and the other was almost complete. He buried them five or six years ago but not in the same year. The house where we had skyped with him belonged to his daughter-in-law and the young man who helped us with the technology was Ahmo's grandson.

Ahmo testified six times at The Hague, including against Ratko Mladić. His statement was also used in the trial of Radovan Karadžić. He smiled as he told us about being with the other witnesses and how they coped by laughing and making jokes. He said it was the only way to get through it.

He also testified in Boston against a war criminal who was living there. Prosecutors from the U.S. came to interview him in Bosnia and then later he made the trip to Boston. His impression of the U.S. was that it was orderly and things ran well. What he remembers most vividly is being in the elevator of a building that had over 20 floors.

On the night we talked with him, he said that he was enjoying being back in Bosnia

Chapter 1. Execution Site Survivors 43

visiting and seeing people. He did not receive any financial support from the BiH government but he did from the government in Belgium, where he was living. At this point, he was comfortable talking about where he currently lived and said that we could share this information about him. He was obviously proud of his two grandchildren with whom he lived. He specifically talked about his granddaughter who is in the first grade. He spends his time doing what he wants to do.

> I walk if I want, I nap if I want, I watch TV. I don't go out much because I don't speak the language.

Ahmo and Hakija know each other. Hasan told a story about Hakija on the plane to London[13] and Ahmo had a good laugh. It was the perfect way to end the evening.

Ahmo got up and walked to the car with no fanfare, no time to really thank him or to say goodbye. He got in the front seat of the car and Šefik closed the door and walked to the driver's side. I walked up to the window on the passenger side and put my hand on the glass and caught Ahmo's eye. He put his hand against mine on the other side of the glass and we smiled at each other. I doubted that I would ever see him again.

That turned out to be true, as Ahmo passed away in September 2019. What an honor it was to have met him.

Today, Branjevo looks just like any other field. In July 1995, 1,200 Muslim men and boys were killed there.[14]

The Branjevo execution site (photograph by Kristian Skeie, July 14, 2013).

Hakija Huseinović

The first time I met Hakija, I was crammed into the back seat of a small car traveling from Srebrenica to Sarajevo. The curvy roads didn't matter as much as they usually do since I was in the middle of Hasan and Saliha and I couldn't have been happier. I met Saliha for the first time in that cramped car on those foggy roads and while I didn't know that we would become dear friends, I knew for sure that I wanted to see her again. The three of us in the back seat talked nonstop. In the front seat, however, it was a different story. Our driver from the British Embassy joined in the conversation at times but Hakija, the man sitting in the front passenger seat, did not say one word. He did not say anything that entire trip, which took three hours. I remember it was a few days before the July 11 burial day at Potočari. Tuesday, July 9, to be exact. The reason I know this for sure is because of something that happened on the road just a short way outside of Potočari. It was foggy and suddenly out of the fog, on the other side of the road heading toward Srebrenica, loomed two large semi-trucks. They had Bosnian flags draped over them and the sides were covered with flowers. That was the first time that I saw the trucks on their journey from Visoko to the Genocide Memorial in Potočari with the remains of those who would be buried during the annual commemoration. In Potočari, the trucks would be greeted by grieving family members who would watch as the coffins were unloaded and taken into the building where they would stay all night and the next day. As the trucks went past us, Saliha began to cry and Hakija remained silent.

I needed to get back to Sarajevo and I was able to catch a ride. The British Embassy had sent a car to pick up Hasan, Saliha and Hakija because they would be spending the night in Sarajevo before leaving in the morning for London. They were all to be honored guests at the "Remembering Srebrenica" event, along with Hasan Nuhanović who would join them later. We had coffee in the hotel in Sarajevo where we were joined by members of the British Embassy, including an interpreter, who would be accompanying the Bosnians to London. The interpreter arrived with sandals for Hakija to wear on the plane because he was having problems with his foot. Hakija tried on the sandals over his warm thick socks and nodded that everything was okay. It was only later that I learned that Hakija wore those thick socks and sandals each day during the very prestigious event, even though his colleagues tried to talk him into wearing his other shoes to such a formal occasion. Hakija had his own ideas and knew what he needed to do, which seemed to be the way he lived his life. I thought he might owe his survival in 1995 to this strong will, although he had a different explanation.

A few years later, Hakija agreed to meet with us to talk about his experiences. We visited with him on a warm afternoon in the small village where he was then living. As it turned out, it was the same village where Saliha's husband's brother now lives. Bosnian haystacks look like the ones in Monet's paintings and a huge one was right next to us. Baby goats jumped and played in the wildflowers. The table was quickly piled high with Bosnian coffee, cookies and many kinds of treats. There was no other place that this could have been except Bosnia.

That day Hakija had a lot to say.

He was born in 1944 in the village of Bućinovići, just like his father before him. He lived there his entire life and was a farmer of land and cattle.

> When I was a boy I had to help my father farm. Even if I didn't want to I had to. I had to obey the elders. Sometimes in the summer we'd go up to a village near Žepa for grazing.

Hakija was the fourth of six children, one of two boys. He experienced death in his family at a very early age, as his mother died when he was in his first grade of primary school. He went to school until the fourth grade and he thinks that was enough. With good humor Hakija described his time in school.

> I would not trade my four grades for someone's university. There are some people who graduated university and they are dumb.
>
> I never loved school. I finished only four years. I had the best marks, fives, in all subjects. But when it came to behavior I had a bad grade, a three. I was naughty. I couldn't sit still on the bench. I got involved in fighting. Some guys who were stronger they would beat me and those who were weaker I would beat them. I don't have any regrets.

After leaving school, Hakija continued farming. His love for farming was as strong as his dislike of school.

He served in the Yugoslav army for two years, beginning in 1964. He was stationed in Slovenia for five months and then stood guard on the border of Albania in the Prokletije mountains, a stunning place also known as the Albanian Alps.

Hakija came home from the army in early February of 1966 and was married five weeks later. He had known his wife his entire life. She was from a hamlet about 40 minutes from his village. They lived with Hakija's father and brother for about eight years until his father died. At that point, he and his brother built separate houses.

He described his life before the war with fondness.

> The life before was beautiful. My life was amazing before the start of the war. I wouldn't trade it for anything. If my wife was still alive I wouldn't be here in this village. I was very content in my life. I wish I could have it again.
>
> The years are passing by. I am again a refugee here.

Before the war, Hakija continued to farm and to hunt and to do something that he loved and misses to this day: horse racing.

> I never missed any horse race. I used to go with that guy Azem from Srebrenica. We went everywhere, Serbia, Sarajevo and a lot of other places.

When asked what he liked about horse racing, he smiled and looked off into the distance.

> When I saw a horse, someone bringing a horse, I would stare, I would just sit and stare at the horse. I loved a good horse. I had one horse but he was not a racing horse. He was workhorse, medium size, and he would carry things, as did the oxen that I had.
>
> Before the war I was no longer going up into the mountains with the cattle so I sold the horse because I didn't need him anymore.

He knew the war was coming because in 1992 political parties were organized in Sućeska and the other villages. In late spring of that year, several villages were attacked near Hakija's home. The day of our interview, as a train whistle could be heard in the background from where we were sitting outside, he told us the story of one day in 1992.

> On the 17th of May the Serbs started to attack, looting the villages and burning them down near where I was living. Sućeska, my village has 15 or 20 hamlets and in the center is a place called Brda. They started to attack with tanks and armored vehicles and one guy that I know waited for them and threw a handmade explosive. The armored vehicles caught on fire which chased the Serbs away.

His youngest sister died from shelling in 1992, leaving two small children.

After that initial attack, Hakija was able to stay in Sućeska until 1995, with his wife and his two daughters. They had to defend their meadows and themselves from the Serbs. It was necessary to farm the exposed meadows during the night because they could not protect them during the day.

Tuesday, July 11, 1995. Everyone in this book remembered that day, as well as the days before and the nightmare days that followed.

Hakija and those around him were talking amongst themselves, saying that they should go to Potočari. Earlier in the day, his brother-in-law had come with a horse, the horse that Hakija had sold to him back before the war. Hakija gave his brother-in-law his backpack that contained a change of clothes and some bread, and hoped that he would eventually catch up with them.

> On that Tuesday, the 11th of July, people around me decided to go to Potočari because everyone was saying we couldn't go through the forest. I told them that I couldn't go to Potočari because I didn't have anything to eat and no clothes to change into because everything was in my backpack that I gave to my brother-in-law.
>
> Then I went through the forest to look for that horse. I found my brother-in-law and his horse around 10 in the morning on the 12th of July near Buljim. We ate something for breakfast and then after we ate I never saw him again. We got separated on that hill and that was the last time I saw him.

Hakija was captured on Kamenice Hill, above Ramiz' place.

> I didn't know where I was. I didn't know anything, the terrain or anywhere. We were surrounded and they were calling us to surrender. I finally sat down when we reached Sandići meadow.

There were so many people in the meadow and Hakija knew many of them.

> There were Dahmo and his father from Gladovići village, Mekanić Junuz who used to be Imam in Pomol village and Ragib Mehmedović who was a mechanic. Everyone was talking to each other. One guy said he thought there were 2,000 prisoners there.

Hakija didn't count. He said he didn't need to count. They were surrounded by soldiers but Hakija said that they were not beaten at that time.

Then Mladić came.

> He introduced himself. He asked everybody if we knew him. Some said yes, some were silent. His first words were "Naser Orić left you, he ran to Tuzla." He told us "It's difficult to wage a war with a Serb. A sheep cannot leave the farm until the owner allows it."

Mladić told them that their families were almost all evacuated and that they were staying in Tuzla, Kladanj and Živinice. He also assured the prisoners that they would be exchanged, taken to a cooler place, given food and be reunited with their families. In reality, none of this happened.

They weren't taken to a cooler place, weren't given food, weren't reunited with their families and they weren't exchanged.

> After 15 or 20 minutes, we were walking in a column four people across. We ended up at Kravica warehouse. It was Thursday around four or five o'clock in the afternoon.

More than 1,000 men were forced inside the warehouse. Once it was full, others tried to get in but they were shot by the soldiers guarding the door.

> Then they started to shoot inside from all over the place. I was sitting in a corner with Redžic Salko from Vlasenica. We got on the ground and tried to protect our heads. They were shooting and throwing hand grenades until the dark fell. Then the shooting stopped. There were no prisoners alive outside and you couldn't hear anything inside.
>
> Inside it was total silence. Outside the soldiers were laughing around the building. On Friday morning at dawn I took two dead bodies and put them on top of me.

During that day, the soldiers kept asking for those who were still alive to come out and join their army. Hakija didn't dare look, so he doesn't know how many people went out. All of those who went out of the warehouse were put in a truck and driven away.

> Then they said that anyone who is wounded should come out and they would be taken to a hospital. Some wounded people went out. I don't know how many. They killed them right away.

When it got dark, a loader came and picked up the dead who were in the door of the warehouse. They were loaded into a truck and driven somewhere. Hakija doesn't know where. Then it was time to deal with all of the dead inside the warehouse.

> They put hay on top of us and I thought they would set us on fire. I said to myself that I wish I would have been killed rather than set on fire. But they didn't set us on fire. I don't know why.

It was now around one in the morning on Saturday. Hakija had been in the warehouse underneath dead bodies since Thursday. He didn't hear any soldiers around the building so he decided to get to his feet, but then he didn't know where to go.

He heard two men whispering and he went over to them. They were sitting down and he realized that they were survivors. One of the men was from Lolići which meant that he would know the terrain. The other man, Ramiz Muškić from Cerska, was deaf. Hakija begged the man from Lolići three times to go with him to find the way out. The man refused but gave him some basic directions.

Hakija and Ramiz left together and it turned out that Ramiz could hear if you talked loud enough. Hakija discovered this when they encountered a soldier who yelled at them to stop but they were able to run fast enough to escape.

They crossed the river and went through a cornfield to the forest. When they sat down, Hakija realized that Ramiz knew the way.

> He said we were going to Kaldrmica-Cerska-Baljkovica. He kept me with him through this area for five days. He knew the area as well as I knew my Sućeska. We came to an asphalt road and there was no chance we could cross it.
>
> I said to him let's go back to Sućeska. He said there are ambushes there, I'm not going there. I said to him we will die from starvation here. I said let's go there, there is some food there, corn and wheat and some potatoes. He wouldn't go with me. He brought me to Jelah village.

Hakija knew many people in this village and they were trying to decide what to do. They had learned of ambushes in several places so knew that there were some routes they could not take. Hakija was determined to get back to Sućeska. By then it was Sunday. One man agreed to go but Hakija didn't know him and therefore didn't trust him. They discovered that they had a neighbor in common, Hasim the forest officer. But Hakija still wasn't sure.

> I said if you know Hasim how many children does he have? He said three so I asked for their names. He knew the children's' names. I asked for his wife's name. He said her name is Munevera and she is nicknamed Banana. So I knew that he knew Hasim. So then we parted ways. I went to Rogač Mountain with Klasim and Šaćir.

Hakija knew the way to Sućeska once he reached Rogač Mountain. Along the way he found Anesa's boyfriend Popara. They made their way to Žepa where they met up with Muhamed and his father. After eight days, Žepa fell and Hakija went back to his village of Sućeska and stayed there until the ninth of September. They then decided to head out to try and reach the free territory. It would take them ten days.

> I left the village and on the 18th of September I came to the free territory. There were eight of us going from Sućeska to Kladanj. Only one did not make it. Ramiz, the deaf guy. He lost his mind. The rest of us survived.

When Hakija arrived in Kladanj, he couldn't find his family. He then, like so many other people, went to Tuzla to the airport to try and find them. He didn't find them there, but he did learn that they were in Živinice. He spent the night with a former neighbor and they left in the morning to find Hakija's family.

> They were in a flat and they were very surprised that I showed up. We stayed in the flat for five months then we left and went to Vozuća.

Hakija and his family lived in Vozuća for six or seven years until they returned to Srebrenica sometime in 2001 or 2002.

> I didn't have money to buy anything in Tuzla or anywhere so we went back to Srebrenica. I felt good returning, like it was my home. I would talk to the Serbs but I wouldn't trust them. I used to go to the towns of Srebrenica and Bratunac and nobody said a bad word to me. Nobody threatened me, nobody said anything. I have to be honest and say that.

Hakija testified at the ICTY four times. During one of those times, he learned the fate of Muškić Ramiz, the deaf man who he had been with when he escaped Kravica.

> Hasib, Ramiz' neighbor, testified one of the times I was there. He told me that Ramiz wandered through the forest for 72 days and then stepped on a mine and died.

He also learned that there was another survivor from Kravica.

> I didn't know about him at the time. He was wounded but he managed to jump out of the warehouse through the window. He was lying on the ground and the soldiers thought he was dead. He crawled through the river to the forest when some guy put him on a horse and took him down to Žepa.

In one of this book's chapters, Mevludin Orić talked about being with Hurem Suljić. Hakija later met Hurem who had survived the massacre at Orahovac. Through his conversation with Hurem, Hakija learned that some of those who survived Kravica were later taken to other execution sites and killed there.

Chapter 1. Execution Site Survivors 49

> Hurem said that he met the Imam from Sućeska, Tuefik Djozić, when they were both at the Orahovac execution site. Teufik was telling the prisoners that a massacre had happened in Kravica when he was there with me. When I learned this I realized that they later took survivors from Kravica to other execution sites.

Hakija continued to describe the time he spent at the ICTY.

> I testified four times at the ICTY against Tolimir, Krstić, Karadžić, and Mladić. Four times. I said to Mladić, "When you came to Sandići meadow, you thought that we would never see each other ever again."

Mladić had a lawyer who questioned Hakija about his time in Kravica, asking if bullets or bombs or shells were more dangerous.

> I said to him, "Sir, you're an educated man, what kind of silly question is that? A shovel or any tool can kill. We shouldn't speak about weapons. These are people." He took off his headphones and he said to me, "You offended me, you insulted me." I said to him, "You insulted me." I took off my headphones and put them on the table. And then the prosecutor told Mladić's attorney that he had the right to ask the last question to a witness but then he said he had no further questions.

When Hakija went to The Hague, Hasan Nuhanović came and picked him up and took him to Sarajevo to catch the plane.

> On the plane there was an entourage and from the other airport they came with a car. It was like an entourage that Tito would have. They took me to the court building then on the way back it was the same thing. Then another time someone else came to get me.

The prosecutor Ibro Bulić came on a number of occasions to see Hakija in his village of Bućinovići. Other people came to talk with him as well. We wondered what Hakija's neighbors must have thought about all of these visitors.

> My neighbors thought that they were bringing me a lot of money. When I went to The Hague, women in my neighborhood would tell my wife, "He will come back with pockets full of money." She said to them, "Not the pocket but a whole bag."

Hakija described the other trip he took, the one to London, as great, the best.

Does Hakija think about what happened to him in 1995 at Kravica and afterward? Before he returned to his village, somewhere around 2000, ICTY investigators met him at the warehouse to ask him questions and to film him. It was a terrible experience for him.

> I went with Hasan Nuhanović two times to Kravica. There are still bullet holes everywhere. Then all of a sudden the picture of what happened came back to me and I said to Hasan that I was nauseous and I had to get out of the warehouse. They were filming everything from inside the warehouse. I went outside to a jeep and they were walking around inside and outside and I said to Hasan, "Call them, I don't feel safe here."

Hakija hadn't told his family where he was going and when he returned home, he told them he had been in Srebrenica.

He recently had hip surgery and, in spite of having no income, he had to pay for the entire procedure which was the equivalent of about 1,500 U.S. dollars. Life was not easy, yet Hakija retained his dignity and his sense of humor even after all that had happened.

The Kravica Warehouse execution site (photograph by Kristian Skeie, July 15, 2013).

> Many people ask me if I am normal. Are you in your right mind? I think maybe for some people I'm not. Muhamed's father Izet asked me that question. We were going from Sarajevo through a roundabout to Zenica at night and he said to me cousin, where are we? I said, "the Zenica roundabout." Then he said, "Oh you are smarter than me. Do you know why I asked you?" I said, "I don't know." He said, "I asked you the question to see if you are in your right mind."

Since only two people survived the slaughter at Kravica, we wondered how Hakija explained that he was one of them.

> Only God saved me. Nobody else. Nobody could save me, only God. There was no chance for me to survive and I only believe in God.

It was hard to say goodbye to Hakija but we had to, given that the afternoon was quickly turning into evening.

Today Kravica Warehouse is hard to see from the road. The Bosnian Serbs have planted tall trees to obscure the view and they use the building to store farm equipment. It still has large holes from mortar shells and bullets, both inside and out. In July 1995, 1,300 Muslim men and boys were killed there.[15]

Mevludin Orić

We drove down so many roads to find him. We went on a narrow road under the bridge that goes over the river Bosnia. There were sheep and dogs everywhere. When we finally got to his house, his family was standing outside. He was almost 45 and a grandfather. After we picked him up, we went to a restaurant to talk but it was too noisy. The second place we found was quieter and was owned by a man from Srebrenica.

Mevludin had been interviewed by reporters many times, which wasn't surprising given the story that he had to tell, including the part where he made the trip *into* Srebrenica on a couple of occasions while everyone else was trying to get out. Even though it was obviously painful for him to talk about what happened in 1995, he generously spent several hours with us, telling his story in painful detail, sometimes having to pause and go outside for some time in order to continue. Like so many other people who participated in this book, Mevludin was willing to go through the pain of recounting his story because he wants history to be known. He wants people to know the truth about what happened.

> Let people find out. It's no problem talking about it. I'm doing this for the truth to be revealed, to be found out. The world doesn't know anything about what happened in Bosnia.

As hard as we tried to have our interviewees talk about their lives before the war, as much as we wanted to know them in that way, it was sometimes almost impossible. The intensity of what happened during the war seemed to make it difficult, if not unmanageable, for people to think about or talk about life before that insane time. Whether that's because it was too painful to remember or because it paled in comparison to the importance of their desire to get the truth out about what happened to them in the 1990s, we were in some cases only able to know these amazing people through the events of the 1990s and the aftermath.

Mevludin was one of our interviewees who glossed over his early life. We did learn that he was born in the village of Lehovići, the municipality of Srebrenica, on the second of February 1970. That is also where he grew up.

> I had land and I was growing tobacco. Fifteen thousand plants. I had a contract with an agricultural company so I could make money. I did that for two years.
>
> The third year was the year when the war came. If I knew how expensive tobacco would be later I would have saved it. I was just giving everything away to people. Sharing everything. Then later tobacco became so expensive. Halal, from the bottom of my heart. Maybe that's why God saved me. When people were coming to ask for food I never was yelling at them, I would give as much as I could. I would never insult, I would never raise my voice. I had two sisters with families, refugees, so I had to help them as well. So, in '93 I only had 20 kilos *[44 pounds]* of maize and I carried the whole thing to the mill. That was the only food left for my family. I could have said to my sister I can help you a little bit but I need to save the food for my family. I don't have the heart for that. My heart would break if I would send someone from my house without giving them at least something. She needed help. She did not have food. Nothing.
>
> In 1992, I went to Croatia and I got back in July '92. I went to Croatia because I was looking at the injustice when the Yugoslav People's Army gave all the weapons to Serbs. Then they were killing people in Croatia. Then I went as a volunteer to Croatia. Maybe it was a mistake but I think not.

When Mevludin went to Croatia, he left behind his mother, father, niece, and his pregnant wife. He returned to Bosnia because his daughter was born.

> I could have left Croatia and gone to Germany but I made a pledge in front of the mosque in Zagreb either I will die or see my child. Nobody knew that I was alive. In Croatia,

I could be in touch by phone until the 15th of April. My daughter was born on the second of April and later all of the connections were cut off.

Then I moved back. I was in uniform. I was in the north part of Bosnia, Orašje for a month and was fighting there. I got back to Zagreb and then I followed a humanitarian aid convoy passing through Bosanski Brod and Gradačac, three days before Bosanski Brod fell. I was one of the last people who passed through Gradačac and that area. From there I got to Tuzla.

Mevludin was in Tuzla for a month before he left with 47 others to head through the woods to bring medication to Srebrenica, which was a five-day trip. It was the first of two trips he made in that direction. He stayed in Srebrenica for around 20 days when the local commander, Naser, told him that he had to go back to Tuzla and bring a surgeon, Nedret Mujkanović, to Srebrenica.

I said I know the way and it's really dangerous and he said you have to go. Naser said you, by all means, have to protect the surgeon because we need him, people need him. We were given orders to stay away from trouble, from fighting, engaging with fire, and anything like that. We were supposed to bring just one surgeon with us and the medication.

Five of us went back through the woods and it took seven days to reach Tuzla. We had some ambushes along the way. I stayed in Tuzla for 15 or 20 days. We collected soldiers for carrying the medication. On our way back there were 545 soldiers and Nurif Rizvanović, one of the commanders. He came with me in that group. He didn't have an order to come to Srebrenica. He just volunteered to come. I was not supposed to bring him as well but he just joined me along with his soldiers. From Baljkovica to Snagovo was the most difficult.

In 1993, the inhabitants of Srebrenica had to surrender their weapons when the area was declared a UN Safe Area.

Someone comes and guarantees your safety, takes your weapons and then lets you go. Then they go and tell the enemy to go and do whatever they want. Hitler did the same thing, it's even worse. We had to surrender our weapons in April '93 when the UN came. We gave up everything. I didn't want to give up my guns. I gave my gun to a village Glogova.

When we gave up our weapons then the army didn't exist anymore. We had to give up Buljim to the UNPROFOR, the UN.

Buljim was a very important hill because it was a UN observation post and was also the exit toward Tuzla. From there it was possible to walk to Konjević Polje.

But then the Serbs kicked the UN out and the UN just gave up their position to Serbs. From that hill they see Potočari and everything.

The local commander Naser told the UN that they have to chase off the Serbs from there but they didn't want to do it. Then we got to that line we said to the UN, this is our border and you have to respect the border. And that hill was very important for Srebrenica. So many soldiers before died defending the line and we didn't want to give it up. When you give them a position they would just give it to Serbs.

So in the morning, we went there and we made Serbs leave. This was in '93.

I was a member of a maneuver unit and later I had a gun. I defended this stronghold with eight bullets. No more. Two times I met the UN soldiers face to face on Buljim. They would come from one side and we would come from another side pointing guns at one another. Then we would just walk by each other.

In 1994, Mevludin was the commander of the maneuver unit on Buljim hill. One day when he was lying down with his gun beside him, he fell asleep. When he woke up, there were nine UN soldiers around him and he was alone.

> I was arrested and they handed me over to the civilian authorities of Srebrenica like I was a criminal. I was in prison for ten days in Srebrenica because they found a gun with me.

The prison commander was Mevludin's cousin. He told Mevludin that he was using him as an example for other people to behave and that he had to put him in prison so that other people wouldn't think he was doing favors for a family member. The conditions in prison were less than ideal.

> There were maybe 15 or 20 other people in prison. Bugs were the biggest problem. Fleas and bugs. It was even worse than being in prison for a year somewhere else. When I came home I had to shower outside of the house. I threw away my clothes to not bring the clothes into the house. I survived many things.

Because Mevludin was in an army unit, he had to go wherever people needed him. His family was still living in the village and by 1994 he had another daughter. His life consisted of going to the front line to support a position when it was under attack and then returning home to grow fruits and vegetables to support his family and others in the village.

In early July 1995, Mevludin was asleep in his sister's house when the shelling woke him up in the morning. He was surprised at what was happening and he ran to his home.

> I knew that they would attack Buljim and I was supposed to be there with my people to defend it. When I got home they continued the shelling every day, every night. On the 11th I was on Buljim on the front line. The UN had fled, they abandoned that line then I had to come with my 10 people. We were hungry throughout the whole day. In the evening, nobody was bringing food to us. We didn't know what was happening. Nobody had any information.
>
> Then in the evening when I got to the village Jaglići a woman had a backpack and she was walking, crying. When I asked her what's wrong she said Srebrenica fell. We didn't have any other information. I said to my friends, let's go to Šušnjari village and see what's happening because they were not attacking that hill. When I got to Šušnjari around eight in the evening so many men were there.

The group gathered at Šušnjari was discussing strategy to escape through the woods to the free territory of Tuzla. Because of Mevludin's knowledge of the terrain and his experience going between Tuzla and Srebrenica in the woods, he was asked to go first and to lead the way. He was hesitant to take on this responsibility for several reasons.

> Everybody came there. Sead Ademović, Naser's cousin, said to me, you know the way, you used to go to Tuzla. Like I was supposed to go first and show the way. When I saw how many people were there I said I'm not going to take this responsibility. I knew what we had to go through. Streams, hills, sloppy terrain, mines, everything. In the first place I said, many people will die if we go all together. It's a long journey. Probably 80 percent of the people didn't know the terrain. They couldn't tell where to go. When I heard that people would walk in a column one by one I knew that it would be a catastrophe. I couldn't take over the responsibility.

> The mistake was, there were some people with weapons, we should walk in two columns. And those who had some weapons could maybe protect those two columns. Maybe less people would die, I don't know.

Ultimately the decision was made for everyone to leave together and walk in the same direction, single file, with Mevludin at the back of the column.

> The mistake was that everybody would be walking in the same direction one by one. Almost 15,000 men. Some of them were on Udrč mountain. On the 12th of July, I was in the back of the column leaving for the free territory from Srebrenica. That's how long the column was. That's how long it took.
>
> Chetniks were shooting against the trees, the branches. On the 12th of July, early in the morning, I got separated from my father. He went to one side, I went to another one. That's when we separated. We were among the last people in the column. I never ever saw him again.

Mevludin's father had brought a backpack with some food and when they got separated, Mevludin didn't have anything with him. He didn't eat anything except mushrooms on one day. After being separated from his father, he kept on walking.

> They started to shoot at us and shell the column. They hit the column. They were watching from the top of the hill and they knew where people were going. Maybe after 500 meters of the walk 8 men died, killed by shelling. Then in Kamenice hill that big ambush, at least 500 men were killed.
>
> Some people saw my father there for the last time.
>
> I kept asking everyone if anybody saw him. I was close to him in the column. I asked people if they saw my father and then they said he's over there. As I started to go to him they started to shoot. I never saw him ever again. Nobody saw him ever again. Many of them who saw him, they died. He died either there on Kamenice hill or he went to Kravica. Those who made the turn on the right headed straight to Kravica. I know the terrain, either there or on Kamenice hill, I don't know.

Mevludin's father's remains have been identified but they have not yet buried him in Potočari. Families often make the decision to wait to bury their loved ones in the hope that more remains will be found.

> They found some of his remains but they didn't tell me where. The Chetniks used to move the graves from the primary to secondary sites. They found his skull and the lower leg and the lower arm. We haven't buried him yet. Maybe this year. Probably. Because I have a sister in the United States, in Boise, Idaho. She will come to Bosnia so we will do it this year.
>
> After the ambush on Kamenice hill the column totally fell apart.
>
> The groups were then created and I was in one of the groups. They were setting ambushes, shooting from all over the place, killing people. People were running all over the fields so when they shot from the hill they couldn't miss. People from the column were unarmed. I saw them with guns heading toward us but I didn't have a gun. They were throwing grenades and everything. Killing people, I couldn't respond with anything.
>
> There was a group of 500 men. Between 400 and 500. A man came up to us and said that he knew the way, that he would tell us the way.

Mevludin was very familiar with the terrain and he did not recognize this man. Therefore, he was very suspicious.

> He said we should go down the hill. But I knew the terrain. That there was an asphalt road down there by the Chetniks. Then I said to myself, no no no don't go there. I didn't recognize him. I knew almost 80% of people from Srebrenica by their faces. I would see them in different places and he was totally unknown to me. His speech was unknown. I totally doubted who he was.
>
> I separated my small group from that big group and I told them not to go down there because Chetniks are there. Some people headed to the asphalt road anyway. We headed to a field and when we got to the middle of it the shooting started down there where the Chetniks were. People were giving themselves up, being shot and killed. I just went back to the forest. I didn't look back. I was running. They were shooting heavily. When I got to the forest nobody was with me. Nobody was there.
>
> All of my neighbors, everybody who was with me, they are buried now in Potočari. They went down the hill to the field. They were probably captured and killed later.

Mevludin fell asleep in the forest, woke up in the morning and joined some other people that he knew who were passing by.

> We got to a hill at Konjević Polje, I was meeting people who were coming back, going forward. I was waiting for the night to cross the road, the road that leads to Nova Kasaba, the main road. They were patrolling, they used nerve gas.

Mevludin was certain that nerve gas was used.

> I know by the color of the shell. The smoke. People were giving themselves up in big groups. You would see a group heading to surrender. I saw my cousin, I just grabbed him, so fast. I put him in the back but he pointed the gun at me and he just went on leading the group to surrender. He chased them, seven people, and his own brother was saying don't do that. He said let's go to surrender. His eyes were so red probably because of nerve gas. I saved the people around me, I pushed leaves on the ground to make a small hole. Then we pressed our faces against the soil because of the poison. I knew how to do this because I was in Yugoslav People's Army, in the Croatian army.

That evening there were 13 of them together. They went to the road and were then rounded up by Serb soldiers who had surrounded them. They were told to lie down.

> They were searching our pockets and they took everything from us. Then they pushed us to Konjević Polje. I recognized a Serb and he also recognized me. His family name was Simić. He lives in Bratunac now. I knew him before the war and we went to school together. He asked me where I was in the army. I said I was in the JNA in Kosovo. He asked me where else I had been. I didn't want to tell him so I said nowhere else. He could have killed me then. He could do anything to me. He could do whatever. I told him later I was in the Croatian army and he could tell other soldiers. But he didn't.

They were all taken to the petrol station by Konjević Polje. There was an agricultural company building and a warehouse nearby and they were pushed inside.

> We sat there and a commander from Serbia came. His shirt was unbuttoned. He was cursing, saying where are your guns? I was thinking that if I had a gun you wouldn't have

> captured me. I didn't say it but I was thinking it. He told us to go to the woods and bring our guns where we left them.
>
> I believe that he was trying to save us. Maybe he wanted us to go to the woods to run. But at the same time, I couldn't trust him. We didn't have guns. Maybe he tried to save us, I don't know. He brought us beer, water, and cigarettes. He said we don't have food because the dogs ate it all. Like, dogs, his soldiers. He sort of protected us there.
>
> I could tell the soldiers were from Serbia. They were disciplined, they shaved. The rest of them were dirty and messy.

They were all put on a bus. They asked a soldier what would happen to them and he said that it was his duty to send people to prison and to take them to Bratunac.

> He was a Serb soldier. When he lifted his t-shirt, there were bruises. He had been beaten because he didn't want to go to the army. He is from Kalesija, he went to Serbia when the war started. In Serbia, they captured him and brought him to the Serb army. Some of them were forced to be in the army. In Kalesija he said we had Muslim neighbors, we had good lives. He said he didn't want to fight. He lived in Serbia. They captured him, beat him, and sent him back to Bosnia to fight. He was a guard.
>
> We got on the last of those buses and sat on the seats in the back. We went to Kravica where they filled in three buses of men. So many of them were left in the fields. I saw so many prisoners by the roads, by Kravica, by the warehouse. They filled in those three buses and those who were left there they were killed.

As they were heading to Bratunac, Mevludin saw the buses coming the other way taking refugees to Kladanj.

> We headed to Bratunac. We spent the whole night on the bus, no water, nothing, with our hands tied behind our backs. I fell asleep, my hands dropped. Then from the outside they shouted put your hands behind your back. I was hungry, thirsty. Since the 13th I'd had nothing to eat. Around midnight they brought water in containers. We were there the whole night. They had the names, lists, taking people out. They called the name of Nino Ćatić[16] who was a radio amateur. He was on the list. He says it's me and they took him away.

People were being pulled off the bus, beaten and killed. Some were taken to the school.

> During the night, we could hear screams from that school. Throughout the whole night they were killing people. The door was open, people were screaming and everything.

At this point Mevludin thought that they would be exchanged because there were so many of them. It didn't make sense to him that they would kill everyone. Later two additional buses came which made a total of five buses.

> In the morning, they said we would be exchanged in Kladanj and we started moving. On our way out of Bratunac they stopped. They said they were waiting for the UN. Then we were asking to go to pee and we were allowed to go in a ditch. By that ditch I saw an additional four trucks full of prisoners. Five buses and four trucks. The UN came, but it was the Serbs on UN APCs. They were kissing one another, all Chetniks. We headed to Konjević Polje.

Even though Mevludin realized that the soldiers were not from the UN, he still thought they would be exchanged or perhaps taken to a concentration camp. It didn't make sense to him that they would kill that many people. Mevludin was in the back of the bus and even though they were ordered to cover their eyes and to look down he was able to look through the window and he realized that they were not being taken to Kladanj but rather to somewhere else.

> When we got to the school there is a Memorial, a stone Memorial. They turned to the right. As the buses were being emptied, more buses and trucks were coming, We had to run from the buses to inside the school. If you had something in your hands you threw it away. Like in front of the doors elderly men were throwing their berets on a pile. Then later stuff was found there. The Hague investigators found berets there. In front of Grbavci school.

They were held in a big gym and there were already 300 people in there. They kept bringing more people in. It was hot and everyone was thirsty and hungry. After about two hours, they started bringing water in but there was not nearly enough and people began fighting over the water.

> It was hot inside. We were sitting, my knees were against my cheeks. It was chaos. Hot. We were thirsty, hungry. It got tighter and tighter and tighter. Later I saw there were classrooms in the rest of the school, and they were also filling in that part of the school with men. They started bringing water in a container and people started fighting over it. They said we won't bring any more water because you fight over it. It was so crowded. Your arms would be upwards and your knees close to your chin and you can't breathe. Elderly men were fainting.

Mevludin got a little bit of water and gave some to his cousin. He was talking with other men when he heard somebody say that Mladić was there.

> He was standing by the entrance where there were two benches. There was a big military gun, other soldiers were very well armed, he was with them, spoke with them. He was looking inside, was happy. He wasn't there for long. I can't tell if it was one or two or three minutes. Ten minutes after he was gone they said we would go to the concentration camp Batković.

Once they left the gym, they were given some water and were blindfolded. Mevludin realized that they were not being taken to Batković as they had been told. Batković was at least 45 minutes away and the trucks were leaving the school and returning in five minutes.

> Me, Haris and my cousin, Hakija, his son Esad, many people, Haso's father Edhem. We were by that entrance. My cousin asked me what would happen to us. I told him I didn't know.
>
> I wasn't that scared. They were killing people and I was with everybody so if they kill me so what. In the end whatever happens, happens. I'm together with people. Those were small trucks, maybe 12 or 13 people could fit in. The truck started moving for just two minutes then they said get off of the truck. My cousin Maid was on my left side. As I jumped off the truck I said where are you, come here. I grabbed his hand. He said they will kill us. I said they won't. Then they started to shoot and the bullets were flying all over. Then he started to scream and I felt his grip. I sort of moved, I fell down, the bullets didn't hit me. He fell against my back. He was shaking then he passed out.

At that point there was a long silence and then Mevludin left the interview. The questions about whether or not this is a good idea resurfaced for me. He said he wanted to tell this story and it needed to be told but it seemed like it is torturing him to have to tell us.

Mevludin returned to the interview and we offered him the option of stopping. He said he wanted to continue.

> It's difficult for me, especially because of him. Another thing, we used to go to school together. We grew up together, my neighbor. To die, why? For nothing.
>
> I had to let go of his hand and to get down. It was good that he didn't suffer much, just a couple of minutes. He wasn't wounded, he was just killed.
>
> I was lying on the ground and then later during the day I heard the wounded screaming. They just kept bringing people by trucks. I could hear everything. The wounded were crying and screaming but they wouldn't finish them off. They let them suffer. It was better for people to die immediately, not suffer more. They would say, let them suffer. There were so many wounded. They were bringing people, bringing people. Then I heard them speaking, joking and everything, saying things like, old man, are you wounded? We will take care of your wounds. They would swear about your Turkish mother, it is best when you are dead. They were saying many things, they were calling themselves Muslim names, joking, Zulfo, ex Muslim commanders, making all of those jokes. I heard them say things like, one's running away. I asked myself, who is running, I couldn't believe that someone survived. One started running through the forest and I heard shooting.
>
> They kept bringing people. I was lying down and they were killing people beside me in a row. When they said someone is running they started to shoot, then again, they would say another one is running. I was hearing all of this.
>
> I was still lying there. Then the commander said, there are people still alive. You didn't finish everyone off so you should come and shoot everyone again. Then they started shooting everybody, finishing them off. Then I said to myself, it's all over. I thought about my wife, my mother, my children, if they will survive. Nothing else. I wasn't thinking of myself but they were killing everybody so I could also die. Then he killed one person and the blood sprayed all over my face. He stood on my heel with his boot and he shot my cousin again. I was waiting for the bullet but nothing happened. He walked away. I was thinking that I might be in Heaven. Then I heard the conversation again. Nothing hit me.
>
> God protected me, hid me, angels, for them not to see me, for me to be the witness to stay alive. I could see lights through my blindfold. I removed my blindfold. I lifted my head. Lights were shining on me. I couldn't run. They were still killing and killing people, elderly people who were screaming that they shouldn't be blamed for anything.

That evening Mevludin woke up and it was raining. He got up and he headed for the road. He knew that Kemal had escaped via the railroad and headed through the cornfield.

> Maybe five or six hours passed. I don't know because I was unconscious. I was afraid and thirsty but the rain started which was a miracle. Then the clouds came and there was no more moonlight. But when the clouds cleared it was a full moon light and you could see everything. Then the commander said, we finished everything here. I believe there were just 10 soldiers guarding. They were swearing, we're tired, everybody's dead, tomorrow we will get back early. I heard an excavator digging a grave. All of that machinery had lights. I was afraid that they might push bodies into the grave and I would be buried alive.

Chapter 1. Execution Site Survivors

> They passed by the grave. They turned off the lights and they faded away. They didn't bury everybody.
>
> It was dark and I was lucky. They left but I was listening for 10 minutes to see if they were still there, maybe it was like a set up to see if there were more survivors. I waited for an additional 10 minutes. But I could only hear insects. It was total silence.
>
> When I tried to get up I couldn't. I couldn't feel my legs, my arms. I was trying to get my cousin off of my back. I was trying to touch my arms to see if I could feel them. When I finally got up it was full moon light and you could see everything, even tiny things. The meadow was full of bodies. I was really afraid.
>
> I started to scream and I couldn't stop. I tried to stop but I couldn't. Hurem Suljić, another survivor, he stood up, he asked me if I was wounded, I was still screaming, I didn't think he was real, like a ghost, or a Chetnik. I wasn't able to speak. First, I was screaming and then later I couldn't speak. I couldn't believe that someone survived, not just me. I was stepping on the dead. It was slippery, slippery, blood, very slippery. I got to him and asked him who he was, why he limped, he said it's another story, he was looking for his shoe. Before the war he fell from the fifth floor and broke his leg. Only the bone was left, not the muscle. He couldn't bend his knee, he had to move his entire leg. I told him not to worry about his shoe, just find a t-shirt to wrap around your foot and he did that. I was afraid they would be back. Let's run.

There were two other men who were alive at that point. Both were screaming from their extensive wounds and although Mevludin tried to help them, they both died.

> Then we ran through the woods. In the forest we found some bushes and there were thorns and a nearby house was burned down. We couldn't go any further. We were inside of the bushes and we slept there. In the morning, it was sunny. We didn't know that we were just 100 meters from the site. We thought that we were kilometers away. We could hear people screaming.

At that point, another survivor ran toward them. His name was Smail and he was bleeding. Smail had crawled over the dead bodies to get out and while doing so he took cigarettes and lighters. He knew that they would want to smoke at some point. The lighter helped later when they were able to start a fire in a stream. They cooked mushrooms, which were wormy, but they didn't care because they tasted good.

Mevludin didn't know the terrain until he climbed a hill near Crni Vrh and recognized the area. It was the same area he had gone through when he brought the surgeon from Tuzla to Srebrenica in 1992.

> When I recognized that terrain I yelled and screamed that I knew the way. Then we went straight to Baljkovica.

They saw dead people along the way and they realized that they were behind the Serb line. He wondered how far they were from the free territory. They waited for night to fall before continuing and they eventually made it to the free territory of Nezuk.

> We were totally exhausted. We could barely see. I got to Nezuk to the free territory, to a Muslim village. I picked some pears and I went back to the bushes and went to sleep. When I woke up in the morning I took off my socks. I walked back to the same path leading to the village. Smail and Hurem were not with me anymore. They couldn't walk up the hill

because of so many thorns and bushes. They followed the road straight. Then they came across our soldiers, Bosnians.

Our soldiers were so close and I spent the whole night still wondering where the free territory was. When I woke up in the morning, there were raspberries everywhere, I was eating them. I threw away all the pears. Through the meadow, through the stream a man was holding a gun and he said, I'm not the enemy, do not be afraid. I couldn't believe it.

At this point in his story, Mevludin paused for a long time before continuing.

I couldn't believe that I made it. When I finally made it I was thinking of the dead left behind. Why did I survive? Why me? Why people as old as 80 were killed? Children as young as 15 were killed. They were all unarmed. Nobody was a soldier. Why would you kill the elderly or children? They were poor children. They were not even 15.

He testified in The Hague three times and saw one of his fellow survivors on two occasions. The man came from the United States to testify and Mevludin said that when they saw each other they cried. Another survivor currently lives in Switzerland.

Mevludin reported that the images he saw and the experiences that he went through are all still in his head.

I cannot sleep without asking the question why. Why people were killed. What kind of Bosnia do we have today? My people died. So many people were killed, women, children. Women and girls raped. We need one state. Not Serbs, not us, none of us have a good state. Why did people die. Today I'm unemployed. I have nothing. My house was destroyed. Not just mine, thousands of people's houses.

We just suffer. Serbs suffer as well. For nothing. Then everybody has Bosnian passports now. They can shout Republika Srpska, I'll never recognize that. My country is Bosnia, Republika Srpska is not Republika Srpska, it's Bosnia. They'll never be able to take Bosnia away. If they try it again, next time they will be in trouble.

It's clear from talking with him that Mevludin loves his country.

Yes, I do. Not just for Muslims, for all of us. Why should people mind each other. It is obvious who started all of this and who did all of this. My schoolmates, we used to go to school together. We used to visit each other during the holidays. The war was because we are Muslim. Why?

Mevludin is able to sleep but it is never a restful sleep.

I can sleep but all the things are going through my head. I keep thinking. It's all stuffed in my brain and I cannot get rid of it. It's impossible to get rid of it. You can use medication, whatever, and it doesn't help. You can't forget.

When I go to Potočari and Srebrenica I get sick. I cannot even survive the burial day. I get nauseous and I faint. The last year there was so hot that I fainted. My daughters tried to help me. They put me into a car and brought me back here. My heart cannot stand it anymore. I buried my sister's son, Mirza, he was 14. He loved me more than his father. And I loved him too. I taught him many things. Why should he be killed? I buried my brother. He was found in a mass grave at Nova Kasaba.

Some people were hiding in the woods for nine months. My brother returned, he made huts in our village. They had a stove and they cooked, they stayed the entire winter.

We told Mevludin that we would do our best to tell his story and let him know that we were sorry it was so hard for him to talk to us.

> It is hard because there is still injustice. The Republika Srpska, as they call it, is based on genocide. There are people working in the police who were killing people in the war. They laugh at the returnees. They are laughing like they want to say we killed your loved ones. They should just pray to God that another war doesn't start. How much anger I have. I wouldn't touch children and women. This time I would have a gun then we would see. What kind of fighter are you to kill civilians. When you come into the woods and you face a soldier you run like a rabbit. That's the kind of people they are. I couldn't believe it. Before the war I lived with them. I spent time with them. I spent five or six years in Belgrade. I couldn't believe that they had such great hate inside of themselves. I know we are Muslims but why do they hate the Catholics? They were also killing them. Who's good enough for them? Nobody is good enough in the world.
>
> When they were killing us, they were calling us Turks. I'm Bosnian from Srebrenica. It will always be my town. They can name it Republika Srpska but in my heart, it's not. Children are being born and I hope and I see that children will be more civilized without hate. They could feel the hate but they don't. Our children are living in the United States and in Europe, we are successful wherever we go. Our children have their businesses, they work hard.

Mevludin said that he wanted to talk to us because people don't know what happened in Bosnia and the truth needed to be told. He hoped that through this book people will find out what happened in Srebrenica.

> We should tell the stories. Nobody else can do it for us. The policies of the European Union are such that they keep silent. From Buljim I saw the planes. They were targeting a stream and only animals were there. The bombs fell and Serbs would just leave an old tank to be destroyed intentionally then they would say that they intervened. They were lying to everybody and to people of Srebrenica the most.
>
> There were smart people from Srebrenica. Before the war, so that's why Serbs didn't like us. We had good companies, only a few people were unemployed. We had good lives. People were going school, becoming lawyers, judges. Serbs did not like that. They said let's just finish them off. Let's get rid of them because they are getting smarter. Now children are being born and the truth will be passed to them. They will be aware of what happened. My parents didn't tell me the history of what happened from 1941 *[to]* 1945. Chetniks also killed many people in Višegrad, Rogatica and Foča. Nobody taught me that. Even today I'm not a nationalist.

Mevludin talked about how beautiful Bosnia was before the war.

> Those who tried to destroy the country did so just because we are Muslims. I don't care if you are from another faith. You can have friends of different faiths, Orthodox, Catholic, but those who did this don't believe that, even today. They still continue what they started. They don't want a life with us. It's not up to us, it's up to them.

Our conversation with Mevludin came to an end. As we all walked out together, the restaurant continued to be very noisy and the music remained very loud. Outside the evening was quiet.

The Orahovac execution site (photograph by Kristian Skeie, July 14, 2013).

Today, Orahovac looks like any other cornfield by the side of the road. You would never know that in July 1995, 1,000 Muslim men and boys were killed there.[17]

Nedžad Avdić

Standing with Nedžad in Sandići meadow today, it's easy to imagine what it was like in July 1995. Especially when he points to the house across the road that is still standing in a state of disrepair. You can still see the balcony where Nedžad was taunted by Bosnian Serb soldiers. He can still describe exactly what they yelled at him while they mocked him. If the meadow wasn't already haunting enough, now the image and sounds from Nedžad's tormentors become part of the story.

We have Nedžad to thank for the inspiration for this book. The first time that he spoke publicly on the July 13 memorialization day at Petkovci school in 2014, he could barely get out a complete sentence without needing to pause for breath, or for tears. Hasan Hasanović stood by his side, supporting him and encouraging him while the women who had gathered in the school listened without breathing. They were desperate to hear the details of what happened in that school, the details of the final hours of their husbands, sons, and brothers. Between gasps of horror at the story Nedžad was telling, they also murmured words of support for this shy man, calling him sweetheart and other terms of endearment. Even if the details were horrible, it seemed like it was better to know what happened than to only imagine it. So many times in life what we imagine is far worse than reality. That is not the case at these execution sites around Srebrenica.

After Nedžad spoke in the school, we all went up to the aluminum factory dam at Petkovci where most of the killing happened. In between Nedžad's poignant, though hesitant, presentation at the school and arriving at the dam, it was like he had gained strength and confidence with each turn in the narrow, curvy, gravel road that we had to follow to get there. Outside, at the base of an enormous dam, he continued the story of those horrible hours and days in 1995. That time, though, his voice was strong and it was easy to hear him as he described the terror that occurred.

It isn't surprising that Nedžad now has truly found his voice and is a frequent speaker in Bosnia and elsewhere. He speaks at conferences and for the media, among other events. When I saw him last year, speaking to the entire camp the second night of the Peace March, I knew that he had become a powerful voice for truth. At the time of Mladić's sentencing he was quoted on the BBC: "'This is my response to Ratko Mladić,' says Srebrenica genocide survivor Nedžad Avdic holding his beautiful family," along with a photograph that was taken inside of the cemetery in Potočari in front of the grave stones. What an eloquent rebuttal for the world to hear.

Like so many others, Nedžad came from a small village. He was born in Zvornik in 1978 and then lived in Sebiočina, a village near Nova Kasaba until the spring of 1992, at which point he was 14. He lived with his three sisters and his parents in Nova Kasaba until the Serb army invaded his village.

Nedžad's father usually worked in Zenica but during that time he happened to be in Belgrade, Serbia. Since his father was gone and there were young girls in the family, it seemed safer to build huts in the forest rather than stay in their house. Sometimes they also slept in barns. They didn't know what was coming but they knew something was happening. During the days before the war started, Nedžad's village would run out of power and they saw the Yugoslav People's Army (JNA) in the hills, practicing, training and shooting. They didn't realize at first that the JNA had become the Serb army.

> They were in the hills trying to intimidate people. From the end of 1991 to May of 1992, it was the JNA training but the JNA in name only. They were driving military vehicles through Nova Kasaba by my school, heading to Croatia. They often shot at the houses. We were really scared and my teacher, who was a Serb, said that those were probably just "crazy people." They had JNA uniforms and JNA weapons but they were all Serbs. They used to raise three fingers, the Serb salute.
>
> We all thought that the war would last for a couple of months and that's it. Maybe a couple of months or a couple of weeks and then everything will end. Nobody thought that the war would last for two or three years.

In the early morning, after hearing his neighbor shouting that the Serbs were coming, Nedžad and most of his family quickly put on their shoes and started running. They had grown used to leaving their house since they had been sleeping in the forest for days before this. They felt safer sleeping in the woods because they knew that the war had started. They could hear detonations and shooting and they also knew what was happening because of the coverage on the television.

They could see the soldiers coming and could hear the shooting. In fact, the shooting could be heard down in Nova Kasaba and in other villages. Nedžad's relatives who lived in Nova Kasaba were running too, but they didn't know where to run so they went through the forest.

His father stayed behind to close up the house.

> We followed the women and children until we got to the next village where Muslims lived. We heard that the Serb soldiers had caught our father and some other people and had taken them to Milići. We got worried and we didn't know what to do but we were with other people, with other refugees.

> After a day they let my father go along with the rest of the men who were caught. They asked questions about the guns but he had nothing. They said they were going to search the house. As my father told me later, they wouldn't wait for him to open the door but rather they just broke into the house.

Several days later, the Serb soldiers burned down the village along with other nearby villages and towns. Those who were unable to escape were killed. A neighbor man was captured and to this day Nedžad doesn't know what happened to him.

Nedžad and his family ran to the next village near Konjević Polje. They were reunited with his grandparents and other relatives who had escaped from Nova Kasaba when the Serb soldiers came. They stayed in the village until February or March of 1993. Nedžad and his immediate family lived in the basement of a house while his grandparents lived elsewhere.

> In that village we lived in the basement and there was shelling on a daily basis.
> At night, as I slept, I told myself it was safe because we were in a basement and we wouldn't be directly hit.
> But lots of my relatives were killed by the shelling in that village.
> I saw my cousin, who was seven, killed, his father got wounded, then our neighbor woman, then another boy close to my house was hit by shelling. In December of '92 planes were flying above and bombing the village. I was scared the most of the planes and I didn't know where to hide from them. They were fast planes, MIGS. People asked where they came from and some people in the village said they were from Serbia. I don't know why but I was so scared of those things.
> There were some other things, maybe worse, but especially I remember the first time people shouted "planes." We were on a meadow and I didn't know where to run to. They were bombing many villages and they bombed the school where many refugees were. We heard the detonations, the explosions.
> Before the planes we thought that we might hide from other things. Then we realized that you can't run. Every day we were waiting to be shot, to be killed.
> The whole time there was shelling of that area, every day. In that basement I would stand by the window and it was a relatively safe place. We lived under a hill. We were targeted by tanks and I saw how they were targeting the other villages from the hills.
> We didn't have enough to eat and I remember one day I was eating bread and watching targets being hit. My father kept saying, "He will eat all of the bread. The next day we won't have anything to eat." My mother said, "let him eat."

Like people all over Bosnia during this time they spent their days trying to find ways to get food. Before their home village of Sebiočina was burned down his parents would return there to try and find food. The family, including Nedžad, would try and find work in the fields so that they could get paid in food.

So many people talk about the difficulties of living in Bosnia during the war and many of them say that one of the worst parts was to have to beg for food.

When it became necessary to move again, some people went to Tuzla through the woods and others, like Nedžad's family, decided to go to Srebrenica where they had relatives.

> In '93 the offensive started against these enclaves of Cerska and Konjević Polje. Then we heard the UN came to Konjević Polje and everyone was hoping that the UN would save people. But they didn't.

We couldn't tell where to run to, where to escape. If we had somewhere to run to we would. Our father didn't want to go far away from our village. He thought if we went to Srebrenica we could return faster to our village when the war ended. And the journey to Tuzla was very dangerous and much further and at the same time we didn't know the way. We went to Srebrenica.

When asked if he wondered why this was happening, why somebody was doing this to him and his family, Nedžad replied:

In the moment I wasn't thinking. I was just surviving. I was just trying to save my life. I wasn't thinking who was shooting from what territory or a plane and who did this. I saw shooting like this in the movies but it was totally unlike the movies.

Nedžad set out for Srebrenica along with his mother and sisters. Once again, his father stayed behind to organize some things to bring and to try and find out any news about what was happening. He followed the family a day or two later.

As refugees we thought that it's best to keep heading to Srebrenica where we hoped to find food or a place to stay. We were walking through the woods, all in rags, almost barefoot and the night before we didn't have anything to eat.

We kept coming across people all the way to Srebrenica, refugees, walking at night. Even if we didn't know them we could tell they were refugees. It was scary at night and even in the evening. It was dark. I think we walked at night and the whole day. We arrived to our relatives' home, which was an old house full of refugees.

When we got to Srebrenica there were fires all over the place in front of the houses because there were so many refugees there. Some people were starting fires in the street, some people were driving people in wheelbarrows, there were lots of cattle and goats, people were all colored by smoke from the fire.

Before the war on TV I saw the Kurds in Iraq and I was sorry for them. But now I thought we were in the same position. I thought we were the same sort of thing, refugees were like the Kurds.

Nedžad's parents found a garage near the school where they could stay, along with relatives from his mother's side. During this time, the trucks with humanitarian aid were bringing food. When the food was all unloaded, they would then use the trucks to evacuate the wounded and other people as well. Nedžad's grandparents and some of his other relatives were able to leave Srebrenica on one of those trucks. Nedžad's father wanted his children to get evacuated and he took them to the trucks to make sure that they got on.

Everybody but me wanted to get on those trucks. There was a huge commotion and you had to fight to get into one. My sisters were small so they couldn't do it. I was 14 or 15 and I was able to get on a truck on my own but I didn't want to without my mother or my sisters. I didn't know why. There was something that made me not want to go.

My grandparents and some other relatives left on the trucks, along with some of my schoolmates. My grandmother died in 1993 in Tuzla from a stroke. She was an elderly woman and maybe she was squashed in the commotion of the trucks. My grandfather died after the war.

I had a cousin who also didn't want to leave. He kept saying to me, "Don't go, don't go, don't go." I didn't want to leave. My father wanted to stay and I wanted to stay with him. He thought that if the war stops then we could go back home. My father was trying to save us, to make sure we were on the truck to get to safety. I was in the crowd hiding and trying to stay. I can't explain it to myself. Maybe I wasn't aware of the situation.

When the UN commander Philippe Morillon came to Srebrenica, the shooting and the shelling stopped.

At that time people were thinking probably this will be different, that the war would end. Some thought that the UN would save people but others didn't think so. Regular people thought that but not the decision makers.

Like most everybody else who was in Srebrenica at the time, Nedžad remembers what happened in front of the primary school shortly thereafter.

There was shelling where so many people died. One of my cousins, he went to play football but he survived. I was supposed to go play that day but I decided not to go because I heard shelling. I was so happy we stayed under a bed in the garage. Later we learned that it was terrible and that so many people had died. My cousin, the one who survived, came back to the garage and he kept talking about what had happened and saying how terrified he was.

After that the UN came, demilitarization started and the shooting stopped. We lived in the garage for a while longer.

As was the custom at the time in Srebrenica, Nedžad and his family used to go to the villages to beg for food. Humanitarian supplies started to arrive and food was being dropped from planes on a daily basis.

Every day we would try and get food but it was a rare situation when we got something. So many people were trying to do the same and you could never tell where the food would drop.

At some point Nedžad and his family moved out of the garage and into the secondary school to live. They stayed for a month or two, after which everyone living in the school had to leave. There was a plan for the building to be renovated so that children could once again start going to school.

The Swedish government built a refugee shelter in Zeleni Jadar. Then they took us from the school and brought us to that shelter. Some of my relatives didn't want to go but we had no choice. We were afraid to go there to live because the Serb soldiers were close on their positions. The front line was so close and the refugee shelter was between Serb lines and the UN position.

Around 3,000 people went to the refugee shelter. About ten of us lived in one of those houses. My family was there along with my uncle, his wife and his child. There was also an elderly man, a refugee from Vlasenica. His family was expelled from Vlasenica to Kladanj near Tuzla.

This man couldn't see well so Nedžad wrote his letters for him which were then sent through the Red Cross to his wife and daughter. He told Nedžad what to write in the letters to his family.

He would have me write that there is hope, that we have information that the war would end soon, that the roads would open up and we will see each other again soon. Then he would ask them to send him something because he didn't have anything. He didn't have his glasses and he needed his glasses. He didn't even have his regular pants so he sort of improvised pants out of a blanket. Even so he went with us on a daily basis to beg for food to some villages.

Two years ago he was buried in Vlasenica in the cemetery where the victims of Vlasenica are buried. I didn't know if he survived but he obviously didn't. When the shooting started in 1995 he picked up his belongings and he ran from the refugee shelter. He went to Potočari and you know what happened.

He was my roomie.

Nedžad and the others lived in the refugee shelter until the beginning of July 1995 when the shelling and the attacks started. He remembered being deprived of food but also remembered something else.

It may seem a little bit strange but I spent the best years of my life there. For somebody from the outside it is difficult to understand this. This was before the killing started.

After going from one village to another we came to this refugee shelter. When we got there we thought that the troubles stopped and we were safe. The shootings stopped, the killings stopped.

There was a river. As children we would make sort of a lake and we would swim every day. We would play football with the UN soldiers. They had sneakers and we didn't have any, or we had sneakers that were totally worn out.

People were building small dams trying to make power. Whoever managed to steal a motor from the factory would use it for a dam to make electricity. They improvised a structure out of wood and made a cinema inside on a TV. So I would go sometimes to watch a movie. We had to pay the entrance fee to the cinema with food but we only had a few cans of meat so I had to steal a can to get in.

Because we didn't have any food I was worried. I would look and see that all we had was a small amount of flour then I would ask, "what will we eat tomorrow?" Whenever I would make that comment it made my father mad. He would always say back to me, "Let's see if we will live." I wasn't aware of the whole situation but he knew. He was aware.

People in the refugee settlement had water during that time but not enough food. This was when they had to go 20 or 25 miles to the villages of relatives to work in exchange for food. This was also when they were begging for food in other villages. He remembered that one time his father had begged for some milk for the family and Nedžad accidentally spilled it. He still remembered his father yelling at him for that.

We would often go to Žepa to look for food over the rocks and the streams. We headed through the canyon of the Drina and we had to be quiet so the Serb soldiers didn't kill us. We got on the cliff of the rock and saw a canyon below.

Nedžad thought that the cliff and canyon were so beautiful that he vowed to return there if he survived. But he never went back there again.

In Žepa we would ask for food and they would give us as much as we wanted, as much as we were able to carry. I don't know why they had food there. It might be that they were getting more aid. In Srebrenica they wouldn't let humanitarian aid come that often. Once in Žepa they gave us so much food that we had to go back for the rest of it and, as far as I remember, there was 70 kilos *[about 154 pounds]* of flour. It was impossible to bring all of that at once through that canyon and the snow.

Every day the kids would go see the Dutch UN soldiers at the observation point. It was interesting and the soldiers would give them posters of Ajax, a famous soccer club. The soldiers were often eating and they didn't share food with the boys. Nedžad and his friends would just stare at the soldiers and watch them eat.

> We accepted them as our saviors and friends. But I'm not sure that they looked at us in that way.

Nedžad and the others stayed in the refugee settlement until the shelling started again in June and July of 1995. This time it was heavy shelling.

> At the end of June or the beginning of July people started to run for their lives. The Serb soldiers had taken over the Dutch positions. Some people were heading to Srebrenica but we headed to other villages because it wasn't safe to go to Srebrenica. Some people were even killed. We were in the woods for several days with many refugees when we heard that the Serb army got into Srebrenica. Nobody knew what to do. Our father said to me, "you decide." Where to go? My mother and sisters wanted to go to Potočari to the base. Several of our relatives followed them. Our cousins also went to Potočari.

Though just a teenager, Nedžad had to make his own decision about where to go. Should he go to the UN base in Potočari with his mother and his sisters or should he try to escape through the woods?

> People were saying that the men and boys had gathered at Šušnjari and would go through the woods to Tuzla. My father said that he would go there to Šušnjari. He told me "Either you go with your mother and your sisters or you come with me." At that moment he was right. I know now that he was right. He was afraid that if I went to Potočari maybe some Serb soldiers would take me and so I decided to go with him, to follow him.
> At that point we separated from my mom and sisters. They left and followed the path to Srebrenica. They first reached the small Dutch Base in Srebrenica then they were supposed to head towards Potočari where the large base was.
> So we kept walking and I followed my father until we reached the village Šušnjari. Once we got there, close to the forest, a huge shelling started. It was dark by then. There were many people in those meadows and so many horses. People kept arriving on horseback or bringing a horse or walking.
> When the shelling started it was chaos, total chaos. We were hiding and then I got separated from my father.
> I never found him later.

Nedžad had the same experience of so many in the column. They moved so slowly toward the forest, walking for a yard or two and then stopping. He describes commotion and chaos while he was trying to find his father.

> Everybody was looking for everybody. I didn't manage to find my father. I asked to join people but they all said no. It's very difficult to understand that moment but everybody was trying to save himself.

Nedžad, surrounded by thousands of people and animals, felt alone. Finally, in the evening the column started to move and they reached the first forest about 20 hours later. By then it was around three the next afternoon. He estimated that they covered only one or two miles over all that time.

> So at the end of that time we got to the forest and the shelling started again. We saw the smoke from the villages around Srebrenica being burned down.

At the entrance to the forest were Muslim men with weapons who stopped Nedžad and others from entering. Nedžad described that the armed men wanted to go first and have the civilians follow. When the column started moving through the trees, the civilians were in the back. They went single file and for a while didn't hear any shooting but the silence didn't last long. Once the shelling started again everyone was side by side lying on the ground and Nedžad remembered the leaves from the trees flying around and landing on him. They didn't stay on the ground for long.

> The column started to move again and we ran. At this point I didn't know anyone I was with but later I found someone. We were running. People were getting shot, wounded. They were crying. A boy was crying, "please don't leave me," and nobody turned around to help. We just kept running and there was a moment when I jumped over some dead people.
>
> We just kept moving and moving on and on. I came across my uncle who had lived with us. He was alive at that point. I wasn't afraid to die but I grabbed him in case I got wounded and he could help me because I had learned that people were not helping each other.

The column kept moving forward and the shooting didn't stop. At one point, Nedžad heard Serb soldiers shouting through megaphones.

> They were yelling, "where are you running?" I got lost and I was alone again. In the morning I saw many people who were dead, some of them who I knew.
>
> A man I knew gave me a small amount of water. He was with his son but they didn't survive.
>
> We were crying, stepping on the dead as we wandered through the woods. One man that I knew was holding the small boots of his daughter. He was wounded in his head but still he kept those shoes of his daughter in his hands.
>
> He didn't survive.

The Serb soldiers started calling for them again through the megaphones.

> "Come out, come out. Give yourselves up or the shelling will start. You will be treated according to the Geneva Convention."
>
> I didn't know what that meant. I didn't know anything about conventions. I know that they just kept saying that.

Nedžad was alone again and didn't have any family members to help him decide what to do. Some people were running through the woods, others were not. He decided to follow the crowd. There were wounded people being carried and there were wounded who were left in the woods. He remembered seeing a classmate who had broken legs.

At one point they got out of the forest. Nedžad didn't know where he was or where he was supposed to go. They could hear tanks and when they got closer Nedžad saw a small hill and a lot of people who were giving themselves up, heading toward the tanks.

Nedžad followed them. He and the others were so desperate for water that when they came across a stream, they drank the water even though it wasn't pure. They kept getting closer to the tanks until they came to a bridge where some soldiers were standing.

> We came out to an asphalt road before Konjević Polje and Bratunac. Watching those videos today you can see those armored vehicles shooting at the hills from that asphalt road. They asked if anybody had any weapons and nobody did. If anybody had any weapons probably they were in the front of the column or they got away. I didn't have any weapons but I had a few things with me. The food that I brought I had eaten a long time ago. I still had the bag with some family photos and some clothes. I brought those things with me hoping that we would survive and that I would save the photos. If my mother and sisters had taken the photos with them to Potočari they would probably have been taken away from them.

Nedžad remembered that the Serb soldiers were "not that rude" until the moment when almost everyone got out from the forest. It was then that the soldiers started to yell and swear and demand money. Those coming out of the woods also encountered wounded people lying in front of them.

> I remember there was a tank and some other weapons and there was a sign written on the tank that said "the queen of death."

At that point Nedžad saw buses and trucks coming along the road from Potočari. Unbeknownst to Nedžad, Hajra was on one of those buses.

> Then the buses and trucks came from Potočari full of refugees and I saw my schoolmate, a girl. There were so many of us on the road that the buses couldn't get through so we were told to start running along a path and the soldiers ran along the side of us. Many of us prisoners were carrying wounded and those who weren't were forced to raise their hands with three fingers, that Serb salute.

The women and others in the buses were crying as they saw their relatives being held prisoner on the road. Nedžad later learned that his aunt had been on one of the buses and she saw him. Once she reached the safety of Tuzla, she found Nedžad's mother in a refugee camp and told her that she had seen Nedžad alive and that he would probably survive.

They ran for one or two miles, past a dead man on the road, and all the while soldiers were beating them with guns. They were told to turn into a meadow on the left and Nedžad saw that the meadow was filled with people. This was Sandići meadow.

He recognized the meadow as a Muslim village that he and his family had passed through in 1993 on their way to Srebrenica. He also remembered it from a year earlier when he and his father would come to the village from Konjević Polje with wheat to grind. This time, however, it was a very different experience for Nedžad and the others.

> There were wounded people in front of us, there was a tank and we were surrounded by soldiers. Soldiers were sitting on the balconies of those burnt houses. One of the soldiers started to speak to us saying, "Why haven't you surrendered before? You see your wounded friends now. If you had surrendered before they wouldn't have been wounded."

By then Nedžad had found his uncle and was sitting beside him. A soldier continued speaking, telling them that they would be taken that night to Bratunac to hangars where they would stay and be reunited with their families in the following days. He told them that they would not be having dinner that night, that other soldiers were coming and that they would not be harmed.

> Then he said, "We are from Serbia." I don't know why he said that. I didn't notice that he had a Serbian accent. Maybe he was from Serbia but I'm not sure.

Chapter 1. Execution Site Survivors

The other soldiers came.

> We were ordered to lay down on our stomachs. We were ordered to clap behind our necks. We were forced to shout, "Long live the king, long live Serbia." This went on for two or three hours and there was shooting all around. As we were lying on the ground I felt as though someone was stepping on us. Probably some soldiers were picking some people and taking them away.

They were then ordered to stand and they saw soldiers shooting into the front of the burned houses. There were no more wounded people in front. Nedžad assumed that the wounded had been taken into the houses and killed. His uncle told him that earlier a neighbor who had been in front of them now was gone. All the while buses and trucks with refugees from Potočari kept heading past them down the road.

Later around 8:00, big canvas trucks arrived to transport the prisoners. There was a sign on the canvas of one on them that said "Transport Tuzla" but in reality, the trucks were headed to Bratunac. Nedžad was forced to run to get on the trailer of a truck and he made it onto the last one. The prisoners were being beaten while being forced to get on to the trucks.

> As we got there we were told not to try to escape. A police car followed us and they had guns. It was crowded inside those trucks and I'm not sure if everybody from the meadow got on. The truck moved fast and then we came to Bratunac where we could see the buildings because the back of the truck was wide open. It stopped by a building and we stayed on board the whole night. We were asking for water. We were shouting and screaming for water. I was so exhausted I couldn't feel my body. A soldier was hitting the canvas. He would swear and say keep quiet.
>
> I was on my knees in the back of the truck by the side of the trailer. I could look out and see people on their balconies who were looking at the prisoners being taken away.

Nedžad saw soldiers sitting under some trees in the backyard of a house. He saw children his own age riding bicycles.

> Some people in the truck saw UN APCs there and they were hoping that they would be saved. At that moment nobody thought that almost everybody would be killed.

They were still on the truck in the morning. By then there were many trucks and buses stopped in Bratunac. Nedžad thought there were probably some buses from Potočari. He saw a bus full of people that had stopped.

> The backside of the truck was wide open and it was hot and we were looking for water. I stood up to see what was happening. The driver had a gun with him which he pointed at me, giving me a sign that I had to sit down. Someone brought a canister of water and started pouring it into people's mouths.

Before the trucks started to move again the prisoners were told to close the backside of the truck because of safety. It was terribly hot inside and Nedžad was breathing through a hole in the canvas.

> We passed through Konjević Polje, Zvornik and by the Drina river. People were wondering if they would give us up to the Bosnian authorities or were they driving us to the concentration camp in Bijeljina.

> Nobody thought would they kill us. If they had wanted to kill us they could have already done so.
>
> We expected the truck to turn toward Kalesija but it didn't. We thought they would take us there to give us up to the Bosnian authorities. We were on some unknown road and people couldn't tell where we were heading. It was terrible inside.

After a while, the truck stopped and Nedžad looked through the hole where he saw empty buses in front of a building. There was a concrete playground in front of the school but at first, he didn't know it was a school. He just saw a building.

> People were shouting to please open up or kill us inside. We couldn't take it anymore because of the heat and we were dying from thirst.

After an hour or two, the truck was opened up and the soldiers started to swear. One of Nedžad's cousins was unconscious and people were stepping on him. Another man was drinking his own urine. The prisoners jumped out of the truck and walked in a line into the building where they stood on the stairs. The soldiers were standing in a line and they started hitting everybody. When the first soldier in line wasn't able to reach all of the prisoners, they sent people through the line individually so that everybody was beaten.

> I was so close to a soldier who asked one of the prisoners, "Do you know me"? The prisoner replied, "I know you brother, how could I not know you?" He was terrified. The soldier then said, "Who do you know," and started hitting him. Then all soldiers started to beat him with everything, with their legs, with their guns.

It seemed impossible to escape the beatings but somehow Nedžad was not beaten at that point. He did not know why. The man who was being beaten just crawled into the corridor and Nedžad went in, too.

> As I got inside in the corridor we took the stairs and a soldier shouted a question, "Whose country is this?" We were silent. The soldier replied, "This is a Serbian country, it always has been and always will be." Then he asked, "Who does Srebrenica belong to?" He replied, "Srebrenica is Serbian, it always has been and always will be."

The prisoners were forced to shout and repeat those words.

Once they got inside a room Nedžad realized it was a classroom and he was in a school building. He could hear commotion from the other classrooms and he was in either the last or second to the last one. As the classroom filled up very quickly, he saw a chalkboard but no benches.

> The soldiers started asking everyone for money. Some of my neighbors and my friends had money that they hid, hoping to save themselves. Some men had amulets and the soldiers threw them away. Some people were giving money, some people were shouting that they were terribly thirsty. Some of the soldiers would give some water then some soldier would bring one loaf of bread.
>
> In all of this maybe there were some soldiers who were not wanting to kill. It was difficult to know at that point. Maybe.

Soldiers kept coming into the classroom and taking away people. They were asking for people from certain villages, from certain towns. The prisoners in the room heard horrible screams from the corridor. Nedžad described the situation as impossible. Everyone was desperate for water and desperate for air.

> In the same classroom we had to pee, we had to do everything. Someone tried to open a window and then the soldiers were shooting through it. Some people got wounded including one of my neighbors who was wounded in the neck. We were trying to hide but the bullets kept ricocheting.

When it got dark around 8:00 or 9:00, the soldiers started to tell everyone to come out of the school, calling them "Balijas," a derogatory term for Muslims. Shooting could be heard until midnight. In Nedžad's classroom, some people were saying that prisoners were being killed in front of the school while others were disagreeing, saying that people were not being killed. There was talk about trying to escape through the window.

> I was terrified. Until the last moment some had hope that they wouldn't kill people. Then it was our turn. The soldiers said that we should go out because the Red Cross would register us. This was all lies.

Nedžad thought that the soldiers were trying to calm down the whole situation because they believed that people might start to run.

> Then people started going out. Someone who was with me gave me a t-shirt because my clothes were wet with urine. I took off my t-shirt and put his on. I wasn't aware I was going to an execution. My uncle said that we should not go out together.

Nedžad kept his head down as he went out.

> In the corridor was a soldier with long hair in a military uniform who told us to take off our shirts and our shoes. I didn't have any shoes, only worn out socks, and he told me to take those off.

There were a lot of soldiers and Nedžad was ordered to put his hands back. On the fence, there were a lot of things to tie people up with and a soldier chose something sharp.

> He tried to make sure that my hands were tied tightly behind my back, then he pushed us toward another classroom. In this classroom it was dark, unlike the previous one where we had light.

When Nedžad's eyes adapted, he saw people's clothes and other personal belongings.

> Probably when they finished everything they filled the classroom with personal belongings but still I had some hope. They told us to get out single file. I went out and I realized this was the end. Do you understand how I felt? In the moment you know that you will be killed. You don't think of anything, you just obey. I was walking with my head down and something was sticking to my feet. It was dark, there were piles of dead on both sides, I didn't dare look. Probably they killed people on the concrete in front of the school before the stairs and it was blood sticking to my feet because of the dead. My feet were covered with blood as though I was wounded myself. There was no light outside, my head was down and I kept walking through.

When Nedžad got to the concrete playground, he saw a truck turned in the opposite direction from which they had come. They were ordered to get into the truck and once it was full the back part was closed. They were ordered to sit but they couldn't all do so because the truck was so crowded. They were crammed up against each other when it seemed like soldiers started shooting through the truck. This is the most probable explanation of why people inside the truck started screaming as they were most likely hit with bullets.

We were terrified. People pushed against each other trying to get down to protect themselves. I was on my knees in the middle of the truck and they drove it for maybe ten minutes. I realized it was a rocky road because the truck was shaking. I recognized my teacher from the school in Srebrenica who was behind me in the truck.

The shooting had started before we stopped. It was sort of raining against the canvas. When they opened the truck they ordered people to come out by fives. I was on my feet by then. As each group got out the shooting started.

Then it was Nedžad's turn.
Nobody wanted to go out.

One of the men in the truck was screaming at a Serbian soldier saying, "You should be ashamed, what are you doing, you are killing innocent people. I took care of you and your mother." He knew the name of his mother. I don't know how he recognized him in the dark. The soldier didn't say anything but another one said, "Get out or I will shoot."

People started to go out of the truck. A man that Nedžad knew from Srebrenica untied himself and asked Nedžad if he wanted to be untied, too.

I said no, I don't want. I was so afraid and I thought I was going to die so why should I.

The man jumped out of the truck acting like his hands were still tied behind his back. Once he was out, he started pushing soldiers and they started to shoot him. He didn't survive.

The other people were coming out. We were hiding behind each other, wanting to live one more second. It's difficult to describe but I was hiding as much as I could. Then, I had no more room to hide behind anyone. I jumped from the truck barefoot and the rocks hurt my feet.

I was walking with my head down and then they said find your space. When I got closer I saw piles of dead people. When I got closer they would kill five then the next five and go on and on and on. I was getting closer. Everything kept happening so fast.

In the moment I was thinking I will die quickly and I won't suffer.

I was so thirsty, I only had one wish, just to drink some water. When we got to the place soldiers ordered us to get down. Our hands were tied behind our back and we started to fall.

I was thinking that my mother will never know where I ended up.

The shooting started. From that moment I don't remember what happened. I do know I was shivering. They were still shooting. I was shivering and the right side of my chest was in pain, my hands and my arm were hurting me probably because of small rocks which were chafing me.

I was just moving and waiting for the bullets to hit my body. I was so afraid and maybe, probably, I was unconscious and wasn't aware when I was hit by a bullet. Lying down I saw how they killed other people and at the same time I was shivering. When they finished one group they would start with another group behind me.

Then another bullet hit my foot. I was in total pain and I wished I could have screamed but I didn't dare. Probably at that moment I had a desire to live, even though I wanted to die. Then a soldier came and killed the man next to me.

When they finished, one of the soldiers said, "Jovo, you have to check everybody to see if their body is still alive and you should shoot them in the head." I was lying down

> and a boot stepped by my head. Then a soldier shot a man in the head who was moaning by me.
>
> They were just searching and killing and finishing off people. I was waiting for them to come and finish me off too. I was thinking of calling them to finish me off because I was in pain. I simply thought I couldn't endure the pain anymore.
>
> When they finished everything I didn't dare shout. Then the truck left.
>
> I was thinking they will bury me alive.
>
> I didn't dare shout at the soldiers but I was praying to God to please bring those people to finish me off. I couldn't take it anymore.
>
> Then they were gone and I was left there waiting to die. I was waiting to die. I never thought I would be saved, not ever, never.
>
> I never thought to run, to escape. It was impossible to escape from those soldiers. As I was lying down the little rocks were hurting my cheeks. I tried to lift my head and turn it to the other side. As I lifted my head I saw a man moving in the pile in front. I asked him if he was alive he said, "yes, come and untie me." I told him I couldn't. He kept calling me and I kept telling him I couldn't help. He kept calling me and then somehow I was rolling and kept rolling and rolling then I got to him.

Nedžad was able to reach the man's mouth with his arms. When the soldier had bound Nedžad's hands back at the school, he hadn't tied them tight. Even though he had pushed Nedžad's arms to make sure that his hands were tightly bound they actually were loose. Nedžad and the man were able to untie each other, the man using his teeth to take off Nedžad's rope and Nedžad using his teeth to start cutting the man's rope.

Nedžad would later realize that the man was slightly wounded in his head. At that moment, the man was unable to move because of the pile of the dead.

Then they heard the sound of the truck again. Nedžad realized he was also wounded in his hand, although he was still able to move it.

> I kept on cutting the ropes off and then I saw the lights of the truck. I said the truck is coming again and he begged me to keep cutting off his rope, which I did. I helped him somehow get on his feet and he was stumbling all over the dead.
>
> It was moonlight and there was a light nearby from a watchman who was keeping an eye on that dam. The man I untied was walking but I couldn't.
>
> I tried to crawl over the dead. It's a terrible image, dead bodies. I got to the end of the dead bodies and I rolled myself into the bushes, somehow stumbling into a ditch.
>
> In the meantime the truck arrived and they started to shoot again, much less but still shooting. It was the last truck and they were trying to use up all their ammunition while shooting the last group of prisoners.
>
> In the ditch was another survivor, that guy who had stumbled over the dead. He had been brought to this place by Serb soldiers from the stadium by Nova Kasaba. They didn't make him take off his t-shirt or his clothes. He was only barefoot. Now he took off his t-shirt and rolled it around my hand then he took my underwear and he rolled my foot which was wounded as well. He told me his name and where he was from, a village near Srebrenica and I told him where I was from.
>
> As he was helping me I fell asleep in his lap. I was exhausted and was bleeding.

Around 5:00 the next morning as daylight was coming, they were still in the ditch. The man tried to wake Nedžad up and said that they should figure out where to go and should run. Nedžad realized that he couldn't walk. The man was trying to lead him into the forest when they saw the watchman and got back into the ditch. The man left for a long time looking for water and brought some back in a shoe.

They then took off and the man would look for water or some apples and would bring them back to Nedžad. They hid in the forest and slept in the grass near some Serb houses.

During the day when they were walking down from the hill, they saw a truck coming to pick up the dead from the school playground full of bodies. The truck kept taking the dead someplace. On that day and other days, only the man was walking, not Nedžad. They wandered for days through streams with the man carrying Nedžad, who kept begging the man to leave him.

> I couldn't walk and he was carrying me. We would collapse together and then I would feel pain because of my wounds. It was raining during the night and we were freezing. One day we reached a Serb cemetery. Some days before Serbs were coming to the cemetery bringing food for their dead. It's a Serb tradition. I was lying there and my friend brought me coca cola and I drank it. It was full of ants but I still drank it.

The man then took off one of the shirts from a cross in the cemetery and put it on Nedžad. They were so dirty and Nedžad was covered in blood. One day they were sitting by the road and Serb soldiers passed by the woods but they were not discovered.

Eventually they were in the forest near a village when they overheard a man and a woman talking about Srebrenica. They were talking about so many people being killed and the woman said that Allah will punish those who did it, so Nedžad and his friend knew this was a Muslim village.

> My friend said I'm going, those are our people. I said I can't go. He went and I stayed. But then I started to crawl. We got to a stream and the man and woman were sitting and we could see that they were wearing Muslim clothing. My friend asked if we could come over to them and they said, "yes, come, come." They weren't looking at us though because they were talking to each other. Both of us were so dirty and I was covered in blood.
>
> When they looked up and saw us they started to run and my friend said, "Don't run, we are from Srebrenica, we are from Srebrenica." But they ran away.

Someone took Nedžad and his friend to the front of the house and gave them water and food. Nedžad was lying down, so exhausted he was unable to move. An ambulance picked them up and took them to a small hospital that seemed like a military hospital, where Nedžad had some sort of surgery.

He remembers screaming.

The next day Nedžad was driven to Tuzla where he was taken to a larger hospital and his friend went to look for his family. At that point, Nedžad thought his father was still alive but he later learned that he did not survive. He was shot in the back of the head near Nova Kasaba by the stadium.

Nedžad's mother came to see him and initially she was relieved because she was told that he just had a slight wound. It was only after Nedžad told her what had happened to him that she realized the seriousness of his condition. Later he was moved to a retirement institution in Tuzla because the hospital was full and he couldn't stay there any longer.

> One day I remember they brought me from the hospital and I fell asleep. I was dreaming and I started to scream. I screamed, "Move this bed, there are dead people here." My

mother and sisters kept saying, "No, no, no it's not real, calm down." Then they started to move the bed and I realized and said it's okay, it's okay.

At night I still have those nightmares, even today.

Nedžad feels so lucky to have escaped with his friend. They never stepped on a mine and they were never seen by Serb soldiers. It wasn't easy for him afterward, however, just as it isn't easy now.

I'm not sure how long I was in the hospital. They put me in this retirement home, there was a doctor there and my mother and sisters kept driving me to the hospital. It took two or three months for my recovery, the whole thing. I know that school started. They signed me up to go to school. I was only 17. I started to go to school with bandages on my arm and stomach but I hid my bandages with clothes. At the beginning I had no clothes in the hospital, I just had pajamas and they were not new. A woman gave me some shorts and some t-shirts. At the beginning I didn't have any clothes to go to school, proper clothes. My mother would find big pants, big, big pants with pockets where they're not supposed to be. She would use tricks to make the pants so the pockets would be on opposite sides.

His mother did what she could to take care of him.

The man who survived with Nedžad was from a village near Srebrenica. He no longer lives in Bosnia but he and Nedžad stay in touch. He doesn't want to have anything to do with Bosnia anymore, which Nedžad understands. He encouraged Nedžad to join him outside of Bosnia but Nedžad didn't want to go. He finished school in Tuzla and has had many chances to leave Bosnia, but he has chosen to stay.

When asked how he was able to concentrate in school after all that happened to him, Nedžad says that it helped him to be in school.

During all that time I never said to anybody that I survived all that I survived. When I got to Tuzla there were a few students, survivors, but my generation most of them died. There was a boy who went through the woods and one girl, those two knew about what happened to me and they told others but myself I never said anything. Same thing at the faculty too.

My life was not simple. I had a lot of problems. I used to go to a psychiatrist in Tuzla. My mother, she had a stroke afterwards, she couldn't take it anymore. Eventually my friend maybe was a little bit angry with me because I didn't want to go with him outside of Bosnia.

Nedžad explained that he still had those dreams.

I constantly have those problems but different. It's not that often, it depends on the moment. Sometimes I think of those memories then it causes the dreams. I still have the idea that I will get rid of those dreams but talking to a psychiatrist he said it's part of my life. I have to deal with that, learn to live with that.

Nedžad was very clear about why all of this happened and how he has learned to deal with it.

God, that's it, that's all. I didn't even try to escape from the execution, seeing all those armed soldiers. It's so obvious it was impossible to escape. God saved us. Nothing else. We could have survived that but later we might have stepped on a mine. It was a very dangerous area, a soldier, another soldier that was passing by could have killed us but, thankfully the man who was with me who survived was so brave. All during the night we were sleeping and during the day we were walking. The last day when we were walking through the village he was carrying me and the Serbs were working in the field and he was taking me through the village, carrying me. I begged him, no, no please don't. Just leave me and you go. He kept saying we'd better go like this. We shouldn't hide, they won't pay any attention.

Nedžad has buried his father and his uncle.

My uncle who was with me, he was found 30 kilometers *[nearly 19 miles]* from Srebrenica. He was found there, in a secondary mass grave. He had a daughter, she lives in Bosnia.

People who survived the genocide have to decide what to tell their own children about what happened. At the time of our interview, Nedžad had two daughters, ages 4½ and 2½.

The older one she knows now. I go to the cemetery and I bring her there, to Potočari. Then I say to her this is my father, your grandfather. And she asks who killed him. I tried to lie to her in the first place. I didn't want to put this burden on her. She asks those questions. If I lied then she would remind me, no you didn't say that, she remembers so I decided not to lie, to be straight with the story.

Nedžad feels differently about telling his children the specifics about his own experience.

I can't say anything. She asked me who killed my father and I said some bad guys. I can't say anything more. She asks why is my grandpa in the cemetery? Why? How come? I said to her, bad guys, bad people did this. Not all people are good, there are bad people as well. Then she says, "I'll get them." She watches the cartoon, Lucky Luke. She said, "I will shoot them." Then I said it is not a good thing to do then she said, " not for real."

I don't want to put this burden on her. It will be part of their lives as well unfortunately. If we stay here to live, I want to stay here, it depends on the situation. If I think about them, about their future, I want them at a certain point in their lives not to survive what I survived. I got married, I have children, but at the moment I think I have to leave here because of them. Then I say I shouldn't have gotten married.

I testified in The Hague Tribunal. When I got back I was sitting in faculty with my colleague. He said, "Yesterday I heard a testimony on television, the voice was like yours." I didn't say anything.

It's understandable that Nedžad wouldn't want people to know about his testimony. It wasn't as clear, however, why he didn't want to share his experiences at all with others.

I got to the company in Srebrenica. People didn't know except a few of them. All of my friends, they knew. They told some people and they knew that I survived something, somewhere. Somebody saw me on television. The Serbs were working there too. Maybe some of them were curious, maybe some of them needed to know, maybe there are some of them who maybe did something to me, I don't know.

One Serb said, "I saw you on the news in Petkovci school speaking to people." Another one said, "I saw Nedžad and I read his testimony." They saw on television and read in the paper. In a way maybe they wanted to understand. Hopefully more of this will happen in future. I used to travel with a Serb coworker because of my job. I stayed in a hotel room with him and we spoke about some other things. He said, "I don't understand people who can kill that many people." He wanted to me talk about it but I didn't, I wasn't ready. That's just one example. We will have more in the future.

Nedžad continues to struggle with the fact that so many people were killed.

Even if a similar thing happened now, even now I wouldn't believe that they would be able to kill that many people. At the beginning of the war people were being killed and we heard stories that many people were killed in neighboring villages. We were afraid. I thought they can kill 100 people but even today I cannot understand how they were capable of killing thousands.

Nedžad's voice continues to get stronger. Recently, there was a book promotion in the Srebrenica Cultural Center. The author of the book is Dušan Pavlović and the book denies the Srebrenica genocide. The mayor of Srebrenica and representatives from the Orthodox Church supported this book and were present at the promotion. When he heard about the event, Nedžad decided that he needed to attend. He wanted to hear what they were talking about.

I was there and it was very bad and I don't know what to say but I all the time I listened with dignity. And I was calm all the time.
Not only did they deny genocide and the international judgement, they deny mass killings they deny everything. They say that we killed ourselves in suicides or in confrontation with the Serb Army. They said that some small groups were killed in mass killings and that mass killings had no connection with Ratko Mladić and Karadžić. That people who killed those small groups of Muslim people are not part of the Serb Army.

Nedžad listened and he waited for the time when the audience could ask questions. He stood up and introduced himself, even though it was clear to him that many people in the audience knew him.

I said my name is Nedžad Avdić and I'm a victim of the genocide. I survived one of the mass executions as a 17-year-old boy. I was in the first class of high school here in Srebrenica and I was taken to be killed and I survived. But before first of all I want to say hello to everybody and I'm not here to deny Serb victims and I'm just here to say to you that I don't agree with your promotion this evening. It is shameful for Serb people.

Some of the event organizers tried to stop Nedžad from continuing but he insisted on talking.

One local Serb postman, he said to me, "You can see that guy behind you, his sister was killed by a Muslim." I said, "I respect that. I want to listen to that because I'm not here to deny your victims. The problem is that all the time you deny our victims and you offend us." I want to say to Serb people hear me please. The author of this book forgot to say about mass killings of men and boys. He all the time is saying about suicide but he forgot to say about Karadžić and Directive 7. You know that Srebrenica was defeated in a military way. Why you did kill us, so many men and boys, without any reason, tell me. Author Dušan Pavlović did not say anything all the time he just was looking at me and someone said that he was smiling ironically but I didn't notice that.

The Petkovci Dam execution site on the annual July 13th memorialization of main execution sites by mothers and survivors (photograph by Kristian Skeie, July 13, 2014).

> Prosecutors in Hague Tribunal mainly charged Serb officers because of separation of men and boys and because of mass killings. You didn't say anything about that. You said in fact that behavior of Serb army toward the Bosnian civilians was one of the brightest moments in this war and atrocity. At that moment they interrupted me and we left that place. I just remember that there were police officers there and later I was told there were 12 of them.
>
> They take Karadžić for a hero but I think history will show that he is war criminal. It is not a problem that we have denial from individuals. It is a problem that they are supported by institutions, by the mayor who should represent all the people here in this community but unfortunately it is not so.

Today, neither the Petkovci dam nor the Petkovci school show any indication that over 1,000 Muslim and boys were killed there in July 1995.[18]

Chapter 2

Death March Survivors

Dr. Fatima Dautbašić-Klempić

The day we interviewed Dr. Fatima Klempić-Dautbašić was a busy one for her. As always, she greeted us with her warm, beautiful smile. I'm always struck by how shiny her brown hair is and the kindness in her brown eyes. After meeting with us, she was going that night to a wedding with her family. She always makes time to share her story if she thinks it will be helpful to someone. She frequently talks with my students and always has a lasting impact on them. What stood out on this day, as it does with every day that I talk with her, is Fatima's devotion as a physician and her desire to help people in that capacity. It is one of her greatest sorrows that she was unable to help the wounded in the Death March as they tried to escape the genocide. It remains painful for her to talk about to this day.

Fatima is a natural-born scientist who always wanted to be a doctor, even though there were no other doctors in her family. From the time that she first remembers, she didn't want to be anything else, even for a minute. She used to play doctor and would always tell her mother when she read articles about medicine because they were really interesting to her.

> Nothing else was so interesting to me other than medicine. It's still like that.
> I liked every kind of book when I was little. I remember that I was happy to read about space, about medical things, and all books by that German author about the Bermuda triangle. All of his books I finished by the time I was 12. When I went to the town library the woman working there told me "you are too young to read these books." But I told her that I liked them. In secondary school I really liked physics.

She was born in Sase, a village that contains a lead and zinc mine. Originally, it was a silver mine which is how Srebrenica got its name. *Srebro* means "silver" in Bosnian. Fatima lived there until she was five years old, at which point her family moved to Bratunac, a little town just over 6 miles (10 kilometers) from Srebrenica. It was in her house there that Fatima was reading all of her science books and dreaming about becoming a doctor. A year after the house was built, her father died from some type of infection.

> I went to school in Bratunac and the main thing that still connects me there is my house. My father built that house for his wife and children and then he died. He was 28 when he died and he lived in that house only 1 year. That house is where my memories are. I was 6 years old when he died.

Fatima, her brother and her mother lived in the house in Bratunac until the beginning of the war. Once they left, they didn't have any information about their house during the war. Her mother wanted to return to their house once the war had ended.

> My mother had dreams that we could go back. She thought that my brother could work there, and live there. She tried to go to Bratunac. She spent about 3 or 4 months there but she had a lot of problems with the people around her. They didn't want her to live there and so we decided to sell the house.
>
> And now whenever I go to Bratunac I walk nearby my house every time. I want to see it, just to experience the smell of my childhood.

Many people from around Srebrenica are related to each other. As it turns out, Fatima and Hasan are cousins. They talked about many people in the family being good in physics including Hasan's twin brother Husein, who was killed in the genocide, as well as his surviving brother Omer. Omer is named after Fatima's father. They wondered whether or not Fatima might have become more interested in medicine because her father died from an infection, something that could have been treated today. Hasan's grandmother is Fatima's aunt. He told Fatima that his grandmother was always proud of her because she was a doctor, that having a doctor in the family is a big deal.

Fatima was a young doctor when the war started. She had been out of medical school for just one and a half years and was working in a small health center in Bratunac.

> I had some dreams, I had my family, and I was really satisfied with my life. I was 25 years old. And suddenly my dreams were broken by the war.
>
> I had to leave my home with my mother and brother and we went to Srebrenica. But it was also in Chetnik's hands and so we had to go to a village and we spent two months in my cousin's house.

Life at her cousin's house in the village was a difficult time for Fatima.

> At that time I was really sad, I didn't know what to do. I didn't have even clothes or food and I was dependent on my family. I didn't work as a doctor anymore. I didn't know what would happen next. Everyday shelling started and I was really afraid for my life, for my cousins, my mother, my brother and others. It was a really hard time.

In 1992, four months after the town of Srebrenica was liberated, the hospital reopened. From that time until the end of the war, Fatima worked in the Srebrenica war hospital as a doctor while living in the building next door.

> It was a really horrible time for me, for all of us because of the shelling and I can say there were thousands of wounded people. We had to do what we could do. We didn't have enough medication, enough bandages, especially in the beginning of the war. People from Srebrenica brought us everything that they found inside of their houses.

People living in Srebrenica brought sheets, some bandages, and some small boxes of mostly opened medications to the hospital. The medical staff cleaned wounds with a cream made from natural herbs. They did what they could to help but it was particularly difficult because of the large number of wounded people and the lack of basic and necessary supplies.

> During surgery we used some anesthetics but it was especially poor during the beginning of the war. We had to, without anesthesia, cut legs. We couldn't cut bones so we did it in the knee, in the joints. Without anesthesia it was really painful for the patients and also for us.
>
> You have to do that but you don't know how to do that because it's really not easy to

be a doctor in that condition when you are trying to help but you have to hurt them. It's really difficult. It was like that the whole first year of the war. A lot of shelling, a lot of wounded people, no food, no clothes, no bandages, no anything.

In the middle of 1993, Doctors Without Borders (Médecins Sans Frontières, MSF) came to Srebrenica and saw how difficult the situation was. They started bringing medicine and supplies to help.

During 1993 Srebrenica was demilitarized and it looked like it was going to be a lot better situation. But it wasn't much better. It was a little better because of some medication, some doctors who came to Srebrenica and we could give people a little bit better help. But shelling continued, people didn't have a lot of food. They had to go to the Chetnik territory around Srebrenica to take food and they had a lot of injuries because the fields of food were mined. Every day we had injured people because of the mines. Many children were injured, many women.

It was also really hard to be in Srebrenica because if you are surrounded, you can't go anywhere from town. Even if nobody shoots you. It really felt like a prison. Chetniks were all around Srebrenica, on the hills. And I felt like in every moment they could see what I was doing. And you can imagine that situation where you were a prisoner like that and there is heavy shelling.

At that time Srebrenica was a really small town. Before the war there were around 6,000 people living there. At the end of 1993 and 1994 in Srebrenica lived around 66,000 people. In my family's flat, at one moment we had 42 people. Can you imagine? Only 1 bathroom. That flat had a kitchen and 3 other rooms—2 bedrooms and 1 living room, and 42 people. We slept everywhere and we lived like that for eight months and after that some convoys went from Srebrenica to Tuzla. It was the UNHCR bringing food to Srebrenica and people jumped into the trucks and nobody could stop them. They were desperate to go. But, I had to stay. I was a doctor and I couldn't go anywhere because people needed us. I felt obligated and nobody would let me go. My mother was there, my family, all of them stayed. At that time my mother was 52 years old, my brother was two years younger than me, so we stayed. But we didn't know what would happen next, to us and to the other people in Srebrenica. We just waited without any hope. We didn't even think that somebody might help us to survive, to get out.

At the beginning of the war there were six doctors in Srebrenica, for 60,000 people. One of the doctors, Nijaz Džanić, was killed by a bomb in 1992. So then there were only five with some intermittent help from Doctors Without Borders. Sometimes the doctors worked two or three days straight, without a break. Because of the small number of doctors and huge number of wounded people, it was not possible for the medical providers to work in shifts of any kind.

MSF came with some medications and they came to help sometimes. We tried to have some scheduled times to work in the hospital, but if you have a lot of injured people every day you can't stay at your home if somebody needs your help. We spent days and nights in the hospital. Sometimes I didn't go to my home for two or three days, even to wash myself or to eat, even to sleep. We worked as long as it was needed.

Fatima feels fortunate that there were any physicians in Srebrenica. There were some nurses and they trained others who had any type of medical or nursing schooling or relevant experience.

> I can say that we were lucky to have even five doctors. But we had about 20 nurses in the beginning of the war and we tried to train some new ones who had been in school before the war, even if it was their first or second class. We trained them and they started to work with us.

On April 12, 1993, there was the massacre at the playground. Hasan and several other people in this book were at the playground that day.

> People were very tense because of feeling like prisoners and they wanted to have some fun and they went together to that school and they played football, they played some music and into that crowd, maybe ten grenades fell.
>
> That day I was working in the hospital. My really close cousin's son was killed in the mine fields the day before and she came to the hospital to see him and I was with her, crying together and looking at the body of her son. He was about 20 years old. It was in the morning and we heard the shelling start again. I didn't know what happened outside because shelling was the usual condition for Srebrenica and if you heard it every day it seemed normal. I wasn't really upset because of that shelling. I didn't know in that moment what really happened in the schoolyard. And just maybe ten minutes after that crowds came to the hospital, many, many wounded people. We didn't have enough places to put all of them, in corridors, everywhere, there were wounded people everywhere. It was a really bad situation. So bad that my cousin who I talked about told me, "don't cry with me about my son, leave me alone, I will stay with the body of my son, you have to go and help those people." She forgot about her pain. She lost her son, but in that situation with so many wounded people, so many crying, so many, I can't explain how bad it was that day. She told me, "I can see. I will stay with my son. You need to go and help the people."
>
> Later, when we counted the numbers of wounded and dead people, it was 66 dead and more than 100 wounded. The next day some helicopters came from Tuzla and evacuated about 70, maybe more people to Tuzla and some of them died that night and, as I know, some of them were saved. They were evacuated to Tuzla and also abroad somewhere. I think it was the UN helicopters who evacuated them. I know about 11 children who were evacuated, but many of the people killed immediately at the school were young. It was 66 people. It's really strange that nobody writes about this situation. I don't know why. Not many people talk about it. After that when I passed the school, on the fence of that school, many many days after that you could see parts of bodies, human tissue attached to the fence.

By 1995, things had begun to deteriorate significantly in Srebrenica.

> There was a lot of shelling, a lot of wounded people, starting in maybe March or April. We could feel that something bad was going to happen in Srebrenica to all of us but we couldn't do anything but wait.

May 25 of that year was memorable to Fatima for two very difficult reasons. On that day, which was one day before her birthday, the massacre at the Tuzla gate happened. Just a few hours before that massacre, the town of Srebrenica was shelled and two grenades fell.

> I wanted to walk around a little bit because it was May, nice weather, I wanted to be with my friends. I tried to make a cake. To prepare any cake in Srebrenica, it was really difficult. It was like a miracle if you could do it. Months before I tried to collect some sug-

ar, and everything I would need. I just finished that cake and said to my mother that she needed to do the rest because I wanted to go for a walk. And I went. It was like my fate, my destiny, to be at that place at that time when the grenade came with my name. I walked with my cousin, I was in the middle. One side was my cousin and the other side was my friend at that time. But now, today, the man from my right side is my husband. The shell hit just me, between them.

She showed us her arm where she was wounded.

All of the bones were broken. I had to have an arm support done. I couldn't do operations. But I think I was really lucky because I could move my hand.

The work at the hospital continued and they tried to remain positive. But at the beginning of July, something changed and it seemed clear to them that something drastic was going to happen. Fatima said it felt like the end was near.

Chetniks started to attack again from the hills around Srebrenica and they came closer, they attacked even UN soldiers at some of the observation points. We knew it was going to be the end. That day, on 11 July we had a full hospital, lots of badly injured people in the corridors and everywhere. Two or three months before that they stopped humanitarian convoys and food and medical supplies and everything else was running out. I was at the hospital and many many injured people came. We heard that the Chetniks were already in Srebrenica and we had to do something with our wounded patients. We decided to evacuate them to the Dutch UN base called Bravo[1] which was in town. We put all of them in trucks and went to the UN base but we had a little problem. They didn't want to accept the patients. They told us that they are not responsible for them and we have to go to some other place with our patients. There was no other place. They were our only option. We told them that they had to take our patients, they must take responsibility for them, we don't have any other place to take them.

After that we told them if they don't take the patients we will break the gate because we had no choice. They finally opened the gate and we took the patients in. We had evacuated the entire hospital and we went back to check and make sure that it was empty. You know, we are doctors. We couldn't leave our patients in the hospital and just go. We first had to take care of them.

By then it was early afternoon. All of the doctors quickly grabbed some medicine and some clothes and went to the post office, across from the hospital, where a lot of people were gathered. There was a great deal of confusion and nobody was quite sure what to do. By that time Srebrenica was falling, and many people had already made the decision to flee to the UN base in Potočari, mainly women and children but also several hundred men who did not join the majority of men attempting to escape through the woods. Fatima's mother was among those who decided to go to Potočari. Those who went to the base did so because they thought they would be protected by the UN. Fatima had serious doubts about that.

I knew that the Chetniks were so aggressive, that if they wanted to kill, they would kill you in front of the whole world. They weren't afraid of anything, of the world, of justice. Nothing would stand in their way. I knew what they did. I saw it every day at the hospital.

I was worried because of my mother. I decided that me and my brother would go to the mountains with many men, but I couldn't bring her with me so I had to let her go to

Potočari. It was a really hard decision and I wasn't sure that it was a good decision. I wasn't sure that I would ever see her again. It was the worst decision of my life. She couldn't come with me because she wasn't that strong to walk.

There were two UN bases. One was a small base called Bravo on the outskirts of the town of Srebrenica. Bravo is where Fatima and her colleagues took the wounded when Srebrenica fell. The other was the main base, called Charlie, located in Potočari in an old battery factory. Charlie served as the UN headquarters. The Battery Factory was a huge structure that could accommodate everything the UN needed. There was also a lot of empty space.

Fatima told her mother that she couldn't accompany her to Potočari and they separated in front of the hospital. Her mother went with the other women and some cousins down to the base while Fatima and her brother left to join the group that was planning to go through the woods and the mountains in an effort to reach the free territory.

I just told her that she had to go with the other women, that I couldn't go with her, I didn't have time. We separated in the front of the hospital and me and my brother went to the mountains and she went to the UN base with other cousins. Srebrenica hospital is at the end of the town. Maybe after a ten-minute walk you are in the woods.

Fatima didn't know what to expect in the mountains. She knew it wasn't going to be easy but it turned out to be far worse than she, or anyone, could have imagined.

Nobody can explain what happened and how it was there in the mountains. I felt like a small mouse in the hand of a cat. Like somebody was playing with me.

I told you that we brought with us some medication, some IVs and it was all in one big bag. In that bag I also had some food and some clothes to change. During the first day we lost the bag when the shelling started again. We had to run and we lost it in the mountains. After that I didn't have anything for the rest of the time for six days.

The majority of the survivors of the Death March arrived in Tuzla on the 16th of July. Fatima feels lucky that it only took her six days. She knows of many men, including her husband-to-be, who spent months in the woods. He didn't arrive in Tuzla until September, long after she had given up hope that he had survived.

He came to Tuzla on the 12th of September. On the second day of walking at Kamenice hill he lost his brother and his father. He hid in a small woods for four days, without food, without water, without anything. Chetniks were walking around but luckily they didn't find him. And after that, during the night, he walked back to his village near Srebrenica and spent two months in the woods. He and maybe 20 men found some food and some water there. After that he felt strong enough to try again to reach Tuzla. After two months I didn't think he was coming.

Once she arrived in Tuzla, Fatima and her friend went every day to Dubrave, where the airport was. At Dubrave there was a tree where a list was posted of people who had arrived the day before. As like everyone who had made it to Tuzla, they were looking for names of their family, friends and all the people that they knew, hoping that they had arrived the day before.

There is debate whether or not nerve gas was used during the genocide.[2] Those who were on the Death March are certain that it was used and many describe a scene that happened on the second day in the woods. Fatima is one of those who is certain that nerve gas was used because of what she observed in so many people around her, in particular hallucinations. It has been argued that these hallucinations could have been caused by exhaustion, lack of food, water and trauma. Fatima reports that it would have taken longer than two days for these types of symptoms to occur if they were caused just by exhaustion or hunger alone. She might have expected to see people hallucinating toward the end of the Death March but not after just two days in and not so many of them.

> Yes, I'm sure nerve gas was used. Every day and everywhere around us there was shelling. On the second day after we left Srebrenica many many people started to hallucinate. We could all see that it wasn't just because they were exhausted. They didn't know where they were if you asked them. They were screaming, running around, they didn't want to listen when we told them they had to be quiet. They had to calm down because Chetniks were around us and they were putting all of us in danger. We were trying to calm them down but it was impossible because they didn't want to listen to anybody. If you asked them, "Do you know where you are?" They said, "Yes, I know very well. I'm in my town, my village." We asked, "What do you see around you?" Many of them told us that they saw some buildings near the top of the woods.
>
> This was happening to a lot of people. I can say it was happening to half of the people around me. They were running around and many of them ran to the mountains. They didn't know what they were doing. We never saw them again. Many of them died that way. It was more than hundreds for sure.
>
> I can't say that the Chetniks called them because I didn't witness this. But, people didn't know what they were doing and they ran to the mountains and in the mountains were Chetniks.
>
> You know we were walking in a line, thousands of people. I couldn't see all of them because we were in a line. I could see maybe a couple of hundred around me. I didn't have symptoms but my brother did. He was a little bit disorientated. But if you are lucky to be together with your brother or other close people you could take care of each other and you had the opportunity to survive. If you were alone it was really hard.

Fatima didn't think about how this all might end. She was focused on survival which she knew meant staying in the line by keeping track of those who were walking in front of her. It was strictly about survival. They had been instructed to stay in single file on the same path because the areas through which they had to go were mined and if they veered off the path, they were in danger of stepping on a mine.

> I had to walk. I was only worried about what would happen if I lost the people who were walking in front of me. I was just concentrating on that. They told us that we had to go step by step. I put my step in the step of the man before me. And we went to Tuzla like that. You can't imagine. We had to do this because of the mines, because of the shelling. I didn't know. This was my first time to be there. I was really afraid to be lost in the mountains.

While it's difficult to know for sure, it's estimated that there were a few hundred women at most in the Death March. We know from Nura's story that she started through the woods but was not able to keep going because she was rounded up along with her sons.

Fatima and her brother shared a half-loaf of bread and a can of food that he had in his bag. That's all she had to eat for those six days. She is still surprised when she remembers that she didn't get hungry along the way. But she did get thirsty. So very thirsty. That is a feeling she will never forget.

> I didn't feel any hunger but I was thirsty. I was really thirsty. And even today if I don't have enough to eat I'm not worried. But if I'm thirsty, if I don't have anything to drink, I still feel nervous. Like in a sort of panic. There was not drinking water. Not at all. We had some small rivers and some people had some small bottles, and they would fill it with the water and we shared. One swallow for everyone. We were desperate to drink but we had to share it with the others. Some people who came with us were wounded and we had to take care of them and we had to take care of that bottle of water if those people started to drink. They wanted to drink all of it. So we had to hold the bottle and give everyone just one swallow. We had to give it to everybody.

Fatima then goes on to say that it isn't just thirst that triggers her memories of those horrible days in July 1995.

> Every moment everything can remind me of that time. Smell is a strong memory. I say it's the smell of that time. But you know, our lives continued. Now we have families, children. We have jobs. And it's like normal life. Same as other people but it's not the same because we are not the same. You can't be calm, you can't be happy. That's true. We are different. And, in every moment, if you start to talk about people who were killed, it's our families, the loved ones, friends, neighbors. People we knew, people we loved and we can't forget it. We can't even forgive it. It's really difficult to explain but at any moment we can start crying. It never stops. It's never over. I'm sure that we will feel like that until the end of our lives.

Even with all of this, there are times when Fatima does feel happy, but never completely.

> I can't say that I never feel happy. I have children, I have friends, I have people who love me and I try to be a warm person, to keep my warmth for my friends, for my family. But deep in my heart I'm sad. They took a lot of things from our hearts. I'm just trying to continue my life. You know all of us, we try to not let them kill us. We try to not let them make us unhappy, to become cold people. To show to them and to all the world that they didn't kill us.

Fatima has children, a fifteen-year-old daughter, Samra, and a thirteen-year-old son, Fedhad. Like everyone in this story who is a parent, she has had to decide what to tell them about the war and about her own experiences.

> It's difficult to find some good balance to tell them everything and to not make them as sad as we are. I told them a lot of this. I talk to them about that time. And some of the people that I lost are also their cousins. I tell them that man and that man and that girl were killed by shelling. They have to know that I loved those people and that I still feel sad about it. But I don't put in my children any hate. I try to explain to them that they have to remember but they don't need to feel hate and sadness. I don't know if it's a good way but I am working on it.
>
> In Tuzla after the war I couldn't find a job here in the beginning. I went to Zenica. I found a job there and I spent 3 years there. Delivering babies. And after that I was married and my husband was working here in Tuzla and that's why I came to Tuzla. I knew him in Srebrenica. His brother was wounded in the beginning of the war, heavily injured, and now he is paraplegic. I found my husband with his brother in the hospital. He was taking care of his brother. For many years we were just friends and after that…. My husband is named Smail. I say that he is my smile.

> I now work in a hospital in the delivery room. I always say that now I'm working for the beginning of life and I love it. I think it's the only place where I don't feel hopeless.

Fatima talks again about the sadness that she feels in her heart, sadness but not hatred.

> I feel sadness in my heart and it can't go out. I try to put it out but it's impossible. But I can't say that I feel hatred. It's really strange. It's not easy to explain how we feel after that. If somebody hates, we are done. Because we have kids. We can't be warm if we hate and that's why we try to not hate and because it would change our personalities. I don't want to change my warmth. I don't want to do things, bad things, that people did to us. I don't want to do those things.
>
> To hate somebody is really painful. Nothing we would do to them can bring our cousins back. I have some colleagues who work with me, I go to Serbia, to Belgrade every year and I talk to Serbs and I don't have in my head that they are able to kill somebody. I try to think that the people who killed our cousins, they are not here, they are not between us. And I don't know how I would feel if I came eye to eye with some of them. Definitely I do not know how I would behave in that situation. If I know that he killed my cousin I would hate him. But I don't think that way. I think that people I meet are not these people.

Fatima talks about her family helping her deal with the deep sadness that she feels.

> Luckily I have my family and my husband went through the same situation and sometimes we talk about it. When I'm so sad I just want to be with my family. And really, it's hard to understand but I feel good when I go to Potočari Memorial Center and sometimes I sit between the tomb stones and I feel peace. I often go to Srebrenica and every time I go to the Memorial. It's not easy to explain. I like to go there alone and sit. To spend a couple of minutes in peace. I feel like I talk to them. I think that they know that I come. Every year we bury people. I lost many cousins. All of them are buried there.

Fatima's explanation of why she survived is familiar. It's the same as most of the people whose stories are in this book.

> I survived because of God. I was just lucky that I survived but it didn't depend on my strength, my cleverness, my brain, it was just luck. Somebody could survive only if God decided.

Her sorrow about not being able to help those who needed it on the Death March comes up again.

> I can't forget some people I met in the mountains, some wounded people who couldn't walk and who died in the mountains. I still think about how hard it was for them to stay in the mountains like that. They couldn't walk and they saw other people go by. It was a situation where nobody could really help. As a doctor and as a person I couldn't help because it was too far to carry anybody. If he wasn't able to walk he had to stay.

Fatima's hope lies with the next generation and she feels strongly that they need to know what happened.

> You can see that it's hard to tell this story. I know that I have to talk about it because it's really important for the next generation, for my children and children in the whole world. I don't want for anybody to be in the situation we were in. I will be lucky if all children around

the world are positive without any hatred and without any prejudice. Not to be willing to kill. And that's why it's important to talk about how we feel after everything.

We talked some more about how hard it is to tell her story and how strongly she feels that she needs to tell it. It had to be especially hard to do so before going to a wedding.

> I have to sleep. I have to spend some time with my children and my husband and I think I will come out of it and get back to my normal routine. I go to weddings, I go to New Year's Eve and everything, but I don't feel the same way as other people. I don't have that kind of laughter. After I was alone living in Zenica for a few years, some of my friends asked me to go with them to a New Year's party and I went there. They were laughing, playing music, drinking, and in one moment I started to cry because I wasn't able to be that happy like the rest of them. They didn't have the experience I had. They are lucky. But all of us, we try to live.
>
> I'm always thinking that there are many people who feel worse than me. I'm sad, I'm a survivor, I spent a very bad time but I'm still here. I have family, I have my job, I can't say I'm satisfied but I have something that keeps me occupied. But what about those mothers who lost everything, their future. That's why we say that they didn't kill only 8,000 people, they killed generations.

Fatima is so proud of her children and says again that hope lies with the next generation. She smiles whenever she talks about them.

> My son likes mathematics too but not my daughter. She is interested in languages. She speaks English very well, and German, and she likes history.

As we finished up, I was surprised to learn that this was the first time Hasan had heard Fatima's story. When I asked about that he replied,

> As survivors we never talk about these things. As Fatima said, we try to stay positive.

Hasan Sejfo Hasanović

If you are familiar with film footage from the Srebrenica genocide, then you have seen Hasan Sejfo Hasanović (not to be confused with Hasan Aziz Hasanović, who is a coauthor of this book). In one of the most heart-wrenching scenes from the end of the Death March in Nezuk, Hasan can be seen carrying and laying down his lifeless brother Hasib who was killed earlier in the march. It is a haunting piece of film that is, however, neither the beginning nor the end of Hasan's story.

In 1991, only four days after graduating from secondary school in Bratunac and just right before the war started in Croatia, he joined the Yugoslav People's Army (JNA) and began his service in Belgrade, Serbia. He was just 18 years old. He did not stay long with the JNA, only about two months.

> I was part of a specialized unit known as the most capable and the most trained unit in the JNA. At the beginning of the war in Croatia and after the fall of Vukovar I deserted. I ran away from the army because I realized that army did not serve all the Yugoslav people. It just served the Serbian people.

In 1991, Vukovar, a town in Croatia, was devastated by the Serb-dominated JNA and Serb paramilitaries. Thousands were killed trying to defend the town, several hundred civilians were brutally attacked and killed and many thousands were expelled. The extensive damage to the town has been compared to that of Stalingrad during World War II.

Hasan spent 58 days on the battlefield in Vukovar which was the determining factor for him to leave the JNA.

> I was working on the checkpoint on the entrance to Vukovar, the village Negoslavci. When I returned to Belgrade the first day I ran away, I deserted.
>
> I saw what they did, the so-called JNA, they were actually just Serbs instead of the whole Yugoslav people. I didn't have access to see what was happening inside of Vukovar, I was just outside of Vukovar. After the fall of Vukovar on 24 November 1991, my unit retreated for a vacation to Belgrade and I deserted and ran away.
>
> The only thing in my mind at that time was to run away. There were a lot of Bosniaks and Croats in the army. Many of them deserted. I just decided to run away, to escape trouble. I deserted without thinking because I've noticed that a lot of deserters never got back. Why should I stay. Another reason was the Serbs, the people coming with the beards and a lot of paramilitaries and that was bothering me and I didn't see the army anymore as JNA.

Hasan ran to his village in Srebrenica, pursued by military police who were trying to find him.

> I was hunted for a month. My parents and the whole village had to act like I didn't come. Because I deserted in November all December 1991 the military police, every second, every day were coming into the village looking for me.

He hid in the woods because he did not want to go back to the JNA.

> My village is on sloped terrain and anyone who would come to the village would come from just one direction. Small children would see the soldiers and military police they would quickly spread the news. It all lasted for a month.

Hasan stayed in his village along with his family whom he describes as "a second class family, workers." Both of his parents were there, along with his two older sisters and two younger brothers.

> Life went on normally until Bajram[3] in April 1992. Even during that time in Yugoslavia there was peace during the three days of Bajram. We had some fairs, some celebrations. But on the fourth of April in Bijeljina there was a massacre and the news spread quickly. People got worried all over the country.
>
> People hearing the news about [the] Bijeljina massacre [and] all of a sudden the fear spread among the people.

Hasan's father decided that the family should leave Bosnia but they were unable to do so. They had relatives in Switzerland, which is where they tried to go, but not everyone had a passport. It was difficult to get any documents during this time and nothing could be issued quickly. So they stayed in Bosnia.

A few days after the massacre in Bijeljina, the first shooting started in Srebrenica and Hasan's village was under fire the entire night.

> On the seventh of April in the meadow we had a meeting of some representatives, both Bosnians and Serbs where we talked about the situation.
>
> These were people that we were living together, eating together, sharing everything,

going to school together, we trusted them and believed that if someone would come from Serbia to attack us that they would stand with us and defend us.

As it turned out, that wasn't the case. Describing the end of the meeting in the meadow, a neighbor told Hasan and the other Muslims,

> If I just blow a single whistle signal, 50,000 soldiers will come from Serbia…

The situation calmed down in the village for the next ten days or so. They heard that there had been some civilians killed in the town of Srebrenica which was around four miles (seven kilometers) away. There were 25–30 people killed, including intellectuals, doctors and artists.

> Among those killed were Jakub Abdurahmanović, the principal of my primary school. Also Asmir Redžić, an engineer from the mine in Sase. The news spread quickly because those were people who used to work there and we knew them, everybody knew them.
> Then there was an incident at the same time in Potočari. Civilians from Srebrenica got kicked out from Potočari as well, houses were looted and houses of faith were burned down, military vehicles kept passing through. On that same day, the 18th of April before the dark, all of the residents of my village were arrested, the entire village.
> I knew what was going on, knowing what happened in Croatia. I knew that it will be even worse for us. It didn't surprise me because I was a member of the JNA army and I knew what was happening. Other people were surprised because they trusted their neighbors. During the Second World War people used to protect each other very often.
> On that day, the soldiers came up to me and my neighbor Suad Ademović, and he leaned against the fence. They wanted to kill both of us. One of the Soldiers pointed a gun and said, "I killed one Muslim in Zvornik and now I'm going to slay one of you and feel how it is to kill." However, during the night they closed us in our houses, he didn't shoot at us, he was just trying to scare us off. So they pushed us into our houses and they encircled the village.
> I didn't recognize the soldiers. They had beards, they had JNA uniforms, they were dressed in the same uniforms and had weapons. I didn't recognize any of them. I wish I had recognized at least one of them. I would be able now to report him.

Having been in the JNA, Hasan understood tactics and strategy. He knew that the Serbs were trying to frighten the people in his village but that they had most likely run away. Given this knowledge, he organized his village, going from house to house to awaken everyone and have them go into the woods. They stayed in the woods during the night and then during the day some people would sneak back to their houses for food. There were also people in the woods, people from other villages who had to flee.

Hasan assumed that people would be killed. They hid in the woods until mid–May when half of his village was burned down along with the barns and the haystacks. The rest of his village was burned down on May 15 and the killing started.

> A shell fell killing my cousin on his 14th birthday. He died on his mother's lap because he was shot in the back of the stomach in Pećišta village.
> So the war for me in Srebrenica publicly started on the 15th of May 1992 when people were being killed massively. From then on every day we had frequent shelling.
> From that moment I decided to join the BiH army. From that time I was officially in the Bosnian army. I was still 19 years old. I was a soldier without a gun, without boots, without

a uniform, without anything. After our resistance we got some weapons from the enemy, some soldiers left their weapons and we took these. However, sometimes you have a rifle and you run out of ammunition and the rifle is useless.

Hasan described that the Serbs were going from village to village where Muslims lived, burning everything and killing people. On a daily basis, refugees from villages in eastern Bosnia were arriving in Srebrenica.

These people had to run and walk so many kilometers to reach Srebrenica. When refugees arrived we had more than 45,000 people in winter of 1993. Babies were dying, people were hungry, Philippe Morillon came to Srebrenica with some soldiers as his entourage. Srebrenica was proclaimed a demilitarized zone and UN Safe Area. By that time we already had thousands of victims, casualties, women, children, elderly people, disabled, people.

By then, Hasan was a soldier in the Bosnian army on the front line, keeping guard, unarmed.

There was a big hatred, [an] indescribable amount of hatred. And we knew why. There were many women who were raped, like in Drinjača village. Some refugees came to Srebrenica from that village, some refugees went back to Tuzla. Many killings happened to elderly people and children.

As a soldier in the regular army you learn all the laws and they teach you that you don't kill civilians, and if you kill civilians on the opposite side you will meet resistance, you will feel hatred.

General Philippe Morillon, Commander of the United Nations Protection Force (UNPROFOR) in BiH from 1992 to 1993, came to Srebrenica in 1993. During his stay, there was the massacre at the playground and Hasan was there.

During Morillon's stay in Srebrenica we had this huge massacre in front of the primary school where 74 young people were killed. One of the first people who came to help, was me. And in the hospital one couldn't step a foot on the ground because everything was filled with the wounded.

I came to the house near that sport center. I broke the door of the house. I was just bringing the wounded in. I saw two or three bodies completely torn up. All those children were civilians, there were no soldiers there, they just wanted to come and play some sports, psychologically to relax.

We started to bury people whose remains were mutilated.

Hasan went on to describe Morillon's visit, the declaration of Srebrenica as a Safe Area and the subsequent disarmament of the Muslims.

Philippe Morillon, instead of staying in Srebrenica, he left Srebrenica. He left Srebrenica and said that all the Muslims should be disarmed. All the weapons that we got in a fight with Serbs were being given to the UN.

Hasan was optimistic when Srebrenica was declared a Safe Area. Even though they had to surrender their weapons, he thought that the UN would protect them.

In 1993 when Philippe Morillon came he managed to fool us with a promise that the main headquarters of the UN in BiH would move to Srebrenica.

> I was thinking we would not have a war and that we were protected. For 11 months in Srebrenica we hadn't had any humanitarian supplies. There was a big starvation. When the first humanitarian aid came they distributed some flour and salt and some ingredients in grams.

While some humanitarian supplies did start to arrive in Srebrenica, Hasan's optimism that the shelling and sniping would stop turned out to be false hope.

> I thought that the UN resolution says that they would make Serbs remove heavy weapons 30 kilometers *[18 miles]* outside of the Safe Area and that military operations would be prohibited in Srebrenica. But on a daily basis Serb snipers were targeting civilians. Civilians were either being killed or wounded on a daily basis. All the time.

On April 18, 1993, peacekeepers arrived from Canada. Hasan reported that there were positive things about the Canadian battalion.

> In '93 we had some peaceful times, some troubling times, and we had those Canadian soldiers. When Morillon left the Canadians came. They were from Quebec. I have to say we were protected then. I had contact with them. They wanted to communicate. They had the mandate to respond and fire. The Canadians were there for a short time.
>
> When the Canadians left, when the Dutch came, the humanitarian aid was scarce, the Dutch soldiers didn't respond to the fire, the killings of civilians started and the situation started to deteriorate. The Dutch came at the end of January 1994 and the Canadians left.

In June of 1993, Hasan was 20 years old. At that point, nobody lived in Hasan's village because it had been destroyed by fire. Some people had started to grow food in the garden but this did not help Hasan's father. On the 25th of that month, his father died at the age of 43.

> He died from hunger. The Canadians helped me to fulfill my wish that I bury him in the cemetery of my family back in my village. The cemetery was underneath a hill and the Serbs could see it and were targeting that cemetery very often.

While June brought tragedy to Hasan's family, August of the same year brought a different kind of event. Hasan was married that year to Hajreta, a woman who is still his wife.

> I got married very young in August of 1993. That was the period when there was peace but still war. I met her four days before I got married. She was underage. Sixteen and a half.

Because Hajreta was underage, her mother had to give written permission for the wedding to occur.

> She was from Zvornik and her family was expelled by the Serbs who forced them to flee.
>
> We had a wedding, we had cake. After I married her she and her mother lived in my house because they had no place to stay so they stayed with my family.

At the end of March 1994, Hasan's son, Haris, was born early. Dr. Fatima Dautbašić-Klempić delivered him and took care of him following his birth.

> My son was born on the 7th month of pregnancy. Fatima was the doctor. She fed him for 34 days through his nose. She took care of him and gave him a nickname, a little finger.

> There was no incubator. After 33 days he got some weight, 3½ kilograms [7.7 pounds], and he got out of the hospital.
>
> At that time it was peaceful, we had the UN, we thought that military action had ended, we thought everything was done. For food you got two or three grams of flour and some powdered milk. My nephew had a cow and he was bringing milk, that cow milk was my son's only food.
>
> Lots of babies were being born. In the houses five or six families lived together. Thirty adults in one house. Nobody fought. Nobody argued. People had sympathy for each other.
>
> We were living with 17 people when we had our baby. It was my uncle's house, a small house. It was me, my wife and my son and my mother-in-law and my mother, two brothers, my father and my sister. In the basement there were two families, from Osmače and Podčauš villages and all of us were living there like a family.

During this time, Hasan was waiting to return to his village and for life to return to normal. As he recounted what happened, Hasan went back and forth in time as he remembered events. Story telling is like that. Stories are rarely linear.

> I was waiting to return to our village. I never thought that we would be in a position to shake hands with Serbs. I hated them. I hated them so much.
>
> Before my father's death in '93, my 70-year-old grandmother was killed by shelling. She was killed just two months before his death.
>
> My father wouldn't have died if war hadn't happened.

As Hasan's story continued, it became clear that Dr. Fatima, along with her colleagues, took care of everything that needed to be done for everyone in Srebrenica. Earlier, Hasan had told us about her delivering his premature baby and later about her trying to help his dying father. We also later learned that Hasan encountered her along the Death March.

> My sister was with my father when he died. He was in hospital for seven days. Fatima tried to keep him alive, giving him IVs and some medication. But there was nothing she could do. My father had problems with his lungs. He was a miner in Srebrenica. He used to work in the mine in Sase.

Hasan described feeling like the war might never end.

> In '94 time was passing and Srebrenica was already, in my opinion, like a concentration camp. You could walk but you could not get out of it and that's it.

He then began to describe the events of July 1995. Everyone's story ultimately got around to those days. Hasan had already experienced what is arguably a large number of traumatic events. Being in Vukovar, being hunted by the JNA after deserting, and losing his father and grandmother to the war. In his case, however, like for so many others in our story, the worst was yet to come. It's important to remember that the people in Srebrenica in July of 1995 had already endured years of a siege, starvation, death, and other war-related trauma. They were already shattered physically and psychologically by the time Srebrenica fell.

Hasan reported that he still had hope and trust in the international community when the shooting started again on July 6, 1995.

> When the shooting started there were more than 450 Dutch soldiers in the UN base. The shooting went on every day and on the 9th and 10th it was getting worse. You couldn't

> even notice a second without any shooting. Every second in front of the Dutch soldiers shelling was taking place and they didn't respond.
>
> On the 11th of July we saw two big pillars of smoke outside of Srebrenica as the UN tried to navigate the airstrikes. I think they just wanted to fool us pretending that they were trying to do something to help us. They didn't help.

Like the others, Hasan had his own story of that day in July when everybody made the decision to flee. But where to go was the question for everyone.

> My mother Nezira went to feed the cow. I looked through the window and I saw the river of refugees fleeing towards the UN base in Potočari and I knew what would happen then. I knew I couldn't go to the UN base because I was an able-bodied man. Even if I wasn't a soldier, I wouldn't go to Potočari. That was true.
>
> I knew it would not be good for me to go to Potočari even though I didn't do anything wrong. I would never do anything wrong.
>
> The worst thing for me, it was horrible, with my wife and my son. He was 14 months old. With every shooting he got scared, he was afraid. I wanted to say goodbye before the Potočari Dutch base. My wife had a necklace with the Muslim sign, a crescent and a star. She gave it to me. She was afraid that people might see it and bother her. I tried to say something to my wife but I couldn't. I was sorry for all the people.
>
> My conclusion was that this was a big judgement day and nobody would survive.
>
> I stayed in Potočari for a while hoping to find my brothers, in the center of Potočari 500 meters [a third of a mile] from the base. My wife, with my mother-in-law, and my son they ran to the base. I didn't know if I should cry or pray to God.
>
> The Dutch soldiers kept driving dead people on the trailer of the truck. There are some images on YouTube that you can see. I saw this. The trucks were passing with so many people, dead, wounded and alive people. People didn't know where to go or what to do. Everybody waited for death.
>
> My mother ran to Potočari.

Hasan headed to Šušnjari village up in the mountains, where he waited for his brother. He found Hasib but not Hajro at that point. They waited in the village until around 3:30 in the morning on the 12 of July. He was unarmed, as was Hasib.

> We headed in the column two by two. During the night of the 12th we reached Kamenice hill. I was among the first who got to that hill. In the back of the column we heard detonations, bombing. The column was broke up and around us shelling started.
>
> My brother Hasib and I sat. Our neighbor came, Osmo Osmanović who was 15 and he said that his brother was killed. I couldn't believe it. I said to him please take me there I want to see that. He brought me there and we saw six dead people.

Among those six dead people was Hasan's brother Hajro.

> I found my brother Hajro lying on his stomach and there were another five dead people near him. I rolled my brother, his back was against the ground. He had three wounds, I saw there were big holes in his chest and a big hole on the back. I just turned him and covered his head.
>
> I started moving and I lost the sight of Hasib, my other brother. As I got back to Kamenice hill it was late and I saw there were so many people there. Everybody was silent. Before the dark there was a very strong explosion. One big tree fell. Serbs maybe they knew and they set up an ambush there. The shooting started from everywhere.

> People were running in all directions, they couldn't tell where to run to. I ran through this steep terrain and I reached a stream. I was waiting there. I couldn't go anywhere. I was afraid of everyone.
>
> I realized that I had reached Kravica. I reached the cultural center later where so many people were killed inside. I saw two, three buses of prisoners parked. I was trying to orientate myself to where I was supposed to head.
>
> Udrč mountain could be seen from there and I was supposed to go back and head straight to Udrč. I went back to Kamenice hill where the ambush happened. If you can believe it there were so many killed people you couldn't even step your foot on the ground because there were so many people lying down dead. There were even some people still alive, moaning, asking for help. I couldn't help.
>
> I was alone. I was so afraid. I was like lost.
>
> I was weak, but at the end of the forest I managed to get my act together and to get myself on the path towards Udrč.

Hasan went through several villages and eventually reached Burnice. He now knows the names of all of these villages because every year he participates in the Peace March which takes him back through this route.

> By a big house, I found a young boy sleeping there. He had a red tracksuit on and I tried to see if he was alive. He was crying and mentioning his mother and he kept saying that his father ran to Tuzla. I realized there was something wrong with him as he might been affected by a nerve gas or lack of sleep or I don't know what was wrong with him. When he woke up he washed his face and his mouth and he said to me, "I know the terrain. I know the way."

The young boy kept insisting that he knew the way so Hasan decided to follow him. Hasan was struck by the fact that the boy did not seem to be afraid. They came across a terrifying scene on their way.

> On the right side of the road we found a man, he was sitting on a chair with his legs tied down and his face was cut and it was hooked to his ears. His lips were red from blood and he was totally massacred.

He was still alive.

> I got scared. This image was the thing that scared me the most. I kept asking myself what will happen to me. I couldn't help him because there was no way to do so even though he was not dead yet. I didn't dare to do anything.

Many survivors talk about their fear of being captured and tortured. For some, this possibility was even worse than their fear of being killed. It was difficult to imagine the fear that Hasan experienced when encountering this horrific scene, a scene that showed the fear of torture was based on a very possible reality. Hasan was surprised that this young boy was not afraid. He was different than the others Hasan encountered along the way. For someone so young, it was surprising that he was so helpful and fearless. The boy helped Hasan cross the river Jadar and then told him to continue to try and reach Udrč. Like the others on this journey, Hasan experienced extreme thirst.

> When we crossed the river I was so thirsty and I couldn't help myself. I tried to drink water from the river Jadar *[but]* it was not enough. Later I learned that the Jadar river was contaminated with nerve gas.

Hasan described being afraid before reaching Udrč but once reaching there he was no longer afraid, even though he assumed that he had reached the place where his life would end.

> There were thousands of people at Udrč and we were waiting for the dark to fall. I was waiting for my turn to die. I didn't know if I will die in a minute or tomorrow.
>
> The image was coming back to me from Kamenice hill and I thought that all of us would be killed. On Udrč I was moving around through the dark to look for my brother, Hasib. I decided to go back to where I came from to look for my brother. I had to look for him wherever he might be.

Hasan set off to retrace his steps in hopes that he would find his brother Hasib. He saw the boy again. He was bringing over 60 people with him and one of them was Hasib, who was barefoot.

> Hasib didn't feel like talking too much. He was probably very tired. I didn't want to ask him much. I asked what happened there and he said many people gave themselves up and he saw lots of dead and wounded. Later I understood that they also crossed Kamenice hill and they saw the same thing like me.

Heading from Udrč, Hasan and his group were ambushed several more times. Many more people were killed. Hasan still lives with the images of people that he knew being wounded and killed, as well as people screaming for water.

> It was so dangerous and difficult to withstand heat, hunger. For all those days I only had 100 grams of salt. I fetched water where I could. The thirst was constant. I was really hungry but the thirst was the worst.
>
> We reached Križevačke Njive. The terrain was flat, it was not hilly, so the Serbs could see all of us down there. We entered the forest around four in the morning on 16 July where we came across some mines.

The mines detonated and many people died or were injured, including Hasan who was wounded in his right leg. He described the detonation as blowing him off to the side. He then got himself back to the group and started to look for Hasib among the dead and the wounded. He found his brother and the news was not good.

> I found him and I touched his belly and I kept my hand on it. He was wounded, his stomach was wide open. He kept whispering, "Be careful I am wounded."
>
> I carried him like for 200 meters *[220 yards]*, then I went back and carried my neighbor. People didn't care, wouldn't help everybody, they were trying to survive. Some people didn't help their family. When my brother was wounded I saw a man saying to his son, "Go on anyway I will be killed."
>
> That was a moment when I felt nothing, no sorrow, no joy. All my body felt nothing.

As we know from her story, Dr. Fatima was also on the Death March, trying to help in an impossible situation. While carrying his horribly wounded brother, Hasan found Dr. Fatima in the crowd. She told him that Hasib would probably die in about ten minutes.

> But he actually didn't die in ten minutes. He lived seven or eight hours longer. He was still conscious. He was just asking for lots of water and I couldn't give it to him because of

his condition. The doctor put all his intestines inside where they belonged but it was still visible. They gave him some medication in an IV. They tried to help but nothing could help.

This happened in the village above Baljkovica.

> My brother asked me to put him down. I put him down and he said to me just to lift his head. I did it and he passed away. And that was the most difficult moment of my life. People were saying I should bury him there. But I didn't want to do that.
> Everything made it more difficult when I learned there are only a few kilometers to the free territory. I carried him down for five kilometers [about three miles], there is a steep terrain. I decided even if I die I will bring him to the free territory and leave him.
> I was carrying my brother and also my neighbor. I was also wounded. Four other neighbors came and they helped me. Without them, I wouldn't have managed to bring him to Nezuk, the free territory.
> When we reached Nezuk, Hasib was only the second body brought there. There were also two people killed right after they crossed into Nezuk.
> I stayed there [a] very short while and one elderly woman brought some food but I lost my appetite. My brother was left there on the ground and they drove me to a hospital.

After three days, Hasan found his mother and his sister at the Dubrave airport in Tuzla. He experienced what the other survivors have described. He was one of the few men who came to the airport and he found only women and children there. With the knowledge that both of his brothers had died on the Death March, he struggled with what to say to his mother.

> She said she heard that I was killed and that both of my brothers were alive. She totally fainted. They took her to emergency room.
> Maybe it would be better if they survived and I was killed.

Hasan spent two and a half months looking for Hasib's grave. He found him by chance. Hasib had been buried in a cemetery for atheists. Hasan's friend, Abdulsamed Djozić, knew that someone from Srebrenica was buried in that cemetery. Hasib's remains were moved to a cemetery in Tuzla.

If you haven't lived through a natural disaster or a war, it is likely that you have photographs of yourself, your family members and your friends over the years. For so many people in Bosnia, it is rare to have any photographs, since the majority of pictures were lost in the destruction caused by the war. Hasan does have one photograph of Hasib, although it is not the one he wishes that he had.

> A medical examiner in the Tuzla Clinic took a photo of my dead brother. The only photo of him is that one of him dead taken by the pathologist.

Once the Memorial was established, Hasan wanted to bury Hasib in Potočari. He was in contact with Amor Mašović, the head of Institute for Missing Persons. Mr. Mašović suggested that Hasan wait to see if his other brother Hajro would be found and then he could bury both of his brothers at the same time.

Hasan had let people know where his brother Hajro and five others had died. He was told that only five bodies had been found on that site. He later learned that Hajro's body had been taken to Grbavci[4] school where it was intentionally cut in half in order to frighten the others who were being held there and who would later be killed.

> He was in that condition, cut in the middle. The top was found at the beginning of 2009 in a mass grave in Snagovo. The bottom of his skeleton and his legs without some bones were found four months later. The bottom of his skeleton was found in three different mass graves. So the parts of his body were found in separate graves. The top of his skeleton was found in a mass grave with 200 other skeletons. He was the only incomplete.

Once Hajro was identified, Hasan contacted Mr. Mašović at the ICMP to request that Hasib's remains be exhumed from Tuzla so that both brothers could be buried in Potočari. These burials happened on July 11, 2009. Hasan also buried his uncle on that day even though his remains were incomplete.

> My brothers *[were]* buried in Potočari and they are silent witnesses. It was so difficult for me to deal with it. I buried my uncle without his head.

Hasan spoke candidly about the impact that all of this has had on him.

> It affected me all this trauma that I survived during the war. After the war it was difficult to live.

He continues to deal with the trauma that he experienced, struggling with all that he witnessed and experienced.

> I'd rather not talk to my family about it. Then I go to bed and I wake up and sometimes I see these images coming through my mind. I think it's easier when you talk about it.
>
> I'm a believer. My faith definitely helps me. I try not to burden my family. If people want to speak I will speak. But I will say my story is not the most difficult story. There are mothers who lost everything, six sons. My mother lost her husband, two sons and three brothers. Some of the mothers lost brothers, a husband and sons. My mother knows many of these women.

Hasan is working on a book about his own experiences. He is finding that it is not an easy project.

> My desire is to write a book. I have the desire to publish it but it's difficult. When I write my book I write two lines, take a walk through my backyard then I go back. I pray to God not to let me exaggerate or to add any lie.
>
> I want to write about what I saw in the column. If you were 100 meters in front or behind you didn't see the same thing. So I'm just going to write what I saw. It's slow to write. Ako bog da[5] maybe next year I'll have it published.

He wondered how it is possible that a person is able to kill other people and thinks about what their punishment should be.

> I wouldn't be able to even kill a chicken. Dražen Erdemović[6] said he killed 72 men and he probably killed more. He was sentenced to five years, it is not any punishment. The only punishment would be that he is brought to the Srebrenica mothers. Probably they would not hurt him, maybe they would let him go. I supposed it's difficult to be a perpetrator, but I don't know.

When asked why he thinks he survived when so many others did not, he responded in a way that was very similar to most of the people in this book.

> I think God. It's my destiny. When I go back in time then I say to myself, is it possible that anybody survived? We had just a few rifles and a little bit of ammunition. They had really good weapons and everything. They had 30,000 soldiers and now Bosnia has 10,000 as a state.
>
> I think that God saved me. God gave me strength to find my brother and to carry my brother.

The footage of Hasan carrying Hasib to the free territory is quite famous. Hasan became aware of this footage when a friend told him of its existence.

> One of my friends said that there is a video of me and my brother and that Ahmed Bajrić Blicko has it. It was made by Muhamed Mujkić when he filmed people coming to the free territory in Nezuk.
>
> My mother listened to me when I told her that I carried my dead brother to the free territory and she did not want to believe it. But then she saw the footage. She also has his photo from the pathologist.
>
> There is the footage in Potočari which is shown in the documentary film to visitors at the Memorial. One time on the news Aljazeera showed where girls from England came to visit the Memorial and they saw the footage of me and my brother and they held their breath.

A photo was made from this footage, a picture of Hasan carrying Hasib.

> In Vienna there was an exhibition about Srebrenica. The head of the exhibition called me and said he wanted me to allow him to make a photo out of the footage of me and my brother and that he will donate money to Srebrenica children. All of the photos that they don't sell they will send to Potočari.

Hasan said that he hoped that one day the photo of him and his brother would be exhibited at the Memorial in Potočari.

His children know everything about his experiences. They accompany him to Srebrenica each year on July 11, the burial day.

> My son is 19 [and] he looks identical to my brother. I took him to the Peace March. I explained to him in detail but the Peace March doesn't go through the exact route. But I tried to explain to him where both of them died and where all major atrocities happened. I took him because he can't learn from the history books.
>
> When he came to Potočari he said to me, "father, if you even bother me sometimes from now on I will carry you on my back if you want. I will never say no."
>
> When it's hard now to live I remember how it was during the war when it comes to everything. I gave my shoes to my brother Hasib and in the footage I was barefoot which totally was strange because I was lost and did not even notice that at the time. I lost all the feelings for everything.
>
> As I said before I wish my brothers had survived, and I was killed, for them to have their children but it is destiny. One was 18 and the other one was 19.
>
> Hasib was very shy and very reserved. When he was five he started to speak but around company he didn't dare to say anything. He was quiet. He had no girlfriends as a teenager, he was so shy. That's life.
>
> I continued my life after this somehow because of my son and my wife. I had to go on.

It is difficult to find anyone in Srebrenica and other parts of eastern Bosnia who did not lose someone in the war. Hasan lost 40 family members, including seven males from his mother's side. Among others, he also lost his father, two brothers, and four twin cousins.

Hasan believes that there were more people killed in the Srebrenica genocide than the stated number of 8,372.

> I forgot to say that not more than 6,000 people came to Nezuk, maybe even less. That's why I think the number of male victims in Potočari is even higher. There are entire families nobody reported their missing status and they were killed as well. There are still people missing. Not all of my family has been identified.
>
> At the last burial I buried my aunt's son, he was 16. Nobody was there to put him in the grave. I was the only family member. After his death his daughter was born. She studies medical sciences and she is a good student.

Hasan is not alone in the anger he feels toward the United Nations and the international community.

> I think that Srebrenica is a black stain on the UN, Europe and the rest of the international community. I hope that a pillar of shame will be built in Potočari. When people come to visit that they will see those that should be blamed as responsible.
>
> I think anybody who committed these crimes should be brought to justice. I'll never forget. I was trying to raise my children not to hate but not to forget. Never forget. I will never forget but I will never forgive. I will never harm anybody. I will never have in my mind to harm anybody. I was in Slovenia with President Pahor a few days ago and he asked me if I hate anybody. I said no I don't hate anybody. I work with the people of different ethnicities. They've never had any problem with me and they will never have any problem in the future.

In his time with us, Hasan described in great detail the trauma that he endured and his sorrow about his brothers and other family members. His mother is sick and he has to take her to the Potočari cemetery very often. Yet, he still says that he is a happy man.

> My wife and I are still married. We have a daughter and a son and we have a happy life. They are well-raised kids staying out of trouble. My daughter, she's 14. I hope she will be a great artist. She loves to draw portraits but in our religion it is not allowed. It's her big passion.
>
> Both of my kids are excellent students. My son made an application for Google in Tuzla. That's his work. He won the first prize in Europe for that. I'm so proud of them. They are good kids, they do not drink alcohol or take drugs.

There are other artists in the family as well.

> My nephew is one of the most well-known painters in Croatia. My daughter, she was good at drawing as a little girl. She was the best in her school at drawing. Every year she wins the first place prize in Bosnia. There is Earth Day when they make drawings and she won a prize. She got 8,000 euros but she donated all the money for some children with special needs in Tuzla. That was her wish. She saw the children on TV and she wanted to donate it.

Hasan said that he is not artistic. From the time he was young he wanted to be a mechanic. His neighbor had a workshop in his garage and Hasan would sneak over there whenever the neighbor was home. He finished secondary school focused on becoming a mechanic, even though he described it as very dirty work. He said that he is still a good mechanic. He finished criminal science faculty after the war but it is not his job now.

Like others in this book, Hasan told us his story at great emotional cost to himself. And like so many others, he thanked us for listening to him.

> Thank you for hearing me. When I tell a story to someone else I like to be heard. When you share the pain and when it means something to someone then it is easier. I saw that you were crying. Unfortunately that happened and if I could change my life I would. If we don't write people will forget. That's also why I'm writing my own book.

Hasan exhibited boundless care and empathy for those in need during the war and it didn't stop there. In 2014, he was honored by the Broadcasting Service of BiH (BHRT) for his heroic actions during the floods that devastated the country in May of that year. Natural disasters pay no attention to borders or ethnic differences and neither did Hasan. In addition to rescuing several members of his own family who were fighting for their lives in Živinice, he also saved nine people, including three children, in Šekovici, a municipality populated 100 percent with Bosnian Serbs.[7]

Hasan Aziz Hasanović (coauthor of this book)

If you visit the Srebrenica Genocide Memorial you have a good chance of meeting Hasan Aziz Hasanović. In his job as curator and interpreter, he works with people all day long who are interested in learning about the Srebrenica genocide. He works with large and small groups, academics, royalty, heads of state and groups of students. He is one of those people who treats everyone the same regardless of their station in life. It's one of the many endearing qualities that he has. He is also the person who is always anticipating what needs to be done, noticing what should be fixed, planning and making things better, all the while having one creative idea after another.

I've seen him in front of countless groups, talking about history, culture and the political nature of the genocide, while also sharing his personal story. Sometimes he paints his story with a broad brush, and other times he talks about the pain and anguish that he carried for a long time after the genocide killed his father, twin brother Husein and other male family members. Hasan, like the other survivors in this book, sees it as his mission to raise awareness about this particular genocide and the warning signs that it could happen anywhere.

A few years ago, Hasan wrote a short memoir in English, *Surviving Srebrenica*, about his experiences growing up in a small village, moving to the larger town of Bratunac and ultimately ending up in Srebrenica along with 50,000 other people. His story is also available in the media, in documentaries, on YouTube and elsewhere in the national and international press. It's a story of an early life that was rich with family and experiences in a tiny village, followed by the horror that war brings. His experiences included living in the woods, running from burning villages, dodging snipers during the siege of Srebrenica, starving, finding ways to play Beatles music with friends when there was no electricity, experiencing trauma after trauma, and ultimately escaping the genocide through the harrowing six days of the Death March.

He is frequently interviewed by the international press and the BBC and has been a keynote speaker at events in numerous countries. He has addressed the Scottish and

Flemish Houses of Parliament. His memoir has been published in Italian and Dutch, and has been translated into German and Turkish. His story has not always had such a wide reach though, fortunately, now it does.

When I first met Hasan, his powerful story reached just those who came to the Memorial. At great emotional expense, he told his story several times a day, at least five days a week. There were certain parts of his story that stood out for him, and for anyone listening. One was the day in April 1993 at the playground when the mortar shells hit the soccer field, killing 74 and wounding 100, mostly children and teenagers. Hasan literally had a front seat to this massacre. Like the others who were there, he described the feeling that it would be safe to play outside that day because Philippe Morillon, the UN commander was in town. There had been days of shelling and people were wanting to go outside, play soccer, and walk around.

Hasan was with his friends and they had heard about Morillon coming. They agreed that they would all go out together to the sports fields in front of the primary school. It was the perfect day to finally be able to play football. When they got to the school, there were so many people, who all had the same idea, thinking it would be safe to be outside. A group was already playing football when Hasan arrived with his friends, so they sat down on the bleachers to wait.

> I sat on the first stand and there were people sitting next to me and above me on other stands watching football. I heard explosions in the distance.

One of Hasan's friends was worried that the shooting would come closer, maybe even hitting the football field. Hasan was not worried because he thought Morillon was probably already in town and the BSA wouldn't dare attack when he was present.

> Just a couple of minutes later, like four meters *[about 13 feet]* in front of me, I saw black smoke, then an explosion. I fainted, I don't know what happened but something happened.

After regaining consciousness, Hasan looked around at the people next to him and above him on the bleachers. What he saw is an image that he has never forgotten. Even with all of the traumatic sights that came later and that remain etched in his brain, the image from that day at the playground stands out to him.

> They were armless, legless, headless people covered with blood. That image is difficult to explain how people looked. People were screaming. Then I just got on my feet and I stumbled over the dead. I went up a couple of meters to the top of those stands and I had to lie down. I had to get down because I was thinking that they might shoot again, I just had to protect myself.

When he realized the shooting had stopped, Hasan saw a house on a hill across the street and he ran there, going into the basement. There was a crowd of people inside.

> All people inside were slightly wounded. Then I was wondering if I was wounded.
> I didn't know what was happening with me. My right arm was a little bit wet, my sweater was wet. I thought it was blood but it was just sort of salt water. I was happy because it wasn't blood.

When he realized he wasn't wounded, Hasan looked out the window to see what had happened actually on the playground.

> There were so many people on the ground and everybody was dead. A couple of hundred maybe, I'm not sure.

He expected the UN would come to help with the wounded and the dead, especially since Morillon's entourage was in town. As it turned out, just one APC showed up with just one soldier. People in the crowd started helping the soldier load the wounded into the APC. Hasan, just 17 years old at the time, watched all of this from the window.

He and a friend then decided to run home to the building where they were living in Srebrenica. It was close by, the tallest building in town. Hasan lived with his family in an apartment on the ninth floor.

> In our flat where my family lived, there was a big kitchen window, a really big one. I knew that they were looking through the window and they knew that I was at the playground and they thought that I was dead. I knew that they thought that I got killed.

When Hasan arrived home and his family saw him on the doorstep, they were happy and relieved to see that he was alive. Other relatives and friends showed up when they heard that he had survived.

> My father wasn't there, he had run to this playground to search for me. He was looking at the dead trying to find me. He couldn't find me and later he got back home and he saw me alive and he was very happy.

There are too many traumas to count in this story: Hasan's experiences, his family watching out the window, his father searching through the dead for his son. This is not unusual for people who lived in Srebrenica during this time. Even though Hasan had been in Srebrenica for about a year and experienced shelling on a regular basis, he was not afraid of it until that day on the playground.

> Until that moment I wasn't that afraid of shelling and shooting. From that moment on, when I would hear the sound of shelling I would hide under a table and I was more scared.

In spite of the traumatic events of the day, Hasan and a friend decided to go search for food that night. His friend had been wounded in the stomach at the playground yet he still agreed to go with Hasan to try and find food.

> It was just survival. You would do anything to survive as if you would be stuck in a jungle, alone, and you would be afraid of dangerous animals. You would try to get food and to defend from dangerous animals, to try to escape. That's how I felt. My mind was working differently then. It was the mind of a survivor.

He described what he meant by "the mind of a survivor."

> Looking for food, trying to stay out of trouble, avoid shelling and to protect myself but at the same time trying to live, trying to spend time with my friends, trying to live as a human being, to feel. We desperately wanted to live; we desperately wanted to see more of life. When you are trapped in a siege you live under impossible conditions.

For three and a half years, Hasan tried to remember the taste of a banana and of Coca-Cola. He forgot what chocolate tasted like and how it was to enjoy a good meal.

> All of those things we used to have, before the war, we had everything. So imagine being trapped in a siege and being deprived of all of these things which you had for years. I was hungry. Sometimes I wasn't that hungry because maybe I had a meal which I could barely call a meal, it was just a survival meal. Today I wouldn't eat that meal, no way. Maybe even somebody's cat or dog wouldn't even want it. In these conditions it's natural that you would remember what you ate before, what you had. Before the war we were able to buy anything that we wanted. We had everything.

Hasan considers himself lucky because he had at least one meal a day, even though it wasn't at all appetizing. It tended to be meager because the small amount of food that they had was shared among six people.

> I don't remember a day when I didn't have at least one meal. I always had to be careful that I would eat just my portion, not to cross the line, not to get into someone else's portions. I love my brothers, my mother and my father and my uncle of course and I would never take anything from them.
>
> We always ate unsalted food because we never got any salt in Srebrenica and the food was so bad. It was terrible, the taste. My mother used a lot of tricks to make a meal and today when I think about it I wonder how she was able to do that. Imagine mothers trying to figure out what to do to make sure that the family had at least one meal a day, when they barely had anything to cook with.

Like the others in this book who lived in Srebrenica during the siege, Hasan experienced days that alternated between boredom and terror; between finding ways to keep busy and trying not to get killed. When Srebrenica fell in July 1995, he decided to go through the woods to Tuzla, starting the journey with his uncle, father and twin brother Husein. Hasan was the only one who survived.

For a long time, he thought of himself primarily in terms of what he survived. A short while ago he said to me, "I am so much more than a genocide survivor now." He is absolutely right.

In 2003, eight years after the genocide, Hasan buried his father at the Srebrenica Memorial. The burial was made more difficult by the process it took to get to the cemetery. He was on a bus traveling to the Memorial when they were stopped in Bratunac. The local RS police told them that they couldn't go any further because there was a traffic jam in Potočari. U.S. President Bill Clinton was inaugurating the Memorial and there were over 50,000 people attending the burial ceremony. Hasan and his family got off the bus.

> I thought okay, we will walk. I walked the Death March so walking a few miles could not make a big difference, even it was a very difficult day for me. We got to the crossroads in downtown Bratunac by the traffic lights. Then all of a sudden to the right and to the left, on the side of the road I saw a few hundred local Serbs. As we walked past, the RS police stood in front of them to make sure there was physical contact between them and us. The Serbs were yelling out unbelievable insults, calling us Turks and animals. They were spitting on us. And there were war criminals in that crowd. So, as I was going to bury my father, they were spitting on me and it made me feel like I wasn't human.

Two years later, Hasan buried his twin brother, Husein.

> It was probably the most difficult day of my life. And I honestly thought that I would not survive his burial. But I did, and then I spent years dealing with the consequences of the genocide. It was my personal confrontation with the past.

> Before those two burials I had a normal life. I was an interpreter for the US Army and I was a university student. With those two burials everything had changed.

Like so many people who survived the Death March, Hasan had nightmares where he was being hunted. These went on for a long time.

> Later, when I graduated from the university, I thought that I could help to raise awareness of the genocide at the Memorial. So, I was always wondering if there was a job vacancy there. And I also thought if I go there, that it would help me to cope with what had happened.

Fortunately for so many people from all over the world, Hasan did get a job at the Memorial and started working there on February 2, 2009. It wasn't easy returning to Srebrenica.

> It was of course, very difficult to adapt there because I lived in Srebrenica throughout the whole war, survived the siege there, and later the genocide. And returning there was not an easy thing. Everything, every building, every house, reminded me of what had happened there. Reminded me of people who I knew who are not there anymore, some of them, most of them actually, are buried at the cemetery as victims of genocide. But I had a very clear mission. I did not come there for just a job. My intention was to raise awareness of the genocide at the Memorial as much as I could.
>
> So, I kept doing what I was doing. Meeting people from all over the world, telling my story, and every time it was very, very difficult. It is hard for ordinary people who haven't lived through a genocide, even to be at the place or watch a documentary. You can only imagine how it is difficult for those who survived to be there, not to mention to work there.
>
> But I never thought of giving up, because I had in my mind my goals to raise awareness for my brother, father, uncle, and everybody else who was killed during the genocide. Over the years I met unbelievable people, from all over the world. I probably have met hundreds of thousands so I would never know the exact figure.
>
> In 2013, I also started to go on the international stage, to try to raise awareness as much as I could. My first trip was to the University of Denver Graduate School of Social Work. The more I traveled, the more people were interested in bringing me to different events and places like universities, schools, parliaments. I've had receptions with Prime Ministers. At the Memorial I've guided Presidents, Prime Ministers, Minsters, Members of Congress, and other very important people.

Hasan is interested in raising awareness about the genocide with heads of state and school children and everyone in between.

> So, I think I have succeeded in getting many people interested in this subject of genocide and my intention is to create an interest among all people and students wherever I speak. I encourage people to come to Bosnia and to come to Srebrenica and I think it really works. Today, I spoke for the first time in one of the Bosnian schools. It's been almost six years since I've been traveling abroad to speak and for the first time today it was in a school in Sarajevo. I spoke of my personal and professional experience regarding the genocide.
>
> I will continue to give my contribution at the Memorial and individually abroad when people engage me to tell the story of the genocide, just to make sure it's not forgotten. That it's not going to happen again. For me this is a mission. Otherwise I would have given up on this a long time ago.

For Hasan, it's important that people come to the Memorial to learn about the Srebrenica genocide. Many people know nothing about it. Even though the world pledged "Never Again" after the Holocaust, it did happen again, in Cambodia, Rwanda, Bosnia and elsewhere. It's still happening today. Hasan believes that educating people about the genocide, particularly though personal stories of survivors, is an important step in trying to stop future mass atrocities and genocides.

When I bring students to Bosnia, and particularly to Srebrenica, they realize how often Hasan tells his story. They often wonder if we should be asking him and the other survivors to tell their stories. They wonder if it's helpful or retraumatizing given how painful the stories are. Hasan explains his viewpoint on these questions.

> From my experience, not just my own but from the people who have survived genocide, war crimes, trauma on different levels, all of them want their stories to be heard. They think that their pain will be recognized by retelling their stories to those who don't know. When students come to visit the Memorial, when survivors tell their stories, they also want students to pass on their stories to those who don't know. Survivors, and myself individually, we never feel we are made or compelled to tell our stories. Nobody can make you do something if you don't want to. People who survived genocide and horrific war crimes, they think they didn't survive it because of pure chance, they think they survived because of destiny and they think that they should in return, tell their stories. When they tell their stories, they also tell the stories of those who were killed. It's sort of a debt toward those who were killed. I think the best judge of whether or not to tell their stories are actually the survivors themselves.

Hasan feels that those who listen to survivors' stories and who then educate others as the survivors have requested are considered advocates.

> When advocating for us, you are not just standing up for us, and those who were killed, you are standing up for humanity. Because the crime of genocide is not just a crime against a particular targeted group. It's a crime against the whole of humanity. It makes it an international matter. It should be a concern of all humanity. It is not a private matter.

Hasan also discussed another aspect of personal narratives. It's an ethical consideration of when and how someone should share stories that are not their own. As he said earlier, he interacts with too many people to count. Included in this are journalists, researchers, and academics with an interest in genocide in general and/or Srebrenica specifically. Sometimes this has a good outcome and sometimes it does not.

> There are people that have good intentions and there are also people, unfortunately, with very selfish intentions and interests. Some of them spend just a bit of time in Srebrenica and they write their pieces. Then they go back home and they claim to be experts on genocide. They educate others about it and of course what they know is a really, really tiny portion of what they should know. Sometimes those individuals scrutinize, impose ideas on what should be done, and criticize what was done. Sometimes those individuals, they say, "Why didn't you do this, why didn't you do that," and they would never say that in some other place like Auschwitz. Because I think for them, we are some sort of an experiment.
>
> As I mentioned before, of course the crime of genocide is an international matter, it should be of concern to every human being, in the sense that people should advocate for the victims. When it comes to [how to] compose the narrative and to how it should be told

to others, it should be those who have lived through it or those who are living in that country or that particular place. And I think it's us, survivors, families, Bosnians and Herzegovinians who should decide how the story is told because it's our story.

Hasan and the other survivors are grateful for people on the outside who take a genuine interest in them and their experiences. Those with stories to tell benefit from people who take the time to learn from them and then go on to raise awareness of the Srebrenica genocide around the world.

It is very important for us to have friends from the outside too, because we cannot be everywhere. True advocates always tell this story in a really sensitive, dignified, respectful way, so we are always very thankful for all of those individuals who stand up for us.

Another reason Hasan and the other survivors tell their stories, and want to control the narrative, is to help counter genocide denial that is so rampant in the RS and in Serbia. It's hard to imagine how difficult it must be to have survived a genocide, lost family members and loved ones, and then have people denying that it ever happened.

The Srebrenica genocide has been judicially established by the two highest UN Tribunals, the ICTY and the ICJ. And many countries, including the European Union, have passed resolutions condemning the Srebrenica genocide and encouraging education about it. Much of the world has accepted it as genocide but not our neighbors. The RS, Serbia, their elites, meaning political elites, media, academia, they have constructed a counter narrative, opposite to the narrative of the truth which was established by the UN Tribunals. Their children are taught that it was a civil war. That they tried to prevent genocide against them. That all sides committed war crimes equally, or that the other side committed more crimes than Serbs themselves. They teach them that Karadžić, Milošević, and Mladić are heroes, not war criminals. They're poisoning the young generation of Serbs with these distorted facts which makes our process of reconciliation impossible. Denial is a wall between groups who are supposed to reconcile.

Hasan sees the process of reconciliation as closely connected to denial.

Many people who don't know, who have no experience in our story, in what happened, they think that some other model that has been applied to some other countries as a success can be also applied here, which is not true because everything is different here. In my opinion, reconciliation is possible only through a political decision, meaning that a decision about this has to be made by political elites, primarily in Serbia. The Bosnian Serbs would follow because they follow everything that Serbia does. The international community should play the role of mediator in this very important matter. I would say that victims, survivors are always ready for this process. Even more ready than anybody else.

Hasan sees reconciliation as much more than politicians visiting other countries or states who are in need of reconciliation. In addition to political symbolism, there needs to be an implementation plan for true reconciliation. The first step to this is a genuine admission, without any exceptions, by the perpetrators, that genocide happened in Srebrenica.

When people say, "genocide happened in Srebrenica but...," they are trying to equalize, downplay, the actual genocide in comparing with something else. If there is a recognition and admission, then victims, survivors are always ready to talk about reconciliation. Then laws should be enacted to incriminate denial of the genocide and the Holocaust. There needs to be a certain standard of acceptable behavior established. School curriculum should teach the established truths about the genocide to educate young people.

Hasan thinks it's important for local people to visit the Memorial, including the younger generation. If they did visit, and if their school curriculum taught established facts, then the process of reconciliation might be able to move forward. Hasan reiterated that the Memorial is the only official memorial in the RS.

> The Memorial is the only place where there are actual victims who were identified through DNA and buried in a cemetery. It's very important that there is a place where we can tell our stories, where the story of genocide can be told to people who don't know. Where people from all over the world can come to learn what Srebrenica has to teach them and where Bosnian students can come to also learn the valuable lessons of the Srebrenica genocide.

When he said the Memorial in Potočari is the only official memorial, he was referring to the main execution sites where most of the men and boys were killed in July 1995. These are the schools and fields and other places that the mothers visit every July 13 to memorialize the executions. The Pilica Cultural Center is the hardest for Hasan to visit.

> One place is really significant for me, it's where 500 men and boys were killed, among them my father. You come there and it's a cultural center. The ceiling is basically going to collapse. It's dilapidated inside, with graffiti on the walls glorifying Ratko Mladić. Locals put trash inside and sometimes manure from chicken coups or pig sties. When we get inside it's impossible to breathe because of that horrific smell. So, we usually stop outside and I tell the story of what happened there. Families and mothers lay down wreaths. They say a small prayer then they get on the bus and go home.
> In front of that cultural center, there is a memorial dedicated to partisans from the Second World War. But there is also a memorial dedicated to Serb soldiers, with their pictures, who might have participated in the genocide. The same memorial, painted in the same color as if they fought for the same thing. But there is nothing which would tell that 500 human beings were murdered there in July 1995. As if nothing has happened. Local Serbs there live in total denial and I'm sure they all know what happened there. But they don't want to talk about that. Anybody visiting there is not welcome.

There were no survivors from the Pilica Cultural Center. Much of what is known about what happened there comes from the ICTY testimony of Dražen Erdemović. His testimony includes information about the coffee bar that is directly across a narrow street from the cultural center.

> In his testimony he said he came to the coffee bar and he saw commanders inside. He heard gunfire from the cultural center and they told him that people were being killed inside. That's when he learned about killings.
> Now that coffee bar is being renovated with a big sign that says "New Life." New life for what? For who? They will go on with their lives, they will never speak up.

There is a large, thick book that lists all of the mass graves and where individuals were found. It was in that book that Hasan learned where his father and brother had been

Chapter 2. Death March Survivors

killed and where they had been buried. Without that book, he wouldn't have this information. He feels fortunate in a way because most people don't know where their loved ones were killed.

The cultural center is the hardest execution site for Hasan to visit and it is also the most difficult for me. I have been in that cultural center three times and I hope to never go in there again. The only reason I would go is if I was asked to do so by my friend Hasan. He has already described the conditions inside and outside this building. In addition to the disgusting state of the building, the emotional toll that it takes for anybody to go in there is immense. This is particularly true, of course, for those intimately connected with the genocide.

The last time I was in there, was on a July 13 with the group memorializing the execution sites. Inside there is trash everywhere. In addition to the pro–Serb graffiti Hasan described, there is also animal and human feces inside, and on that day in July it was also piled in the doorway in an effort to keep people out. When you go in, you enter a place that you wish you had never seen, because it is an image of nightmares and slasher films, but it is real. Twenty-plus years of neglect have only worsened the horror of the bullet splattered ceiling and walls, holes made by grenades that were lobbed into the crowd of 500 people imprisoned, and a performance stage under which people attempted to crawl for cover. If you tried to, you could not count the number of holes in the walls made by bullets and grenades. You don't want to know how many holes there are, because you don't want to stay in this place for the amount of time it would take to count that high. It is impossible to avoid imagining what it must have been like in there. You can feel the horror and the fear. You can almost see and hear people trying to crawl under that stage, trying to get away from the inevitable.

During one conversation that we had, Hasan told me about the first time he went into the cultural center. When he saw all the bullet holes and the stage where people tried to hide, he wondered what it was like for his father. Did he hold onto hope up until the last minute? How squashed were all of them in there? Was he tortured before he was killed?

The pain of this is evident on Hasan's face each time I've seen him inside that building. It's one of the few times his defenses seemed stripped away and the extent of the trauma he has endured is unmistakable. He still manages to talk to the group of mothers assembled there. It is beyond my comprehension how he is able to do that. It's a time when the personal and the professional collide yet he pushes through.

On a daily basis, Hasan moves forward with his self-imposed mission. He does so with a drive that is selfless and single minded. He often keeps an almost maniacal pace of organizing, arranging and attending to detail. He is always anticipating what needs to be done and is the first to jump up and do it. I realized some time ago that this is what it takes for him to keep his feelings at bay. But even when he is whirling at his most extreme, he remains gracious, generous and thoughtful. That is the strength and charisma of his character.

He carries an additional burden. Most males his age from Srebrenica were murdered in the genocide. Therefore, he represents for many of the mothers how old their son would be now and what their sons might be like. Hasan is aware of this and treats the mothers accordingly, with love and compassion.

In Srebrenica, he is everybody's son.

The Pilica Cultural Center execution site where Hasan Aziz Hasanovic's father was killed (photograph by Kristian Skeie, July 14, 2013).

There were 500 Muslim men and boys killed in the Pilica Cultural Center in July 1995. Nobody survived this execution site.[8]

The Kozluk execution site is now used as an unofficial trash dump. There are piles and piles of trash where over 1,000 Muslim men and boys were killed in July 1995. There were no survivors from this execution site.[9]

The Kozluk execution site where Hasan Aziz Hasanović's brother was killed (photograph by Kristian Skeie, July 14, 2014).

Haso Hasanović

Haso Hasanović (not to be confused with the two Hasan Hasanovićs in this book) was 16 years old when Srebrenica fell. He was born in the hospital there and lived in the village of Lehovići above Srebrenica his entire life. His father worked for a construction company and his mother took care of the home and the children. His school was in Potočari and he made the two-hour trip on foot every morning and afternoon. He walked with his younger brother, his older sister and children from his village as well as the surrounding area. There were around 50 pupils in that school.

> We went to school for as long as we could. When we stopped going to school I knew that something was wrong and the shooting started. We would go to school for a month then we would stop going for ten days. When there was a ceasefire we could go back to school. We used to have a normal life, going to school together, sitting together on the bench. Then all of a sudden something happened. Because probably it was about people who were making the decisions.
>
> Refugees from other municipalities started coming to Srebrenica. Then the Serbs called for the Muslims to surrender their weapons and we knew that the war was coming.

In July of 1995, the situation in Lehovći changed dramatically. Suddenly soldiers were going through the village saying that Srebrenica had fallen. People from other villages started to pass through on their way to Potočari.

> We tried to stay in the village but then we had to go. All the people had to pass through my village to go to Potočari to the UN base. Then we knew what was happening. So all of the people from the village gathered on the road. Then some guy came and said that men shouldn't go to Potočari, only women and children should go. Only women and female children and boys under 13 were going to Potočari and boys who were older than that were supposed to go through the woods. Some man told us. This information was being passed. So I decided to go through the woods with my father.

Haso said goodbye to his mother and his siblings on the road.

> All of us were crying, thinking that we might not see each other ever again. They went to Potočari and we headed to Šušnjari, to the woods, toward Tuzla with the men.
>
> When we started going from Buljim near Šušnjari to Kamanice hill we came across ambushes during the night. They started shooting from all sides. People started to scream and cry and run, people were getting wounded, it was chaos. Then I lost sight of my father and I never saw him again.
>
> I started to run downhill, I fell on a tree and there was a pain in my chest. I was unconscious. When I came to I was alone. Nobody was there, only the dead and the wounded crying and screaming for help. They were screaming and the wounded would say, "Do you have a piece of paper to write that we were left here to tell our families where we were left?" I circled around the place for two days. I didn't know the way. I couldn't find the way to Tuzla.

All of this happened to Haso when he was just 16 years old. Unfortunately, it didn't end there, and the situation got a lot worse.

> The place where I was I saw maybe 50 people dead and so many were wounded. From the whole site they were screaming for help. I didn't know where the column went and I tried to figure it out but I was just making a circle around the place. When the enemy started shooting again, the shelling, I started going. I came across a road and I followed the road. Then all of a sudden, from the ambush, two men jumped and they captured me. I didn't know where I was. I didn't know anything.

Haso's hands where then tied and he was ordered to follow his captors. They told him that they were going to let him go.

> They brought me to the Kravica warehouse and put me in that yard with a fence around it, in front of the warehouse. There was the Serb army there all around the place. Then they brought my schoolmate Nukić Nermin. We used to go to the same class. One of the soldiers shot his legs. Then he fell and started screaming. Then another soldier said, "Why did you shoot a child? We should bring bandages to help him." Then Nermin was taken by two Serb soldiers. They took him behind that warehouse. He never showed up again. After the war he was found and he was buried. One of the Serb soldiers said to me, "This is what will happen to you when your turn comes. There are so many people that we have to kill before your turn."
>
> From the warehouse they were taking ten people out and they would line them up against the wall and shoot them. When I was there, maybe five or six groups they brought out and they killed them. They would kill them then they would make the rest of the Muslim men load them onto the truck. Then they would kill those who were loading the truck then they would do the same thing to the other group.

Later they untied Haso's hands and told him that it would be impossible for him to escape because the entire place was surrounded by Serb soldiers. As it turned out that was not the case.

> The Serb soldier came to me and gave me a bottle to go to the woods to fetch water. He told me where the water spring was behind the warehouse. He said to me, "Don't dare to run because we will hunt you and we will find you." As I got to the water spring there was a sort of hose and water running from it from the earth. I found a little girl by that water spring. She was still alive, she was shaking, with blood running out of her. She was slain, she might have been 16. Probably that girl was taken out of the bus of refugees. She was wearing pants and a blue jacket. When I saw that, I circled around the water spring, and then I sort of lost my mind. I thought I was looking for water around my house, where I lived.
>
> Then I said to myself, I should run, I don't want to go back and I jumped into the river. When I was crossing the river and was about to reach the forest they started to shoot at me. I managed to run away from the site but not for long.
>
> Maybe they sent me to get water just to see the girl who was laying there. They sent me there to see that to scare me off. They didn't send me there so that I could try to run.
>
> I wasn't free for long. Wandering through the woods I came to the Muslim hamlet Burnice. I found a full village of people because people couldn't find their way to Tuzla. They tried to cross the asphalt road but every time they tried they failed.

Haso had caught up with those who were trying to get to Tuzla through the woods. It was a relatively small group of people who were stuck attempting to cross the road that goes from Konjević Polje toward Nova Kasaba.

> I saw many people. Then I wasn't alone, I was happy. Some of my neighbors were there. But I wasn't happy for long.
>
> When I met the neighbors I asked them if we could go further and they said no. We tried to cross the road but we failed. That night we tried to cross the road again. When we reached the asphalt road the Serb soldiers starting shooting then we had to go back again. I was running through the meadow which was pretty steep then people were being shot and they kept falling. We got back to Burnice again and we slept there. We didn't have anything to eat.

Haso had lost his food near Buljim at the very beginning of all this. He hadn't had anything to eat since then and, in fact, for the 16 days that his entire journey took the only thing he ate was small wild apples.

> We were in Burnice the whole day. In the evening around six the Serb army encircled the village. They brought military dogs and wherever people tried to hide they found them. Then we were all caught and our hands were tied with wire behind our backs. They pushed us toward a small meadow and they were counting people. One of them who was counting was swearing saying that "Because of you Balias[10] all of Serbia got involved. We thought that we would find many more men." They lined us up into a column and we started going downwards toward the asphalt road. One man tried to run from the column, an elderly man, maybe in his 60s. But he was shot. Then we were walking to Konjević Polje down the road. From the road we continued to Lolići hamlet. As we got there they pushed us toward the meadow.

Before Haso and his group arrived at Sandići meadow, people had been killed there. There were piles of bodies and they were forced to lie down on top of them. The Serb soldiers moved a distance from the prisoners and started to shoot. They weren't shooting at people but rather shooting just to scare people, including young Haso who had already encountered numerous horrific experiences along the way. Eventually buses and trucks arrived at the meadow.

> The commander said, "we will put you on the buses and trucks and we will take you to Bratunac." They told us to get up but we couldn't because we were tied. They were kicking people, then they were releasing people and pushing them onto the trucks. The commander asked if there were any children there. Two of them got up and they were younger than me. They were maybe 10 or 11. Their father was there and he told them not to tell their family name, Orić. They lied about their family name and they were let go. They put us on a bus. There were three of us. Already on the bus was a boy who had been taken prisoner earlier. The Serb army came on the bus. They came from Bratunac, from the military barracks. There were trucks in front of us with the other prisoners and we went to Bratunac. When we got there we got off the bus and the soldiers asked the commander what they were supposed to do with us. He said, "you know where the killings are being done, Vuk Karadžić school."

Haso and the others from his bus were not taken to the school although the other prisoners from the meadow were taken away from Bratunac in buses. Haso was taken to a military barracks in Bratunac along with three other children.

> We got inside, they put us in a cell a sort of prison and four of us children were there. It was dark, no lights. We also noticed that there was someone else in the room. I was

afraid *[of]* who was there, maybe some Serb soldiers. In this military barracks they played music, they sang, and they were shooting as if they were celebrating because Srebrenica fell. There was a man in a cell who stood up and he lit a cigarette. His name was Fadil from Drinjača. He was also in the woods trying to get to Tuzla and he was in the cell with us.

It wasn't until morning that Haso realized they were in an actual prison. He looked at the walls and saw that people had written how many days they had been there and signed their names. He then knew it was a prison for that military barracks and he thought it was for Serb soldiers who wouldn't go to the front line earlier.

In the morning they started to take people one by one to interrogate them. They asked me where the Bosnian Muslim soldiers were, what they ate. When I said in the woods they probably ate snails, they didn't believe it. Three Serb soldiers were interrogating us. They were not commanders, they were soldiers. Then a Serb officer came and he started to ask questions, all the same questions as before. I said, "they are in the woods," they asked, "what did they eat" I said, "they ate snails."

When I said that the Bosnian Muslims ate snails the officer turned toward his soldiers and he started to swear at them and he pushed them from the office. He said, "you are total idiots and you have a great lunch and they ate snails and you are not able to capture them all."

What followed was an extraordinary turn of events. As Haso told it, there was a Serb captain who had been captured by Bosnian forces. Haso's current captors had the plan to release Haso and the other children so that they could carry a letter to Naser Orić, the Commander of the Srebrenica defense. The letter contained information about exchanging the captured Serb captain.

The officer said to us, "You're lucky that the captain is captured. You're lucky because he is a captain and not an ordinary soldier. That's your luck."

They stayed in the cell in Bratunac for two days. On the third day, things changed.

They took us out to play football and they said this is a football game between Muslims and Chetniks. They gave us the ball and we were barefoot. My feet were bleeding and we had to play football with soldiers. They were recording everything. Then they took us back to the prison. After an hour a vehicle came in front of the building. It was a jeep *[with]* the sign UN. I knew those signs from the war. The soldiers had UN uniforms and helmets but they were Serb soldiers.

We got inside the vehicle and we headed to Zvornik. When they started to speak I realized that they were Serb soldiers. In the police station they started another interrogation. Asked the same questions. Then they let those children go but they kept me. I was older than them, they were smaller and younger. They put them back into the car.

The Serb soldiers told him to stay with them. They then asked the drivers why they brought Haso there because of his age, and the answer was because in a year he would be fully grown and would be able to carry a gun and fight against the Serbs.

Then a Serbian soldier took a radio and called Bratunac. He talked to someone who said that they had to let me go too with the letter. He said that I was supposed to carry the letter and hand it to the Bosnian authorities. Then the commander of the police hit my back with a club and also kicked me in the back. Then they let me go. I still had the letter.

> They put me again in a jeep with those three children. He turned off the asphalt road down a rocky road. We were driving for an hour when the car couldn't go any further because of the road. They were just guiding us by walking. We came across four Muslim men who were trying to get to the free territory. The soldiers tied them and left them to sit in the meadow. They were talking between themselves and said, "once we get back we will kill them later."
>
> We kept walking. We got to the front line, no man's land, then they said to us that we were supposed to sit, that they would go ahead and demine the path. We sat for an hour. The soldiers were saying to us, "you should stay with us to live, it's better for you," all that crap. I asked them if we could go to Tuzla with them. We were crying and kept begging them to let us go. The Serbs kept saying that we will go to Tuzla and they cursed our president.
>
> The soldiers demined the path and they showed us where to go. They said, "go there and you will see that place, it's your army, your government, your authorities." We got there and we couldn't recognize our army. They had uniforms like the Serb army. In Srebrenica our armed men didn't have any uniforms.
>
> When we got there, they started to kiss us and they asked us why we were there. And I asked them if Naser Orić was there and I said I have to give a letter to him. They said he was here but that he left and was gone. They said, "Just give us the letter and we will hand it to him." I sort of fainted.

They were put into a house for the night and in the morning were taken to Tuzla to the Dubrave airport. Haso met neighbors and people from the village, but he could not find his family. At that point he thought that they were dead. He then learned from his neighbors that his family was living in Tuzla with his father's brother.

He thought Tuzla was close, so he started walking. He didn't realize it was so far away. As he was walking a taxi stopped but it would have cost Haso one German mark for a ride and he didn't have any money. A woman from a grocery store saw Haso and took him home to sleep. In the morning, he went to Tuzla with her son.

When Haso got to Tuzla, he found his mother and his sister but the rest of the family had gone back to Dubrave to look for him. Many years passed before he learned the fate of his father. The information came from Mevludin Orić whose story is also told in this book.

> Mevludin told me that he was with my father. He was with him at the execution site. He told me that my father was killed and many of my neighbors were killed there. My father was buried during the second burial at Potočari, July 2003.

It is almost impossible to count all of the traumatic events Haso endured for those 16 days. He continues to struggle with the images that haunt him.

> After talking like today, it takes me ten days to get rid of them. I have the biggest problems with sleep, with dreams. I dream of going through the woods and all of the images come back to me. Sometimes I get up and I start to yell and scream.

One of my ongoing dilemmas with these interviews was knowing how retraumatizing they would be for many people. Balancing that with people's desire for their stories to be heard and told continued to be an ethical dilemma. I told Haso that I was sorry he would be heading into a bad ten days because of telling his story to us.

> I hope that by telling my story people will listen and that this will never happen again. It's evil, similar things are happening all over the world. Even here, being Muslim here and a returnee was very difficult. When I got back I lived in a tent. The situation will never be as it used to be. It will always be important who you are. Wherever you go to get a job if you are from the right nationality group then you have rights but if you are from the wrong nationality group then you can't get a job. Also our authorities are not paying attention to us. I should be able to get a job in Potočari school as a handyman but it's difficult to get a job even after what I survived.

Even with as difficult as it is to live in Srebrenica, Haso is glad he returned.

> I kept changing places as a refugee. I was in Tuzla, then Gornja Tuzla, then Banovići, Vozuća, etc. Wherever you go you aren't accepted, you are a refugee. I decided to come back to my land, to my village, where my father is buried and where we lived. Memories brought me back to Srebrenica.
>
> I tried to go to the States a long time ago, it didn't work out. We were going through Zagreb, we had interviews with some military people. It was 1997. Maybe because of the numbers we were not accepted.

Haso said his children know everything about the war and his experiences.

> I just keep telling them to make sure that they don't forget. Even without telling them they go to the Memorial to see that big cemetery. It's enough for them to know.

Haso met his wife when they were both refugees in Vozuća.[11] She's originally from Sućeska near Srebrenica.

> She lost her mother, two brothers, and her father. We understand each other. We never fight and respect each other. When I wake up screaming my wife puts her hand on me then I come back to reality. I take sleeping pills. I also take a sedative. Like this one (he takes a sedative). It helps.
>
> I took one before this interview too. I just wanted to make sure that I didn't have to stop and go out. That's what happens with me now.

Haso believes that he survived because of God.

> From all the people who were killed, it's a miracle that I survived. It's God, so that I can tell who did what. Why should we be silent, we should tell the story. Speak up. For the truth to be told, for us who survived to tell the story.

He acknowledged that it is very hard to do.

> But if we all stay silent, if we don't speak up, all of us, then the truth won't be told.

The year before he met with us, Haso testified against Mladić at The Hague. His first experience with the ICTY was back in 1998 in Tuzla when he was in his second year of high school. Investigators took him from school to the Tuzla Hotel where he gave a statement. His experience last year at The Hague was different but his statement was not. Haso reported that he never changed his story or his statement. He was there for ten days because the trial kept getting postponed. Finally, the day came when it was his turn to testify with Mladić in the room.

> When I spoke in front of Mladić and I told the story he said, "No, it's not true. It's true that Muslims killed themselves." During the trial he said, "You killed your selves," with a

> smile. He can smile but he's not a free man. He is in prison, on trial. He looked at me. I was able to look him in the eyes. I wasn't afraid. I didn't even mind his smile because I know what kind of a man he is, what he is capable to say and do.
>
> When I testified against Mladić he smiled at me and his attorney tried to confuse me. He tried to use any tricks. He did everything just to confuse me. Asking a few questions with the same meaning and turned everything around. But he failed.
>
> At the trial the judge came and he shook hands with me and he said, "Congratulations, you were so straight. We've never had such a calm witness." This was last year.

Haso carried the weight of responsibility for that letter. He doesn't know exactly what happened with it.

> I don't know. I never found out. The people from the front line took the letter and probably it was given to the right person. I know that the exchange happened.
>
> It was our ticket to freedom and maybe to save some more people who were kept as prisoners. Maybe more people were exchanged because of that letter, it was a very important letter for more people to be exchanged.

Haso knew there were a lot of prisoners who could possibly be exchanged.

> Wherever we were we saw prisoners. Along the road, wherever I ran, I would see killed and wounded people.

The day following our interview would be Haso's birthday. He said he would celebrate at home with his wife, his two children and his mother. His daughter was in her third year of secondary school and his son was in 8th grade in a private school.

As so often happens in Bosnia, an intensely difficult conversation ends on a light note. As we were saying our thank yous and goodbyes, Haso showed us his tattoo, which is a set of initials. He explained that he got the tattoo because of a girl from a long time ago and those were her initials. When we asked what his wife thought about that, he started laughing and told us that both women luckily have the same initials. *Sudbina*,[12] perhaps.

Ramiz Nukić

Ramiz Nukić ("The Bone Man") still lives in the house where he grew up. When he was a young man, no one would have ever guessed that at this point in his life, once he finishes his days caring for his animals and his crops, he would head into the woods above his home looking for bones. Every day. He looks for bones every day. He considers it a bad day if he doesn't find any bones because that means he hasn't helped someone identify a missing father or brother or son or uncle.

When we sat down to interview him in a café in Srebrenica, I needed to let him know how much of an impact he always makes on my students. He graciously allows me to bring my students out to his house to meet him when they are in Sarajevo for the summer. I told him he was a huge hit with my students. When he replied, "that's just the way I am" with a smile, I couldn't help but smile back. I find that I often smile at Ramiz because even when he is telling his story about the war, even when he is talking about his daily hunt for bones in the hills above his house, his humor comes through his dark eyes and his marvelously lined face. If life had been different for him, if he didn't wear his sorrow and trauma on every line in his face, if he hadn't been through the ravages of war, he would look like a movie star. The fact that he is a shameless flirt and wickedly funny also makes it impossible not to smile at him. He is charming and I always look forward to seeing him.

His sense of responsibility may stem from being the oldest of seven children. He was born in Pobudje, Kamenice hill, in the municipality of Bratunac on April 16, 1961. He lived there growing up, along with his parents, four brothers and two sisters.

He tells me it's the house that I visited in his village, about 9 miles (15 kilometers) from the town of Srebrenica. The modest house that sits up on a hill, a now infamous hill that was the site of a massacre that began on the evening of July 12 and continued throughout the night. Ramiz was trying to get down the hill toward his house when the massacre started. When you look across the valley from his house, you see nothing but beautiful countryside—hills covered with lush forests, fruit trees, grazing sheep and a beautiful sky with unforgettable light. I have seen this view at all times of the day and into the evening and it is always lovely and ironically peaceful. Every visit to Ramiz's house ends with him insisting that we take home large amounts of raspberries and other fruits. Knowing that Ramiz ekes out a living partially by selling the things that he grows in the local market makes it difficult to accept his generous gifts but he insists, every time. Once he sent us home with enough fresh berries to feed at least ten people. He is as generous as he is funny, as generous as he is haunted by his memories of July 1995.

The first time I was there, I walked up the hot, dusty road quite a way before we headed left up a hill and into the woods. Along the road there were cherry plums, a fruit I had never seen before, which were juicy and delicious on such a hot day. I have looked for them every time since but that was the only year there were so many on all of the trees.

Ramiz began working as a construction worker in a Srebrenica firm in 1979, the same year he married Fata.

Ramiz liked the construction job and wishes that he had the job now. He worked there for a year, got married, and two months later went into the army for a year. While he was in the army, Fata stayed with his parents. When he came back in 1981, he started working with another firm where he stayed until the beginning of the war.

Ramiz's first child was born in 1980 and the other four arrived between 1983 and 1991 (1983, 1986, 1989 and 1991). He and Fata had several little children during the war.

Ramiz knew war was coming because he "saw some things that were happening." He saw that "it wasn't any good." Even though he is a man of few words, it is always clear what Ramiz means when he talks to you.

> Like everybody else we stayed in our home. We tried to resist against the enemy. We were able to stay in our home until '93. Then we moved to Srebrenica. We were in Srebrenica until 1995. It was as if we were in a big concentration camp. We couldn't go anywhere. We could barely move. No food. No shoes. No clothes. But we somehow endured the whole thing. I wish that this genocide had never happened. Even with living in those conditions we would have somehow been able to survive.

Ramiz was with his family in Srebrenica until July 1995. He was on the front line when the severe attacks on the town began around the eighth or ninth of July.

> When I came back to the place where I lived I saw that many children were fleeing towards Potočari. I sent my wife and children to Potočari. When I sent them off I almost died. I sent them off from that village and it was difficult for me. I'm sending them off and I don't know where. I'm going in some other direction and I don't know where.

When Ramiz lined up in Šušnjari with the others on July 11, he knew they would be going through the forest but he could not have known what would happen on the hill just above his house.

> We sort of lined up and set off through the forest. We started moving and there were obstacles all the way until Kamenice hill near my house. And when we got there it was terrible. They rounded up so many people there. There was shooting from all sides. I got down on the ground and thought whatever happens, happens. By some miracle I survived. I didn't know what happened to my brothers. This all happened on that hill above my house. There was a large number of both dead and wounded. I stumbled on the wounded who begged me to finish them off. A wounded man, he was begging me to kill him but I couldn't. I didn't have the heart to do that. I would have a bad conscience throughout my whole life if I had done that. I don't know what happened in the entire Death March but I know what happened to me. I know my own experience.

That is where Ramiz last saw his brothers. They were together on the hill when the shooting started. Ramiz hit the ground and after that, he couldn't find them.

> And I didn't find them until the last three years. I buried my father this year, I buried my brother last year, I buried another one two years ago, I buried an uncle in 2010 or something like that.

So much trauma and so many people lost that he can't remember when he buried his uncle. He is not the only person in Bosnia who can't remember such things. There is just too much to remember. The story is so big. And so terrible. Ramiz had to wait a long time for his brothers and father and uncle to be found and identified. Because of this, he started looking for bones.

> I waited a long time. So, all of this encouraged me to do this thing with collecting bones. I started collecting bones in order to find my loved ones.

Because of the massacre he had escaped above his home at Kamenice hill, he knew there would be many bones and personal artifacts to be found. He moved back into his home around 2001 to the best of his memory, and at that point he started searching for bones. He had lived in Banovići near Tuzla from 1995 until he returned home.

> I started collecting bones in order to find my brothers and my father. Then when I saw that I couldn't find them I just decided to collect all the bones to make sure that those bones don't stay there on the soil in the forest uncollected and unidentified. I didn't ask for any compensation or anything. Nobody knew about me doing that until this year. This year people found out. I'll keep on doing this as long as I can.

At first it was easier to find bones because there were more of them. Now it's more difficult because many years have passed, yet Ramiz still finds bones. It is estimated that over 200 people have been identified through the ICMP because of the bones Ramiz has found.

> I found some bones recently. I still go to look for bones. I don't know who those bones belong to and I don't care. It's important to find them. It's important for a mother or brother or sister to be able to have closure and the identification.

When Ramiz finds bones, he keeps them where they were located and covers them with leaves or sometimes a tarp to protect them. He then calls the authorities who follow state protocol to retrieve the bones and begin the identification process. Ramiz never knows whether or not the bones are linked to an individual and he isn't concerned about that. What he wants is for surviving family members to have a chance to know that their loved ones have been identified.

Ramiz is so tender in the way that he protects the bones once they are found. He covers them to keep them safe so that animals in the woods won't get them in the time it takes for the authorities to come collect them. Once Ramiz showed me a small jacket made out of parachute material that he had found. It doesn't make sense that seeing a child's jacket sewn out of a parachute would be more difficult than seeing human bones on the floor of the forest, but that was the case. That small jacket represented so many things. It must have been the only fabric a mother had to make a coat for her young child, her child who was living in a war zone. The coat might have protected the child at one time from a cold wind but here it was, deep in the forest, some 20 years later, among a pile of human bones that had been found only because a man had decided to make finding those things his life's mission. Ramiz lives his life knowing he is surrounded by bones.

He realized long before the time he started looking for bones that his father and brothers were dead. When he survived the Death March and got to the free territory in July 1995, he started looking for his family, including his father and brothers.

> When we started moving from Srebrenica I ate just once. My second meal was on the sixth day when I reached Tuzla. I didn't eat for six days and I stayed alive. I found some water and a little fruit which saved me.
>
> I was in the group in the front of the column and I got to Tuzla. I spent a month looking for them. Then it was clear to me that they were killed, that they had died. I don't know what else to say.
>
> When I got back home I started doing this, looking for bones. Still my life is completely difficult and different. It's very difficult to live my life. Four people in my family died. Two brothers, my father and an uncle. Those were my closest siblings. I was wounded, my sister was wounded and another brother was wounded. I was wounded in the neck but I stayed alive. They couldn't kill me.

Ramiz thinks he stayed alive because of *sudbina*, destiny, but that isn't all. He thinks it's also because he had no fear during the Death March.

> On the way from here to Tuzla I had no fear. I was aware of everything. I had a clear mind. I knew that it would be difficult. Somehow I made it to Tuzla.

He was surprised that he had no fear because that was unusual for him.

> I was surprised because I knew how I used to be before the war. And when the war started I was fearful. I didn't have any experience with a war. You get used to fear and then all of a sudden you become fearless. Then at the end I was fearless.

Ramiz is no longer fearless. He said that he is back to normal. For many people who survived the genocide, their new normal includes memories of the horrors that they witnessed. Many people report that they cannot get the pictures out of their heads. Ramiz is no exception.

> I can't get rid of those pictures. Those pictures are always there in my mind. Sometimes I tell myself that I should forget. Because when I go back in time and think about it,

it becomes more difficult. Then I just forget it and make jokes and everything just to forget those terrible images.

There were people who went crazy because of the fear and something else there were people who lost their minds. It's interesting it happens in two or three minutes. When I was crossing the river Jadar and reached Konjević Polje there was a man in front of me. He was in his right mind then when we crossed the river Jadar. As soon as we crossed that all of a sudden, his mind sort of cracked up. Then we had to put some cloth in his mouth and to tie his hands to make sure that he doesn't shout, to make sure that we weren't discovered. Then after ten minutes we untied him and he was okay. It was just for moments. I think it's fear. Just like a consequence of that fear. If you are in your right mind it's possible to just go crazy in moments for no reason.

I cannot tell you the exact reason for that but I know that those who were very fearful had those moments when they lost their minds. I was not thinking of myself. I was thinking of my wife, of my children, where they were. I didn't know where they were. I got to Tuzla [and] I didn't know where they were.

When Ramiz got to Tuzla, he found his sister, who knew that other family members were in Banovići. He didn't know where that was, so he got on an army truck and started looking for them. He finally got to a sports gym in Banovići where he found some of his family members, including his wife and children.

It was crazy, horrible. I hope that this will never ever happen to anyone ever again. There we so many people inside you couldn't get inside that gym. I came and I didn't have a place to sit. Those images are even worse than those images from the forest. Everybody started to cry, ask questions about the fates of their families. I said to one of the mothers that her son survived and came out of the forest with me. I couldn't prove it and I kept telling her that he will come, he's coming. I couldn't persuade her until he came physically.

I tried to answer everyone's questions about their family members but I failed. I couldn't. Nobody believed it. It was even worse than my trip from Srebrenica to Tuzla. When I got in that gym it was total chaos, women and children everywhere.

Ramiz's experience and his memories are his motivation to keep looking for bones. He finds it helpful to search for bones but it is hard for him when he doesn't find any.

It helps me to look for bones. When I go into the forest if I don't find any I feel sorry. I feel sad. If I find a single bone my heart is that big, so big, so you understand what I'm saying.

Since the 20th anniversary of the Srebrenica genocide many more people have "discovered" Ramiz. There are more and more people who are coming to talk to him. This has not necessarily been positive for him.

They've made my life more complicated. I don't want to lie but many people promised me help but they lied. It doesn't matter, I'm going to live. I don't like lies but what can I do? Maybe they were born with that problem to lie. I wouldn't lie. I'm just saying the things that I have seen and survived.

When I told Ramiz how grateful I was to talk with him, I also let him know again about the impact he has had on my students, that they talk about him long after they leave Bosnia.

> They are talking about me as someone who is an important person.

I agreed with him and let him know the students felt such admiration for what he does, that he does something he doesn't have to do. They know he does this just to be helpful.

> Yes, that's true. Nobody does this in Bosnia except for me. The new American Ambassador mentioned my name at the United Nations and I felt pleased. This famous journalist named Almasa from Dnevni Avaz, she told me about it. She came to see me because she heard about the Ambassador's speech at the United Nations on the television and she came to see me.

Ramiz's family is happy that he is searching for bones. Like him, they feel this is a very important thing to do. They don't, however, help him as he is more comfortable going into the forest alone.

> It's just me who goes. I don't want to take my children and take any risks because of the land mines. I just go alone. If I see a mine I just mark it and I go away. But sometimes I take it out.

Ramiz's children were too small during the war to really know what was happening. As they grew older, they knew about some details and now that they are grown, they know about what happened in Srebrenica and on the hill above their house.

> I keep telling them what happened, I keep telling them my story. I try to describe things to them in order for them to know. Sometimes when I tell the story they ask questions. Many people ask me those questions. I try not to talk about it because it's difficult. I just try not to talk about it.
> I found my father after 20 years and I almost forgot about him. I buried him in Potočari. I wanted to die. It was so difficult for me. Even though it's been 20 years. Even now when I drive by Potočari it's difficult because I know there are four of them lying there. It's not just my family, it's so many of them. But we have to move on.

Ramiz had come to the end of his story and, not surprisingly, he asked if we would like another coffee.

Chapter 3

UN Base Survivor

Nesib Mandžić

It's always nice to find yourself in the right place at the right time, however, none of us enjoy being in the wrong place at the wrong time. That expression holds particular meaning for Nesib Mandžić, a man who was a professor and director in the secondary school in Srebrenica during the 1990s. It seemed like that was the right place for him given the stories his former students told about him. They talked about what a great educator he was and how important he was in providing structure, discipline and a demand for excellence from students who were living a nightmare in Srebrenica.

What about the wrong place at the wrong time? Nesib found himself chosen as a representative of the refugees who had fled to the UN base in Potočari following the fall of Srebrenica. He had recently had surgery and so did not join the other men and boys who decided to flee through the woods in an effort to reach the free territory of Tuzla. He was chosen to meet with Ratko Mladić in a sham "negotiation" which was held over a two-day period on July 11 and 12, 1995. The meetings were filmed by Mladić's film crew to be used as propaganda to show that he was negotiating in good faith. During one of the meetings, pigs were being slaughtered outside of the meeting room. This thinly disguised aggressive act toward the non–pork eating Muslims in the room could not be missed. What else could not be missed is the ghastly shrieking of those animals that can be heard on the recording of the meeting. At times it is so loud it drowns out the human voices in the room. I had the opportunity to view these videos on many occasions and had read Nesib's testimony from the ICTY trials at The Hague. To meet him in person was such an honor.

While the most well-known part of Nesib's story is his time spent with Mladić in July 1995, his story neither begins nor ends there.

> I lived in Srebrenica before the war. I lived there most of my life except for the time that I was at the university in Sarajevo. Before the war I was a professor in secondary school in Srebrenica.

Nesib's native village, Skelani, was across the river from the Serbian town of Bajina Bašta.[1] Skelani was about 125 miles (200 kilometers) from Belgrade. At the end of fall, 1991, the village faced economic sanctions from Serbia. Then, Serbian guards were placed on the Serbian side of the border crossing. The tremendous power of propaganda was evident during that time.

> We were helpless at the time. The Bosnian state fought for the right to be recognized as a state, independence. That area around my village, close to Serbia, had poor

communication with the rest of the country because of the location. On the other side was the politics of Bosnian Serbs and politics of the regime of Slobodan Milošević. In this area between Bosnia and Serbia, it was a tense atmosphere. The regime of Slobodan Milošević controlled the media of Belgrade, Serbia, Serbian television. The television represented this area where Bosnian Muslims lived as an area where jihadists lived. They created an irrational attitude, animosity toward Bosnian Muslims. Someone who lives 200 kilometers [125 miles] far from Skelani in Belgrade what does that individual know about Skelani? They would accept what has been broadcast on the television. The media ruled the world.

Nesib was living in Srebrenica as refugees started arriving and there was no place for them to stay.

In the spring of 1992 the school had to be shut down. Almost for two years refugees lived in that school. From Bratunac area, Žepa etc.

When the school closed, Nesib joined the resistance, which would later be called the Bosnian Army. In January of 1993, he was wounded and was relieved of his duties although he stayed in the Army until April of that year. The school was remodeled and reopened in December 1994.

In 1993–94 they had this idea to reopen the secondary school again because by then students had lost two years. We reopened the school even though we had only empty classrooms. We got some benches from UNHCR and some of the chairs we made manually. Then we had to improvise in terms of the teaching equipment. We had 1,300 pupils from 15–20 years old. Around 700 males and 600 females. Around 17 teachers.

They had to be creative with their teaching since they did not have any educational materials.

We organized ourselves, we got some literature from the library in Srebrenica, we got some from the police, from houses and families. Some pupils brought some. Under those circumstances we organized the lectures and I think we had good lectures.

He teased Hasan, saying that he could tell me whether the lectures were good or bad. Hasan arrived in Srebrenica May 1992 so missed two and a half years of school. He was able to start in December of 1994 when the school reopened and Nesib was the director. Hasan remembers Nesib as a strict disciplinarian who insisted on structure and appropriate behavior. He describes this experience in detail in his own memoir, *Surviving Srebrenica*.[2]

Nesib said the pupils did not ask questions about what was going on in the town or with the war.

I banned all the politics. We needed our unity. Everybody, teachers and kids, all together.

He insisted that the school focus on education.

When you have good, pure intentions, when you realize the conditions under which you work and live, I presented those circumstances to the pupils. When you come into difficult times you get serious. Look at the child who is playing and all of a sudden there comes a danger like a snake then the child understands that he or she is in danger. He or she would shout out loud for help, they'll think about how to get away from this danger.

That's how we had to organize our students during those bad times. When I was a student we studied, we worked we used to have fun, we would go out. Students in Srebrenica didn't have any of this.

Nesib was honest with his students.

We are here, under siege. I know that none of you have two meals a day, the question is maybe you don't have even one. If you want to survive you have to learn and work.

As hard as it was to make the decision, on July 3, 1995, the school needed to close again because Srebrenica was under constant fire.

I went to check on the school, we had meetings, people who worked there, but we knew we couldn't afford to have the students come because of the shooting. We couldn't have students there because a shell could fall.

The days leading up to July 11 became increasingly difficult.

We were afraid that the worst would come even though each one of us had hope that the Dutch might save us. One moment you think you might get killed and on the other hand you think the Dutch might save you, that's how it went, on and on. This agony lasted for 10 or 11 days until the 11th of July.

Nesib had had surgery in mid-June of 1995, and he was still recovering on July 11. He wanted to join the other men in the woods but he knew that was not possible given his physical condition.

The Battery Factory today, site of the UN Base in Potočari (photograph by Kristian Skeie, June 12, 2010).

> The Republika Srpska army entered Srebrenica, they pushed people to the end of town where one of the battalions was. I was in a dilemma where to go. A month before I had surgery. I wanted to go through the woods but I couldn't. I didn't have the strength to walk knowing that it was over 100 kilometers *[62 miles]* of a march. Then I decided to go to the base of the United Nations. That's how it developed.

Nesib describes all of this in great detail in his testimony at the ICTY.[3] On the day he talked with us, he gave us a summary of what had happened and even with this shortened version, it was possible to imagine the scene and his fear as his role unfolded.

> The first night I was outside the base and then the rest of the nights I was inside.
> So many people were there, probably over 30,000 mainly elderly sick men, children and women. A couple of thousand men of different ages, from children under 13 to the elderly over 80. On the 11th of July in the evening the RS army encircled the base of the Dutch battalion. Totally encircled. The UN soldiers did not react. By not reacting they jeopardized the refugees.

On July 11, Nesib learned that Ratko Mladić was in Bratunac, at Hotel Fontana, holding "negotiations." He had requested that a representative of the Bosnian Muslims join the meetings to negotiate the evacuation and other needs of the refugees. The UN chose Nesib for this role.

> They selected me, I don't know why. I didn't want to be selected. I was terrified. Many times Dutch soldiers kept repeating that Bosnian representatives should go from Potočari to Bratunac to meet and to negotiate. They were telling this to me directly. They were trying to talk me into it.
> In the evening I remember that I was sweating, I was left out of breath. I asked them if I could wash up thinking about going to see Mladić. It terrified me. The Dutch commander, Karremans, tried to persuade me that this was the only way out. I knew we didn't have any support from the Bosnian government or the UN. Karremans mentioned that the Dutch soldiers in Potočari were also in a very bad situation. Then he said that we would represent the Bosnian side and we would tell them what the situation was like in Potočari. It was just me who went. It was my destiny. Sometimes in your life you come into a situation where you don't want to be.
> The Dutch soldiers took me to Bratunac to the Hotel Fontana. It's a restaurant. There is a video of the meeting on YouTube in English.[4] It was me, Mladić, his associates, local commanders. It wasn't a real conversation, it was just Mladić's own monologue, just him speaking and he was dictating. He criticized Bosniak politicians, he spoke about surrendering our weapons, all that stuff. I was there for less than an hour and a half. Then they took me back to the base.

The next morning, July 12 around 10:00, another meeting was held at the same place and on that day, Nesib wasn't alone. This meeting was also filmed by Mladić's press people and can be seen on YouTube.[5]

> Ibro Nuhanović[6] and Ćamila Omanović joined us. Mladić and his men exerted pressure on us, tried to intimidate us. He was in a bad mood. He put us in a very difficult position, especially me. He said to me, "Nesib, the destiny of your people is in your hands. Either you will survive or disappear."
> You feel helpless, used. You don't have a way or the possibility to say anything. Total

abuse. There was no negotiation, it was just a TV show. He wanted to send a message to the Netherlands, to the States, to NATO for the negotiations then people would reach a compromise. We were his prisoners, not negotiators. When they mentioned this refugee evacuation? We managed to add just one sentence regarding the evacuation which says that the buses and the trucks would be followed by the Dutch.

It was like a show. Even today they manipulate with this all over the world.

This is a short version. In The Hague there are statements, big statements, time-related statements.

Footage of both meetings was used as evidence at Mladić's trial in The Hague. It is hard to watch these videos where Mladić is pretending to negotiate for the safety of the Muslims knowing that the killing had already started. Seeing Nesib put in such an impossible, vulnerable position is both poignant and infuriating.

Later in the afternoon of the 12th, Mladić came back to Potočari.

He came back, terrifying and intimidating people. Men were being separated from women and you are helpless, I was helpless, everybody was helpless. Your heart is in pain.

Nesib remained inside the base for another 10 or 11 days, he doesn't remember exactly.

Serb soldiers, they didn't want to let it go so they were intimidating everybody. They made a small group stay, interpreters, families of interpreters, Doctors Without Borders. Maybe 60 or 70 people. The Dutch soldiers were there too.

On the 13th they took away Hasan's father Ibro Nuhanović and Ćamila Omanović tried to commit suicide afterwards. I was left. We didn't have any communication.

There were negotiations between the Dutch and the Serb side about how we will leave. I was not part of that negotiation. On the 21st or 22nd, I cannot remember, they told us that at 12:00 we should leave Potočari. We were ready at 11. An hour was like a day. When we left we got on a small bus. Around 15 or 16 people. The rest of the people were in the other vehicles. They all were brought out. We got out of Potočari to Serbia.

Nesib frequently asks himself why he survived when so many others did not. He has decided on an answer for himself.

It is destiny. God. Someone has to survive, like people surviving the execution sites. God leaves witnesses, eye witnesses. It is up to the witnesses to tell the stories, it is their obligation.

Nesib does feel obligated to tell his story and acknowledged how hard it is to do.

It upsets me to tell this story, whether it's *[to]* you or anybody else. But I have to deal with it. To speak up, to explain. Regardless of the fact that we survived Srebrenica, I always tell the same story to Serbs. In a very reasonable tone, for them to understand. I'm not blaming an ordinary man. I know that my Serb neighbor is maybe not to be blamed. It's the regime. I'm telling this story in terms that nobody should follow the regime.

He also felt strongly that the story needs to be told because there are concerning dynamics happening around the globe.

This is our sudbina, fate and it's also my destiny. In the upcoming time I'm really concerned for the future. The youth, the young people. I'm not thinking about myself. This

> situation is not any good, currently. Not just in Bosnia, all over the world. There's nationalism all over, division, religious and ethnic lines, it's more visible, it's sad, intellectuals participating in this division. It's happening all over the world.
>
> You see how many people die and suffer in Ukraine now. They are brothers there and they kill one another. Here in Sarajevo people are not interested in what is happening over there or someone from Berlin or elsewhere. However, if you don't deal with this problem similar things might happen in other parts of the world.

I told Nesib that his willingness, along with that of others, to tell their stories was so important for my students to learn what happened.

> They will be good. If they don't go into politics. It's applicable not to just them but to everybody, all over the world.

The other topic of conversation with Nesib was the recent ruling from the International Court of Justice (ICJ)[7] which he found frustrating. A case had been brought before the Court in hopes that the 2007 judgment that exonerated Serbia for the genocide would be revised. Nesib was of the opinion that the process was flawed, particularly when it came to Bosnia's lack of documentation and use of witnesses. He was concerned about future ramifications of this recent verdict.

> With this verdict from the ICJ, which isn't binding, tomorrow any country can go ahead and commit genocide all over the world without fearing any consequences.

He was also frustrated about the international community's current attitude toward Bosnia and the region.

> The situation in the Balkans is irrelevant to the rest of the world. All of us are sinking, Serbia, Croatia, Bosnia. Ordinary people are dealing with their own problems, how to survive. The ruling regimes manage people how they want. On the other side in Bosnia we have relevant organizations from Europe but I don't see that they care about the progress in Bosnia. They are trying to stay to the side. The Council of Europe, OSCE, they try to stay out of things using any excuse. "You Bosnians should decide about your own problems." In all of these countries, Bosnia, Serbia, Croatia, men choose how to survive with their families.
>
> Twenty years ago everybody was abused, let down. Now it's the same thing but in a different way. Now people have to think how they will survive, the basics. Twenty years ago people were forced to leave their houses, many people were killed, many people were in prisons. This population that survived all of this is the more vulnerable population. The system didn't offer them any protection or any resocialization. They don't have jobs, it's very sad. I'm not talking about myself. For a Bosnian person I have a great life. I work hard and I live well. But I can't be happy and satisfied if someone in the morning walks to the trash bin looking for food. That's how it looks like.
>
> Sad. In this sense we were supposed to be supported by the international community. We would get rid of the corruption and many other things. When you get rid of the corruption then the rest of the things will be fine.

Nesib credits hard work with helping him move forward.

> Yes, we did survive, we had to endure. Every day I work hard in this field of energy with solar panels, just to forget what I survived. The more I work, the less I think. If we think

about what happened on a daily basis then we would be gone in three or four years. The work liberates you from frustration.

When I thanked him for spending so much time with us and for his willingness to share his story in spite of how difficult it was to do, he replied:

> It's nothing. I say again it's destiny. A man has to survive to do much. When you survive something it makes you stronger. God had predetermined what will happen to all of us. Do you want another coffee?

Not surprisingly, everyone had more coffee.

Chapter 4

Mothers of Srebrenica

Hajra Ćatić

It wasn't the weather when we climbed the hill to see Hajra that made that December day so memorable. It was winter in Srebrenica, which meant it was foggy and damp as it started to get dark on that late afternoon. We had hoped to get there earlier, but we ended up spending more time than planned in Potočari. We had walked from Hasan's office over to the cemetery, followed by the black cat that hangs out there. For the first time, I saw them replacing the green grave markers with the white tombstones. I'm assuming it takes half a year for that process since it had been about that long since the burial day on July 11.[1] During the winter, the cemetery is so quiet when just a small number of people are there.

By late afternoon, we were walking up the hill to see Hajra. We walked past the small Klas pasta factory and passed the house on the left where the owner of the Misirlije restaurant[2] lives now. We were heading further up the hill when we heard a knock on the window to our right. There was Hajra, who had been looking out the window for us. It's good that she was since we were heading to the wrong house. We took off our shoes and were let into a lovely, elegant home. She said she does something new in her house every year. The first thing I noticed was a painting of a young man on the wall, which was unlike any painting I had ever seen. We soon learned the story behind this painting and why it hangs in such a prominent place.

Hajra's home was not only elegant but also immaculate and welcoming. She immediately served us juice and three desserts she had made. As is always the case in Bosnia, you don't make a choice between three desserts, you eat all three. I think this is the first Bosnian house I have been in where there were a number of portraits on the walls and numerous framed pictures of people on the sideboard in the dining room.

Although this was the first time I had the chance to talk with Hajra, I had seen her many times at meetings and events, and also on TV and in documentaries. Each time she had been advocating tirelessly for the continued search for those still missing from the 1995 Srebrenica genocide. She has a very personal stake in this since her son Nino has not yet been found. It's clear, though, that her advocacy efforts go far beyond those of her own interests. She has been organizing and advocating for most of her life, in one way or another. She is a community organizer extraordinaire.

At the age of 70, Hajra was as elegant as her home. As she often does, she wore a beautiful black headband and clips and some other tasteful decorations in her hair.

She was born in Srebrenica on the same street where she currently lives. The house she grew up in was destroyed during the war, however, and is no longer there. There were four children in the family, two boys and two girls, and she was the youngest. She is the only living sibling at this point. Hajra's brothers lived in Srebrenica and her sister moved to Sarajevo after getting married.

> When we got married in 1965 we lived in a different building and then we built this house and moved in. My husband Junuz was also from Srebrenica. We knew each other our whole lives. He finished faculty in Zagreb. He worked for Feros and then applied for a new job in Sarajevo and I didn't want to go there.

As it turned out Hajra didn't have to move to Sarajevo because Junuz got a job with the municipality of Srebrenica instead. They had two sons, Nermin and Nihad who was known as Nino.

Before the war Hajra worked for the municipality of Srebrenica for 32 years where she earned her first pension. She was the president of the workers' union. She described a very active life with a lot of female friends. Her best friend and colleague, Vukica, was Serbian and they spent most of their time together, including holidays.

> I had lots of female friends, both nationalities, even more Serbs. We were really good friends. Vukica was a secretary like me. We worked for the municipality of Srebrenica, in administration.
>
> Vukica and I were never apart. She didn't know how to make a pie and she would say "I want a pie. Can I come over to your house and you can make a pie?" She had two sons and I had two sons. Our children were friends.

Now, it's not like it used to be before the war. It was still hard for Hajra to talk about Vukica's betrayal of their friendship. Vukica left Srebrenica for Belgrade in 1992, before Arkan's Tigers showed up.[3] She didn't let Hajra know what was coming, even though Hajra was sure Vukica knew in advance.

> She knew what would happen and she left Srebrenica for Belgrade. I trusted her. I didn't think she would have left without telling me. I was here with my family and I was crying. She called my phone from Belgrade. I was crying and telling her that Arkan's Tigers were here. It was the middle of April, 1992 at the very beginning of the war. I knew that she went to Belgrade because she had relatives there.

It was very clear to Hajra that her friend knew the war was coming, as did her Serbian coworkers.

> As the situation deteriorated, many Serbs went to Ljubovija, Serbia.[4] They would come back to work in the morning as if they were fearful of something.
>
> We all had the perception that we hadn't done anything to anybody so why should we leave the town?
>
> Vukica knew. That's why she moved. When she called me from Belgrade I said there are no Serbs to protect us from Arkan's Tigers. She said she would try and call someone to come and protect us.
>
> Not all Serbs had left at that point. A man named Branko was still here. I knew him because we had lived in the same building before we built our house. When our sons were young they were friends. I told Vukica to send anybody and Branko came to the house. He was looking out the curtains and the windows and he didn't say anything.

Hajra's oldest son, Nermin, had gone to Ohrid, Macedonia, in 1992. He had a lot of friends and some of them from Skopje invited him to come there because they were worried that troubling things would happen in Bosnia. Hajra wanted Nermin to take Nino with him, but Nino didn't want to go.

> I said to Nermin, don't go without Nino. Nino doesn't want to go to Ohrid and you should persuade him to go. Nermin is older. In the morning Nermin said that he didn't sleep all night because he was trying to persuade Nino to go with him but Nino wouldn't go. Nermin then went with his friends to Ohrid and Nino stayed here.

On the day in 1992 when Branko was at the house, Hajra's youngest son Nino was 22 years old and was living in Srebrenica because he had not gone with his brother to Macedonia. He and his friends had built a lookout shelter in the hills above the town so that they could look down and monitor what was happening. He came home from that shelter and asked his mother why Branko was there at their home.

> Nino came here and he saw Branko outside and asked why he was here. I said that Vukica called and sent Branko to check on us. But he said, "Mom, with binoculars we saw from the hill that Branko's sons Predrag and Nenad are standing guard by the big market. Arkan's Tigers got in that big market and were robbing everything, stealing everything." Branko's sons were part of Arkan's Tigers.

Hajra was betrayed by several friends.

> Those were fake friends. I considered them as friends and then they all changed. We said to Branko we wanted to go to the village.
> So we went up into the forest above Srebrenica. Nino was still up there with his friends. Me and my husband and some cousins and some neighbors, we were looking from the forest and they set this street on fire. Everything was on fire. On another hill we saw Chetniks who had set the fire. They were looking at Srebrenica on fire and were singing. That was just at the beginning of the war.
> We stayed in the village for 20 days after the fire.
> I came back from the village to Srebrenica when the Serbs left. A Serb who used to work with my husband would come up there and tell us everything.
> I moved back in here to my house with my husband and son. Nermin moved from Skopje to Sweden. He had a girlfriend that he dated for ten years, she went to Sweden to join him. When he got to Sweden she came to Sweden from Rijeka and they got married there. They stayed in Sweden. They have two children, they are students now. A son and a daughter.

Hajra worked during the war because her skills were needed in the municipality building. It was difficult to go back and forth when the city was being bombed from the air.

> I used to work for the municipality during the war helping to establish an administration. On the way from the municipality building to here you couldn't escape the planes. I was so scared. I would hide in the basements of some houses nearby to try to save my life. All the windows shattered because of those bombs. The municipality building was in the same place as it is now.
> Before the war even when I was working in that building, I used to come here on my lunch breaks. I knew that I needed five minutes to walk from the municipality building to here and another five minutes to walk back.
> Now I need more time.

Chapter 4. Mothers of Srebrenica

Throughout the war, Nino was part of an amateur radio station, Voice of Srebrenica, that broadcast from the second floor of the post office building.[5] The UN military observers were in the same building, in the basement. All throughout the war, reports were sent out by the amateur radio operators to anybody anywhere in the world who would pick them up.

> When my son would walk through the town everyone would stop him and ask if his reports would reach the public. He said, "those that reach the audience will reach the audience. It isn't up to me."

On July 11, 1995, Nino broadcast the last report sent out of Srebrenica. Hajra has that broadcast recorded on her phone, and she frequently listens to it. Nino made a plea to the world.

> Nino sent a report about the situation in Srebrenica, about the terrible situation in the town. At the same time the military observers sent reports that things in Srebrenica were settling down. My question is what kinds of reports were being sent by the military observers. This is all to say that the Europeans and the Americans and all those who let us down believed the observers more than our amateur radio reports.

Nino's last broadcast said:

> Srebrenica is turning into the largest slaughterhouse. Killed and wounded are being brought to the hospital non-stop. No words can describe this. Three deadly projectiles land on this town every second. 17 killed, 57 heavily and lightly wounded are in the hospital right now. Would anyone from the world come here to see the tragedy that is happening to Srebrenica and its residents? The crime against the Bosniak population of Srebrenica is unprecedented. The population of this town is vanishing. If Akashi, Boutros-Ghali, or someone else is behind this, it will not matter to Srebrenica anymore. I am afraid.[6]

When Srebrenica fell on July 11, Hajra and her family had to decide where to go just like everybody else in town. Hajra and Junuz wanted to see Nino, so after they got dressed that morning, they went to the post office where everybody was packing up. Nino thought his parents should go to Potočari and he planned to go with his friends through the woods.

> The farewell was terrible. Then there was the big column at Kazani[7] so we said goodbye and I don't want to even speak about that. He said, "Mom, I'll see you in Tuzla."
> The young people were amazing in Srebrenica during the siege. I saw them walking in the column to the forest and all of them were so beautiful even though they had to live through the war. I kept looking at them as they faded away through the forest. That is the last time I saw Nino. At the petrol station. Then he faded away into the column.

After saying goodbye to Nino, Hajra and Junuz went to Potočari where they spent two nights outside of the base. There were old, used Srebrenica Express buses with no seats where they slept along with many other people. They gathered hay to put on the floor.

> We didn't want to sleep outside. There were around 5,000 people in the base. Then they closed all the entrances and they didn't let anybody else in.

Conditions in and around the base were terrible. By the second day, Hajra wanted to leave. Late in the afternoon, buses began to arrive and started deporting refugees.

However, Hajra and Junuz spent one more night in the bus and it wasn't until the next morning, July 13, that they decided to leave.

> Serb soldiers, Chetniks, got among the crowd and they were looking at everybody. They were taking men to the places where they killed them and they were raping girls. You start to make your own peace and then all of a sudden you hear a scream from far away, someone probably being either killed or raped and I couldn't take it anymore. On the third day, early in the morning, I said to my husband that I'm not going to stay here any longer.
>
> We stood in line, there were two APCs on both sides of the road, with a tape across it, and they were letting people go two by two, toward the buses and trucks. When I was close to a truck, like four meters, they told my husband to go on one side and told me to go toward the truck.
>
> My husband was separated from me in Potočari.
>
> I said to them, "Why are you taking him away? He's sick." In 1991 his kidney was taken out. His situation had deteriorated, it was swollen. That Serb Chetnik pushed me with his rifle and I started to fall, reaching [for] the ground with my hands.
>
> I got on the bus and I sat by the last window looking out at Junuz. They took him to the white house[8] and I could still see him. I just want to say there were so many men separated before him and when he reached the white house he had to dispose of his backpack. You couldn't see the basement of that house because the pile of those backpacks was so high. I saw him when he sort of made a turn and entered the house. I never saw him again.

The bus left Potočari and they were stopped along the road by the Serb soldiers who were asking for money and for gold. Hajra could see prisoners on the side of the road and she kept hoping that she would catch a glimpse of Nino.

> I saw prisoners on the side of the road at Sandići, maybe 200 or 300 prisoners. Police officers were surrounding them. I was just looking to see if I could see my son. All that way to Konjević Polje we were seeing prisoners on both sides of the road.
>
> I was on the bus and I reached the Dubrave airport in Tuzla.

When she reached Tuzla, Hajra's cousin who lived there picked her up and took her to her home where she stayed for a while, continuing to hope that Junuz and Nino would show up.

> I was waiting to see if my husband and son would come. I couldn't even think that they might be dead. I was working in the administration helping the Srebrenica people who survived. I took the job primarily to find out what happened to my son and my husband. Because there was a big exchange of information when people were coming, and I also had other missing family members. I just wanted to know what had happened to all of them. I started the job a few days after I got to Tuzla, after I had a rest. People who survived the Death March they would come to register themselves.

It is remarkable that Hajra went through all of those horrible days, living under siege in Srebrenica, saying goodbye to her son Nino, seeing her husband separated and led away, and after just a few days started working and organizing the efforts in Tuzla to register survivors and to look for those who were still missing. It's as if she sprang into action much like she had been doing her entire life. There was a job to be done and Hajra was the one to do it. In spite of her trauma and her worry, she started working on all the paperwork that needed to be completed for those survivors who came out of the forest. In addition, she needed to make a living.

In the process of working on paperwork for those who survived the Death March, Hajra went with the Red Cross to knock on many doors of people living in Tuzla. There were so many missing men and as just an ordinary individual she couldn't really do anything to help in the search for people and information. She realized that she needed to form an official association so they could search for people and for information separate from other NGOs.

> We were looking for our loved ones and we could see that there were many missing men. We were knocking on many doors with the Red Cross but basically you couldn't do anything as an individual. Then we registered the Association of Women of Srebrenica. It was the first association registered. Once we formed the Association we could knock on many doors and ask for the information.

After working all day, Hajra sometimes talked with a psychotherapist named Irfanka Pašalić in Tuzla. Dr. Pašalić had left Srebrenica before the war.

> I felt like something had happened to me and she would talk with me. I was so glad to see her. I would just jump from my chair and I would run to her. I'm still in touch with her today.

The association Hajra started while looking for her family members is still active today in Tuzla. Anyone who has looked at pictures from the war and the genocide will recognize the current headquarters of this association. The office is wallpapered with pictures of men and boys killed in July 1995. It is almost impossible to breathe when sitting in that room.

The Association of Women of Srebrenica started sometime in 1995 with the goal of fighting for peace and justice and that fight continues to this day. Starting in 1996, on the 11th of each month, they have the tradition of holding a Peace Protest in the square in Tuzla in honor of those who have yet to be found. Many families of the missing, other ordinary citizens and other associations come to support them each month. The Women in Black from Belgrade[9] have been supporters from the beginning. In addition to the monthly Peace Protests, they also write articles and publish books about what happened, not just in Srebrenica but in Bratunac, Zvornik, Vlasenica and other places as well. They produced 52 issues of a magazine and 2 books: *United Nations on the Pillar of Shame* and *The Srebrenica Deadly Summer*. Hajra worries that the number of association members decreases every year. She talks about mothers being tired and that many of them are deceased. There was a particularly tragic loss for the association three or four years ago.

> I can never forget Munib from the village of Bajramovići. He was the only father in our Association. He used to tease us that we weren't just an Association of mothers because he was a father. He would come on the 11th of every month for many years. The transportation company from Kladanj was so generous, they always gave him a free ride to the protest. His wife was wounded and she died. He lost four sons and on the 11th of every month in Tuzla he was there.
>
> When two of his sons were identified he wasn't ready for it. He couldn't take it anymore and he committed suicide. In the year he was supposed to bury two of his sons he hung himself in a mosque.

When Hajra started the association, she was no longer living with her cousin's family.

> My husband's school friend found out about me. She lived in an intermarriage with a Serb and she gave me her flat. Then later I was sleeping in the Association house and now I sometimes still sleep there.

For many years, the association rented a house in Tuzla. An Italian woman, Nedda Alberghini, who was involved with the Women in Black from Italy came to a protest on the 11th. She had a developmentally disabled son who had been killed in an automobile accident and she had dedicated her life to humanitarian activities all around the world in his honor. When she came to the protest, she could see that the rented house was very narrow and there was not enough space for women to gather. She offered a sum of money to buy a house for the association.

> We found a house to be near the place of the protest and to be near the ICMP identification center. We bought the house and she still pays our bills.

The association translated all of the documents into Italian so that the donor could see the work they are doing and they are still in contact. A picture of the donor's son hangs on one wall in the meeting room. It is larger than most of the other pictures and in some ways, it seems out of place. In the most important way, however, it is exactly where it should be, as a symbol of solidarity among women whose sons died far too early.

Tuzla, which sits on large salt deposits, is home to three salt lakes in the middle of the city. The monthly Peace Protest begins at one of the lakes and winds its way to the main square of the old town, making a circle and stopping at a beautiful building near the Tuzla Gate. On May 25, 1995, on the Yugoslavia Day of Youth, the Bosnian Serb Army launched an artillery attack against the town of Tuzla, killing 71 young people and wounding 200 at this gate, an event known as the Tuzla Massacre.[10]

The marchers carry a long quilt made of pillow shams containing the picture of a missing boy or man, along with his name and other information about him. Hajra showed us some of the quilt squares she keeps in her house. There is also a large quilt that is kept in the association office in Tuzla that is brought out for the July 11 protests.

> We don't invite people, they just come. We used to have a lot more people but many are sick, many died. So now it's a small number of people. That square is named the Square of the Victims of the Srebrenica Genocide. We stand at the Gate, journalists come and they interview the families. Afterwards we go to the mosque to dedicate our prayers to the souls of our loved ones.
>
> The Red Cross in Tuzla made a good arrangement for us. All people after the protest can go to one of the cake shops to eat cake or drink coffee. Everyone can talk with each other and it's all free.

The day before we met with Hajra, I had the opportunity to accompany the association to a small village called Kozluk outside of Srebrenica. A mass grave had been discovered and the mothers were paying their respects as the remains were being exhumed. Also in attendance were all of the necessary personnel from the ICMP including the main pathologist and the main prosecutor. The mayor of Srebrenica was also there.

Unbeknownst to me at the time, Hajra's husband had been killed near there.

> My husband was killed in Kozluk by that mass grave which we visited yesterday. There were other mass graves by that one called Čančari 1,2 and 3 and he was exhumed from that secondary grave. In 2008 I buried him. Of course I felt terrible. It's easier when you find the remains and you sort of make peace with yourself.
> But then you think he got into their hands and I can't imagine what they did to him before they killed him. These thoughts are devastating for all of us. I think that those killers are monsters.

I can't imagine what it must be like to have to think about that.

It was at that point in our interview that Hajra played the recording of the last report her son Nino sent out on July 10, 1995, from the post office as Srebrenica was falling. Even through the crackly static and the language barrier you can hear the desperation in the man's voice. I told her I had heard it before, even before I knew her and I always wondered what it must be like for the mother of the person making this report, what must it be like for her to hear his pleading, desperate voice going out on the airways in hopes that someone in the world would hear and do something. Here I was, sitting with the very person I had always wondered about. I asked her what it was like to hear her son's voice.

> Some people say they can't look at a photo of someone who died and I live with this. I did all the research on his life to know everything. He used to write poetry. He had written a play for a theater but they didn't make it.

After returning to Srebrenica, Hajra had a couple of interactions with people she had known before the war. She hoped to gain more information about Nino from them but she was not successful. There was a couple Hajra knew, Danica and Miloš, who are Serbs. Hajra and Danica worked together at the municipality before the war.

> When I got back to Srebrenica for the first time Miloš saw me and he came up to me and he wanted to say hi. Before the war Nino would come often to drink water at home and Miloš would come into the municipality building and he would say "I saw your beautiful son." On this first visit after the war he was coming up to me to talk to me and I said, "What did you do to my beautiful son"? Then he just walked away.

A few years ago, she ran into Danica, who Hajra said is always trying to talk to her. On that particular day, they had a conversation.

> She said to me, "I want to tell you something. When they kicked the Muslims out of here, they made the Serbs clean the public buildings, clean the town. When they made us clean the buildings I found Nino's theater play book." I almost cried and I asked her if she saved that notebook. She said no, she didn't, that she had just thrown it away.
> I told her I would give her the whole world for that. She said she didn't keep it because she thought we would never see each other ever again.

Hajra's son Nino has not yet been found. Many people have told her where he was killed and she has gone to some pretty extreme steps to try and find his remains.

> Everybody told me about the location of his death, Bočin Potok.[11] It was mined.
> So we got to that place where a witness told me that my son was wounded and we could not find his remains. Actually at that place we didn't find any bones.

Hasan's brother Omer, who is a journalist, accompanied Hajra to film her search for Nino's remains.

> We were walking through the woods nearby that creek. We saw those mines around and I was afraid that my group and the other people that were there might get killed by the mines.
>
> I saw a skull lying on the ground. I knew that the creek would swell and I was afraid that the skull might get washed away so I put the skull in a bag.

Hajra took the skull and kept it for one and a half years. She knew the procedure, that it should be reported to the prosecutor's office. She didn't do that, however, for quite some time.

> For one and a half years the skull was in a drawer in my Association. When I was appointed to the advisory board to the Institute of Missing Persons, I called Lejla Čengić, spokesman for that Institute, and I told her the story. I was on a bus and she called me three times saying that when I get to my Association they will take over the skull. So they took it.
>
> The minister of human rights has to be present during the meeting of the advisory board of the Institute of Missing Persons. So they knew that this creek was mined. I filled out a first request to the ministry asking them to demine that area. So they did it. Then they collected some tiny bones.
>
> When I was with a journalist at PIP and saw everything on the table I asked if this was all from Bućin Potok. Dragana[12] said yes. And I was asking for the results of the DNA, to see if it came and she said no. She pulled open a drawer and I saw a blue bag. I said is that the skull which I brought. She said yes. I asked if it was identified and she checked on the computer and said it wasn't identified. I don't know if it belongs to him, that skull.

Hajra picked up the skull three or four years ago. For the past two years, it has been at the ICMP morgue in Tuzla.

> We're still waiting. Those five bodies which were found after the demining, they found two incomplete skeletons. I called the main pathologist, Rifat Kešetović, last year before new year's eve. He said that he would send on the 12th a sample for the DNA for those five bodies. Until now they haven't done the identification. Those who were supposed to do the DNA maybe they didn't produce the results which haven't come yet. I am disappointed in all of this. Maybe they are just trying to prolong this. Families are dying, mothers are dying.

Hajra was finally able to return to her house in 2003, but she tried several times before that.

> When we came for the first time the Serb police didn't let us come through the town. They led us to the cemetery near the petrol station where Saliha's first son is buried. They made us get back on the buses so we just said prayers at the cemetery and got on the buses and headed back. Families were on those buses, mainly women.
>
> We asked for permission to visit another cemetery. Then they didn't let us through again so we came through Milići. We left buses at the Misirlije restaurant. Then we got to the cemetery and I was looking at my house but I couldn't reach it, I couldn't get to it.

Eventually Hajra was able to at least get to her house although she still wasn't allowed to return and she was at the mercy of those living illegally in her house. They could decide whether or not she could even enter her own home.

> I used to come even before 2003 for short visits. I used to come with journalists. Two families were living here in my house, one on this main floor here and the other upstairs from Semizovac near Sarajevo.

Hajra was still hoping that she would find the play Nino had written.

> We came to Srebrenica with police officers, we came with IFOR international forces, we came with the buses full of women. We would come here to my home with a police officer. The officer would ask the family if we could come in. If the family said yes we would come in, if they said no we couldn't come in. They let me in. I asked them if there were any of my son's written papers. They said there is nothing.

In 2003, everybody had the right to get their property back. Like others returning to Srebrenica, Hajra had to get the necessary papers and permission. When she moved back in, there was an unfortunate situation across the street.

> There was a store in that building right across from my house and the Serbs would get drunk and sing. They would sing and yell, "What else is left, we killed you and raped you and kicked you out from here, what else is left."

The owner of that building decided to sell it and Hajra thought that her association should buy it and evict those who hung out there. They put together a proposal, which was funded by an organization in France, and her association bought the building. They opened a store on the first floor.

At the same time, Hajra's doctor from Tuzla who had been so helpful to her had an Italian NGO called Amica. They had the idea that they could use the space in the building to make pasta and sell it.

> Some Italians bought us some machines for making pasta and my doctor continued to help us. When Italians would come to visit her she would send those Italians to us. They donated the money for the machines and everything necessary for making pasta. We went several times with her to visit Italy.
>
> Later another big company from Sarajevo took it over. They wanted for the returnees to be employed here. Now there are four people working here. It's a small capacity. Four young people work there, they have space and they are happy. I don't have anybody to work there but I am happy that some other young people work there.

Once Hajra was back in Srebrenica she received a phone call from Vukica, the friend who Hajra felt betrayed her, who went to Belgrade when the war started.

> She returned to her apartment here. She lives in that building near that main market. She called and said she wanted to come for a morning visit. I just hung up the phone. I didn't want to talk to her.

Throughout her life, Hajra has been a community organizer and she continues with that work. Her association was instrumental in getting Potočari designated as the site for the Genocide Memorial. She credits Hasan Nuhanović with helping the association in their quest for a Memorial in Srebrenica-Potočari.

> I work for my town. I love Srebrenica. This is the best town ever. I could have gone to Sarajevo when my husband got a job but I didn't want to go. Hasan Nuhanović was working helping the organization and Hasan said that the women should ask for the location in

Potočari for their loved ones to be buried. If anyone deserves to have a name in Potočari Memorial it's Hasan Nuhanović.

There was pressure to have the Memorial located at the Eagle Base in Tuzla. There were numerous meetings with the American ambassador Thomas Miller who then pressured the High Representative to designate the land in Potočari as the place for the Memorial. The women wanted to bury their loved ones near to where the genocide took place.

In 2003 we had the first burial. That year we had three burials, 31st of March, 11th of July, the 20th of September. We had to have three burials because there were so many identified people to bury that year.

In 2004, there was just one burial day in Potočari, July 11. It remains that way today.

Hajra's association continues in their advocacy for justice. She showed us a photo of women from her association protesting in front of the State Police Station in Tuzla.

The High Representative made the RS establish a commission to establish the facts about genocide and as a result is a list of those people who participated in the genocide. On that list there was a man who was working in the state police SIPA[13] in Tuzla. Not only was he working in the state police he was working as an investigator in the war crimes unit.

So we held protests in Tuzla in front of the police station and he was removed.

We were interested in how Hajra keeps going. What gives her the strength to continue doing all that she is doing? Before she answered, she served us huge pieces of baklava and another Bosnian sweet called tulumba. She also insisted that we have juice.

I live with a hope to find the remains of my son and that is the only wish of mine. Nermin, my other son, sometimes he doesn't like it when I deal with the past, when I focus on my son Nino. I'm not saying I don't love Nermin and his children. Wanting to find Nino is something else. I live with that.

Hajra feels strongly that people need to tell their stories and to speak out.

We have to speak. If we don't speak, if we don't write, if we don't make recordings then people in the future wouldn't know what happened. I'm aware of that.

Hajra showed us pictures of her granddaughter and other interesting photos. Then more pictures of grandchildren came out before she continued.

We have to tell the stories. I keep saying to the families, please tell the stories, please speak up.

We agreed that it's very important that people hear these stories, not just in Bosnia but around the world.

If the world doesn't help us we can't do anything.

We were still interested in the picture hanging above Hajra's sofa. It is a pastel of a young man with a large white flower and words from a poem tumbling down the right side of the portrait. Hajra explained the origin of the picture to us. In honor of the 20th anniversary of the Srebrenica genocide, she was at the Bosnian Embassy in The Hague where she saw this painting and knew that it was Nino. It was done by a Bosnian artist, Zekira Kira Ahmic,[14] who now lives abroad. She painted it in honor of Nino, capturing his image and also representing his poetry. Hajra asked her for the painting and ten days later, she received it from the artist.

Hajra continues to wonder what Nino would look like now.

> I have a tenant who is head of the UNDP, Alex. He's Belgium. He's the age of my Nino and when I look at him I keep imagining how old my son would be now, what he would look like.
>
> Everybody loved Nino and he was very attached to me, emotionally. He always said that he wouldn't date for as long as his brother did. During the war people would ask Nino why he didn't get married. He would say that he wasn't ready because there was a war and he had other things on his mind.

Unfortunately, Nino never had the chance to decide if and when he was ready to get married.

Nura Mustafić

Like so many women in rural Bosnia, Nura Mustafić makes woolen socks in the traditional way, soft socks in bright colors. The day that she sat across the table from me in the café in Srebrenica was as cold a day as I ever remember feeling. When she pulled the hand-knit socks out of her purse to give me, I gladly accepted them since my feet had not been warm since I had arrived in Srebrenica several days before. Receiving the socks as a gift was lovely but not surprising, since the generosity of these women was well known to me. What did surprise me, however, was when she reached into her bag and pulled out a large piece of cooked pumpkin, insisting that I take it for later. Who could refuse warm socks and warm pumpkin on a freezing day?

Nura was born in Han Pijesak in the village Podžeplje, which was about 40 miles (64 kilometers) from Srebrenica on the way to Sarajevo. She was very smart in school but had to leave after the fourth grade. Given that she was the oldest of six children she was needed at home to work in the fields, where she planted trees and looked after the sheep. Her teacher used to ask her to come back to school and finish all eight grades but that was not possible. In those days, in her village, men used to say that female children shouldn't go to school because they didn't need school.

Nura's family owned their property and grew wheat, corn, rye and barley, among other things. It was hard work, especially combined with caring for the farm animals. Oxen helped pull timber out of the creeks.

When Nura was 19, her father died at the age of 56 from a stomach ulcer. After that, there was no income and no pension so, like many of their neighbors, Nura and her five younger siblings worked the fields to survive. Nura remembered her mother saying that they all needed to work hard so that they wouldn't have to knock on people's doors for money or for any other kind of help. Though life was difficult Nura proudly described how close her family was and how they stuck together all the time.

For entertainment, Nura used to come to Srebrenica to watch bike races and it was there, at age 20, that she met Hasan, who she would marry in Srebrenica two years later, in 1969.

Hasan worked in several places around Yugoslavia. Early in his career, he worked for a company that built dams in Belgrade as a driver for Hidrotehnika. Back then, it didn't matter if you worked in Serbia or Croatia or Bosnia, it was all one country. In fact, it was on his last route from Zagreb to Belgrade in 1992 that it became clear to him that war was coming.

Nura and Hasan lived in Pančevo for two years together and one of her sisters came to stay. Her family missed her and she missed them. Once Hasan was sent to Montenegro to work for a while, Nura moved back to her mother's home since she was pregnant with her first child, Mirsad, who was born in Han Pijesak in 1971. Over the next four years, two more sons were born: Alija in 1973, followed by Faud in 1975.

As Nura continued her story, I held my breath because I knew what was coming. I had talked with her a few times over the years and knew that she lost all three sons and her husband during July of 1995, but I didn't know the details. As she wound her way around the story, the details came spilling out. She freely shared the basic facts along with the horror of those days in the early 1990s. Like most everyone who agreed to share their story for this book, there were moments when Nura had to pause, sometimes to remember dates or details but more often to regain her composure as she told a story that no mother should ever have to tell.

Quiet, strong, broken-hearted Nura.

Nura described a happy existence with her husband and son. Hasan was eventually able to transfer his work to Bratunac and then to Srebrenica, meaning that he was working closer to home. Nura and Hasan were finally able to build their own house in the village of Bajramovići, about three miles outside of Srebrenica town, and moved in with their two sons on May 15, 1975. Shortly after that, on October 3, their youngest son Faud was born. Nura recalls that when they moved into this house in Bajramovići, she was very quiet. Her husband asked her what was wrong, then he turned on the music and he said, "Let's celebrate, we should be happy, this is our own place. No more living in other people's houses or flats. We're not paying rent anymore." When recalling this moment, Nura smiled and even laughed a bit and then sat silently for some moments. She later described the times that she is still sometimes quiet and the reasons behind that. Again, I held my breath, becoming very quiet myself.

Nura described daily life with her husband and sons and you could not help but notice her pride. This was a woman talking about her family just like so many women love to talk about their families. She smiled when she described how smart her boys were, how well they did in school, particularly Mirsad and Faud. Her middle child, Alija, decided not to go to secondary school and instead went to be with Nura's mother and worked in a timber company. It was impossible not to be struck by how hard working this family was.

They stayed in their house in Bajramovići for 20 years, only leaving in 1995 when they had to. Nura started to notice things changing when she heard people suggesting that the police and the municipality should be divided, one belonging to Serbs, one belonging to Muslims.

> Everybody was saying that war will not happen, though, because it wasn't the same situation as after the Second World War, that circumstances are different so war would not happen. But then we found out that people were killed in town, that the town was empty, that people were burned in their houses and flats. We heard this because my village was so close, it's just right behind the hill.

By that time, Hasan wasn't working and was at home. People had started to leave his company and finally he was the last one there. It was a State-owned company, a transportation company in Potočari. After making that final drive between Zagreb and Belgrade in April 1992, he decided to bring his truck home, realizing that war was coming. Even though they no longer had an income, the family was still growing crops and they had a cow which helped with providing food for the family. This was familiar to Nura as she had been in this situation as a young woman at home after her father died. Being able to grow food and make food from cow's milk meant that there was enough to eat. It also helped that they had sheep.

There was enough to eat until the refugees started arriving and the nonstop shelling began. The first refugees were Nura's family, who came to her house from Han Pijesak. At some points during 1992–1993 there were up to 15 people living in her house, including her husband, sons, mother, sisters, two brothers and other relatives. Prior to the war, in Nura's small village of 40 houses, about four or five people lived in each house. During the war, all houses swelled with refugees who had to flee their own villages.

Nura was as relieved as everyone else when on April 16, 1993, the Srebrenica enclave was proclaimed a UN Safe Area. Everyone thought things would be fine but in reality, the food supply was running out because there were so many refugees in the villages and in the town of Srebrenica. Nura described refugees coming from five or six other municipalities. When the NATO food airdrops began, Nura and her family could see all the people on the top of the hills trying to get the food. She remembered, and described with a smile, the day that one of her sons was able to bring home some flour from the airdrop. She said to her son,

> "Let me look at this, this is real food." We made everything. We even got some oil and rice. Even though the houses were full, we were smiling, laughing, and sharing food. Even if you have just one meal, if you are with your family things are easier.

Nura said that all along they had the perception that Srebrenica would never fall.

> We thought that the UN would rescue us and stop the Serb attacks. We always trusted them. We trusted the United Nations. It was called the Safe Haven. We thought that in a few minutes they would come with planes to protect us.
>
> On the 10th of July, when they said that Srebrenica was falling, they said that women and children should go to Potočari and men should go through the woods. I was in my house and my husband asked, "where are we supposed to go?" Our children said that we should just follow people. I left my husband and children in the village and went down to Srebrenica with the other women. When we got there we heard news that Srebrenica would not fall. I decided to return home to cook something for my children but soon I was on the move again because they kept shelling the village. They were shelling everywhere.

When Nura returned to her village from Srebrenica, her husband was surprised to see her and asked her why she had come back.

> I told him I came back because of the shelling. They were shelling everywhere. So many people were heading down the road to our house so we knew that Srebrenica was falling and that we had to leave our house. We decided to join them, to follow them.

Like everyone who was trying to escape, Nura and her family had to decide what to do, which route to take. There were only two options. One was to go to the UN Dutch base in Potočari in hopes that they would be protected by the UN. The other option was to set out for the free territory through the woods.

> So then we started to move again, all of us together. It took an hour to get from my village to Srebrenica. I started to go through the woods with my husband and my sons from the village. We started to move toward Buljim. We stayed there at Buljim for the night. Everyone else went to Potočari. Before Srebrenica fell I told people that if it falls I will go with our children wherever they go.

Nura paused for a long time. This story was becoming increasingly hard to tell. We offered to stop but Nura wanted to continue.

> So when we were on the move, over the hill the shooting started. I was with my husband and I lost sight of my oldest son Mirsad at the start. I was still able to see the other two, Alija and Fuad. When the shooting started, I hit the ground. Later I was looking for them. My husband Hasan said that we should go on with the people but I said that I wasn't going. I needed to find my sons. One boy asked me what I was looking for. I said that I have two sons. He told me that they were both wounded. I found them and they were carrying Fuad in a blanket and my other son Alija was able to walk but was still wounded. One of my cousins said to me "here are your sons." People were carrying them. Then we started carrying them and we got to a meadow.
>
> We stayed in that meadow. Everybody was leaving. My husband went to fetch some water for my sons. Then he went again to get more water and he didn't come back.

Nura waited as long as she could, starting to realize that her husband was not coming back.

> I was left with my children in the tall grass. I tried to put some clothes on their wounds. Fuad couldn't walk and Alija was wounded too. People were just passing us. My sons told me that we should give ourselves up. But then a military vehicle passed by and we hid from it. I told my sons that we should stay in the forest and not give ourselves up.
>
> They were shooting all over the place, and shelling. I lost all feelings, I didn't care if I would die. I was in the middle of hell so I didn't care what would happen to me. Some people were wounded, some people were just passing by, near Buljim. I was still waiting for my husband to come back but he was not coming back. I was crying and my son said, "Someone has to die. Maybe they will save us if we come down to Sandići, maybe they will spare us because we are wounded."
>
> There were so many beautiful boys around us. They all said that we should go down and give ourselves up. They took my sons. There were ten of us and we were coming down to Sandići. There were artillery armored weapons on the road.

Nura continued down the hill with the help of the others.

> When we got to the road there were so many soldiers with guns. I realized that some were from Serbia. Later when I got to Tuzla I found out that they were from different parts of Serbia, the JNA. At the time, I just saw soldiers. They kept calling men to come down and surrender. They kept saying that we wouldn't be harmed, that we would be treated well. On that meadow, there are still those two houses. The meadow was full of prisoners.

Nura and her family had made it to Sandići meadow. It is estimated that at one point 2,000 people were in this meadow, including Nura, Saliha's husband Ramo, Haso, Hakija and Nedžad. Today, in the museum in Potočari, there is a picture of hundreds of prisoners in this meadow against a backdrop of the buses containing women being transported from Potočari. Many women saw their husbands or sons or fathers or brothers being held prisoner in this meadow.

When asked if the soldiers saw her and her boys at this point, Nura nodded her head yes.

> I was in this group of ten boys. They just kept shelling the forest around us. I saw severely wounded boys with open stomachs, open wounds, crying for help, begging people to kill them. I thought that the soldiers on the road were the United Nations. If I had known they were Serbs I probably wouldn't have gone down there.
>
> It was so hot during the day, they brought some water in the truck. One Serb gave me a bottle of water and he said that I should go into the house and give some water to the children. My boys were in the house. I was crying and my boys told me not to cry. Nobody could speak. You couldn't say anything. My two sons who were wounded were inside the house and my other son was somewhere, he was not with us. We got separated.
>
> One soldier said that he wanted to put me and my boys on a truck and we would all go to Kladanj. They put us, in one of the trucks with the women coming from Potočari. When we got to Tišća near Kladanj, people were leaving the trucks and buses. They put stairs by the truck for people to be able to come down. When we were coming down the stairs, two soldiers, Serbs, they took my children. I said they are wounded. All the people were gone so I was waiting there for them to give me my children back. They took my children. One of the soldiers pushed me with his rifle and I kept following the people. I was all in rags. I lost all my clothes, even my shoes and a scarf. I was walking in my socks. I didn't care about any of it. Everything was totally lost.

When Nura left the house in Sandići meadow and got onto the truck with her sons, she thought that they were going to be okay.

> When we were in that house and I was giving them water and putting water on their cheeks I told them that we were safe and that we would reach the free territory, that we were going to Kladanj and that we would be okay. I told them that their wounds would be cared for and that they would be fine.

As it turned out, that was not the case. When Nura got to Kladanj alone, she went to Dubrave airport where a large refugee camp had been set up. She described going from place to place, barefoot, looking for her family. She routinely checked in with the hospital to see if anyone knew anything about her husband and sons.

> I knew that Hasan was wounded because he didn't come back from the water spring. I didn't know anything about my oldest son Mirsad who got separated from us. When they took my two wounded sons they said to me "Mom you should go ahead, maybe Mirsad survived and maybe he will come later."

Mirsad did not come later. Over time Nura learned that Mirsad and Faud did not survive and she was still, twenty-one years later, waiting for news, any news, about her son Alija.

Nura stayed in the refugee camp at the airport for a month or so. She then moved to Tuzla where she was given accommodation in a school. Along with so many other women she continued to try and get information about her family. She went to the hospital and checked every room and every place to see if she might find her husband or her sons.

Nura moved from the school to refugee houses which had been built by a Dutch NGO outside of Tuzla. While she was living there, mass graves started to be discovered, at which point she realized that "everybody was gone." She reported her missing husband and sons to the Red Cross and then later she gave a blood sample at the ICMP. She told them everything that had happened, including the place where she last saw her husband and sons. She doesn't remember when it was that she met with the ICMP, but she will never forget when the first burial happened at Potočari.

In 2000, Nura moved back to her village where she lived in a tent before moving to the Slavinovići refugee camp built by a Dutch charity. She lived there with her mother and sister, both of whom died within the past three years.

> When I got back to my village first I lived in a tent. Then I learned that they found my husband. I had told them where he was by the water well and they found him there, almost the complete skeleton. Just those tiny ribs were missing. Then later they found my two sons. My oldest son was in Snagovo. Then they found the youngest one Fuad in Mršići. I'm still looking for my middle son. The two who were wounded, one is found and buried and I'm still looking for the other one.
>
> The medical pathologist from Tuzla wanted to wait until all three were found before we buried them. They weren't sure about the identity. They couldn't tell the difference between the two sons until they found both of them. I said that I want to bury my two sons who have been identified while I'm still alive. He said, don't, let's wait for the third one to be found. But then I told them that one of my sons had broken his ribs when he was younger and then they were able to identify him.

At the ICMP, which was established in 1996, identification is made through DNA testing. In a situation like Nura's, however, the DNA could only tell her that two of her sons had been found. It could not, however, tell her which sons. It was up to the forensic anthropologists at the ICMP to reconstruct the skeletons with any identified bones and then determine which belong to which son. When Nura told them about one son having a history of broken ribs, they were able to determine which son had been found.

> In 2010 I buried my husband.

We told Nura that she protected her sons as long as she could, that she held on to them and did everything possible. She had also been taking care of her husband and her sons, even after they died, by telling this painful story so that others would know what happened and what life was like for those left behind.

> God let me live to look for them. I said I want to bury my two sons. I'm not going to wait for the third one. In 2011, I buried both of them. I'm still looking for Alija. I left a spare place by their graves. My husband and two sons are together, buried side by side. It's been 20 years but it's as if it was yesterday.

Like Saliha, Nura wanted to return to the home she had shared with her husband and sons. Both women wanted to be in the place where they can imagine the footsteps of their sons. Nura's house was rebuilt on a smaller scale and she said that the small space is fine because she is alone.

> It's been 20 years but I will never forget it. I can't forget it.

Nura's blue eyes filled with tears and she started to cry.

> None of my sons were married. I am alone. I would have given my life. I wish they had killed me, not them. They would have their families later and they would mention my name, that I died for them. They would have their children, their family, now nothing is left.... Three gravestones and still looking for the fourth one to be erected.

Nura has a good friend, Mafija Hadžibulić, a neighbor who also lost her sons. They spend a lot of their time together, eat together and Nura sleeps at her friend's house so that neither of them are alone. She says they understand each other and they are always together, wherever they go.

Nura starts to laugh.

> Sometimes we fight but it's okay. All good friends fight. I tell her I'm coming over for a cup of coffee and that she should make coffee and she says, no, you're younger, you should make the coffee.

When asked why she thinks all of this happened, Nura talked about those in power who caused the war.

> It was big powers and also we are of different faiths and different ethnic groups. Those of us living in the village, we didn't care about the politics. We were just ordinary people and ordinary people didn't want war. Srebrenica was a safe haven zone and we thought we would survive. I thought that at least one of my sons would stay alive. None of them survived. But I'm still alive. I fight for justice and I hope that the younger generations will fight and will follow in our footsteps and fight for justice and this cause.

We asked Nura why she thinks she survived.

> I keep asking myself that when I'm alone. How could I survive when they separated my children? I ask myself, even today, how. Maybe there is something strong which gives me strength. It's Allah's power. I believe that. His will keeps me going, keeps me alive. Imagine a situation when they take away your wounded children and you are still alive and you are able to survive all of that.
>
> I'm still happy to meet people, to speak to people, to tell them my story, for people to know. Whoever comes to see me and visit me, I'm so grateful. It's not just me. There are thousands of women left alone by themselves, it's not just me.
>
> When you climb up that hill in the cemetery and you look down and you see that endless field. You imagine the mothers mourning.

Nura is still waiting for news about her son Alija and, like many of the mothers, will not be able to believe he is dead until his remains are found.

> Hopefully I will find Alija. I think and I imagine that he is somehow still alive. I can't imagine that he is dead. If he comes and he knocks on my door, I hope I'm still alive. I'm not that sick. My health is still pretty good.

Nura believed God allowed her to survive so that she could tell the story of her husband and sons. She lives among those who deny the genocide, which she feels is another reason it is so important that her story be heard.

> It's a true story. I always say that this is my life, I lived through this. My father and mother brought me up in a way that I should speak straight, no lies, just the truth from heart and soul. I was taught that the truth and justice prevail. Even if I would have to give my life I would stand for justice and truth.

> There is nothing as bad as losing children. I'm fighting for my children because God let me live to fight for them and to fight for justice in order to have closure.

We wrapped up our time together because it was getting late and Nura's ride was waiting for her. As she was preparing to leave, she gave me the wool socks and the pumpkin from her purse. She insisted that the next time she saw me, she would give me more socks. We said our goodbyes and I promised Nura that I would see her again when I returned to Srebrenica.

Neither of us knew that we would be seeing each other the very next day at a newly discovered mass grave at Kozluk.

Saliha Osmanović

Saliha began our time together by thanking us for inviting her to meet. Anybody who knows Saliha would not be surprised by this. She never seems to realize what a gift she is to those lucky enough to know her. Many people familiar with the Srebrenica genocide would recognize Saliha, as she is the wife of Ramo Osmanović, who was filmed when he was forced to call their 18-year-old son Nermin down from the woods during the Death March, down from the woods to a certain death. That film is one of the most infamous taken during those days in July 1995. Saliha may have become famous because of Ramo, but to those who interact with her now she is a hero in her own right. Her beautiful face is lined with every experience she has had since the war began. I love her face and her deep laugh. Her eyes more often than not fill with tears yet she still laughs.

Saliha was born in Zalužje in 1954, the youngest of five children. Her father died when she was two years old, the first of many important males who would be taken from her.

> I don't remember my father because when I was two he died so our mother raised all of the children. My brothers and sisters probably suffered but I was the youngest and I was spared a little bit. He was working in the mine and all of a sudden something happened with his lungs and he died. My mother raised us by herself, five of us.
>
> I never felt a father's love but we had a good life because of everybody else.

Saliha finished the fourth grade in school and then had to drop out.

> My mother was not able to provide financially for my further education. When I finished fourth grade I was working in the fields and with the animals. It was our land. My father didn't have brothers or sisters. He was the only one in his family so he had a lot of land. We grew corn, potatoes, beans, all kinds of vegetables. We had cattle and sheep, everything. I lived there for 19 years.

Saliha then married Ramo and moved with him to Dobrak, where they lived for five years with Ramo's two brothers and his parents. Saliha continued to work in the fields and did the cooking.

> I had to work hard. It was the life.

After living with Ramo's family for five years, they built their own house in the village nearby, the house where she still lives now. By then they had two small boys, Nermin who was three and Edin who was two. Saliha described them in a loving way.

> They were good. They were so tidy. They would listen to me and they were smart. They would listen and would do whatever I would say. They started going to school in Skelani, that little town nearby.
>
> Later, a little bit before the war started, Nermin went to school in the town of Bajina Bašta[15] across the river in Serbia.

Back then, it didn't matter if you had been born in Serbia or Bosnia or anywhere else in what was then Yugoslavia. It also didn't matter where you went to school because it was all one country with little attention paid to ethnicity or religion. The first sign that war was coming was in 1992, when Nermin was told he needed a pass to cross the bridge into Serbia to go to school.

> We had to ask the Serbs to give him a pass to be able to go to school like everybody else. He needed a pass to go to Serbia. I was very surprised.

At the time Ramo, who was a carpenter, was working in Belgrade, Serbia. He was working and unaware that the war was coming. In May of 1992, he went home to Bosnia for a seven-day vacation and he never went back to Serbia because the shooting started. Ramo was working in the fields and three days before he was supposed to go back, Saliha looked out of her window and noticed a car that had stopped. Later, Ramo told her what had happened.

> A Serb named Radivoje stopped his car on the road in front of our house. He called my husband by his full name and said, "Come here. It's your turn now. Your village and another village Rešagići will be burned down." My husband told him, "We are not guilty of anything. Why, why should war happen? We didn't do anything wrong to anybody."
>
> You have seen how close my house is to Serbia. They started to shoot and my husband said we needed to run. With just what we had on us we ran up in the hill in the back of the house and into the woods. We started walking through the woods. This was the eighth of May, 1992.

Today, at Saliha's house, it is, in one way, hard to imagine what it was like that day in May. Her backyard where they ran to the hill is now covered in a magnificent garden where she grows enough food for herself and for the animals that come to steal her vegetables. It is a very short distance from her front yard of fruit trees and flowers to the Drina river that divides Bosnia and Serbia. It takes a few minutes to walk from her house to the Drina, which is very narrow in that spot, so narrow that you can skip stones into Serbia. What isn't hard to imagine is how terrifying it was for Saliha and her family when shooting started from Serbia, a place that is literally a stone's throw from Bosnia.

Saliha, Nermin and the boys walked all night through the woods and kept walking. They were trying to get to the town of Srebrenica which was a long way away. So far away, in fact, that it took them a month to get there by foot.

> We were walking during the night and Srebrenica was far. First we went to Osat[16] and we stayed there for a while. Then we went to another village then we came to Srebrenica. I think after a month we got to Srebrenica. All the time from Serbia they were shooting heavily. All the Muslim villages were under fire from Serbs. All the villages were heavily shelled and people were being killed and wounded. When we would come to a village people were bringing food and drinks and something to help but also people from those villages were

getting ready to escape. There were a lot of people in the woods with us, children and small babies. It was chaos. You don't know where to go, you just go. It's crazy.

When asked why they decided to go all the way to Srebrenica, Saliha was matter of fact in her answer.

> Where else would we go? There was a circle in which Muslims were trapped and the only place to go was Srebrenica. I was thinking that my family and everybody would survive. I was just thinking that we would stay alive and everybody else would too.
>
> We got to Srebrenica and we found a house with a room, there were just walls, nothing else inside. No mattresses, nothing to eat or to drink. My life today, sometimes I have the feeling that I shouldn't eat or I shouldn't drink. I lost my sons, my husband, I lost my family, I lost my life. There is not a day when I don't think of them. I talk to people but it doesn't help that much. In my soul I suffer.

Saliha remembers the day that so many children and others were killed at the playground in April 1993.

> I remember. My Edin, my son was in school there. People were saying that people had been killed there, at his school. Then I went to the school and I saw dead people on the ground. I went back home and Edin came from school. He was inside the school building so nothing happened to him then. I was so scared thinking it was him who had been killed. Everybody loves everybody but you care the most about your children. I felt sorry for everybody.

Later, Saliha's fears came true and Edin was killed.

> On the sixth of July 1995, five days before Srebrenica fell, my son Edin was killed. It was Thursday at nine in the morning when the shelling happened. There used to be a coffee shop maybe a mile before the Potočari Memorial and Edin was on the road. He was with two cousins, one was wounded but they survived. Just my son was killed. Maybe they were not close to each other as they walked.
>
> I was making a pie and when you make a pie you share with people. I had a headache and I had to lie down. Then my husband Ramo came and he said our children were killed. "Don't go with me," he said.
>
> But I started walking down the road and someone said that Edin was killed and Ramo was bringing him in a wheelbarrow. When I heard that Edin was killed I fainted. Then some people brought me inside to a room.
>
> We buried him in Kazani, the cemetery at the end of town. They buried him during the night because during the day there was heavy shelling and they couldn't do it then. He was killed on the sixth of July and on the 11th Srebrenica fell.
>
> I will never forget that. I will never forget. I can forget some things but I can never forget this, even in my sleep. When Thursday comes during the week I can't do anything because he died on a Thursday.
>
> But I always say it's not just me, there are thousands of others.

Saliha's heart was broken because of Edin's death and five days later, Srebrenica fell.

> There was heavy shelling, it was scary and you had to run. You don't know where to run to. Then I followed people. Ramo and Nermin went to Kazani to follow the other men.

> I went toward Bratunac to Potočari. I was there with many people. It was hell and Mladić was walking by.
>
> I think I slept two nights in Potočari. I was outside the base where the buses were for two nights.
>
> For me that was something I cannot explain to you. When I was in Potočari I was alone. I didn't know where to go. When we got on the buses to Tišća they let us off the buses but we didn't know where to go. I was alone, on my own.
>
> I got to Lukavac. I was alone. I didn't know where to go, who to live with. They took me to an ambulance and put me on an IV. They had to take care of me. Then they put us in a building for refugees and they took me to emergency. I felt terrible.

Saliha felt alone for a long time. In fact, she still feels alone, and she is alone, which is her greatest sorrow. This woman who is so affectionate, who loves to be touched, to hold hands, should not be alone.

After arriving in Lukavac, Saliha spent the next many months staying in various places with various people, and sometimes staying alone. She spent some time staying with her husband's brother and her mother-in-law in Jasenica. It was there that she first saw a picture of Ramo in the newspaper. It was a picture of him calling to Nermin, although at the time Saliha did not know that part of the story.

> When we were in Jasenica my husband's brother had a newspaper and I took that paper then I said, "This is my husband Ramo, this is him." Then I started to cry. I said, "He is alive, he will come." I was crying and I asked my husband's brother "I saw my husband in the newspapers, where are those papers?" I said to him "He is alive," and he was just comforting me. He knew, but I don't know how he knew. Then I saw the picture of my husband on television and I thought he must be alive.
>
> When I moved to Sarajevo I tried to find news but every day I saw that there is no news about Ramo or Nermin.
>
> I expected that someone would bring good news and tell me that they are alive. I expected that someone would say something about that, that someone would say something. I can't remember how much time had passed.

Saliha eventually went to live with her brother in a house that he bought. He told her that she shouldn't be spending time in other people's houses, that she should come to live in his house. By that time there was a VHS tape of Ramo calling to Nermin.

> There, in that house I saw my husband Ramo on the tape. I saw everything when he was calling my son to the Serbs. I saw those soldiers around him who were swearing and who were rude. When I saw that I thought he was still alive. He was calling my son to come down to surrender and I thought that he might be alive.
>
> And they still say that the genocide never happened.
>
> I was in that house maybe five years. I would watch that tape maybe every day and then my family took it from me.

After those five years, Saliha moved back to her village, Dobrak, where she still lives today.

> I got back to Dobrak where my children were born. I'm far away from everything and I'm alone. It's very difficult but what can I do? It's life. You can't change it. Time changes. I wish I could change it but…

Sometime around 2009, Nermin and Ramo's remains were found and identified. Family members thought Saliha had been told but, in fact, nobody had notified her.

> My brother's wife called me and said to come to her house in Živinice. She told me she had something to give me and something to tell me. We were sitting in the house and my brother's daughter called me from the Netherlands where she lives. She said, "Don't cry, thank God that they found them," and I said, "Who?" Then she said, "Ramo and Nermin." She thought that I already knew but I didn't know. Then they put me in the car and took me to emergency immediately. They gave me some medication.

Ramo's brother was the first to know about the identification, but he didn't tell Saliha right away. The family didn't want to call her and tell her on the phone because they were worried about her hearing the news when she was alone at home.

> My husband's brother found out but he wouldn't say anything. Nobody told me, nobody called me to say. I was in Dobrak and I was alone so they didn't tell me to make sure that I wouldn't get sick alone and die from hearing the news.

After learning the news, Saliha returned home to Dobrak.

> This was maybe six years ago, I think it was in 2009. I have all the papers but I can't remember the dates. I was supposed to go to Tuzla to sign all the papers but instead my husband's brother went there.
> It took a long time for them to be found. When they killed them they dumped them in a grave and buried them and then they moved them in other graves.

Around seven years ago, Saliha moved back in to the house where she lived with her family before the war. She explained why she returned.

> I had nowhere to go and I decided to return because my children were born there. Also I wanted to show the Serbs that I came back to my house. It's my house and I will live in the memory of my children and my husband. I will show them that at least I survived.

She still wondered why all of this happened.

> I don't know. I ask myself why. We didn't do any wrong to anybody, my family. I can't imagine that a man can do this to another man, to kill children. Oh my God, to comprehend what happened. I don't know. How is it possible that something like this could have happened? People were not supposed to be killed.
> Today we live together again.
> I don't know how to hate. I don't have any hate inside of me, nothing bad inside of me. Those who did this should feel it in their soul, their spirit and their conscience. They should feel guilty. They should feel guilty.

Saliha testified against Mladić during his trial at the ICTY in The Hague. They offered for her to be a protected witness but she declined. She said that she no longer had anything to lose.

> They kept calling me for seven years to come to The Hague to testify. I didn't want to go there on my own. I wanted them to come to my village to see where I live. I told them come to see where I live, where Serbia is. Where I live you can see Serbia on the other side and they can't say they didn't have anything to do with the Bosnian war, with what they did to us. It's so close.

I testified in front of Mladić and I was looking at him. I saw him with my own eyes in Potočari. I spoke about this in The Hague. The ICTY. I saw him in Potočari. You could tell he was just rolling his fingers against his head and looking down. He couldn't look at me. Then I asked him if he can eat and sleep now, if he can walk, does he have a bad conscience. I said to him, "Don't say that Muslims started all of this. Who shot at who? I lived in my village and Serbia was shooting at my village."

Mladić said no words to me.

Afterwards a woman from Tuzla who works at the ICTY came to visit me in my village. She said that Mladić's attorney was the worst one. He would ask me the same thing twice. He was checking my answers. When he would ask me again I would say "Don't ask me again, I already said it, I don't want to repeat it again, I don't want to speak any more about the same thing."

I said they didn't let the food come to Srebrenica over the yellow bridge. He asked me if I saw that yellow bridge when I was in Srebrenica. I told him to come to see where I lived, come to see that it's impossible to see it from my house. They asked me how many kilometers it is from Srebrenica to the yellow bridge. I told him to go to Srebrenica and measure it himself.

I was okay, my thoughts were straight. I'm glad I went to The Hague for the truth to be known.

Saliha says that she didn't care that she was in the same room with Mladić.

He finished his job killing people and everything. I just came to tell the truth. I was happy to have said to him what I thought. He couldn't say that he wasn't in Potočari because he was. He said no words to me. His lawyers said he was giving bread and water and juices and candies to everyone in Potočari. I said, "Yes and later he killed everybody."

He was just trying to trick people into thinking that he was humane but in Potočari it was hell, just like everything.

What was each day like for Saliha now? Now that she lives in the place where all of her family memories are?

I go to bed with tears. You don't hear people's voices at night. I cry on all the holidays, crying. That's life.

The first thing in the morning I realize that I am alone. Then I say I don't know why I live when I lost everything. It's difficult, very difficult. When I sleep then I don't know.

Somehow I get up and I move and I start doing things. I used to say, "Why did I wake up? I should have died but instead I wake up and I'm alive." I'm alive, what can I do? It's the way it is.

God gives me strength. But I also ask myself how I can get strength. I don't know. I get strength somehow. I have to live. I keep asking myself the same question.

Saliha said that it was difficult to speak about justice after genocide.

In my opinion the truth should be told. They can say to me now that I didn't have my sons. They say to everybody you didn't have a brother, you didn't have a father. They are always ready to deny it, they are always ready. I always say that there are many mothers like me. We should just be telling our stories so that people know. We will never forget what happened.

I told Saliha that everybody who meets her thinks that she is a gift to them. I let her know that my students talk about her all the time. They write in their papers about her, about how she is an inspiration to them. I've brought students to see Saliha every summer for several years. Initially when we talked about the idea, I asked her if we could come work in her garden for the day. She agreed but when we got there, she would not let us help her do anything. She wanted us to wander in her garden and pick whatever we wanted to eat while she cooked us an enormous lunch. We stayed for several hours but it still wasn't enough for anybody. I have now quit asking her if we can help her do anything. She loves meeting and talking with the students and they feel the same.

> I'm so grateful. I'm so grateful. I always love meeting new people. You should always come. And your students should always come.

Will she ever let us help her in her enormous garden? She has other ideas about our visits.

> Whatever you want. I'd rather have them sit and look at their young faces rather than letting them go to the garden. To speak with them. I love to speak to people. I spend all the time alone but when people come I just want to speak to them.

As I always do, I promised Saliha that I would never come to Bosnia and not see her. This is one of the most important promises that I will keep. She said that she noticed that I come to see her each time I am in the country. I can't imagine doing otherwise.

We thanked Saliha for taking the time to talk with us.

> Thank you. You invited me and I came. Just say hello to people, to your students. Pass my greetings to everybody.

Chapter 5

Human Rights Activists

November 30, 2017. The International Criminal Tribunal for the Former Yugoslavia (ICTY). The Hague.

> "Slobodan Praljak is not a war criminal. I am rejecting your verdict with contempt," Praljak shouted defiantly. He then tilted his head back and drank from a small vial. As the judge appealed for him to sit down, Praljak declared: "I have taken poison."[1]

And just like that, on international television, convicted war criminal General Slobodan Praljak committed suicide after his guilty verdict was pronounced during his appeal judgment at the ICTY. The spectacular drama and conspiracy theories reverberated around the world, people calling for an investigation into how he was able to smuggle poison into The Hague. Its aftermath also illustrated a major problem with conflicting narratives in the former Yugoslavia. His death was celebrated by some, while in his homeland he was hailed as a martyr and a hero. The Croatian Parliament held a minute of silence and read out the following statement.

> The verdict does not accept the historical truth, facts and proofs and as such, it is unjust and unacceptable. By the tragic act of suicide, the general Praljak has symbolically pointed out all the injustice of the verdict.[2]

The media reported on the Croatian government's official reaction to Praljak's verdict and his subsequent suicide.

> A former commander of Bosnian Croat forces in Bosnia-Herzegovina's 1992–95 war, Praljak was convicted in 2013 of crimes including murder, persecution, and deportation for his role in a plan to carve out a Bosnian Croat ministate in Bosnia in the early 1990s. Many in Croatia consider Praljak a hero despite his conviction for war crimes. For days after his death, Praljak's photo was on display at Zagreb's main square, where people lit candles. About 2,000 people, including two government ministers, filled the main concert hall in Zagreb on December 11 to attend the ceremony, while hundreds more crowded together into the building's entry and hallways to watch on giant TV screens.[3]

In addition to the crimes mentioned above, he is perhaps best known for commanding Croat forces to destroy the historic Stari Most (Old Bridge) in Mostar, an Ottoman Empire bridge which had stood since 1566.[4] After many years of meticulous work, a replica bridge was opened in July 2004 and is now a UNESCO world heritage site.[5]

Praljak joins an infamous group of men including Milošević, Karadžić and Mladić who are seen as heroes by "one side" and as monster war criminals by another side. Events following his suicide illustrate the major divide in narratives about the war in Bosnia. Is Praljak a war criminal as determined by the ICTY or a hero/martyr as declared by the Croatian government? This fight for control of the narrative defines much of the political situation in Bosnia, Serbia and Croatia nearly 25 years after the end of the war.

The day after Praljak's suicide, we headed to Belgrade, the capital of Serbia, to meet with four Serbian human rights activists, people who have devoted much of their lives to social justice and fact-based narratives, which are not easy tasks in Serbia.

Hasan had not been to Belgrade since a fourth-grade school trip and truthfully, he was very reluctant to consider a trip there. He remembers feeling blind rage toward Belgrade after the genocide. After thinking about it for a long time, he decided that he needed to go to Belgrade for this book. We identified four people who were well-known and respected for their anti-war, human rights work. We were interested in learning about those in Serbia who did not support the Milošević regime, and who do not deny the role Serbia had played in the war in Bosnia. It was our good fortune that they all agreed to at least meet with us and hear more about what we were doing. Ultimately, they all agreed to be part of this book.

With our trusted driver Šefik, we started out from Tuzla in the cold, dark morning around 4:00 a.m. I had lobbied for spending the night in Belgrade given the distance (a minimum of three hours each way) and the length of time we would spend interviewing people but that was more than Hasan could agree to.

We were interested in learning what these advocates had to say about their work. We were also curious about what drives someone to fight for justice while housed in a country or a society with a culture of denial. Serbia continues to deny any responsibility for the Bosnian war, the Siege of Sarajevo, the Srebrenica genocide or other atrocities committed in the 1990s.

In order to begin to understand the complexity of the situation in the former Yugoslavia as it relates to the war in Bosnia and the genocide in Srebrenica, it is helpful to consider the old adage that says "there are two sides to every story." You hear it everywhere under most every type of circumstance. Is it really true though? Are there two sides to every story? When it comes to the Srebrenica genocide, we would argue that no, there are not two sides. While there are certainly two, if not three narratives about the genocide, there is only one set of facts that has been established by the ICTY.

It is sometimes argued that during the 1990s war in the former Yugoslavia, there were war crimes committed on all sides and that all sides had casualties. All families were impacted by the war and therefore there should be no assessing of blame, or no naming of an aggressor. These arguments are an example of false equivalence. False equivalence has been defined as "a situation in which you are led to believe that two things should be given equal weight in your considerations as you come to any given decision, while those two things are not in any way actually equivalent."[6]

A version of this is "false moral equivalence." "Moral equivalence is a term used in political arguments or debate. It is an informal fallacy that says doing X is morally equivalent to doing Y, therefore someone doing X is just as good or bad as someone doing Y, regardless of what X and Y actually are."[7] This same false equivalence is prevalent in narratives from Serbia about the Bosnian war. In fact, it is the basis of that narrative. It is true that in any war there are casualties on all sides, crimes are committed on all sides and families on all sides are impacted. It is false equivalence, however, to therefore conclude that the deaths of soldiers have a moral equivalency to the deaths of civilians, or that genocide is comparable to other war crimes. We heard about this concept from all of the people we met in Belgrade.

Žarko Korač

Our morning began in the Majestic Hotel coffee shop in central Belgrade where we met Dr. Žarko Korač, a psychologist, university professor and longtime member of the Serbian Parliament. His political career includes serving as deputy prime minister in the government of Serbia between 2001 and 2004, and acting prime minister for one day in 2003 after Prime Minister Zoran Djindjic was assassinated. He is a great storyteller and started talking about how he got into politics. We were specifically curious about why he entered politics as a psychologist. He said that he entered politics for the worst possible reason.

> ...Not to be indifferent to suffering isn't a very good reason. I don't think professionals can help politicians very much. When you enter politics, it has its own rules and you have to follow them. Actually, they bend you, you don't bend them. It's quite difficult. Obviously, you face a lot of psychopaths and deranged people but that's beside the point because they get elected. So, the question here is much much more difficult. Others don't see what you see.

He never expected to win. He first ran for office, unsuccessfully, in 1990 on an anti-Milošević platform.

> In 1990 I belonged to the Circle of Independent Elections in Belgrade. I must say it was quite prominent people. Maybe 150 of us, maybe 200, I don't remember. We had meetings every week. Some of the best people in their fields such as linguists, architects, directors of TV, film directors, philosophers and so on, many experts. They opposed the war. I got screwed in those first elections.

Žarko lost in 1990 but he ran again successfully in 1993 and he became a parliamentarian. At the time Milošević was extremely popular in parliament and Žarko was in opposition to him which was not easy.

> I was also in the first democratic government after the war. After 2000 when we extradited Milošević. And from then on, I've been on and off and at the moment I'm still in parliament. It's the last time. I'm 70 and I am old for politics. I will stay a public figure but not in parliament.

Žarko talked about the history of Yugoslavia as a base for the rest of what he had to say. Everyone we talked to in Belgrade shared the same understanding of how and why the war in Croatia and Bosnia began and how the former Yugoslavia got to where it is today.

> After the fall of communism, the three federations in the communist world—Czechoslovakia, the Soviet Union and Yugoslavia—dismembered. The Czech and Slovak separation was peaceful. In terms of Yugoslavia, the whole point was the position of Serbia and how the Serbs saw Yugoslavia.
>
> Serbs mostly were taught that Yugoslavia was an extension of their own state based on the fact that Yugoslavia was formed mostly by the victories of the Serbian army in the First World War.

In the early 1990s, when the Republics started voting for independence, the ultimate goal of the regime was for a Greater Serbia.

> So Serbia let Macedonia go, let Slovenia go, but would not let Bosnia and Croatia go. The reason behind this was that there are many Serbs living there. The idea was to carve another state and Serbs used propaganda. It was actually all very open. It was not concealed. They all the time claimed that the borders are artificial borders meaning from the former Yugoslavia, socialist Yugoslavia, that Serbs have a right now to carve new borders like after the First World War.
>
> They wanted to create a new state, referred to in Bosnia and Croatia as "Greater Serbia." It's interesting that this term was never used in Serbia. Serbs now protest and say that they never used that term at all. It's quite true. They never used this term but they tried exactly to do this.
>
> Like today the RS is an excellent example of the old program. What Dodik[8] is doing today for his cynical purpose to stay in power. He all the time claims that it is normal for Serbs to annex themselves to Serbia. This is exactly how the original problems started in Croatia and Bosnia. The idea that Serbs have a right to self-determination.

Žarko agrees with our other interviewees when he names the cause of the war.

> The main culprit for the war was the Serbian political program when Yugoslavia started to break apart. So Serbia has by far the greatest responsibility for this war and for the start of this war because it deliberately did not opt for the democratic solution for problems. From the beginning, it opted for the violent aggressive solution in which only the Serbian position would be accepted, not any other. But clearly the main culprit for the war and the violence in the war is in Belgrade. No doubt about this. I am not saying the others are without their own sins but the main sin was in Belgrade. They had the largest diaspora and they were the largest nation, they were the biggest nation in the former Yugoslavia and also, they had arms on their side. "We are the largest nation, we have arms, so you have to do as we say."
>
> The JNA army sided with Milošević, with the Serbs, and it became a pro-Serbian army. And that was a huge problem. The Serbs actually had all the arms which was their advantage as well as political and financial support from Belgrade. And the Bosnians had more or less nothing. The Croats at the beginning were not really armed. So, the Serbian army was successful. Belgrade all the time claimed it had nothing to do with these wars. They claimed it was an indigenous uprising in Bosnia.
>
> The idea was if Yugoslavia could not stay together then how could Bosnia stay because it was like a small Yugoslavia with no clear majority.

When the Serbs took over the JNA, it was the fourth largest military in the world. "The Yugoslav People's Army was used to achieve the Serbian leadership's nationalist goals during the 1990s wars in Bosnia and Croatia," according to a report from the Humanitarian Law Centre watchdog group.[9]

Žarko continued:

> The biggest victims of this war obviously were Bosniaks because Bosniaks had nowhere to turn. Turkey is very far away and Islamic countries wouldn't finance or see Bosnia as part of their religion. Because the Bosniak Muslims are probably the most secular group of Muslims in the world. Not as much as they used to be. They were completely secular, you would see only old people in mosques.

Žarko discussed the role propaganda played in this war in order to gain support in Serbia. Even though Serbia is now under different leadership than it was in the 1990s, the propaganda machine remains in full force now as it was then, focusing on nationalism and Islamophobia.

> And this Islamic fear now feeds into this. People say, "oh, you see what Bosnian Muslims do now and you allow them to run the state to be in charge of the area."
> Meaning they want to impose on us Sharia law.
> The majority of the Serb population saw this as a justified war in Croatia and Bosnia preventing their *[Serb]* annihilation. And this is exactly what Mladić said, and this is how *[a]* huge number of Serbs, I don't know how many, at least half of the population, see Ratko Mladić as a hero. They think that maybe some crimes were possibly committed, but that basically Mladić was preventing Serbs from being annihilated from the Islamic influence.

Žarko described this using an interesting phrase.

> Hitler did not make Germans Nazis. They made Hitler their leader.
> People recently said that Ratko Mladić was the first one in Europe to fight ISIS, which is fantastic. Really fantastic. This is what they said. I was startled. He should be commended as the first one for fighting terrorism.
> To a large extent during the war it was an extremely nationalistic atmosphere, it was justified on the side of Serbs. It was always presented this way that Serbs in Croatia and Serbs in Bosnia are fighting for their survival. This justified everything that happened in Srebrenica.

Žarko saw that some progress had been made over the years when it came to acknowledging Srebrenica, at least acknowledging that something did happen there.

> I had a problem when I first wrote about Srebrenica in the beginning if we talk specifically about that. When I spoke for the first time publicly I was accused of being a liar. The first reaction was very strong and it was denial. Of course, we'll come to what they are doing now but in the beginning, they actually denied that anything happened there. Most of the public denied it. I'm talking about ten years ago. Now it's different.
> Actually, it's quite an achievement that today people accept that something happened in Srebrenica. So, public opinion has shifted to the extent that some now accept that there was a crime there.

Žarko talked about the role false equivalency, or equalization of guilt as he referred to it, has played and still plays in rhetoric and attitudes in Serbia about the war. One of the areas where this shows up the most is in any discussion about the number of people killed in the 1990s war.

> By far the biggest victims were the Bosniaks. Of course, there were Serbs and Croats. The numbers are a little bit misleading because there is one fundamental difference. Bosniaks were killed as civilians. I think a little over ten percent were in uniforms. Croats, on the other hand, most of them were killed in uniform which is a difference. Which means that the Croats were mostly killed in battles but Bosniaks were mostly killed as civilians. They were unarmed.

Žarko again mentions equalization of guilt when he describes a Serb monument on the side of the road that has been erected in Kravica, Bosnia, very close to Kravica Warehouse, one of the main execution sites. Like the other main execution sites in Bosnia, Kravica Warehouse is not memorialized in any way.

> The Serb monument in Kravica is a typical example. On this monument they wrote the names of all Serbian victims for all of Podrinje which is an area along the Drina River. This means causalities from all Serbian villages and the Serbian army along the Drina River. This is equalization of guilt.
>
> So people here say, "Okay, there was a crime in Srebrenica but they committed crimes against us, we will forget everything, like nothing happened." I'm talking about the majority of people. There are of course extreme positions where people say that Srebrenica got what they deserved because there were some massacres by the Bosnian army coming out of Srebrenica. So that is an equalization of guilt.

Žarko sees another issue as well, which is an effort to erase memory.

> This is typical of our president who said we should look toward the future not look at the past which is a force for erasing memory. They say, "Okay it happened but we should not talk about this for the future." It's very tempting to say that we have diplomatic relations in Sarajevo, we travel to Sarajevo and we have trade relations meaning we shouldn't be concerned too much with it. It was war, bad things happened, things happened to them, they happened to us.
>
> It is an anti-historical position where you say "Okay, this is past." But these are two positions. In Serbia, the massacres in Srebrenica was not presented in the media. You never had articles like the ones in an independent media. Of course, you had some independent media but they did not reach too much of the population. It was, at the time, B92 radio, it was national "Naša Borba" which was later "Danas," it was this newspaper which is the only really liberal newspaper and it was this weekly which is extremely liberal.

The other major issue, which is an outcome of media control and propaganda, is the denial of genocide. The ICTY determined that the massacre of more than 8,000 men and boys in July 1995 in Srebrenica was officially genocide.[10] Denial takes many forms. There are still people who deny that anything happened in Srebrenica. Others say that something did happen but the Bosniaks deserved it. And still others say that if something did happen, it certainly wasn't genocide.

Ratko Mladić was convicted of genocide and persecution, extermination, murder, and the inhumane act of forcible transfer in the area of Srebrenica in 1995; of persecution, extermination, murder, deportation and inhumane acts of forcible transfer in municipalities throughout BiH; of murder, terror and unlawful attacks on civilians in Sarajevo; and of hostage-taking of UN personnel. He was acquitted of the charge of genocide in several municipalities in BiH in 1992.[11] Mladić was sentenced to life in prison.[12] As of this writing, he has the right to appeal. A verdict was originally scheduled to be handed down in March 2020 but was posponed and is now expected in the first half of 2021.

Radovan Karadžić was convicted of genocide in the area of Srebrenica in 1995, of persecution, extermination, murder, deportation, inhumane acts (forcible transfer), terror, unlawful attacks on civilians and hostage-taking. He was acquitted of the charge of genocide in other municipalities in BiH in 1992.[13]

Both Ratko Mladić and Radovan Karadžić were convicted of genocide in Srebrenica and both were acquitted of the charge of genocide in other parts of Bosnia. This is a difficult situation for those in other municipalities where genocide has not yet been officially recognized. This is evidence of how complicated the dynamics are of this very political issue of ruling an atrocity as genocide.

In 2010, almost 15 years after the Srebrenica genocide, the parliament of Serbia adopted the "Declaration on the Condemnation of the Crime in Srebrenica."[14] Žarko describes the Declaration as rather lackluster.

> On 31 March, 2010, the parliament of Serbia condemned and recognized a huge crime in Srebrenica. The crime had been declared genocide by the international court. This declaration didn't mean that people accepted what the court said. So it's neither here nor there. This declaration was adopted by parliament with a very thin majority.

While it was seen as a step forward and somewhat of a victory that the Serbian parliament acknowledged that a crime occurred in Srebrenica, one of its major shortcomings is the absence of the term "genocide." There were other problems as well. According to one report,

> The sobering process in Serbian society—especially in "patriotic" intellectual circles, in the media and the education system—will be hampered by the still dominant rhetoric of a world conspiracy against the Serbs, whereby the Serb nation is represented as the main, often the sole victim of the 1990s Balkan wars. The parliamentary debate on March 30 was thus perverted into a disgusting—often indeed monstrous—glorifying of crimes committed, tug of war over the number of victims, and celebration of notorious war criminals such as Ratko Mladić and Radovan Karadžić as Serb heroes.[15]

For those who do honor the ICTY facts and judgments and admit that genocide happened in Srebrenica, there is still the debate about whether genocide occurred elsewhere in Bosnia. The primary location that comes up in that debate is Prijedor, a town in northwestern Bosnia where horrible atrocities happened to Bosniaks at the hands of the BSA.

Between May and August of 1992, the BSA killed more than 3,000 civilians in Prijedor, among them 102 children and 258 women. Some 30,000 others were tortured in concentration camps at Omarska, Keraterm, and Trnopolje on Prijedor's outskirts.[16]

Žarko talked specifically about Prijedor.

> We can debate, for example, whether Prijedor was much worse than Srebrenica because there was no war in Prijedor.
> They took people from their apartments and executed them. They put them in camps like Keraterm[17] which is a horrible story. And the way they killed people is terrible. This was an execution. We can debate horror stories, how they executed people there. So, we can open this question. But still Srebrenica became a symbol. It was the first time genocide was declared.

Bosniaks in Prijedor were forced to wear white armbands, reminding people of the way Jews were forced to identify themselves before the Holocaust.[18] There is a movement with growing momentum to acknowledge the armbands and the atrocities that occurred in Prijedor.[19]

Many people in Bosnia, particularly in cities, describe life before the war as one where different ethnicities lived side by side without difficulty. Serbian rhetoric says that this was not the case. There is currently a movement in the RS to separate from Bosnia and become its own state. There are a number of problems with that proposal, which Žarko discussed.

> So the world does not want to have Bosnia as a small Islamic state. They think it would become prey of very radical Islamic regimes. And there is a second thing. I think it

would be a great moral sin to reward aggression and genocide. These things at the moment keep Bosnia together.

Sometimes people have huge problems living together after wars, but not before. Before the war there were no serious problems. It's a big lie that there were more problems in Bosnia than other parts of Yugoslavia. I always thought of everyone in Bosnia as quite similar. They speak the same language, Bosnian, which is distinct from mine. In Bosnia it could be anyone, a Croat, Serb or Muslim. Their habits and behaviors were typical for Bosnians. All I saw was that Serbs in Bosnia are actually closer to Croats and Bosniaks than to me in Belgrade. They have a separate history and a separate culture in which they live. The melting pot worked very well in cities, not in the villages. In the villages ethnicities were divided mostly into Serbian, Croatian and Muslim but in the cities there were a lot of intermarriages. That is a sign. Actually, intermarriages were quite common. In the cities, you wouldn't have this ethnic division. So Bosnia I remember had no specific problems of living together.

What very often happens after the term which is now ethnic cleansing, is that it's impossible to reverse, to go back to the previous. Divided cities like Mostar. So, the future direction is very much up to Belgrade and Zagreb. If they try very hard they could discard this ugly nationalism about Bosnia. If they did not support nationalism I think it would subside. Given enough time, Bosnia would probably heal its wounds, we're talking about periods of 10, 20, 30 years. It's very hard in Bosnia because of crimes committed there and palpable tensions between nations.

While Žarko sees that Belgrade and Zagreb hold the key to the future of Bosnia, particularly in terms of problems driven by nationalism, he also sees issues with Saudi Arabia, other Islamic states, as well as Russia.

In Bosnia, the problem is Saudi Arabia with the money, but not only Saudi Arabia. Europe's view of Islam. Once Bosnia, hopefully becomes close to membership in the EU, they will be faced with the fact that some Islamic states, very radical like Qatar, UAE, actually own a lot of land, and people will start to think whether we need this in Europe. They buy property and have hotels and everything. That might be the problem for Bosnia for the future.

The Russians are very active in the RS. They want to prevent Bosnia from entering NATO in the future. Russia is working against better unification of Bosnia which is very destructive because they want to prevent Bosnia from having an independent foreign policy.

Žarko returns to Islamophobia.

Second, let's be very fair, Islamic terrorism achieved a lot, especially in the west, it's getting more and more upsetting, extremely anti–Islamic attitudes. Right wing parties in Europe, North America, the United States are mostly anti–Islamic. This situation in the USA is interesting. They are right now copying Europe but in America it makes no sense because there are very few Muslims. This is idiotic in the States.

I hope Bosnia stays together because to say that some nations cannot live with another is simply nonsense. It's especially hard to tell this to Americans because if you live in New York, which I did a few times in my life, when you look through the window and look down you always see 15 or 20 nations walking in the street and nobody kills anybody. It's especially hard in the USA to explain to people that people cannot live together because that's how America was created, for all people to live together. It's for everyone.

At the end of our conversation, Žarko asked if we had heard about Praljak drinking poison at the ICTY. He was struck by Croatia's reaction to this event. Unfortunately, he had to go so wasn't able to tell us more about his ideas.

> When you see [the] reaction in Croatia to what happened to this general Praljak, then you can see that their democracy is only skin deep.

In wrapping things up, Žarko talked about sitting in parliament next to Vojislav Šešelj, a convicted Serb nationalist war criminal who was freed on appeal and is now back in the Serbian Parliament.[20] In 2018, Šešelj was sentenced by the ICTY to ten years in prison for the persecution of Croatians during the war. "The tribunal found Šešelj guilty of inciting hate crimes with his nationalist speeches. One speech he gave to a Serb crowd in May 1992 sparked atrocities against ethnic Croats in Vojvodina."[21]

I told Žarko that one of the most memorable pictures I have seen of Šešelj is where he is wearing a Trump t-shirt at a pro–Trump rally he held in Belgrade before the U.S. election.

> I am sitting in parliament next to Šešelj. He's a Trump supporter. They support each other these people, they recognize each other. Serbs had great expectations of Trump. Of course, now they are disillusioned. Because obviously Trump has other priorities and Serbia is not one of them.

Hasan was originally not wanting to go to Belgrade but Žarko put us both at ease. It set the tone for a day that continued to get more and more interesting.

While Žarko's human rights advocacy takes place within the political system, our next interviewee's work can be summed up in one word—protests. She works totally outside of the system and repeatedly says she does not like any kind of connection with the nation state.

Staša Zajović

Finding Staša Zajović's office in Belgrade presented some challenges but we were finally able to locate it after asking several people on the street for directions. After making our way up the stairs, we entered a vibrant, crowded space with walls plastered with posters, information, and pictures in some places two or three layers deep. It was immediately clear that this was a place of and for action.

To say that we received a warm welcome from Staša is an understatement. A self-described feminist, peace activist, anti-fascist dissident, leftist, and disobedient, Staša has been the co-founder and coordinator of the organization Women in Black (WIB), Serbia, since 1991. Buzzing around the office were a number of volunteers, including a Bosnian man from Tuzla who was there for the day interacting with an Afghani family who was staying at a refugee camp in Belgrade. We were just in time for a birthday party for the Afghani boy who was turning nine years old on that day.

If you've ever hosted or attended a child's birthday party, you are probably used to the chaotic and fun-filled atmosphere that typically ensues. On this cold, dreary day at WIB in Belgrade, the four children in the family were running around, taking pictures, playing on WIB's laptops, laughing and making all sorts of noise which you would expect at a birthday party. And at the same time, on their mother's face and in her demeanor was evidence of the hardship and sorrow that had led to her and her family living in a refugee camp so very far from home on her son's ninth birthday We all crowded around a table and delicious food appeared from somewhere, including a birthday cake with a #9 candle. We sang the "Happy Birthday" song in three different languages, shared the cake and enjoyed the huge smile on the face of that cute nine-year-old boy. While this was going on, the boy's sister, who did not seem much older than nine herself, was quietly making sandwiches, wrapping them in napkins and putting them in her backpack in the other room hoping that nobody would notice.

Once we sat down to talk, Staša explained that the staff and volunteers at WIB are doing what they can to help the refugees who are staying in a camp not far from the office. It seems like her desire to be involved where there is a need knows no limits. It's no wonder that she has been the recipient of numerous international awards and that in 2005 she was nominated for the Nobel Peace Prize as part of the 1,000 Women for Peace campaign.

Talking with her makes you want to spend the rest of the day listening to anti-war music, especially songs by Joan Baez and John Lennon, musicians who inspired Staša in her younger days. Her pacifist origins were with men refusing to serve the JNA, and their mothers. Staša comes from a long line of strong pacifist women. It is not surprising that she is a passionate and devoted human rights activist. In her own words,

> I'm from an extremely antifascist background. We are very, very proud that my grandmother was part of the Antifascist Front of Women. I think for social emancipation fighting against the machoism etc., it is not fighting only for social and class emancipation but also for gender emancipation in very patriarchal, political and cultural surroundings.
>
> We are outside of political parties, making visible women's resistance against the regime is extremely important. Since the beginning, we cooperated with the founder of WIB, Neda Božinović.

Neda Božinović, born in 1917, went to the University of Belgrade for law school. She was active in the communist students' and women's movement prior to World War II and was an anti-fascist partisan. She ultimately became a judge of the Supreme Court of Yugoslavia and was a founder of WIB.[22]

Staša describes herself as,

> an activist from a Yugoslav feminist network from before the war. I am a leftist dissident from during the Tito time meaning I didn't want any kind of militarism in any way including the JNA.

Staša founded WIB Belgrade in 1991. Their roots were in the citizen's resistance movement, Not in My Name.

> Our motto is "not in our name" and we are always disobedient to all kind of militarism. The closest group to me politically is Code of Pink: Women for Peace.[23]

Although Staša now loves Sevdalinka, which is Bosnian traditional music, and feels very connected to Bosnian women, up until 1991 she had never traveled there. She decided to make the trip in July 1991 when she learned about an anti-war concert being held in Sarajevo. The concert, Yutel for Peace, was "the culmination of earlier peace protests in Yugoslavia uniting anti-war activists from all over the country with Yugoslavia's most popular rock bands in a collective effort to save Yugoslavia from war and dissolution."[24] It was held in Zetra Olympic Hall which had been constructed for the 1984 Olympics.

> Never ever before the war was I in Bosnia. I was not interested. I never heard Bosnian songs. I'm a generation of rock music, anti-war songs. I have nobody in Bosnia. And then I heard about the Yutel for Peace concert in Sarajevo in July. I was really interested and I said I will go because it is *[an]* antiwar concert. And I decided, it's my history, and anti-war concert and everybody has family in Bosnia.

The importance of the event was later described in the press:

> The evening of July 28, 1991, was the pinnacle of the anti-war movement in Yugoslavia, a movement that hardly anyone remembers today. Only months later, barricades were erected in Sarajevo ... before long Zetra was transformed into a mortuary.[25]

After being at the concert, Staša reports that she was very moved by the Bosnian people, so much so that when she had the opportunity to organize a "Peace Caravan" from Belgrade to Sarajevo, she jumped at the chance. She was familiar with the peace caravans from the work being done by her WIB colleagues in Italy and Israel. When Staša arrived in Sarajevo, people were surprised that WIB had come. They told Staša and the others that they shouldn't worry because there was peace in Bosnia which would continue. They said that the war in Croatia had nothing to do with them. This worried Staša and she started talking to them about Vukovar and she was stunned to learn that they didn't know what had happened there.

Vukovar is a town in eastern Croatia near the Serbian border. Hasan Sejfo Hasanović, who carried his dead brother to the free territory during the Death March, was stationed in Vukovar. In his narrative in this book he explains making the decision to desert the JNA because of what happened in Vukovar.

Prior to the war, Vukovar was populated by Croats and Serbs in roughly equal numbers. In 1991, the Serb forces of the JNA held Vukovar under siege for three months, ethnically cleansing the Croats. By the end of the siege in November of that year, the town had been completely devastated.

BBC News describes the devastation and massacre that occurred in Vukovar:

> It was, perhaps, the most comprehensively destroyed town of any size in either Bosnia-Herzegovina or Croatia during the wars of the first half of the 1990s.
> When the Serb forces took control of Vukovar on 19 November 1991, several hundred people took refuge in the town's hospital in the hope that they would be evacuated in the presence of neutral observers. But about 400 individuals—including wounded patients, soldiers, hospital staff and Croatian political activists—were removed from the hospital by the Yugoslav army [which was now under the control of Milošević] and Serb paramilitary forces. Some 300 men were taken to a farm, four kilometres [2.5 miles] outside Vukovar. The detainees were beaten up. Some died of their injuries and approximately 260 of them were executed and then buried in a mass grave.[26]

Staša knew about Vukovar from an information channel that had been established. The information she had was not from the mainstream media but from other peace activists in Croatia and throughout Europe. She talked more about her time in Sarajevo.

> We had a vigil in front of the cathedral in the center of Sarajevo. I was surprised and very worried. How is it possible that they don't react and they didn't want to know what has happened in Vukovar? They said, "No, it doesn't have to do anything with us," and I said, "You know that 100 kilometers *[62 miles]* from here there is terrible killing." They said, "We don't want to know what happened there." I immediately convinced my friends to organize this peace movement.

During this time, before the war in Bosnia, Staša and Nataša Kandić (who we met later that day) started organizing war protests in Belgrade.

> We organized every night for six months a candle vigil for war victims. For six months, every day, reading names. We held our protests in front of the Student Cultural Center because it was a symbol of the other Yugoslavia. We wanted to show pluralism of opinion during war time. This was when we used the slogan Not in Our Name because in wartime we were against all steps, all decisions of the Serbian regime everywhere. We did not accept any second of their actions or activities during Milošević's time.

Staša knew from their extensive network that the war in Bosnia had started. They did not know from mainstream media as that was controlled by the regime. WIB continued their protests and dealt with the propaganda of the Milošević regime.

> In the beginning, we faced all kinds of problems from the state and society also. The media was completely controlled by regimes. In the '90s and also now. We know how the state media, the regime media, directed and controlled public opinion. The regime used to repeat every day, that "Women in Black are Croat whores, the women on the street are whores, they are Alija's whores." We also faced a lot of physical attacks.

During the Milošević regime, Staša was interrogated by the secret political police "tens of times" and was put on the wanted list.

> Activists were tortured. All kind of persecution, but not rape. During the last year of Milošević, every day they used to come here interrogating. They were taking our documents away and never giving them back to us.

Even with all of that, Staša thinks that in a certain sense, times were better under the Milošević government than they are now under Vučić. She clarifies that the times were better, but Milošević was not better as a person.

In 2001, six years after the Dayton Peace Agreement ended the war, they organized protests every week at the same place, Republic Square.

> This is the place of national institutions, symbolically and politically very important. We were fighting for this place, but with completely opposite messages of the institutions. We used them for protest. We kidnapped their space just like Milošević did and now Vučić does.

To Staša, symbolism is important and WIB uses symbols as the opposite of their original intent: "Wearing black in some cultures signifies mourning, and feminist actions dressed in black convert women's traditional passive mourning for the dead in war into a powerful refusal of the logic of war."[27]

Being visible is another important part of WIB, not only in cities but also in small towns and villages. All generations join the WIB events. Staša described their street protests as including women who are in their 80s and people as young as 18. Sometimes the perception of the public in Serbia is that WIB only focuses on Srebrenica but their activities are more varied than that. In addition to protests and other types of activism, WIB provides support and educational services to women. Two groups of women who have been a focus are mothers of those killed by the Scorpions and women from Srebrenica.

In June of 2005, a video emerged of six Muslim civilians from Srebrenica being executed in the town of Trnovo on July 13, 1995, by Scorpions, a Serb paramilitary unit. The

Scorpions were put on trial from December 2005 to April 2007. A large contingent of women from WIB Belgrade visited Srebrenica and after that, the WIB decided to start speaking up. This became evident during the multi-year trial of the Scorpions.

> One hundred WIB from Serbia attended the Scorpion trials. After every session they decided to speak to our neighbors and said, "I was with Srebrenica women." I asked them why they did this. They said, "because I decided this is my human duty and moral decision to tell them that I was in Srebrenica because Srebrenica is the most known place of human suffering."
>
> In collective memory Srebrenica is present. Not by authorities, but by people, yes. No thanks to politicians. Also thanks to brave Srebrenica women. Because they decided to come to Serbia.

After WIB traveled to Srebrenica and then attended the Scorpion trials, women from Bosnia started coming to visit WIB in Belgrade. It is difficult to describe how monumental this is for many Bosnians, particularly those from Srebrenica, to travel to Belgrade. It is a testament to the power of support and building of trust that WIB has established in Srebrenica. Nura Mustafić and Saliha Osmanović, whose stories have been told in this book, visited Belgrade after meeting WIB in Srebrenica. For Staša, this is so satisfying.

> My biggest gratification, my biggest recognition, is this kind of understanding between women. For example, I used to go visiting the villages of mothers whose sons were killed. I visited Nura Mustafić in Bajramovići village. And I met with Saliha when she came to Belgrade to testify in another trial.

The WIB–organized visits between women have been very successful. In March of the year that we met Staša, 85 women from Srebrenica came to Belgrade. During the time we were in Belgrade, 50 women from Serbia were visiting women in Srebrenica. In addition to providing support and connection, WIB organizes educational courses and groups on various issues. WIB has spent many years accompanying women from Srebrenica to court.

> We are everywhere and I think that living in this aggressor state, with the propaganda and ideas about the war we think this is some kind of reparation that we are doing. Emotional reparation built with community beyond all barriers. This is the biggest joy for us. For example, yes, this is really really nice this women's court we organize together. It is some amazing initiative with Munira[28] and community women. A lot of women, not leaders, I'm always linked with people, ordinary people. I prefer to go to the villages near Sarajevo. I love Sarajevo but I prefer to go to rural zones. With the modest people, without media and so on, I'm more interested in this.
>
> We go the commemoration in Srebrenica but we also like to connect in other ways. For example this year we organized in Djulići five cycles of educational courses with women in power. We have also organized visits to Belgrade to go to a play and so on. Because we understand each other, we support each other and we need to not just go to the Commemoration. We are friends. We spent together a vacation with Srebrenica women and activists from Serbia. This was very nice, very nice.

All of WIB's work of is done in spite of the current leadership of the Serbian government and the propaganda machine that Staša says is more damaging than Milošević's government.

> I know we have to go against this new Vučić propaganda machine. His most important weapon is the *Informer*, a daily newspaper in Serbia which calls itself an independent paper but is controlled by Vučić.

For six days in a row, the *Informer* wrote that WIB has two million dollars in donations from over 25 donors. They put Staša's picture on the front page and said that she is rich and that she bought a fancy car. Staša found out about this when she was on the bus, her daily mode of transportation, given that she doesn't own a car.

> Last year it was really terrible. In the buses people told me they saw the *Informer* that said I have a lot of money to buy a car and my photo was on the front page. I explained to people that they are being manipulated. I pointed out that I am using public transportation like them and I don't have a car. I live in a working class neighborhood in a big building very far from Belgrade. WIB has one donor. It's propaganda which is a weapon of Vučić regime.

The *Informer* also reported that WIB receives a lot of money from the European Commission. Staša explained that in order to even apply for money from this commission you have to cooperate with the state institution, which WIB has never done. WIB receives no money from the European Commission. This was more propaganda designed to discredit WIB and Staša herself.

> Vučić propaganda is more sophisticated than Milošević's. Vučić uses it every day. He has a lot of PR and propaganda people everywhere. They know how to isolate, how to denigrate, how to destroy people mentally. They fabricate every day with this kind of propaganda.

It upsets Staša that the international community does not see Vučić for what he is, in some ways worse than Milošević.

> It's worse now because Vučić is kidnapping everything, he's succeeding now. This is our tragedy. He's convinced the EU and the U.S. that he is a leader of reconciliation in the region. A factor of stability. In Milošević's time, sometimes the international community treated him as a peacemaker for a short time for pragmatic reasons. But with Vučić it is different because he promised them to solve the problem of Kosovo, that he would let it go. Vučić is loved by the international community, loved as a reconciliatory and for us this is difficult.

Staša is also concerned that Vučić is trying to erase his actions during Milošević's government in the 1990s and that the international community believes him. He is attempting to rewrite history.

> After Milošević they wanted to erase, to abolish all crimes committed in our name during the '90s. But also, they intentionally erase all memories about the resistance. Vučić was an active member of war strategy and propaganda and his intention is clear to deny his responsibility for the past. This has nothing to do with any kind of reconciliation. We are very disappointed that the European Union politicians support him as a symbol of stability. It is very dangerous for us. We oppose it because they are erasing and annulling the responsibility of Serbia and the regime and annulling his personal responsibility.

Vučić, the current President of Serbia, served as Slobodan Milošević's Minister of Information during the 1990s war.[29] Vučić once infamously said, "For every Serb killed we will kill 100 Muslims."[30] Staša sees him as acting one way on the international stage and another way at home in Serbia.

> Vučić and this regime, they act in two tracks. One for EU institutions and the U.S. and two, they organize neo–Nazi fascist hooligans from here. They control us and the fascists which is different than Milošević time. Milošević used them but did not control them. But now this fascist organization is controlled directly by Vučić. Vučić is worse.

Contrary to the propaganda published by the *Informer*, WIB has one primary funder, the Mott Foundation. They also receive some funding from the Global Fund for Women. There are five people who work at the office every day, three of whom are salaried. There are a lot of volunteers, and Staša says it is too difficult to tell how many. They organize 2,000 events. When they go to rural areas, it does not cost much money because they stay in the homes of women who prepare food for them as well. They only need money for gasoline and for big events.

There are thousands of activists who work with WIB in Serbia. Not surprisingly they are organized horizontally, rather than in a hierarchical manner. There are also many other people around the country, who Staša refers to as allies, who support WIB in a variety of ways. These are people who do not want to protest in the street and for different reasons do not want to be public in their support, but WIB could not survive without them. Some helped during the war and many are still involved. One example is the support WIB receives from market vendors who know that WIB goes to the refugee camps late in the afternoon. WIB stops by the market on the way to the camps and vendors donate pounds of food for the refugees.

Staša is concerned about the moral compass of Serbia, concerned about the future.

> Future. What does this mean future? Last night we were meeting with a group of very nice people, very nice young students, men and women. We showed them testimony of people from the war and they were shocked. They said, "We never heard, nobody told us." How is it possible to live in this kind of empty historical and emotional reality? What does this mean that we are living in a so called moral society without ethical standards, without empathy? This is the society of zombies. Moral zombies.
>
> I don't want to live where everywhere people say that I'm a liar and I lie about Srebrenica. They can't really deny the Srebrenica genocide because it's true, but they do. They deny other crimes too.
>
> People are scared, dealing with the past, confronting it. We are not just fighting because of Srebrenica or the victims of Vukovar. We are also fighting for how to survive in the moral sense, in the ethical sense. How do we survive?
>
> We are citizens without any political engagement. It is very difficult for us to live, anywhere we live in this country. That's why we support the voices of empathy, of solidarity, and of friendship.

We ended our time with Staša talking about the solidarity of women around the world. She was happy to see the women's marches after Trump's inauguration, saying that this represented a global action.

As we said goodbye Staša thanked us for coming, wished us well and filled our arms with WIB literature and books. She sent us off with as warm a goodbye as her welcome had been.

Sonja Biserko

We made our way on foot to the offices of the Helsinki Committee for Human Rights of Serbia.

We were looking forward to seeing Sonja Biserko, the founder and president of the organization. We first met her the day before in Sarajevo, when she had traveled from Belgrade for a launch of her most recent book, *Yugoslavia from a Historical Perspective*. It was a memorable day for many reasons, including the suicide in The Hague of General Praljak. We had been rushing that morning to meet up with Sonja, so we hadn't heard the news and she was the first to tell us. This dramatic scene provided the backdrop for our discussion about the complicated role that Serbia and Croatia played in the Bosnian war. Sonja is one of the most knowledgeable experts in the world on this topic and she has been a human rights advocate in Serbia for many years. The Helsinki Committee for Human Rights of Serbia describes their mission on their website as:

> Established in 1994, the Helsinki Committee for Human Rights in Serbia began its mission at the time nationalism had not only culminated in disastrous wars, ethnic cleansing, war crimes and genocide in the territory of Yugoslavia, but also in massive human rights violations in Serbia proper. Ever since and through hundreds of projects the Committee has been trying to expose Serbia's prevalent ideology—nationalism—and, inasmuch as possible, alleviate its fatal effects on the entire scope of human rights, the country's economy, the rule of law, regional and global relations and international standing, but, above all, on younger generations and attitude towards modernity and demands of the modern time, vs. deep-rooted patriarchalism, gender bias, etc.[31]

Sonja has been a senior fellow at the United States Institute of Peace as well as a part of many other organizations around the globe. She is a prolific writer. Her work has been recognized by numerous international awards and she was one of the 1,000 Women for Peace nominated for the Nobel Peace Prize. That a person of her status and her packed schedule would generously make time for us, especially on a book launch day, spoke a great deal about her passion for education. Not only did we meet with her on her busy morning in Sarajevo but she insisted on hosting us in Serbia the next day, which is how we found ourselves in her office.

Even before you get to the door of the Helsinki Committee offices, there are bookshelves and tables of books lining the hallways, along with literature on human rights, reports, policies and position papers. It was clear that this was a place where smart people worked tirelessly to advocate for the truth, to write books and other educational materials, and to fight for justice for those whose human rights had been violated. Inside the office there were many, many more books lining the walls along with a collection of interesting human rights posters. It was a professional, busy place even late in the day.

Everything Sonja does is in keeping with the mission of the Helsinki Committee. Just like the others we spoke with in Belgrade, Sonja was clear about the role of the Milošević regime and the role of propaganda in the Bosnian war.

> The role of Milošević regime in the war in Bosnia. It was key. They had a good propaganda machine and were so clever in hiding responsibilities even though they had full control. In the early '90s they used the Kosovo problem to mobilize the Serbs for war.
>
> The fact that Karadžić and Mladić were hiding in Serbia for so long also speaks about Serbia's involvement. Why they protected them for so long. The fact that all these criminals were in Serbia at that time and the international community was not ready to deal with them. There was a 1994 interview in a magazine in Bosnia "Dani" when David Owen[32] gave

an interview. He said there were 20 criminals from all sides and that's it. Each side had 20 of them. The international community had this approach of equalizing sides.

It is important to understand the comments of several people in this chapter within the context of the international court system. The issue of individual versus state responsibility is at the heart of many heated debates about who should be held accountable for the atrocities that occurred during the 1990s war.

There are two international courts that prosecute individuals, the International Criminal Court (ICC) and the International Criminal Tribunal for the former Yugoslavia (ICTY). There is one court that hears disputes between countries and determines state responsibility, the International Court of Justice (ICJ).[33]

It is also important to understand the concept of joint criminal enterprise: "Joint Criminal Enterprise is a form of co-perpetration, which applies in cases where a plurality of individuals share a common criminal purpose and coordinate efforts to commit its underlying crime."[34] Individuals have been convicted of war crimes, crimes against humanity and genocide in trials at the ICTY. While there have been efforts to hold both Croatia and Serbia accountable for these crimes by declaring them to be a joint criminal enterprise, those efforts have failed.

Sonja focused on the ICTY, its accomplishments and its limitations.

> ICTY said that Croatian troops were in Bosnia. ICTY does not establish guilt of the state, just individuals. Guilt was implied because of [the] verdict against Praljak and the others.

Sonja explained that the guilty verdict against General Praljak proved that Croatian troops were present in Bosnia. Implied in that was that Croatia was guilty for crimes committed. She suggested that this is one of the reasons the Croatian government reacted so negatively to the Praljak verdict.

> Croatia now has been sorted out as the only aggressor. Not Serbia. This is a big problem as I understand and Croatia won't let it go easy. It's unfair because Croatia cooperated better with The Hague Tribunal. Serbia was from the beginning very obstructive, not giving complete documentation or archives to the ICTY. They said in all these verdicts they didn't have enough proof to conclude that Serbia was present in Bosnia. They only tackle individual responsibility, not any responsibility of the state, army, police or political leadership. We cannot say that this approach is relevant in terms of clarifying the role of Serbia.

Sonja said that Serbia escaped from an implication of joint criminal enterprise by failing to provide relevant documents to the court. Croatia showed greater cooperation with The Hague and ended up with an implication that they were an aggressor while Serbia avoided such a designation.

> There are many flaws in the work of the Tribunal but on the other hand considering the international context the Tribunal achieved absolutely very important results. All the legacy of the Tribunal is relevant.
>
> It was because of the current government and all of the political elite which come from those past times. They protect and defend and deny all those who were indicted and sentenced in The Hague because they themselves were also part of these projects. It is almost impossible at this moment to expect any kind of acknowledgement from the side of Serbia or facing the past.

The ICTY has been criticized from all sides for various reasons. One area that is problematic for Croatia is the number of Serb leaders who were acquitted.

> These leaders from the Serbian Security Services like Stanišić, Frenki, Perišić and others were totally acquitted. You know Šešelj was acquitted as well.
> For Praljak, so I think Croatia was ready to accept this verdict had Serbia also been qualified as this joint criminal enterprise. It would be much easier for the other side to accept it.
> ICTY tries individuals for individual responsibility and not states or nations. But individuals did not act on their own, they were part of the military, of army, police. They did war crimes under a plan, were given orders as a group called joint criminal enterprise. To tie individuals to a group and to a system but to stop short of naming a country is problematic.

Part of the propaganda that exists to this day in Serbia is that Milošević was innocent because he was never sentenced. What gets lost in that narrative, however, is the fact that Milošević died in prison before he could be sentenced. Does that make a person innocent? Some say yes.

The role of the international community was discussed with Sonja, just like in the rest of our Belgrade meetings.

> Russian penetration is contributing to more uncertainty because they took the side of Serbia, not because they are defending Serbia's interests but because they want to keep Serbia out of NATO and the EU. They are really proving that the EU is not able to handle Balkan affairs. I think there is more attention and more call for bringing the U.S. back to the region.
> There was a recent meeting in Washington of the Atlantic Council calling for more robust presence of America in the region. I'm not sure if that will happen. I don't know but taking into account security issues in the region such as migrants, and new factors not only Russia but Turkey and some other Arab states and Muslim states, may be of concern so this may be a good time to call for more attention.

Today the Helsinki Project focuses on young people. Sonja doesn't know if there will be enough people to be able to continue the work. It remains problematic because of the strong nationalism that is still present.

> Young people grow up on the model of denial not only within the family but also in schools, in factories and state media. Everything is suggesting that we are victims. There are very many bright young people and on another hand many young people are leaving the country and the region. There are more people leaving now than during the war because they are not respected. They are educated and skillful people.
> I think it is very important for this region to stabilize and to have some kind of economic prosperity in order to create younger generations who want to live here and who want to clarify the past in the way that it would open up perspectives to normalization of relations.
> Young people are extremely important because this is a generation which will be responsible without being even born at that time of war. It is a burden that is on their backs because the previous generation did not do its work.

Sonja reported that there was a predictable unleashing of hate language a few days after verdicts from the ICTY were made public.

> So you have this constant war with words which has blocked any other processes in the region. All citizens in the region are hostages of the national policies. Leaders generate nationalism and of course the process of transition and transformational values is totally halted. We didn't install new systems, we just destroyed the old one. There are too many very fragile states like Bosnia and Kosovo and Macedonia. You don't have regional dynamics which would open up the perspectives of normalization and respect for each other. It's really a problem.
>
> I think it's high time to start the dialogue based on the facts, not only on the verdicts and how many years are attributed to this or that war criminal. So many groups have no knowledge of the Tribunal because nobody really tried to explain how the Tribunal functions. For example Milošević's trial was repeated on the TV all the time but in the TV studio there was never an expert who would explain the statutes of The Hague Tribunal. It was a missed chance to explain it because Milošević and others defended themselves politically so for most of the audience in Belgrade it was like a TV show in which they were winning because they were insulting everybody.
>
> When Šešelj was acquitted he was treated like a hero who won the Tribunal.

Sonja talked about the important legacy of the Tribunal, which was the accumulation of accurate documentation.

> There are many facts and materials gathered by the Tribunal which otherwise wouldn't be there. This is a very important legacy and Mirko Klarin and his agency[35] they are really taking it case by case and documenting it chronologically with all testimonies and documents that were accepted in the Hague which is very important time line documenting the war.
>
> We published a book *Conflict in Figures*, edited by Ewa Tabeau, a demographer and her team focused on eastern Bosnia and it is well done. So you can see that it was a campaign of terror from the very beginning. They gave figures before the war, during the war and after it and you can see the change of an ethnic structure.
>
> They were not ready to describe the war in Bosnia as genocidal because the international community was active only in 1995. According to the convention of genocide they should have acted much earlier starting in 1992. If you consider the international community's position at that time maybe it's understandable but not justified. Today the world is in a worse situation than at that time. The genocide in Bosnia is being discussed within the international legal community now because there are so many genocides taking place all over the planet. I understand that they didn't want to attribute genocide to the state. They attributed genocide to the Bosnian Serb Army without Serbia.
>
> We all expected when the war finished, we looked at the Tribunal as an institution which will bring justice and so on. Then you start to understand how difficult it is to change the society stances and how difficult it is to work with the elites which are not ready to acknowledge things. It has to be an enormous effort by the elites.
>
> People's opinions will be shaped by the elites and the current media which is under the control of the political elites. Intellectual, cultural, religious elites and everybody. If you do not have someone with a good intention to change the mindset of the nation then it will be very difficult to do so. It is important to have groups and people who deal with that. Because maybe one day they will start to reflect on it and they will be very happy to have Women in Black and the other groups which care.

We wondered why the international community has not exerted more pressure on these elites to move the process of reconciliation forward?

> Because the EU, which has a mandate over this, has never dealt with putting this kind of pressure on society. They work only with governments.
>
> The EU has to readjust some policies if they want to have a European values system, rule of law, tolerance and so on, which we all talk about but nothing happens. Hungary, Poland and the States are undergoing some processes which they have to handle. I think Yugoslavia was an indicator of what may happen because we were not an isolated case. Maybe by brutality and how it fell apart yes, but the problems which were exposed are not different than other places.

In addition to their work with youth, Sonja's organization is involved with many more projects.

> Our agenda is very responsive. Depending on the developments in the region we have dealt with refugees, minorities, media and so on. Nowadays, one of our main projects is New History which we worked on for three years. We hope that we will be able to continue because we came to the point where without understanding the Yugoslav context you can't explain the war and what happened afterwards, because these elites are denying Yugoslavia and they use Yugoslavia as an enemy.
>
> As if the war is proof that Yugoslavia didn't work. It's extremely important to clarify this past to show the benefits of Yugoslavia but also to somehow show that Yugoslavia was the first European Union which operated on similar principles.
>
> This is what we are working on now, promoting the book and hopefully if we get support for the project we will progress on the outreach with young elites from academia because they are relevant for this new reflection on what happened. National universities and institutes are not willing to fund projects which deal with Yugoslavia. You have many people who agree with that. With this project we brought together 50 interested researchers from the region. We had a conference in Belgrade months ago, they are all interested to continue that.

Other current projects include: defining extremism for young people and helping them understand what it means and how to recognize it; a project on cultural ice breakers with young artists from Kosovo and Serbia; work with refugees; and monitoring of prisons and other public institutions. They write analyses of ICTY verdicts along with their other numerous newsletters and books.

All of this is done with eight staff members and people who consult on particular projects. They have had different funders in the past but funding has decreased in the region because of many other critical areas in the world. They depend primarily on EU funding and are now starting to see an increase in funding because of concerns that the "Balkans will blow up again" with the Russian penetration in the region.

In closing, we asked Sonja about her thoughts on what is happening in the U.S. Her response was sobering.

> I think the EU and the US perceive themselves as modern which is okay. This is something that they are offering to us and at the same time they underestimate problems within societies which have become visible in recent years and nobody was paying attention to it.

Yugoslavia was the first early warning to the world about what may happen because we are not unique but we are unique in the way that we treated our problems. Problems that existed like in the States. Trump didn't come out of a war but whether he has answers to these problems that's another thing. I hope you won't end up like we did because what happened in Yugoslavia happened so quickly.

We left Sonja's office with even more books and we made our way on foot through the now dark, cold streets of Belgrade to find our next and final interviewee.

Nataša Kandić

Nataša Kandić was our last appointment. Our directions told us that her office was within walking distance so we started out. By then it was dark, getting colder and the city was alive with people and Christmas lights. As it turned out, we had quite a bit of trouble finding Nataša's office. Our route took us past the Serbian Parliament and the square where the protests from WIB had occurred. We went into a couple of different buildings before we finally found our destination. Cold, tired, and hungry, we were grateful that Nataša was still in her office, waiting for us along with a large office cat who insisted on being part of the meeting. Nataša was so gracious to have waited for us even though we were long past due. She could not have been more welcoming and willing to talk.

In the course of interviewing people for this book, I had the chance to spend time with some people I already knew and already felt great respect for. There were also some who were familiar to me because I had seen them on videos or knew their story and their connection to Srebrenica but I had never met them. Nataša was one of those people who I had heard about for years in connection with a VHS tape that literally changed the course of history. This tape let the Serbian people know what had really happened in Srebrenica, which was counter to the information they received from the government's propaganda campaign.

At the Genocide Memorial in Srebrenica, in the museum's multimedia room, visitors watch a 30-minute documentary entitled *A Week in July*, produced by Sense TV Tribunal. It tells the story of the July 1995 Srebrenica genocide through testimonies and verdicts of the ICTY. All of the film is hard to watch as the horrible events and aftermath of that time play out in vivid pictures and videos. There is one video segment that is particularly difficult to see. When I take my students to the Memorial, I let them know ahead of time what we will be doing and what they are likely to encounter. I always make sure to let them know in advance about this particular footage and the reason it is included in this film.

The footage shows the Scorpions, a Serb paramilitary group, getting ready to execute six Muslim men from Srebrenica (this was the tape mentioned earlier in our interview with Staša Zajović). The Scorpions force the men to get out of a truck and lay on the ground, where they stay for quite some time. The executions are delayed while one of the Scorpions leaves to get a battery for the video camera, so that they can record what they are about to do. During the wait and the subsequent executions, the Muslim men are taunted by the Scorpions with vulgar words and expressions. When the man with the extra camera battery returns, filming resumes and all of the executions are recorded from start to finish.

The significance of this tape, once it became public many years after it was made, cannot be overstated. It was the first time that Serbian people saw a Srebrenica connection to Serbia. The fact that this tape made its way to the public and to The Hague for evidence is because of Nataša's tireless efforts to bring it to the surface.

We met with Nataša in the office of the Humanitarian Law Center (HLC), Belgrade, Serbia, which Nataša founded. It is out of this office that she conducts her work as a human rights lawyer and activist. Her work is recognized across the globe and in 2018 she was nominated for the Nobel Peace Prize by two members of the U.S. Congress. She has won more than 20 international, regional and national awards for her work with human rights.[36]

Nataša told us about her early days in human rights work. As we had learned earlier in the day, she and Staša worked together. It's interesting that Nataša and Staša started out together and both continued to be advocates in very different ways, one within the court system and one totally outside of any system.

> In 1991 it was clear that our state, our world is changed. Politicians were focused on how to take power, how to replace the former president *[Tito]*.
>
> Serbians started putting out political messages focused on allegedly trying to protect Yugoslavia. The main message was that Serbs have the right to all be in one state. There were other messages about ethnic territories and changing the borders of the former Yugoslavia. The population in Serbia supported Milošević fighting for all Serbs to be in one state.
>
> It was clear that war was coming so many people from Belgrade decided to leave the country meaning they could not influence the war policies of Milošević and the political elite. Others decided to stay and to try and organize against the war policy, against the policy of Serbia, to try to protect minorities.
>
> So it was about human rights and when the crimes started in Croatia, again many people decided to leave the country. But for me I thought it was very important to stay and document what has happened with human rights violations.

Nataša was involved with WIB at the time and as we know from Staša, they protested in front of the presidency every night for six months and soon after that, they started to collect signatures in the streets. These were for a petition that said citizens of Serbia have a right to refuse to go to war in the territory of another state.

She says that Milošević was smart and was strategic in dealing with their protests. Even though they weren't officially allowed to protest, he never sent the police to arrest them.

> He was very busy with more serious issues, with the war in Croatia, with the war in Bosnia, and he wanted to show that his policies were accepted by the majority of people. He could show foreign diplomats that we were free to protest but that we were only a small number from a human rights organization and didn't have much support.
>
> We didn't have access to independent media except one small radio station B92, with a very good program. At that time, it was very difficult to be present in the media.
>
> We had candles for people who were killed in Croatia and read their names. We understood it was important to know the names of people who were killed as civilians or who lost their lives as members of the JNA army and Croatian army.

Nataša had made the decision to stay in Belgrade in order to document the human rights violations that were happening under Milošević. In 1992, she established the Humanitarian Law Center (HLC) of Serbia in Belgrade as a "human rights-based non-governmental organization that would document the egregious human rights violations that were then being perpetrated on a massive scale across the former Yugoslavia, during the armed conflicts in Croatia and in Bosnia."[37] Later they did the same for Kosovo.

> We were trying to document human rights violations by the regime in Serbia against Muslims. For example, we continued to collect more statements from people, especially women from Foča. We were very satisfied when the ICTY prosecutor, Patricia Sellers decided to try to get a legal community together to discuss the new crime, rape, as a crime against humanity. There were many organizations who documented rape during the war but she succeeded regarding the raped women from Foča. It was the first time in history I think that rape was qualified as a crime against humanity.[38]
> We continued to document war crimes, everywhere where it was possible.

In addition to the work she was doing on documenting war crimes, Nataša also began to represent victims in trials at the Serbia Special War Crimes Court in Belgrade.[39] It was during one of these trials that she first heard about the existence of the Scorpion tape.

> Many indictments focused only on small perpetrators without a focus on high-level individuals. In 2002 for example, during one trial for killing children in Kosovo, I heard from one witness that the unit Scorpions were present in 1995 at Jahorina mountain, and that the unit participated in the execution at Jahorina mountain, killing six Muslims from Srebrenica and that they filmed the killing.

Nataša started trying to find the VHS tape. She had heard from many people who had seen the tape but she had difficulty finding it. The footage circulated for a decade among Scorpions and Serb nationalist circles. It could even be rented in video clubs in the small town of Šid, some 60 miles (97 kilometers) west of Belgrade, where most of the Scorpions in the video lived.[40]

> But after that the commander of the Scorpions ordered the members of his unit to collect the VHS tapes and destroy them. In 2004 one member of the Scorpions came to me to tell me that he had the tape which he had given to his lawyer in Tuzla. They told me that they met with Amor Mašović, who at that time was president of the Federal Commission for Missing Persons. They talked with him about the video tape and they wanted to give it to The Hague Tribunal if the ICTY would give witness protection to the owner of the video tape and relocate him from Serbia.
> They promised to give me the video tape if I talked to the ICTY to help the owner of the tape leave the country, which I did. They gave me the original tape and gave the ICTY a copy. The owner of the videotape became a protected witness and he was relocated.

The other part of the agreement was that Nataša could not use the videotape before the owner left the country, which he did on June 1, 2005.

> I gave the video tape to one television station, B92. At that time it was very professional and the public saw the tape. It was the first time that people in Belgrade, in Serbia, had seen anything like that. They reacted very emotionally to it, with passion, they were shocked with the behavior of the perpetrators, they were shocked with the victims because two out of six men were very young and the victims had been very quiet without asking for

> their lives. But the perpetrators, all of them were in the new uniform, with the weapons, they were very harsh. The public reacted very strongly and it was the first time that I saw that people in Serbia had changed. That people didn't see Serbs in uniforms as heroes anymore. The public said, "they are criminals, all of them they should be locked away forever. They don't deserve to be free."

When this tape aired on B92, it was the first time the Serbian people saw actual footage of atrocities being committed in Bosnia. It was the first time that they saw something that had actually happened, not something that had been released by the regime as propaganda. It was a turning point.

Nataša said that this was a good moment but that Serbian politicians did not send a good message in response to the public's reaction to the tape. They tried to protect the state by distancing themselves from the Scorpions.

> They said the Scorpions are criminals, a paramilitary unit without any connection to the state or state institutions. They said that all of them will be detained and they will be jailed. Since the state had information about the Scorpion's locations, they were arrested and accused of crimes.

When the trials started in 2007, Nataša represented the victims who were the mothers and some children of those who had been killed. She convinced some of them to testify and others came to observe. Those who were there heard the testimony of the Scorpions.

> When the judges asked the Scorpions about their salary and who gave them their uniforms, all of them said the State Security Service.[41]
> I was attacked by the prosecutors and some members of the court council, saying that I don't have a right to accuse the state, that it's not a trial against the state, that it is the trial against individuals. All of them were very angry and the judge has the right to not allow some questions and the presiding judge had stopped me from asking questions. But it was clear that all members of the Scorpions said that their unit was established by the State Security Service and that their salary came from the State Security Service, their uniforms, everything.

All of the accused members of Scorpions were sentenced for war crimes but Nataša says that the judgment was not justice because the verdict confirmed that the victims were not from Srebrenica.

> The presiding judge said in explanation that there was no evidence that the six Muslims were brought from Srebrenica. It was very clear to see what the aim was. The court was not going to allow a possibility to see a connection between the unit Scorpions and the Srebrenica crimes. It was political instruction to protect the state.

Nataša described the trial where the testimonies of the Scorpions tied them directly to Serbia, which should have led to Serbia being found guilty of being a joint criminal enterprise. She observed, however, that the court was determined to convict only individuals and to protect the state.

> It was a time when the International Court of Justice opened the trial based on the BiH claim against Serbia for the genocide in Bosnia. I saw, because I represent victims in the court, that the judges stopped asking questions to the witnesses especially members

> of the unit Scorpions about their status, about their connections, *[to]* the State Security Service of Serbia.
>
> It was clear that it was not true but the judgement was that the Scorpions committed the crimes, that it was a paramilitary formation under the RS army, but with no connection to Serbia. It was really very difficult for the families because the mothers testified that they were together in Srebrenica with their sons, and that on the 11th of July the sons went to the woods and the mothers went to Potočari. And for them it was clear that the court said that their testimony is not true.
>
> Some of the Scorpions finished their sentences. Two years ago, Slobodan Medić, the commander of the unit, got the right to spend weekends at home. He was travelling by car with his wife and son and there was an accident and they were all killed. Justice is...
>
> And his brother who was also a member of the unit, is in jail. Of those who served their time, none of them are in the public eye. Some of them were young, maybe 22 or 23 years old. They got a big salary, weapons, a uniform. They said that they got a salary, in 1994 of 1,500 Deutsche Marks. And people here had only 20 Deutsche Marks. Can you imagine? For them, they liked the war, they liked to participate because they got very rich.

Nataša's efforts to obtain that VHS tape continue to pay off every day when thousands of people who visit the Srebrenica Genocide Memorial see the footage as a verified part of history.

She continued in her belief that accurate documentation of war crimes and victims was needed in order to address the facts about what happened during the war.

> And later, after Milošević, I saw that we needed a new approach to deal with everything that happened. We were all citizens of one state and you couldn't tell a difference between Muslims and Serbs.
>
> My idea was that we should use documentation, the legacy of the Tribunal, to see how to address the wrong policies of the past. It's not only Milošević who is responsible for what's happened. That's impossible. Many generals who are free today and many institutions also have a very big responsibility.
>
> Now it's time, after 25 years, to think about our past, and do something that is important. We need to build a culture of memory, to remember the victims, to know all of the victims, to know their names and the circumstances in which they lost their lives. Our culture in the Balkans always focused on the numbers. For example, in Bosnia many politicians will say 200,000 Muslims were killed. Here in Belgrade the politicians will say the biggest number of Serbs were killed, that Serbs were the biggest victims. Albanians will say that they are the biggest victims of Serbs and Serb policies. But we don't have very strong politicians who understand how important it is to take responsibility for the past and to see what to do to prevent future crimes in the region.
>
> The obligation of every state is to try to secure the truth. And we have states who don't think it is their obligation. They think their obligation is to protect accused people, to take care of their families. We have, for example, in every society, Serbs who say that Mladić is a hero. A hero? People in Sarajevo and Croatia would say that he is a war criminal.

In 2006, they started to build a regional coalition network for dealing with the past, called REKOM.[42] The objective was to have all of the countries from the former Yugoslavia form a coalition by signing interstate agreements with the goal of documenting the actual number of civilian victims from each country killed during the 1990s war. The goal is to know everybody's name as well as the circumstances under which they died. There have been previous efforts at this type of documentation but there has been no standardized way to verify the information which has led to exaggerated numbers of victims.

> It means that we take this approach to focus on victims, to know the name of victims, to try to convince politicians that it is their obligation to do this. To give respect to the victims, to apologize to all victims, and to say that all civilian victims as dead people are equal.

Per Amir Kulaglić, Minister of Tuzla Canton government, REKOM is still an initiative but it has stalled. It is supported by a lot of organizations and NGOs from the territory of the former Yugoslavia but the signing of the interstate agreements has not happened.[43]

Nataša remains hopeful about REKOM.

> The commission will be very impartial and independent. All collected information, all documents, will be checked. Everything that The Hague Tribunal established as core facts will be in the hands of the commission. This time I believe that we are very close to this aim because it's not too difficult of a task only to name the victims and to establish the circumstances under which the people lost their lives. I think it's such an important step for the future.

The day ended as it had begun, with a discussion about General Praljak.

> Now for the dead general Praljak, some Croats say that he is a hero. Some people in Mostar and other parts of Bosnia will say that he is not a hero, that he is responsible for crimes, for the death of many people. This is the problem.

* * *

After another three-hour drive, and almost 24 hours from when we began, we were back in Tuzla, exhausted, and full of admiration for those who we had met.

There were themes and ideas shared by our interviewees. Certain points were agreed upon by everybody: the history of the breakup of Yugoslavia and efforts toward a Greater Serbia; propaganda about Muslims predicting the imminent demise of Serbia if Bosnia was allowed to be independent; media control; comparisons of Milošević and Vučić regimes.

Each of our interviewees has a long career in fighting for human rights and social justice in governments that work to do just the opposite. Each of them has faced verbal abuse and criticism privately and oftentimes publicly. They all continue to fight the good fight. They all were generous with their time and information. They are all remarkable. They all are role models for advocacy, whether it be within or outside of the system. And most impressively, each of them has a strong moral compass that propels them toward the greater good. It is through their work and their efforts to educate the younger generations that there is hope for some sort of reconciliation and a way forward.

PART II

Aftermath

Chapter 6

Response

Following the genocide in Srebrenica, a number of events and institutions played a vital role in the pursuit of justice. Several of these are discussed in this chapter, including: the discovery of mass graves, the International Criminal Tribunal for the Former Yugoslavia (ICTY), the International Commission on Missing Persons (ICMP), the women's associations and the Srebrenica-Potočari Memorial Center and Cemetery (commonly referred to as the Memorial).

Mass Graves

Beginning on July 13, 1995, more than 8,000 Bosniaks were detained and executed at various locations. The first major massacre took place in Kravica which was then followed by mass killings at Orahovac, Petkovci Dam, Kozluk, Pilica Cultural Center and Branjevo. All of these execution sites became primary mass grave sites with the exception of two. Those killed in Kravica were transported to Glogova, an area that contained numerous mass graves. Those massacred in the Pilica Cultural Center were trucked to Branjevo and buried there.[1]

Today, the sites of these mass graves are not marked, nor are the sites of mass executions. There is no memorialization of any kind. A person can easily drive by these locations without having any idea that hundreds, sometimes thousands of individuals, were buried there. Even when one is deliberately looking for them, these grave sites are not easily found.

A few years ago, Hasan and I drove through a peaceful, lush valley to visit his father's sister and her husband. We were eating fresh raspberries from their enormous patch and drinking homemade juice just over 100 yards (92 meters) from where the remains of Hasan's father had been excavated from a mass grave. It was hard to reconcile the beautiful surroundings and good company with the fact that we were in an area called the "valley of the mass graves." People from these villages have tried to mark the mass graves in their own way, given there is no official memorialization from state authorities.

Hasan once spoke with a man who returned home after the war, to the village in which we were sitting. The man told Hasan he had been cleaning up his septic system, when he came upon a pair of men's pants with a belt still attached to them. The man then phoned the Institute on Missing Persons, one of several institutions engaged in the search for Bosnia's wartime missing. They sent a team of investigators to the site, where they then discovered a large number of human remains had been buried.

During and in the immediate aftermath of the Srebrenica genocide, military and police structures under the direction of the RS government moved the remains of Srebrenica's victims from primary mass graves to secondary and tertiary gravesites. Often acting under the cover of night, they carefully hid these remains in increasingly far-off locations, in places where Muslims had lived before the war. These remote villages were heavily damaged, sometimes nearly destroyed, during the war. The Bosnian Serb authorities orchestrating this cover-up operation calculated that the Muslims would never return to these places, and that the international community would not search there for mortal remains. They thought that these bones would be hidden forever, and that the crimes which they had committed in Srebrenica would never be brought to light. They were wrong.

International Criminal Tribunal for the Former Yugoslavia (ICTY)

On the North Sea coast of the western Netherlands is The Hague, the seat of the Dutch Parliament. This city is also home to several international courts, each distinct from the other.

The differences between these courts can be confusing and it is important to understand the role of each in the context of the Srebrenica genocide. In understanding the differences between these courts, it is possible to gain a better understanding of the challenges of justice when looking at individual guilt versus country or state responsibility.

> The ICC (International Criminal Court) is a *criminal* court that prosecutes *individuals* charged with genocide, crimes against humanity and war crimes. The ICC is a *permanent* court with global jurisdiction.
> The ICTY is a *criminal* tribunal that is *temporary* and has a limited geographical scope focusing on the former Yugoslavia. It prosecutes *individuals*, rather than governments, in cases of genocide, crimes against humanity and war crimes.
> The ICJ (International Court of Justice) is a *permanent*, civil court that hears disputes between *countries* and determines state responsibility.[2]

Prior to the establishment of the ICTY by the UN Security Council in May 1993, there had not been an international war crimes court established since the Nuremberg and Tokyo Tribunals. The objective of the ICTY, as formally declared by its mandate, is "to bring to justice those responsible for serious violations of international humanitarian law committed in the former Yugoslavia since 1991 and thus contribute to the restoration and maintenance of peace in the region."[3] To this end, the Tribunal indicted 161 high-profile individuals, 90 of which were convicted for genocide, crimes against humanity or other war crimes.[4]

Given the massive scale of devastation and widespread violations of international law committed during the war in former Yugoslavia, including systematic rape, ethnic cleansing, and genocide, this may seem like a relatively small number. It begs the questions, who gets indicted for war crimes? How are these decisions made, and who is responsible for making them?

Interestingly, during the Nuremberg trials after World War II, it was estimated that over 3,000 people should have been tried for war crimes. Yet, only 22 individuals ended up being prosecuted. What was the reason for this shockingly low number of prosecutions? When asked this question during an interview on National Public Radio, Ben Ferenz, an investigator of Nazi war crimes and the chief prosecutor at the Nuremberg Trials provided the following answer: "The answer is ridiculous. The question—how, why do we stop at 22? There were only 22 seats in the dock. Three thousand men could have been tried for the same crimes."[5]

In the case of the violence in the former Yugoslavia, it wasn't a limited number of seats that prevented the ICTY from indicting larger numbers of suspected war criminals. Rather, there were many other factors which impeded this process. Questions of culpability for war crimes are often complicated by notions of individual and collective responsibility. In some cases, the guilt of the top political and military leadership was readily apparent. Slobodan Milošević, Radovan Karadžić and Ratko Mladić were all tried at the ICTY, along with other high-ranking individuals. Yet it is often unclear how far down the chain of command these indictments should go. Should they include all military officers? All those involved in killing a certain number of people? Those who hired the trucks to transport prisoners to the execution sites? What about the drivers? When dealing with a crime as expansive as the Srebrenica genocide, which needed the participation and complicity of large segments of the population as well as both military and civilian infrastructures, the possibilities are almost limitless. The debate over who should be tried for the crimes committed in Srebrenica continues to this day, accompanied by widespread frustration with the relatively small number of indictments.[6]

After 25 years of prosecuting war crimes in the former Yugoslavia, the ICTY is closing. As was always the plan, it has now transitioned to the next stage, called the International Residual Mechanism for Criminal Tribunals, known as, The Mechanism, which will take over the appeals that will be brought forth in the future.[7] Local war crimes courts were established in Belgrade, Zagreb and Sarajevo to try those indicted with lower level war crimes. These courts do not have a time-limited mandate.

The legacy of the ICTY as an impartial database of judicially determined facts about the Bosnian war is critical in the ongoing struggle against the culture of denial and revisionism. The role of the ICTY and other judicial bodies in establishing the fact-based narrative of the Srebrenica genocide and other episodes of violence in the Bosnian war is critical to reconciliation efforts in the former Yugoslavia.

The International Commission on Missing Persons (ICMP)

The International Commission on Missing Persons (ICMP) was established in 1996 at the initiative of then–U.S. President Bill Clinton. The ICMP's mandate is to locate and identify the missing persons from the conflict in former Yugoslavia, and it is funded by a variety of organizations and governments. The ICMP has one administrative office in Sarajevo and one in Tuzla, where the morgue for forensic analysis is also located.

In the early stages of the effort to identify Srebrenica's missing, techniques relied on information from victims' families regarding clothing, personal effects, medical history, and visual identification. Pictures of personal effects were collected and placed in books for families to search through, in hopes of identifying clothing or other articles that had belonged to their loved ones. At that point in time, this was the most sophisticated methodology available. Things changed dramatically in 2001, however, with the introduction of DNA technology which greatly increased the speed and accuracy of the identification process.

The ICMP estimates that between 8,000 and 8,100 individuals went missing from the 1995 fall of Srebrenica. In an effort to identify these victims using DNA analysis, the ICMP has collected blood samples from 22,160 family members of the 7,773 reported victims and compared them with DNA profiles from post-mortem samples excavated from mass graves. Of the 7,040 unique profiles extracted from bone samples, 6,838 persons have now been DNA-identified by the ICMP.[8]

The identification process requires DNA analysis as well as reconstruction of skeletal remains by forensic anthropologists. This is particularly helpful in the cases where several brothers were killed. A DNA analysis can verify that the bones belong to one of the brothers but cannot make a distinction between siblings. By analyzing the skeletal remains, the forensic anthropologists can determine the identity of siblings based on age, prior injuries or dental records.

In 1998, the ICMP started collecting blood samples in Tuzla, where Hasan was living with his family. He remembers that his grandfather initially didn't want to give a blood sample. One of his sons was killed in Tuzla and the other was missing from Srebrenica. He didn't want to give a sample for his son still missing from Srebrenica, because he had hope that this son might still be alive somewhere. Giving a blood sample seemed like it would mean accepting that his son was dead. Several months later, he agreed to participate because everyone around him was doing so. The science of DNA analysis was poorly understood at that time, but ICMP experts managed to explain the process in simple language, and to convince the victims' family members that this was the only way to identify their loved ones.

Hasan describes the process that he remembers. Some people came to their home, completed paperwork with necessary information, then took blood samples from their fingers and put the samples in vials. Hasan recalls that the experience was unpleasant, but also that he and his family understood it was something that had to be done. During that visit, blood samples were taken from Hasan and his mother. His younger brother Omer was attending school in Turkey, so he did not participate at that point. Hasan had heard about the mass graves. This, coupled with his personal experience on the Death March, left him with almost no hope that his father or brother could still be alive.

In 1998, Hasan was a university student studying criminal science. As part of a course in criminal forensics, he went with other students to the ICMP in Tuzla. He didn't know what he was getting himself into. He remembers that there were corpses lying everywhere on plastic outside and that the odor was terrible. It was difficult to breathe. He doesn't remember how he got there or when he left.

The ICMP staff returned to Hasan's home on two more occasions, going through the same process both times. They called the house and came over with photos of what had been found, photos of clothing and other belongings. Hasan's mother didn't want him to be present during these meetings and made him leave. She then tried to hide the documents, however, Hasan wanted to see the pictures left by the ICMP and later found them. They were pictures of pieces of clothing. When the ICMP left after their 2002 visit, Hasan's mother told him they had identified his father. After their visit in 2004, she told him they had identified his twin brother. Many women came over to the house to be with his mother and everyone was crying. When this happened, Hasan remembers that he would leave the house and do whatever he could to distract himself. He has never talked with his mother about the pictures.

Kathryne Bomberger, director-general of the ICMP, shared the following data regarding the scope of identifications that have been made.

- More than 40,000 people were registered missing from the conflicts of the 1990s in the former Yugoslavia.
- Approximately 31,500 people were registered as missing at the end of conflict in BiH. This figure includes around 8,000 people missing from Srebrenica and Žepa UN Safe Areas in July 1995.
- Well over 70 percent of people missing after the conflicts in the former Yugoslavia have been accounted for, a ratio that has not been equaled anywhere in the world.
- In Bosnia and Herzegovina, around 75 percent of those who were missing at the end of the conflict have been accounted for, the highest rate of missing persons case resolution in any post-conflict society anywhere in the world.
- Approximately 1,000 of the 8,000 people missing from Srebrenica are still unaccounted for.[9]

The work of the ICMP marks the first time in any situation that mass casualties were able to be identified on an individual basis.

Srebrenica presents the most complicated forensic challenge in terms of locating and identifying victims. This is because, in an attempt to conceal evidence, the initial mass grave sites were disturbed and mortal remains were removed and buried in a series of secondary and tertiary sites. In numerous cases, body parts of one individual have been found in several different mass graves. If not for the work of the ICMP, the families of Srebrenica's victims might never know the fate of their loved ones. Additionally, the ICMP's analyses have been used as evidence of war crimes in the trials of the ICTY, helping ensure justice for Srebrenica's victims.

Women's Associations

As we learned from Hajra Ćatić, women began the fight for truth and justice shortly after being deported from Potočari to Tuzla in July 1995. They began to organize, forming their own associations which would become some of the proactive forces for truth and justice in post-war Bosnia. With the help of humanitarian activists from around the world such as Jordan's Queen Noor, former U.S. Ambassador to Vienna Swani Hunt, and European Union Commissioner Emma Bonino, they organized the first commemoration at the Mejdan Sports Hall in Tuzla on September 11, 1996. It was an emotional event which quickly devolved into chaos.

> The commemoration program began with news footage. One woman recognized her husband and fainted. Others started yelling and losing consciousness. On the screen, a Serbian general ordered women to board buses. At once there were shouts in Bosnian: "Stop the movie"! More and more people were getting up. The chaos began. No one had control.[10]

This commemoration drew worldwide attention as it was attended by renowned CNN journalist Christiane Amanpour. With the continued support of women from the international community, the women's associations became more organized in Tuzla, Sarajevo and Srebrenica. They began protesting on the 11th of every month in Tuzla, and through their collective efforts, exerted considerable pressure on the local and international communities to address the consequences of the Srebrenica genocide.

Members of the women's associations have testified before the ICTY and local

Tribunals and have worked with victims and witnesses to help them prepare for trials. They have established connections with similar organizations worldwide and serve as consultants for women who are hoping to establish similar associations in their own countries. The women's associations in Bosnia are international role models in the relentless quest for truth and justice despite the most formidable obstacles. Additionally, these associations are allies of Bosnian society's most vulnerable, working to assist local families in need.

Only a relatively small number of women are active in these associations. Saliha Osmanović, for example, is not involved in an association. Her village is far from Srebrenica and it is difficult for her to get into town for events. Being involved in these associations requires energy, time and dedication, which is more than some women can spare.

The Srebrenica-Potočari Memorial Center and Cemetery

The women's associations played a leading role in the establishment of the Memorial Center, and specifically in securing its rightful location in Potočari. Initially, there were calls for the Memorial to be located in Kladanj[11]; however, the persistent advocacy of women's organizations ensured that the Memorial and cemetery would be constructed on the site where most of the families of Srebrenica's victims had lost their loved ones. Through their unrelenting pressure on the international community and the OHR in Bosnia, the victims and their families ultimately prevailed.

On October 25, 2000, the High Representative for Bosnia, Wolfgang Petritsch, issued a decision designating Potočari as the location for a cemetery and a Memorial commemorating the victims of the Srebrenica genocide.[12] This property was donated to the Memorial Center, which occupies the only land that currently belongs to the central government as opposed to one of the two entities (the Federation and the Republika Srpska).

After a hard-won struggle, the Srebrenica-Potočari Memorial and Cemetery Foundation was established.[13] In March 2003, Paddy Ashdown, who was the high representative at the time, made the decision to transfer ownership of the Battery Bactory in Potočari from the owners to the foundation.[14] The Battery Factory was built in the 1980s and was part of the complex that served as the UN base of the Dutch battalion. When Srebrenica fell in July 1995, this was the facility to which thousands of people fled, in the hope that they would find safety and protection inside.

As the building of the cemetery progressed, it soon became clear that burial grounds would be needed before the Memorial was complete. Up to that point, identified remains were being held in a storage facility in Tuzla which was overcrowded and unable to hold the bodies any longer.[15] For this reason, the first 600 identified victims of the Srebrenica genocide were buried in the Memorial cemetery in March 2003, several months before the official opening ceremony for the Memorial in September. During the official opening ceremony, which was attended by more than 50,000 people from around the world and was inaugurated by former U.S. President Bill Clinton, an additional 107 identified victims were laid to rest.

In 2003, there were three burials held. Since then, there has been one annual commemoration held each year on July 11. These occasions begin with a ceremony inside the former Battery Factory in the morning, followed by the commemoration and burial of identified victims in the early afternoon. Thousands of people attend this event each year, and it receives extensive coverage from international media.

When a victim's remains are identified by the ICMP, the victim's family members have the option of burying them at the next July 11 commemoration. If the remains are incomplete, which is most often the case, families can choose to wait in the hopes that more remains will be found. For families who choose to inter their loved ones after the first successful identification of partial remains, recoveries of additional bones and fragments after the initial burial can reopen old wounds and be a source of renewed anguish. For this reason, many families choose to wait, particularly in cases where the victim's skull has yet to be recovered.

In the days and weeks leading up to the July 11 ceremony each year, the victims' remains are prepared in accordance with religious custom. Coffins are prepared in the town of Visoko, 20 miles (33 kilometers) northeast of Sarajevo. Each coffin is the same, draped with a green cloth, and loaded onto a large semi-truck to begin the journey. The outside of the truck is draped with an oversized Bosnian flag. These are the trucks that we saw coming out of the fog as described in Hakija's chapter, on our way from Srebrenica to Sarajevo. In the past, multiple trucks were needed to carry the coffins. As time has passed and fewer people are identified each year, now just one truck is needed. The truck leaves Visoko and winds its way to Sarajevo, where the main street, Maršala Tito, is closed off. People line the streets to pay their respects to Srebrenica's fallen, and a hush falls over the city as the truck passes. There are cords that hold the flag in place over the truck and people use those to decorate the truck with flowers as it goes by. It stops in front of the Bosnian presidency for a brief ceremony, and then continues on its journey to Potočari.

The truck arrives at the Memorial Center in the early afternoon on July 9 where families are waiting. It is a solemn occasion with the silence broken only by the sound of crying. The coffins are unloaded and housed overnight in a building that was part of the Battery Factory and that served as a dormitory for the Dutch battalion. It is a rectangular, barn-like building with windows on one side where the sun pours in. Once the coffins are all unloaded and laid in rows in order by number, a prayer is led by imams. People come on the 9th and 10th to pay respects and they are able to locate a particular coffin by using a list that is hung on the outside of the building.

On the afternoon of July 10, the coffins are moved from the building across the road to the cemetery. Keeping with tradition, each coffin is carried overhead by several people, all in a line making their way from the building to the cemetery along a pathway and street which is lined with people. The coffins remain in the cemetery overnight, with family and friends continuing to come by to pay their respects.

The next day, July 11, is burial day. Thousands of people from all over the world come to attend the commemoration. The ceremony begins mid-morning inside the Battery Factory, with world leaders, politicians, dignitaries and other speakers. Nedžad spoke last year as part of the program, representing the survivors.

Across the road at the cemetery the Commemoration continues. There is the noon prayer followed by dženaza, (a prayer for burial) and then at last, the burial. Family members often spend the entire day in the cemetery. A few years ago, Saliha buried her brother on July 11 and she asked us to be with her in the cemetery.

For the first few years that I brought graduate students with me to Bosnia, we did not attend the July 11 Commemoration. It did not seem like it was our place to do so. Hasan was clear, however, that it was important for us to come to Srebrenica on that day. He

Chapter 6. Response 191

A July 11 memorial service and burial at the cemetery of the Srebrenica-Potočari Genocide Memorial (photograph by Kristian Skeie, July 11, 2017).

said that it was important for the international community to bear witness in order to teach others about the Srebrenica genocide. We started going and always stood outside of the fence of the cemetery during the burial. The only time I went inside was the year that Saliha asked me to. While I still believe that we can support and bear witness, I also believe that our place is outside, at the perimeter, unless we are specifically invited in; the inner circle is for those who are burying their loved ones, those who are intimately connected to the burials and to the violence and struggles which preceded them.

People in Bosnia and from around the world have found many different ways to participate in the July 11 Commemoration. Hundreds of motorcycle clubs from across the region come to Potočari for the occasion, and there are organized bike marathons and foot races. The most important event, however, is known as the Peace March, which has become an integral part of the Memorial Commemoration. First organized in 2005, this event was initially called the "March of Death—The Road to Freedom." It began with about 1,000 participants, most of whom were survivors of the July 1995 Death March, like Hasan, who today serves on the Board of Organizers. In the intervening years, this event has taken on an important role in maintaining the culture of remembrance.

Since its inception, the Peace March, as it is now known, has grown exponentially each year and now includes not only survivors but also people from all over the world. It begins on July 8 in Nezuk, where most survivors came out of the woods in 1995. Walkers cover a distance of about 60 miles (100 kilometers) through the woods and over difficult terrain. Each night they camp, and there is a commemorative program. The Army of BiH provides tents and support while the Red Cross provides first aid medical care. Humanitarian organizations distribute food and water while the entire march is monitored by police and security. It's fair to say that much of the country is involved with the logistics of this event.

Marchers carry flags from various countries and organizations as they make their way back from Nezuk to Potočari. They walk through villages that were pre-war places of residence, pass the "valley of the mass graves" where thousands of victims were buried, over the hills and mountains, and through the water. The route stays as close as possible to the original route of those on the Death March, only in reverse. The Peace March ends in Potočari on July 10 in time to help move the coffins into the cemetery.

For several years, students from the University of Denver have participated in the Peace March. Many of these students are women, and they join a very small overall number of female participants. Hasan and the Army of BiH have made sure that they are provided for and safe in an inherently uncomfortable situation.

During the Peace March of 2018, a particularly poignant thing happened. Several students participated, and that year Nura Mustafić, who we know from this book, and her dear friend Mafija Hadžibulić, who she mentions in her story, decided that they were going to do the Peach March. As we know from Nura's story, she began the Death March with her husband and sons in July 1995 but ended up in the Sandići meadow, which was the last time she saw any of them. For years, she had been wanting to do the Peace March in honor of them because she has felt terrible guilt about not being able to protect her sons along the way. Mafija also wanted to walk in honor of her two sons who were killed.

In 2018, they announced that they were ready. There was no question that they were strong. All of their lives they had been walking, tending to animals, caring for land. But honestly, several of us were worried about whether or not they would be able to complete the March, given the rigor of the terrain and the distance. It was clear that finishing meant everything to Nura and she was determined to do it. Hasan asked my students if they would be willing to walk with Nura and Mafija to help them along the way as needed. Naturally, the students were delighted, as were Nura and Mafija. A bond formed between them during that Peace March that still exists to this day.

What happened in actuality was that Nura and Mafija walked so fast that they ended up waiting for the students on several occasions. The students had good walking shoes and state-of-the-art water bottles. Nura and Mafija wore rubber shoes designed for walking around the village, and warm sweaters in spite of the heat. They carried little else with them. As word spread about the two women throughout the march and the press covering the event learned about them, they received well-deserved attention from many people. They waited for the students on the last day so that they could all cross the finish line together into Potočari. Knowing how much it meant to Nura and Mafija to complete this journey made it all the more special for those around them.

The Peace March has grown from a local event of survivors to an international event of thousands. As one of the organizers of the Peach March, Hasan has encouraged international participation by putting tremendous effort into managing all of the complicated logistics. In 2018, I was invited by the Organizing Committee to be part of the official program on the second night of the March. I was honored to address the crowd of participants expressing my gratitude for welcoming my students and assuring them that we will continue to help spread the word about Srebrenica throughout the United States. That is a promise that we are determined to keep.

Chapter 7

Ramifications

Psychological Responses to War and Genocide

Grief

Grief. Most of us have felt it. Some are no doubt feeling it now. Perhaps we have judged the way that others grieve or have been subjected to someone else's judgment about our own grieving process. Rather than being helpful, the questions and statements with which people respond to others' grief are often full of judgment: "Isn't it time to be finished with that?," "Why don't you just move on?," "Why keep thinking about it all the time?" and "You need to do something to cheer yourself up."

Grief is an unavoidable part of the human experience, and there has been a great deal written on the subject. Grieving is typically classified into three main categories: grief, prolonged grief, and complicated grief. There are additionally various stages of grief, and countless checklists which are used to determine whether a person is grieving healthily, or whether some sort of intervention is required to change the way that grief is impacting their life.

The grieving process is the natural response to losing a loved one. People have ways of adapting to loss, usually with the support of friends and relatives, and everyone does it in their own way. Adapting to loss includes: "accepting the reality of the death, including its finality, consequences and changed relationship to the person who died; adapting means seeing the future as holding possibilities for a life with purpose and meaning, joy and satisfaction."[1] Under normal circumstances of loss, this makes sense. But how must this model of adaptation be altered to accommodate the experience of *total* loss which accompanies war and genocide? What happens when *an entire country* is grieving? Who is available to provide support in these situations?

The grief that occurs in the aftermath of war and genocide can be compared in some ways to a type of anguish known as "complicated grief." Consideration must be given, however, to the circumstances of loss occurring during a war and genocide. It is necessary to be thoughtful about whether or not something is indeed complicated grief or is an expected reaction to loss on such a dramatic scale.

> Complicated grief is a persistent form of intense grief in which maladaptive thoughts and dysfunctional behaviors are present along with continued yearning, longing and sadness and/or preoccupation with thoughts and memories of the person who died. Grief continues to dominate life and the future seems bleak and empty. Irrational thoughts that the deceased person might reappear are common and the bereaved person feels lost and alone.[2]

The Center for Complicated Grief in New York City describes the following behaviors as indicative of complicated grief: maladaptive thoughts, dysfunctional behaviors or inadequate emotion regulation that can interfere with adaptation to loss. "Maladaptive thoughts are described as being not based in fact. They can also be thoughts that are catastrophizing. Many dread the future in the world without their deceased love one."[3] It is hard to imagine what catastrophizing would look like in the Bosnian context. Immense devastation engulfed the country and the lives of nearly everyone in it, creating the backdrop against which massive trauma occurred. In some cases, it would not be possible to imagine anything worse than what actually happened in Bosnia.

> Dysfunctional behaviors are typically related to avoiding reminders of the loss and/or escaping from the painful reality. A bereaved person may try to feel close to the person who died by looking at pictures, listening to their voice, smelling their clothes.... Bereaved people are often inclined to avoid places, people or activities that hold reminders of the person who died.[4]

After a war, it is unusual for people to have any pictures. For many, the loss of photographs is a source of intense grief. Similarly, people are often left without any clothes, possessions, or even their homes in the aftermath of conflict; all of these absences are painfully felt, and serve as traumatic reminders of the complete nature of the loss they endured.

> Inadequate emotion regulation is another common problem for people with complicated grief. Acute grief is typically highly emotional. Most people have a range of ways to regulate these emotions. They balance the pain with periods of respite, giving themselves permission to set the grief aside for a time. People with complicated grief have trouble doing this.... Regular routines including adequate sleep, nourishing meals ... and social contacts may be disrupted, making emotions more difficult to manage.[5]

Bosnians experienced the complete loss of their social circles, and not only as a result of death. The relationships between victims and perpetrators in the Bosnian conflict were often expressly personal. Sometimes neighbors or those considered friends did the killing. Sometimes those considered friends were the perpetrators of sexual violence.

The grief associated with the loss of loved ones can be stalled and intensified when the fate of the missing person is unknown. In Bosnia, 25 years after the war, there are still over 1,000 people killed in the Srebrenica genocide whose remains have not been found. Across Bosnia, about 25 percent of those who went missing have not been located.[6] In these instances, no official burial can take place. People often envision their loved ones being under the ground someplace in a mass grave, perhaps after having been exhumed and relocated to a secondary or tertiary grave. They have not had the opportunity to properly "take care of" the deceased because they don't know where they are or how they were killed. Until a positive identification is made, survivors cannot mourn in accordance with their traditions. They cannot restore any dignity to the mortal remains and are left wondering what happened to their loved ones and where their remains are located. This can then trigger or intensify a grief reaction. As one survivor who is waiting for the identification of her husband, son and brother says, "I am bitter. I am angry at the government and all of them.... It's been 22 years since the end of the war, and they can't even tell us where the bodies are, so we could find our loved ones and lay them to rest. Then I could also rest."[7]

Following a war, the loss is too immense and the trauma is too extensive to be evaluated according to typical standards. There is a concept called shadow grief, which makes more sense when considering the sorrow of so many people in Bosnia. The fundamental idea of shadow grief is that a person grieves not only for the immediate loss of their family, home, or community, but also for the way these losses will impact the rest of their lives. The consequences of such loss are felt particularly keenly when there is a significant event or milestone in a person's life, and important friends and family members are missing. Shadow grief is defined as:

> A dull ache in the background of one's feelings that remains fairly constant and that, under certain circumstances and on certain occasions, comes bubbling to the surface, sometimes in the form of tears, but always accompanied by a feeling of sadness and a sense of anxiety.
>
> Many circumstances may bring sudden unexpected feelings of loss. A sight, a sound, a scent, or a holiday may trigger a sudden burst of sadness that emerges from the shadow of loss. It is easy to wonder what is wrong, when after years have passed there may still be this dull ache. Nothing is wrong. Although we may have joy, our loved one is absent. We yearn for their presence even when the sun is shining.[8]

Impatience with the grieving process can come from within a grieving person or from those around them. It is tempting to attach a timeline to grief in order to define what is an "acceptable" duration for sorrow, and when it is time to move on. There are many reasons for this impatience and judgment, however, it is ill-advised to expect a grieving person to follow a particular deadline for moving on, whatever moving on means for them. Conceptualizing sorrow as shadow grief allows for an understanding that the intense loss will forever be with the grieving person.

> Many people believe that after a year or two has passed, grief passes also. They tend to think that bereaved people have put their emotions behind them and have moved forward to living normal lives. To an outsider, this may appear to be true, but as most bereaved persons will testify, every day is a continued act of healing. Significant loss sticks with us and though we may appear to have returned to our former activities, something inside has changed.[9]

The scale of loss that occurred in Bosnia during the war and the genocide is staggering beyond our ability to comprehend. People lost their entire immediate and extended families, their entire villages, their communities and their homes. Civil society unraveled and it is still trying to recover. What does that mean in terms of grief? What is a "normal" grief response in such an extreme situation? Who gets to say what is "normal"? How can this level of loss, through such unnecessary and violent means, ever be truly dealt with?

It is important is to understand that shadow grief should be expected and met with compassion. The people in this book experienced unimaginable heartache, and yet have somehow managed to move forward and lead full lives. Does this mean that they are "over" their grief, or that they have experienced "closure"? Their resilience and strength have allowed them to continue on with their lives in something resembling a normal fashion, but this does not mean that their grief is finished. Not only are they mourning the events of 1992–95 but they continue to mourn what could have been. With the start of each new season, every holiday, each time their loved one would have been participating in something new, such as school or marriage, poignant grief resurfaces. It is always there for people who have experienced such extreme loss, and it is deeper and more acute during certain times of the year and certain events. It is crucial to check in with people during these difficult times. Most of us are aware that holidays, birthdays and other anniversaries are difficult for those who have lost loved ones. What we don't always realize is that shadow grief can be triggered by the light in the sky or the feel of the breeze, the changing of seasons or a song heard unexpectedly.

In Bosnia, where over 100,000 people died as a result of war and genocide, it is rare to find a person who has not been directly impacted by extreme loss. Acceptance is different when people die in unnecessary and unnatural ways. When death comes not as a result of an accident, natural disaster or illness, but rather as a result of war, another layer of complexity is added to the grieving process.

There have been numerous attempts from the international community to intervene in post-war Bosnia and some of those efforts have focused on various ways to help survivors deal with their grief. As is always the case, it is important for individual or group interventions to be culturally appropriate. There are often assumptions made about what would be helpful for an individual or a community without a full understanding of what is acceptable within that particular culture. Interventions that are not culturally appropriate can be damaging to individuals and communities.

What is needed is a compassionate approach to understanding the extensive grief that continues to occur in Bosnia, an approach that is free of judgment.

Trauma

Grief and trauma have been shown to be distinct from each other, but the vast majority of people in Bosnia have experienced both. Complicated grief appears to be triggered by loss, while the root of trauma is exposure to a life threat.[10]

Bosnia is a country filled with individuals still grieving, which is complicated by the extensive trauma experienced by the majority of the population. Trauma, a deeply distressing or disturbing experience, has many causes, and trauma experienced as a result of war is more complex than most other types. It is multifaceted, multi-layered and cumulative. When looking at grief and trauma, it is sometimes difficult to know which is causing a survivor the most pain.

In listening to people describe their experiences from the war, it is striking how many traumatic events have happened to a single individual. Oftentimes people have experienced so many horrendous events that it is astounding anyone survived with any form of intact mental health. Among other atrocities, people experienced mass destruction, loss of their homes, rampant violation of human rights, persecution, forced migration, starvation, constant shelling, murder of family and friends, mass rape, executions, missing persons and mass graves.

When civil society completely unravels and plunges into the chaos of war, nothing is normal. Cumulative trauma is experienced, sometimes on a daily basis. People in this book experienced one trauma after another. So many shocking things happened that sometimes people forget about significant events. Under typical circumstances, just one of these events could derail a person's mental health for a long time. During a war, however, the traumatic events accumulate to the point that they sometimes blend together. In this book, so many people remember times when they thought they were going to die. This happened not just once, for most people, but on many occasions. Over and over again, they believed that they had reached the end of their lives.

Because of its complexity, it is difficult to assess the impact of war trauma despite the efforts of various institutions. In Bosnia, there were regional variations in the war. Living under siege, which happened to civilians in Sarajevo and Srebrenica, was a primary risk factor for every problematic mental health outcome.[11] The citizens of those two locales were exposed to extremely severe war trauma, especially surviving children and adolescents from Sarajevo and Srebrenica.[12] Young people who have lived through a war often experience post-traumatic stress disorder (PTSD), depression, externalized behaviors and problems in school.[13]

Another factor that can influence the impact of war trauma is knowing the fate of those who were killed or missing. If no identification of remains has been made, families wonder what really happened to their loved ones. They wonder where they are and if there is any possibility that they might still be alive. If just one bone has been identified, it is easy to speculate whether or not this really means that a person is dead. All of this adds another layer to war-related stressors. This is confounded for families whose members were killed as a result of genocide, as there are often multiple relatives murdered or missing. When a loss is unconfirmed, meaning no mortal remains have been identified, it is even more difficult. This can be seen in conversations with those whose loved ones have not been found. Receiving the news that an identification has been made and subsequently being able to bury the family member is an important part of this painful journey. Everyone talks about the importance of identification and the longing for this if it hasn't yet happened. It is possible that living without conclusive evidence is an additional mental health risk factor. For many families, the definitive knowledge about the fate of the missing person as well as the physical return and burial of the mortal remains is of utmost importance.[14] There are many indications that an unconfirmed loss is likely to lead to traumatic or complicated grief.[15]

The healing process for survivors is also affected by whether or not the perpetrators of human rights violations are held accountable and brought to justice. When individual, organizational or state perpetrators are not brought to justice, it makes it more difficult for healing to begin. Not only are people dealing with the trauma of what they experienced or witnessed, they are also forced to deal with the absence of justice. The fact that hundreds if not thousands of war criminals have escaped any sort of prosecution or punishment is not just unfair, it is intolerable. This abominable reality can only impede the healing process for survivors.

People are naturally inclined to believe that an element of fairness should govern social life. The belief that the world is a just place where everyone, at least to some extent, gets what they deserve is called "a belief in a just world."[16] Oftentimes, a perceived lack of fairness can obstruct the healing process. Interestingly, this does not seem to be the case for people in this book. We repeatedly heard that people were able to move forward in spite of this lack of justice. Perhaps this is tied to a firm Islamic belief that justice will be served in the afterlife.

One of the most common mental health outcomes from trauma is post-traumatic stress disorder (PTSD). This disorder was first observed in war veterans and was originally referred to as "shell shock." Shell shock was used to describe soldiers who were "shivering, crying, fearful and had intrusions of memory."[17] PTSD is now understood as a mental health condition that is triggered by either experiencing or witnessing a terrifying event. People who have PTSD may feel stressed or frightened even when they are no longer in danger. It is natural to feel afraid during and after a traumatic situation. Nearly everyone experiences a range of reactions after trauma, yet most people recover from those symptoms with the passage of time. Those who continue to experience problems may be diagnosed with PTSD.

For symptoms to be considered PTSD, they must last more than a month and be severe enough to interfere with everyday life, such as interpersonal relationships or work. The duration varies from person to person. Some people recover within six months, while others have symptoms that last much longer. For others, the condition is ongoing, or chronic.[18]

The National Institute of Mental Health (NIMH) outlines the numerous symptoms of PTSD. Some of these symptoms are familiar to many people in Bosnia and include the following[19]:

- Flashbacks, bad dreams and frightening thoughts;
- Staying away from places, events, or objects that are reminders of the experience;
- Being easily startled, feeling tense or "on edge," having difficulty sleeping, and/or having angry outbursts;
- Trouble remembering key features of the traumatic event;
- Loss of interest in enjoyable activities

There are numerous risk factors for PTSD which include:

- Living through dangerous events and traumas;
- Getting hurt;
- Seeing people hurt or killed

These risk factors are part of the wartime experience of many people in Bosnia and especially for those who survived the genocide in Srebrenica.

Not everyone exposed to traumatic events develops PTSD. Of those who do develop it, there are varying degrees of intensity. There are resilience factors that can help reduce the risk of developing the disorder. These may include:

- Seeking out support from other people, such as friends and family;
- Finding a support group after a traumatic event;
- Learning to feel good about one's own actions in the face of danger;
- Having a coping strategy, or a way of getting through the bad event and learning from it.

Intergenerational Trauma

Trauma does not just impact individuals at one point in time and stop there. There is increasing attention being paid to the way in which trauma impacts future generations. This is referred to as intergenerational or transgenerational trauma. The question then becomes how the experience of human-created trauma suffered by individuals in one generation affects the next generation. A survivor of the Holocaust expresses this concern: "Hitler is dead. Still, he may yet achieve his goal of destroying us if we internalize the hate, mistrust, and pain, all the inhumanity that we were exposed to for so many years."[20] Extensive research on Holocaust survivors and their children has shown:

> that knowledge of psychic trauma weaves through the memories of several generations, making those who know it as secret bearers. Furthermore, ... massive trauma has an amorphous presence not defined by place or time and lacking a beginning, middle, or end, and it shapes the internal representation of reality of several generations, becoming an unconscious organizing principle passed on by parents and internalized by their children.[21]

It is difficult to understand the process by which trauma is transmitted from one generation to the next. To what extent can this phenomenon be attributed to the sharing of stories, being reared by those who have experienced trauma, internalizing their social cues, or feeling responsible for the previous generation? There is some evidence that this process might be a biological one. The field of epigenetics considers the possibility that trauma is passed from generation to generation by actual physiological changes that occur as a result of trauma.[22]

To fully understand the psychological circumstances of those born to people who experienced the trauma of war and genocide firsthand, the likelihood of intergenerational trauma must be considered.

Treatment of Psychological Issues

For treating complicated grief and other psychological problems, Cognitive Behavioral Therapy (CBT) has proven to be effective. This form of psychological treatment focuses on patterns of thought which are unhelpful to the process of recovery or that negatively influence emotions and behaviors.

> Numerous research studies suggest that CBT leads to significant improvement in functioning and quality of life. In many studies, CBT has been demonstrated to be as effective as, or more effective than, other forms of psychological therapy or psychiatric medications.[23]

While CBT has also been used in the treatment of trauma-related problems, another type of therapy has been proven to be the most effective in treating trauma. Eye movement desensitization and reprocessing (EMDR) is a type of psychotherapy developed in the 1990s, during the Bosnian war. "Unlike other treatments that focus on directly altering the emotions, thoughts and responses resulting from traumatic experiences, EMDR therapy focuses directly on the memory, and is intended to change the way that the memory is stored in the brain, thus reducing and eliminating the problematic symptoms."[24] EMDR separates the emotional response from the traumatic memory. The memory remains but the negative feelings and emotions no longer accompany it. EMDR therapy has been proven to be more rapid and/or more effective than trauma-focused cognitive behavioral therapy.[25]

After the war in Bosnia ended, the international psychological community was faced with the challenge of figuring out the best way to help the vast percentage of people who were severely traumatized. The direct experiences of genocide, war crimes and crimes against humanity had dramatic consequences for people living in many parts of the former Yugoslavia, but the most serious and widespread devastation was felt in Bosnia.

Since shortly after the war ended, Dr. Mevludin Hasanović, a psychiatrist currently working in Tuzla, has been a leader in the assessment and treatment of trauma connected to Srebrenica. After the war, he recognized the importance of EMDR in trauma treatment and was instrumental in the training of psychotherapists in this method. Dr. Hasanović is the head of the Association of Bosnia and Herzegovina EMDR Therapists, an organization that is itself a member of EMDR Europe.[26] He and his colleagues continue to provide this beneficial treatment to trauma victims throughout Bosnia.

Fortunately for those in Bosnia who wish to seek therapy for their trauma, there are well-trained therapists who are available to help.

Sexual Violence

Any discussion of wartime trauma must necessarily address the topic of sexual violence. Sexual violence represents a unique form of trauma, and has been used instrumentally in warfare since time immemorial. Crimes such as wartime rape and sexual torture have historically been considered an inevitable part of conflict, and have frequently gone unprosecuted or have been lumped together with other crimes against humanity. During the war in Bosnia, sexual violence was one of the most shocking and widespread practices, and was employed systematically as an instrument of genocide and terror.

It is impossible to know with certainty how many victims, primarily women, were raped during the Bosnian war. In 1993, a European Community Commission estimated there were 20,000 rape victims in the conflict. The Bosnian government put the figure at 50,000.[27] Because of the stigmatization that accompanies sexual violence, it has been difficult for many people to come forward and talk about this traumatic experience and to seek support. This stigmatization is sometimes even more pronounced in instances of sexual victimization of men during conflict, leaving our knowledge of men's experiences of wartime sexual violence even more deficient.

Women, however, are by far the most numerous victims of sexual violence. Furthermore, sexual violence is the means by which women are most commonly targeted. The trauma associated with this kind of violence, both in the course of immediate combat and in non-combat situations, puts women at one of the highest risks of developing PTSD as well as severe problems related to sexual functioning and sexual health.[28]

There were three main types of rape scenarios during the war:

> Women were raped in their own homes, and the word about it spread through their villages. That caused many people to flee in fear that it might happen to them too. The second type of systematic rapes were committed by individuals or small groups during the battles and occupation of territories. This model often included public rapes. The third model was committed by individuals and groups who raped women captured in camps, hotels, and private brothel-camps set up for Serbian soldiers and paramilitary.[29]

Rape occurred throughout Bosnia. Victims often knew their rapists, sometimes even as neighbors, friends, or co-workers before the war. Facilities known as "rape camps," where women were detained and raped systematically over prolonged periods of time, were set up in Foča and elsewhere in Bosnia.[30] The exact number of women and men who were subjected to sexual violence during the Bosnian War is impossible to know. We do know, however, that such practices were used extensively, and that the number of victims therefore was considerable.

The legal definition of a "crime against humanity" includes rape, sexual slavery, enforced prostitution, forced pregnancy, forced sterilization, or any other form of sexual violence of comparable gravity.[31] The formal recognition of rape as a specific crime against humanity by the ICTY was a significant development in international humanitarian law.

> The ICTY took groundbreaking steps to respond to the imperative of prosecuting wartime sexual violence. The Tribunal was among the first courts of its kind to bring explicit charges of wartime sexual violence.
> The ICTY was also the first international criminal court based in Europe to pass convictions for rape as a crime against humanity.... The ICTY proved that effective prosecution of wartime sexual violence is feasible, and provided a platform for the survivors to talk about their suffering.[32]

In 2000, Dragoljub Kunarac, Radomir Kovač and Zoran Vuković were indicted before the ICTY for 33 counts of crimes against humanity and crimes against the laws and customs of war. The three men were accused of widespread and systematic rape of Muslim women at a "rape house" and sports hall in Foča, where women were held captive and raped repeatedly for long periods of time.[33] All three were convicted of these charges, marking the first case where an international war crimes court treated sexual violence alone as a crime against humanity.[34] Dragoljub Kunarac, Unit Commander for the BSA, is currently indicted by the Bosnian State Court for additional war crimes related to sexual violence in Foča.[35]

There have been several resolutions passed by the UN Security Council addressing the use of sexual violence as a tactic during armed conflict. These resolutions are an attempt to dispel the notion that sexual violence is an inevitable part of war. A Security Council resolution was passed in 2008 demanding the "immediate and complete cessation by all parties to armed conflict of all acts of sexual violence against civilians."[36] It is highly unlikely that Security Council resolutions alone will bring about the change that is so desperately needed regarding wartime sexual violence. It is encouraging, however, that the gravity of this issue has been receiving a greater degree of publicity and official attention. In 2009, the Office of the Special Representative of the Secretary-General on Sexual Violence in Conflict (OSRSG-SVC) was established by another Security Council resolution. These resolutions

> signal a change in the way the international community views and deals with conflict-related sexual violence. It is no longer seen as an inevitable byproduct of war, but rather a crime that is preventable and punishable under International Human Rights Law....[37]

In the words of Ms. Zainab Hawa Bangura, UN Special Representative on Sexual Violence in Conflict, "Sexual violence in conflict needs to be treated as the war crime that it is; it can no longer be treated as an unfortunate collateral damage of war."[38] In 2019, the UN Security Council went a step further, adopting a resolution that calls for "warring parties around the globe to implement concrete commitments to fight ... the heinous, barbaric and all-too-often silent phenomenon of sexual violence during conflict."[39]

While the UN is attempting to combat wartime sexual violence at the policy level, there are people and organizations in Bosnia who are working every day to mitigate its effects, by offering much needed services to those who were sexually victimized. These individuals and groups are also advocating for cultural change regarding the stigmatization of sexual violence in Bosnian society. In 1993, an organization called Medica Zenica was founded in the city of Zenica, about an hour northwest of Sarajevo. This NGO promotes justice and support services for survivors of wartime sexual violence in Bosnia, and for the last 18 years has been directed by Sabiha Husić. Sabiha has been recognized worldwide for her work with survivors of wartime sexual violence. In 2014, she received the Woman of the World Award in New York from the women's rights organization Women for Women. She was very generous with her time when I talked with her about the crucial work that is being done by Medica Zenica.

Medica Zenica's website describes their mission and the extensive services that they provide:

> "Medica" Zenica is an expert non-governmental organisation that continuously offers psycho-social and medical support to women and children victims of war and also post war violence, including victims of war rapes and other forms of war torture, sexual violence in general, domestic violence survivors, as well as victims of trafficking in human beings.[40]

Sabiha describes Medica's work as multidisciplinary and culturally sound, with a focus on empowerment, as well as humanistic and feminist principles. In all that they do, the Medica's workers fight to dislodge the stigma faced by survivors of sexual violence. Their team consists of 25 professionals and volunteers, who are dedicated to providing a variety of services for the entire country. These services include a 24-hour hotline, counseling, shelters, and vocational training. Additionally, the staff is involved in research, advocacy and writing. They have formal cooperation arrangements with numerous ministries and institutions throughout Bosnia. They also support an informal network of women who are organizing support groups for sexual violence across Bosnia. Much of their clientele comes to them via word of mouth. As time goes on, more and more women are seeking services from Medica.

Sabiha's research for her Ph.D. showed that many victims of wartime sexual violence choose to share their experiences with their romantic partners. This is an encouraging pattern for those recovering from sexual trauma in what she describes as a patriarchal society. In her research, she also identifies three models for working with survivors of sexual violence. The first model provides support and healing through civil society organizations like Zenica Medica that offer specialized services for the survivors of sexual violence. The second model delineates the role of government institutions in providing access to legal services for the victims of sexual violence who chose to seek justice in court. The final model emphasizes the informal support of friends and relatives which should be tailored to the unique strengths, preferences, and coping mechanisms of each woman individually. Ideally, survivors should have access to all three forms of support.

Medica continues to look for funding and donors to keep the organization operational. A recent donation of 10,000 euros has allowed them to fund safehouses for victims of domestic violence in Bosnia. To date, Medica has established five such safehouses in the Federation and three in Republika Srpska. As the organization branches out to provide services to those experiencing domestic abuse, Sabiha and her team continue to provide much needed assistance to an untold number of women in Bosnia.

Chapter 8

The Responsibility of the International Community

Forty miles from Krakow in Poland sits Auschwitz, the largest of the German Nazi concentration camps and extermination centers. It is, in many ways, the symbol of the Holocaust. Is it conceivable that anyone would be allowed to hang posters in Auschwitz glorifying Adolph Eichmann, the Nazi SS officer who organized Adolf Hitler's "final solution"? Of course not. The international outrage would be enormous.

Why then was there so little outrage when posters celebrating Ratko Mladić were recently plastered in advertising spaces in Srebrenica, the site of the 1995 genocide in Bosnia? An article in *The Sarajevo Times* described the posters which not only featured a color photograph of Mladić but were also printed with the words "There was no genocide" and "Live and be healthy." Mladić is a convicted war criminal.

> The Hague tribunal sentenced Ratko Mladić a former commander of the Republika Srpska Army..., to life imprisonment for the genocide in Srebrenica, of persecuting Muslims and Croats throughout Bosnia-Herzegovina, terrorizing civilians in Sarajevo by long-term shelling and sniping and taking UNPROFOR members hostage in the period from 1991–95.[1]

These posters were put up by a citizen's association called Eastern Alternative and they have made plans to put up the same posters in the neighboring towns of Bratunac and Milići. "The president of this association, Vojin Pavlović, said that in this way they wanted to draw the public's attention that no genocide had been committed in Srebrenica."[2] This is just one example of the numerous ways which Bosnian Serbs glorify war criminals and deny genocide in and around the municipality of Srebrenica. Such displays are only permissible due to the political structure of the Bosnian government, and more specifically, the existence of the Republika Srpska. This is discussed in more detail later in this chapter.

Such outrageous displays are indicative of the failure of justice and reconciliation in Bosnia. The role and responsibility of the international community must be examined in an effort to understand the roadblocks to justice in Bosnia and possible solutions. Looking back to the 1990s, many questions arise about the responsibility of the international community, particularly in three areas—failure to protect, failure to deliver justice and the Dayton Peace Agreement.

Failure to Protect

In the 1990s, the international community failed to prevent genocide in both Rwanda and Bosnia. Following these massacres, the United Nations began to seriously reevaluate the responsibility to protect vulnerable citizens, resulting in an attempt at a definition of "responsibility to protect."

> The responsibility to protect embodies a political commitment to end the worst forms of violence and persecution. It seeks to narrow the gap between Member States' pre-existing obligations under international humanitarian and human rights law and the reality faced by populations at risk of genocide, war crimes, ethnic cleansing and crimes against humanity.[3]

We can argue extensively about when the failure to protect actually started in Bosnia, based on a wide range of legal and humanitarian criteria. Most would agree, however, that by the time tens of thousands of people ended up as refugees in Srebrenica the need for protection was long overdue. By early 1993, the situation in Srebrenica had become increasingly intolerable. Those who were living there during that time, however, recall having a reason to be hopeful in March of that year. That was when Phillippe Morillon, the UN Commander for Bosnia, made his famous pronouncement to the thousands of refugees living in impossible conditions in Srebrenica. He climbed to the top of the post office, opened the window and through a megaphone declared, "You are now under the protection of the United Nation forces. I will never abandon you."[4] This was one of the first official efforts to protect the most vulnerable people in Bosnia.

Today, walking down the road from the town of Srebrenica toward Potočari you pass this same building on your left, which still serves as the town's post office This is the same place where the amateur radio broadcasters were housed in July 1995. Nino Ćatić issued his final broadcast from this building. Across from the post office is the hospital where Fatima worked during the war. It is still the hospital for Srebrenica today. Standing there now, in between these two buildings, it is hard to imagine what it must have been like in March of 1993, with thousands of people gathered there, desperate and waiting.

Hasan Aziz Hasanović doesn't need to imagine because he was there when Morillon made his announcement. Hasan went to the post office with his friends because they had heard that Morillon was coming and they wanted to see what was going to happen. They waited outside in the huge crowd for a couple of hours while negotiations went on inside the building. Hasan remembers sitting under a tree with his friends, waiting. Morillon tried to leave when a throng of women surrounded him, blocking his path. He got on top of an APC and tried to calm the worried crowd, eventually telling them that he had decided not to leave Srebrenica. He went inside the post office and later that day he went up to the second floor, opened the window, and through a megaphone made his historical promise. Tremendous emotion came over the crowd. Everybody was applauding, cheering, crying, and screaming. The video of Morillon climbing on top of an APC and assuring the crowd that he wouldn't leave is striking[5]. Other noteworthy footage shows him speaking through a megaphone from the top floor of the post office when he made his fateful promise to protect the people of Srebrenica.[6]

Not surprisingly, people in Srebrenica again became hopeful because they were officially going to be under the protection of the UN. They heard it directly from the General Philippe Morillon who was charismatic and powerful. They believed him. Morillon made his famous announcement on March 12 and exactly one month later, on April 12, the playground massacre occurred. Several people in this book have described that massacre in great detail. This event was so horrendous that it caught the attention of the international community. On April 16, the UN Security Council passed Resolution 819 declaring Srebrenica a UN Safe Area. The Resolution spells out the specifics of what it means to be a Safe Area, including a demand that "all parties and others concerned treat Srebrenica and its surroundings as a Safe Area which should be free from any armed attack or any other hostile act as well as a demand that allows the unimpeded delivery of humanitarian assistance to all parts of the Republic of Bosnia and Herzegovina."[7] Three weeks later, five more safe areas were designated in Bihać, Goražde, Sarajevo, Tuzla, and Žepa.

Author Michael Dobbs discusses the dangers of what he calls a "feel good response" to mass atrocity, of which Srebrenica is a prime example:

> By a feel good response, I mean action that is designed to look good in the eyes of international public opinion but fails to do anything really effective to protect a threatened population. A feel good response can often wind up making a tragic situation even worse—as was the case in Srebrenica. Examples of such empty moralism abound—from Bosnia to Rwanda to Darfur to Syria.[8]

Days after the passage of the resolution, a Canadian battalion of UN Peacekeepers arrived. They negotiated a ceasefire agreement which included the demilitarization of Srebrenica's Bosniak defenders, who were asked to turn in all of their weapons. Widespread compliance with this measure demonstrates the level of trust people placed in the UN. Living in a UN Safe Area, in the presence of international Peacekeepers, they thought they would be protected, and gave up their arms. As Hasan puts it, "We needed protection, we thought we had protection, and it failed."

About a year later, Hasan remembers walking with a friend near the UN base, which by that time was occupied by Dutch Peacekeepers. His friend told Hasan that his father heard about a genocide happening somewhere in Africa and that the UN had run away. Hasan's friend said that he was afraid the same thing would happen in Srebrenica. They later learned that the African country was Rwanda.

As has been described by everyone in this book who survived the genocide, the mission to protect turned into a failure to protect. In May of 1992, Bosnia became a member of the UN. Therefore, when the country was attacked internally and externally by Serb forces, the UN and the international community had an obligation to protect the territorial integrity and sovereignty of the country. They failed to do so.

Serbian and Bosnian Serb forces carried out an organized military operation intended to exterminate the Muslim population of eastern Bosnia. The genocide in Srebrenica was the culmination of a campaign which included persecution, massacre, systematic rape, destruction of property and destruction of cultural and religious heritage. The international community did nothing to prevent this tragedy.

In April 1993, the UN promised to protect the inhabitants of the Srebrenica, Žepa and Goražde enclaves. With the official designation of a UN Safe Area, people in Srebrenica believed that they were under UN protection and would certainly survive the war. When the BSA overran Srebrenica in July 1995, however, the Dutch UN battalion offered no resistance.

Numerous questions about the failure to protect may never be answered. Various individuals and institutions have attempted to blame one another for failing to prevent genocide in Srebrenica, however, the bottom line is that the international community failed.

Questions which need to be answered in order to establish responsibility for the failure of the international community in Srebrenica include:

> Why did the central command of the UN not respond to the situation in Srebrenica?

Why did the Dutch battalion not allow more, if not all refugees into the base?
What could have been done to stop the killing outside of the base?
What could have been done to stop the separation of the men and boys from women and children?
Thousands of refugees were expelled from inside the UN base on July 13, and handed over to the Bosnian Serbs. By that time, it was clear that men and boys were being killed. What could have been done to prevent this expulsion from inside the base?

Almost 8,000 men and boys were held prisoner after the fall of Srebrenica while the international community made no attempt to rescue them. On July 12 and 13, 1995, several refugees died of natural causes inside the UN base. The Dutch battalion buried them on the grounds of the base in a mass grave and kept the location a secret for 17 years. The grave was found in July 2012, after the details of the location were provided by a former Dutch soldier who had attended the burial in 1995. Ban Ki-moon was the first UN Secretary-General to visit the scene when he went to Potočari in July 2012. In August of that year, five people were exhumed from the grave, including a newborn baby.[9]

Who is to blame for the Srebrenica genocide? The UN High command? The UN Peacekeepers on the ground? The Dutch state? The leadership of the Bosnian Serb Army? The Milošević regime in Serbia? The international community in general?

> Srebrenica has haunted the Dutch political and military establishment. In 2002, as a result of an explosive report written by the Netherlands Institute for War Documentation, the Dutch Government even stepped down, with the Prime Minister acknowledging a modicum of responsibility, although not culpability, for Dutchbat's failures. Subsequently, victims initiated legal proceedings before the Dutch courts against the Netherlands and the United Nations[10]

The Mothers of Srebrenica, led by Munira Subašić, filed a civil suit against the Dutch state. They represented families of the approximately 350 men and boys who were expelled from inside the Dutch base on July 13, 1995, all of whom were subsequently executed by the BSA. In 2014, a Dutch court held the state liable for compensation. In 2017, the appeals court upheld that decision ruling that the Muslims were "denied a 30% chance of avoiding abuse and execution," therefore making the Dutch state liable for "30% of damages owed to families."[11] The case was then referred to the supreme court.

In July 2019, the Dutch supreme court reduced the state's liability to 10 percent, saying that peacekeepers had only a "slim" chance of preventing the deaths of hundreds of Muslim men. The ruling stated:

> The Dutch state bears very limited liability. That liability is limited to 10% of the damages suffered by the surviving relatives of approximately 350 victims. The state did act wrongfully in relation to the evacuation of the 5,000 refugees in the compound, including 350 Muslim men the Bosnian Serbs were unaware of.
> [The Dutch Peacekeepers] failed to offer these 350 male refugees the choice to stay where they were, even though that would have been possible. The chance that the male refugees would have escaped the Bosnian Serbs had they been given the choice to stay was slim, but not negligible.
> In a swipe at the failure of other foreign powers to act, the top court added that the "chance of Dutchbat [the Dutch UN mission] receiving effective support from the international community was slim."[12]

In December of 2001, a 10-member French parliamentary commission conceded that France "carries part of the blame" for the 1995 massacre at Srebrenica. The commission concluded that "French General Bernard Janvier, commander of UNPROFOR forces for former Yugoslavia at the time, was too hesitant about ordering air strikes against Bosnian Serb troops, a move which they said might have prevented the massacre." General Janvier took exception to the findings of the commission in his testimony: "If there had been 400 Frenchmen in Srebrenica it would have been different. We would have fought. The Dutch were ordered to fight. When you get such an order it is your duty to fight...?" One of the report's fundamental conclusions was:

> There was no strong political will to intervene in Srebrenica, not by the French, not the British, nor the Americans, but not even by the Bosnian authorities in Sarajevo.[13]

The United Nations itself cannot be sued. The treaty that governs the immunity of the United Nations is quite sweeping and stipulates specifically that the United Nations "shall enjoy immunity from every form of legal process...."[14] Nonetheless, the United Nations has taken some responsibility for the Srebrenica genocide.

The walls inside the former Dutch base were covered with graffiti, all interesting in one way or another. Several parts of that graffiti have been preserved and are now part of the Memorial. One interesting piece consists of large black letters that say "UN = United Nothing."

Over the years the UN itself has made statements of regret about Srebrenica. These statements are typically made on anniversary years of the genocide. On the tenth anniversary of the genocide, UN Secretary-General Kofi Annan delivered the following message.

> We can say—and it is true—that great nations failed to respond adequately.
> We can say—and it is also true—that there should have been stronger military forces in place, and a stronger will to use them.
> We can say—and it is undeniable—that blame lies, first and foremost, with those who planned and carried out the massacre, or who assisted them, or who harbored and are harboring them still.
> But we cannot evade our own share of responsibility.
> As I wrote in my report in 1999, we made serious errors of judgement, rooted in a philosophy of impartiality and non-violence which, however admirable, was unsuited to the conflict in Bosnia. That is why, as I also wrote, "the tragedy of Srebrenica will haunt our history forever."
> Without justice, there can be no reconciliation, and no peace for the families of the victims, or for society as a whole.[15]

On the 20th anniversary of the Srebrenica genocide, Mr. Al Hussein, United Nations High Commissioner for Human Rights spoke, saying in part: "The United Nations made the mistake of believing what was complicated politically must also be complicated morally, when it was not. That all sides committed crimes was true, but that did not mean all sides were equally *guilty*."[16] At the time of the 20th anniversary, the UN Security Council failed to adopt a resolution which would have formally recognized the 1995 events in Srebrenica as genocide. At the request of the Serbian government, Russia voted against the resolution. Following the veto, those who had supported the resolution expressed their outrage. Mr. Hussein spoke again, calling for unity to counter such crimes as genocide, saying: "When we are running out of words in our outrage, we have to take action and live up to basic values and principles."[17]

Samantha Power, U.S. member of the National Security Council who later became the U.S. Ambassador to the U.N., expressed her displeasure after the resolution failed to pass. She had been a war correspondent in Bosnia and had been to Srebrenica.

> "This was a singular horror. It was genocide," she stressed, noting that it was a fact reiterated by subsequent forums. "Russia's veto was heart-breaking for the victims' families and represented another stain on the Council." She compared deniers of genocide at Srebrenica to Holocaust deniers, as the refusal

to recognize such crimes not only hurt victims, but also reconciliation itself. "So long as the truth is denied, there can be no meaningful reconciliation," she added, reiterating that Russia's veto was a denial of the genocide.[18]

It is worth noting that after the veto, Bosnian Serbs in and around Srebrenica demonstrated their profound gratitude for Putin by putting up posters of the Russian president all around Srebrenica—on windows, trees, kiosks, and advertising boards.

In December of 2014, members of British Parliament visited the Memorial, led by Colonel Bob Stewart, former Deputy Commander of UN forces in Bosnia under Philippe Morillon. Colonel Stewart was welcomed by Hatidža Mehmedović,[19] President of the Mothers of Srebrenica association. She commented that visits such as Colonel Stewart's "mean a lot to the victims, and that all well-intentioned people who fight for justice and truth are welcome to Potočari."[20]

This was in direct contrast to when Philippe Morillon visited Potočari in 2010. The Mothers forced him to leave, expressing anger that he had not fulfilled his wartime promise to never abandon Srebrenica. On that occasion, Hatidža said, "He did not have the right to enter the cemetery where our children were buried thanks to him."[21]

During his visit to the Memorial in 2014, Colonel Stewart recounted his time in Srebrenica in April 1993. His British contingent of UNPROFOR soldiers began transferring people from Srebrenica to Tuzla using helicopters and trucks. He estimates that they transferred 2,000 people before he was ordered to withdraw. He said, "I came to Srebrenica today to remember the people that we should have saved. We should have saved them all and it is the responsibility of the international community. This is a big mistake and a stain on the conscience of the international community."[22]

In the years following the genocide, many have scrutinized the role of the international community and the UN Peacekeepers in an effort to understand what exactly went wrong.

> We must examine the responsibility borne by the United States and other western governments for Srebrenica. While it is clear that primary responsibility for the worst massacre in Europe since World War II lies with the perpetrators, the international community must also bear a share of the blame through its inaction and fecklessness in declaring a "safe area" it was unable, or unwilling, to protect.[23]

Rwanda in 1994 and Srebrenica in 1995 became symbols of the failure of the international community to prevent or stop the most horrific atrocities committed against civilians. In light of these two failures, the UN has taken a critical look at its peacekeeping capacity as well as its "responsibility to protect."

> The UN undertook the development of the doctrine of a "Responsibility to Protect" (R2P) incumbent on the international community to protect vulnerable populations against genocide, war crimes, ethnic cleansing and crimes against humanity. The peacekeeping missions stopped being just passive forces interposed between parties to a conflict; instead, almost all of them were endowed with a primary mandate to protect civilians.[24]

Whether the development of the R2P doctrine or the redefinition of peacekeeping missions have changed the way in which UN Peacekeepers respond to vulnerable populations at risk for crimes against humanity, ethnic cleansing or genocide is a matter of debate.

Individuals have been found guilty of war crimes and genocide. Ironically, only Serbia has escaped responsibility. Efforts have been made to hold Serbia responsible both directly and indirectly, by proving that they were part of a joint criminal enterprise. All attempts have been unsuccessful. This is discussed in detail in Chapter 5 of this book.

In the aftermath of war and genocide, the issue of justice remains at the forefront of Bosnian society. Any discussion of the international community's role and responsibility in post-war Bosnia must take into account the country's current political structure.

Dayton Peace Agreement

Americans often expect non–Americans to know about cities like New York, Washington, D.C., or Los Angeles. The citizens of Bosnia, however, know about Dayton, Ohio. This is because it was in Dayton, Ohio, that the end to the Bosnian War was negotiated.

The General Framework Agreement for Peace in Bosnia and Herzegovina, also known as the Dayton Peace Agreement (DPA), Dayton Accords, Paris Protocol or Dayton-Paris Agreement, is the peace agreement reached at Wright-Patterson Air Force Base near Dayton, Ohio, United States, in November 1995 and formally signed in Paris on December 14, 1995.[25]

The U.S. State Department chose Wright-Patterson as the place to negotiate the agreement for a number of reasons. The facilities were well-suited for the purpose, it was far enough away from any major American metropolis and the weather in November is often unappealing. They wanted to minimize distractions. The overarching objective was to reach an agreement as quickly as possible. Delegations from Bosnia, Croatia and Serbia all participated in the negotiations, and the agreement was ultimately signed in Paris by the presidents of each country: Alija Izetbegović from Bosnia, Franjo Tudjman from Croatia and Slobodan Milošević from Serbia.

The Dayton Peace Agreement successfully accomplished its most urgent objective; it stopped the war. This was also the deal that divided the country between two entities: the Federation (with 51 percent of the territory and a predominately Bosniak and Croat population) and the Republika Srpska (with 49 percent of the territory and primarily Bosnian Serb inhabitants). It also provided for the district of Brčko in northeast Bosnia, a multi-ethnic self-governing area that geographically splits the RS in half. By dividing the country in this way, the agreement institutionalized the ethnic divides within Bosnia. It also, according to many, rewarded the Bosnian Serbs for their genocidal campaign. At the time of the 20th anniversary of the genocide, British journalist Julian Borger wrote:

> Dayton was not just supposed to stop the killing. It was meant to heal the wounds of ethnic division. Yet, two decades on, the country remains as rigidly divided as ever, between a Serb half, the Republika Srpska and a Federation of Bosniaks and Croats. "Its name has come to encapsulate Bosnia's purgatory: life in the absence of war, but never quite at peace. And a long way from happiness or normality."[26]

The Dayton Agreement became the operating Bosnian constitution; however, it was only intended to be in place temporarily. The expectation was that the country would eventually develop and ratify its own constitution to replace the Dayton Agreement. Twenty-five years later, this has yet to happen. The government of Bosnia today, described by some as the most complicated on earth, continues to be paralyzed by ethnic divisions and insurmountable bureaucracy.

The central government is comprised of a tripartite presidency, meaning that there are three presidents active at the same time. One is a Bosniak, one is a Croat and one is a Serb. It also has a full cabinet and parliament. As has been stated, Bosnia is one country comprised of two entities: the Federation and the Republika Srpska. Each entity has its own president and prime minister as well as a full cabinet and parliament. The entities have significant autonomy. Their parliaments have jurisdiction over healthcare, education, agriculture, veterans' issues, labor, police, and internal affairs. The Federation is further divided into ten cantons, each with its own administrative government and relative autonomy on local issues such as education and health care.[27] Compared to the entities, the federal government is relatively weak.

Within the country there are five presidents, three at the federal level and two at the entity level. There are also 150 political parties. Radio Free Europe produced a video explaining the governmental structure of Bosnia.[28] Additionally, TRT World produced a video explaining what it takes to vote in the complicated governmental structure of Bosnia.[29] Both videos do an excellent job of quickly explaining this almost inexplicably complex government.

The degree of autonomy enjoyed by the entities allows them to function almost independently in many domains. This explains why genocide denial persists unabated in the RS, and why the public celebration of war criminals has been able to become common practice. While the RS is primarily populated with Bosnian Serbs, there are still villages and municipalities where Muslims live and sometimes even constitute the majority. Ironically, Srebrenica lies within the borders of the RS, and is therefore governed by those who espouse the ideology of Greater Serbia and extol the legacy of Milošević. This creates an extremely uncomfortable situation for those whose family members were victims of genocide, or who were hunted themselves by Bosnian Serbs in 1995. Not only do Bosnian Serbs monopolize entity politics, they also control the judiciary, the educational system, and the local police. The RS police, among others, were found responsible by the ICTY and the ICJ for the genocide committed in Srebrenica.[30] After these rulings, however, the police force was not abolished. It still exists, with some of the same officers that were part of the organization in 1995.

Discussion of the inherent problems in the existence of the RS has been ongoing for quite some time. In January of this year, an international conference was held in Sarajevo entitled "Legal and Political Violence—Implications of the Declaration on the January 9, 1992, Proclamation of the Republic of the Serbian People of Bosnia and Herzegovina." This conference focused on the illegality of the RS, its solidification under the Dayton Peace Agreement, and the ramifications of its current existence. As an institution, the RS has been called the greatest reward for genocide in human history. At the time of the 20th anniversary of the genocide, Borger wrote:

> Moreover, the near-equal division of Bosnia between the two principal parties, reasonably close to the ceasefire lines agreed in October, had the ring of fairness about it. It seemed fair however only in a moral and historical vacuum. The halving of Bosnia had been created by "ethnic cleansing" through mass killings and deportation.
>
> They hacked Republika Srpska out of Bosnia through repeated atrocities such as the concentration camps established in 1992 around the western town of Prijedor, where more than 3,000 people were killed, and the slaughter of 8,000 men and boys from the Muslim enclave of Srebrenica in July 1995, just four months before Dayton.
>
> The territorial gains made through such methods were carved in stone at Dayton, while Republika Srpska was given international recognition.[31]

There is agreement among many that the Dayton Peace Agreement needs to be revisited and a new constitution put into place. The question, however, is who is responsible for reforming the constitution? The international community or policy makers in Bosnia? There is one office in Bosnia that has the potential for addressing this issue. It was established by the Dayton Peace Agreement and is called the Office of the High Representative (OHR), administered by the High Representative (HR). The HR is appointed by the UN Security Council and is always a member of the international community. The OHR's mandate has a number of sections,[32] however, its overarching role is to ensure that the Dayton Peace Agreement is being followed by those in power. The HR has an important tool at their disposal called the Bonn Powers. The Bonn Powers enable the HR to "remove from office public officials who violate legal commitments and the Dayton Peace Agreement."[33]

Each HR has their own style and interprets the role of the OHR differently. The most active HR was Paddy Ashdown, who held the position between 2002 and 2006.

> Taking over the role after Sweden's Carl Bildt, Carlos Westendorp of Spain and Austria's Wolfgang Petritsch, Ashdown quickly built a reputation as a no-nonsense implementor of tough measures to help the country recover from its 1992–1995 war.
>
> During his mandate, Ashdown sacked corrupt officials and Bosnia completed some painful reforms aimed at strengthening central institutions at the expense of the two post-war entities—the Serbs' Republika Srpska and the Muslim-Croat Federation.
>
> They notably included defense reforms aimed at merging two ethnically-divided armies into one, as well as police force and customs and tax reforms.[34]

Failure to Deliver Justice

Following World War II, the international community reached a unanimous consensus about who the aggressors were in the conflict, and initiated international criminal proceedings accordingly. Trials were held in Nuremberg culminating in the conviction of a number of senior Nazi officials for crimes related to the Holocaust. In later years, Nazi symbols and paraphernalia were outlawed, statues and other public symbols were destroyed, and it became illegal to deny the Holocaust or to glorify war criminals.

Would justice have been served if the Nazis were given 49 percent of Germany as their own territory, governed by their own president, in addition to their own federal executive office possessing one third of the presidential authority of the entire country? Once again, the answer to this question is a resounding no. If, instead of being rooted out in the wake of the Holocaust, Nazis had been given copious political representation in the German government and their own allotment of land on which to glorify war criminals, deny genocide, and champion Nazi ideology, today's Germany would be a vastly different place. As preposterous as this scenario may seem, it is exactly what happened after the Bosnian War, with the Dayton Peace Agreement. This was the beginning of the failure of the international community to deliver justice to post-war Bosnia.

While the trials and convictions carried out by the ICTY did successfully achieve a degree of justice for victims of the war and genocide, its long-term legacy is decidedly mixed. Milošević, Mladić and Karadžić were all indicted by the ICTY. Although Milošević died during the course of his trial, both Mladić and Karadžić were tried, found guilty of all but one charge, and ultimately sentenced to life in prison. Several other high-profile members of the Bosnian Serb army were also tried and convicted in international court. There are, however, thousands of others who participated in war crimes in Bosnia who will never be brought to justice. More alarmingly still, many of these individuals have since been promoted to positions of prominence in government, military, law enforcement, and civil society structures. This unthinkable situation lends itself to a number of further injustices. Bosniak citizens who have returned to Srebrenica, for example, find themselves largely at the mercy of Bosnian Serbs, who occupy positions of power not only in politics, but in institutions like healthcare and education. In some cases, these individuals were directly involved in the 1995 genocide.

One of the more ironic outcomes of the establishment of the RS is that Srebrenica, the site of the genocide, is located in the RS entity, as are many other villages and regions that were also subjected to ethnic cleansing and other atrocities.

Genocide denial is rampant in the RS, and is reinforced at the national level by the Serb member of the Bosnian presidency. For many fighting against this wave of illegitimate historical revision, it can seem unstoppable, progressing with ever greater frequency and daring. The unofficial "11th stage of genocide"—the glorification of war criminals—is one of the most conspicuous outgrowths. Statues and monuments are erected in honor of Milošević, Mladić, and Karadžić, streets are named after them, and a dormitory at a public university was recently named after Karadžić. These instances only embolden those who deny the Srebrenica genocide, giving them the impression that they have won.

With this atmosphere of denial so deeply embedded in the fabric of nearly half of the country, it is easy to see why efforts toward transitional justice or reconciliation have yielded so little success. How can success possibly be achieved when the perpetrators of justice persist in denying the experiences of genocide victims, and the victims of genocide still struggle to make their voices heard and to seek justice for themselves and their loved ones?

Public school curriculum is just one more indication of the failure to deliver justice in Bosnian society. With no department of education operating at the state level, entities have free reign to create their own historical curriculum. For this reason, the judicially established facts of the Srebrenica genocide are omitted entirely in classrooms across the RS. Even in Srebrenica itself, students are frequently taught that the 1995 genocide never took place.

In the absence of a standardized, factual curriculum in public schools, war criminals replace teachers and children are left with ideology in the place of actual history. The narratives which they are taught by their parents and religious and ethnic community leaders glorify war criminals, and in this way ensure that the ethnic divisions in Bosnian society are passed on to the younger generation. In some communities, there is a phenomenon called "two schools under one roof," which is just as precarious a situation as it sounds. One group of students attends school in the morning and the other in the afternoon, or a building is divided into wings, segregating students along ethnic lines for instruction in subjects like history and language. Although there are very few differences between the languages known as Bosnian, Serbian, and Croatian, for political reasons, these languages are taught separately.

The only people who benefit from a divided state are those who are currently in power. For them, division is financially as well as politically lucrative. Nationalist leaders stay in power by resorting to fear tactics and propaganda, especially during election season, when campaign tactics bear a particular resemblance to those used prior to and during the war. Those in power continue to benefit from keeping their own constituents afraid of and hostile to ethnic and religious "others."

In addition to continued calls for the Dayton Agreement to be replaced, there is an ongoing effort to enact legislation which criminalizes genocide denial. Pressure to do so comes from within Bosnia itself, as well as externally from the international community.

Anti-denial laws have been proposed many times, but are always voted down by Bosnian Serb members of the parliament and are never supported by the Bosnian Serb member of the presidency. High Representative Valentin Inzko has stated that he is considering enacting a law himself, with the authority afforded him by the Bonn Powers, if proposed legislation continues to fail in the parliament. He reports that there is wider support for this application of the Bonn Powers than ever before. The OHR is working on a law banning genocide denial in preparation for the upcoming 25th anniversary of the Srebrenica genocide. According to HR Inzko in December 2019,

> Some things which are not tolerable anymore are taking place. The climate in the Peace Implementation Council (PIC), a body made up of foreign ambassadors and heads of international organizations overseeing the peace process in Bosnia, is changing. I never had support for using the Bonn powers to this extent before.
>
> My people in the legal department are working on some elements of that law on banning genocide denial. I think that this is a cultural, moral and ethical imperative and if this would be done, Bosnia and Herzegovina would then be as other countries which punish those who deny the Holocaust.[35]

It is encouraging that the HR is speaking publicly about the need for a law banning genocide denial in Bosnia, as well as expressing his willingness to use the Bonn Powers to this end if necessary. The criminalization of genocide denial is an important step on the road to reconciliation in Bosnia, along with constitutional reform and finding a sustainable alternative framework to the Dayton Peace Agreement. These initiatives, while no doubt slow and onerous, are essential to the country's post-war political and economic development. Justice and reconciliation cannot be achieved while genocide denial is allowed to fester, much less prosper. The key to lasting peace and stability in Bosnia, therefore, lies in pursuit of these objectives. Only after these objectives are achieved can reconciliation begin in earnest.

Chapter 9

Lessons Learned

The story of the Srebrenica genocide is one of enormous complexity. It is impossible to recount this story in its entirety or in enough detail to do justice to the horror and diversity of its victims' experiences. The dynamics leading up to the genocide were the same as in other instances of genocide which came before it, those which unfolded simultaneously (in the case of Rwanda), and those which would come after. There was no shortage of warning signs in Bosnia that genocide was imminent. Thanks to the work of Dr. Gregory Stanton, it is now accepted that genocide unfolds in the course of ten predictable stages.[1] These stages are not always linear or sequential, and several may be observed to be ongoing at the same time. Regardless of the order in which these stages manifest, genocide never happens unexpectedly. There is always an abundance of warning signs present before any actual violence begins taking place. One of the most important lessons to be learned from the tragedy of Srebrenica is that we must be paying attention.

Nationalism

Nationalism is one of the first and primary ingredients for the complete unraveling of civil society which is necessary in order to commit genocide. Often sold as and confused with patriotism, nationalism is distinguished by a number of important factors. Similar to patriotism, or the love of one's country, nationalism is a concept in which groups of people experience a similar pride in shared culture, language, history, ethnicity or borders as members of a nation-state. However, unlike patriotism, nationalism entails the idea of in-group supremacy, in which the collective needs and ambitions of one group exceed all others.[2] In the words of one author, "Patriotism simply entails a sense of pride for one's own national group, while nationalism encourages an orientation involving liking for one's own group and disliking of certain other groups."[3]

There appears to be a rise in nationalism around the globe. This is evidenced in the rise and election of nationalist leaders and political parties, as well as by the increase in nationalist rhetoric and racially motivated violence. There are several types of nationalism and all forms do not always lead to violence. Typically, however, the supremacist nature of nationalist ideology lends itself to the perpetration of violence. One common theme present in violent nationalism is "a national discourse that brands a minority group in the state as enemies of the nation."[4] Pride and love for one's country is not intrinsically harmful, but when these emotions become exclusionary, that is, predicated on the degradation and demonization of others, the potential for violence and abuse is unmistakable. Nationalism can be a motivating factor for individual as well as group behavior.

Ethnic or religious motivated violence can be carried out by lone individuals acting under the influence of nationalist ideologies, or by hate groups pushing nationalist agendas to divide or stratify society. These hate groups often use language intended to convey that they are acting with their country's best interests in mind, and in this way violent supremacy can masquerade as patriotism. "For all their 'patriotic' rhetoric, hate groups and their imitators are really trying to divide us; their views are fundamentally anti-democratic and need to be exposed and countered."[5] White nationalism is a dangerous ideology. Between 2011 and 2017, it was the motivating force behind nearly 350 terrorist attacks worldwide.[6] White nationalist groups promote white supremacist dogmas, often focusing on the alleged inferiority of nonwhites.

In March 2019, Christchurch, New Zealand, was home to a horrific mass murder of Muslim worshippers. More than 50 people were killed and the same number were wounded.[7] The event was shocking because of its scope and location. What isn't widely known is that there was a connection between the Australian perpetrator of this massacre and Bosnia. Prior to the shooting, the gunman posted a video on Twitter showing him driving and playing a song honoring convicted war criminal Radovan Karadžić. "The song … is known as 'God is a Serb and he will protect us' from a propaganda music video produced by three Bosnian Serb soldiers, which warns 'Turks' (Bosnian Muslims) that the Serbs were coming, led by Karadžić…. The song has evolved into a meme known as 'Remove Kebab,' a euphemism for ethnic cleansing against Muslims." Several things were written on the gunman's rifle including *"Kebab removed"* which was in reference to this anti–Muslim song.

> In his 74-page manifesto published on line before the attack he wrote that the motive for his attack was to "create fear" and called for killings of Muslims. According to Balkan Insight, "Serb nationalists enjoy cult status among many far-right groups in Europe where they are admired for their militancy, extreme Islamophobia and—most importantly—for having put words into action in the 1990s, when Serb nationalist paramilitaries killed thousands of Muslims in Bosnia and Kosovo."[8]

Propaganda is the most effective tool of extreme nationalism. In this context, it is used in conjunction with hate speech and is intended to demonize the "others."

During the trial of Slobodan Milošević, a 97-page expert report examining Serbian propaganda tactics during the Balkan wars was filed. It accused Milošević of "launching a ferocious media campaign to help him achieve his nationalist goals. Without the media, and especially without television, war in the former Yugoslavia is inconceivable."[9] The report goes on to say that Milošević's propaganda campaign was based on the same techniques that had been used by Hitler, with the additional reach and power of television. It is estimated that official Serbian propaganda reached more than 3.5 million people across the former Yugoslavia every night.[10]

Hate Groups

Hate groups exist around the globe. In 2018, the Southern Poverty Law Center (SPLC) identified 1,020 active hate groups operating in the United States, a record number and a 30 percent increase over the past four years. These hate groups are organized by ideology, with Neo-Nazi's accounting for the largest membership in these groups, followed by Anti-Muslims and White Nationalists.[11]

The SPLC defines a hate group as:

an organization that—based on its official statements or principles, the statements of its leaders, or its activities—has beliefs or practices that attack or malign an entire class of people, typically for their immutable characteristics ... race, religion, ethnicity, sexual orientation or gender identity—prejudices that strike at the heart of our democratic values and fracture society along its most fragile fault lines.[12]

The FBI uses similar criteria in its definition of a hate crime: "A criminal offense against a person or property motivated in whole or in part by an offender's bias against a race, religion, disability, sexual orientation, ethnicity, gender, or gender identity."[13]

Hate groups deliberately induce fear and hatred of minorities in their communities. They capitalize on civil unrest, particularly when triggered by hate crimes or social injustice, to further their racist ideologies. Where state institutions are not prepared to handle, or worse, are sympathetic to, these forces, the resurgence of nationalism and a proliferation of hate groups increases the likelihood of mass human rights violations and even genocide.

Genocide: Theory and Prevention

The model proposed by Dr. Gregory Stanton, president of Genocide Watch, has become widely accepted by genocide scholars as the key to understanding how genocide unfolds. In this model, Stanton describes genocide as occurring in ten stages: Classification, Symbolization, Discrimination, Dehumanization, Organization, Polarization, Preparation, Persecution, Extermination, and Denial.[14]

These stages might or might not unfold in order, but might appear simultaneously or even in a different sequence. Most importantly, we must not think of this process as inevitable. At each stage, there are preventative measures which can be used to halt the progression to genocide. By understanding these phases of genocide, we can better hope to identify at-risk societies, and prevent genocide in the future. For this reason, a brief description of the stages follows.

   1. CLASSIFICATION: People are distinguished into "us and them" by ethnicity, race, religion, or nationality. The main preventive measure at this early stage is to actively promote tolerance and understanding. Prior to the war in the 1990s, people in all of the republics of Yugoslavia lived in relative harmony in spite of differences.
   2. SYMBOLIZATION: Names or other symbols are given to the classifications of people. This does not necessarily result in genocide unless it combines with hatred and leads to dehumanization. To combat symbolization, hate symbols and hate speech can be legally forbidden.
   3. DISCRIMINATION: A dominant group denies the rights of others through laws or political power. To combat this, discrimination on the basis of nationality, ethnicity, race or religion should be outlawed.
   4. DEHUMANIZATION: One group denies the humanity of the other group. Members are likened to animals, vermin, insects or diseases. Dehumanization overcomes the normal human revulsion against murder. Propaganda in print, on hate radio, or social media is used to vilify the victim group. To combat dehumanization, incitement to genocide should not be confused with protected speech. Dehumanizing language was used extensively by the Milošević regime. It is now unfortunately being used with increasing frequency and viciousness by current administrations in the United States and Europe, targeting Muslims and immigrants, among others.

5. ORGANIZATION: Genocide is always organized, usually by the state, often using militias to provide deniability of state responsibility. To combat this stage, membership in nationalistic or paramilitary organizations should be outlawed.

6. POLARIZATION: Extremists drive groups apart. Hate groups broadcast polarizing propaganda and employ mass media for indoctrination. Leaders in targeted groups are arrested and murdered. Prevention may mean security protection for moderate leaders or assistance to human rights groups. Assets of extremists may be seized, and visas for international travel denied to them.

7. PREPARATION: Plans are made for genocidal killings. Euphemisms are often used such as "ethnic cleansing," "purification," or "counter-terrorism." Prevention should include prosecution of incitement and conspiracy to commit genocide, both of which are crimes. Prevention at this stage may include enforced arms embargos but only if they impact the perpetrators, not the victims. The term ethnic cleansing was and continues to be used extensively to describe and minimize the genocidal operation in Bosnia during the 1990s. The international arms embargo against the former Yugoslavia only advantaged the Serbian and Bosnian Serb forces, who had access to all of the fire power of the Yugoslav National Army.

The following stages were particularly catastrophic for Bosnia. Serb forces used virtually all of the available means of annihilation, and few preventative measures were deployed by those in a position to stop the violence.

8. PERSECUTION: Victims are singled out and persecuted based on ethnic or religious identity. Members of victim groups may be forced to formally register, or wear identifying symbols. Property is often stolen. Sometimes victims are segregated into ghettoes, deported to concentration camps, or confined to a region where they are targeted in order to starve or kill them off slowly. Killings, torture and forced displacement amplify. Genocidal massacres begin. The perpetrators gauge international reaction. If there is no credible call for intervention, they are free and emboldened to commit further atrocities without threat of intervention of retaliation from the international community. At this stage, a Genocide Emergency must be declared. The international community should commit itself to armed intervention and/or provision of heavy reinforcements for any armed contingents of the victim groups engaged in resistance and self-defense. Humanitarian assistance should be organized by the UN and other humanitarian organizations, and the international community should prepare for the inevitable deluge of refugees who will be fleeing the conflict.

In Srebrenica, no armed intervention occurred in time to save the victims from genocide. The Bosniaks were unable to defend themselves as they had been forced to surrender their weapons when Srebrenica was declared a UN Safe Area. In eastern Bosnia, all expressions of persecution were present. Individuals and villages were identified as Muslim and subsequently destroyed. Those who were not killed were forced to flee. In Prijedor, Muslims were forced to wear white armbands. Property was seized or destroyed. Muslims had no choice but to flee to Srebrenica where they lived under conditions of dreadful deprivation as the BSA refused to allow humanitarian relief to be delivered. Prisoners were taken to concentration camps. Killing intensified and was allowed to continue with no intervention from the international community.

9. EXTERMINATION: Killing rapidly escalates to become mass killing and soon genocide. The terminology of extermination is favored by perpetrators, who

perceive their victims as subhuman. Dead bodies are dismembered; rape is used as a tool of war. Destruction of cultural and religious property is used to remove any trace of the group's existence from history. All men of fighting age are primary targets. At this stage, only rapid and overwhelming armed intervention can stop genocide. Real safe areas or refugee escape corridors should be set up under heavily armed international protection. An unsafe "safe" area is worse than none at all.

In Bosnia, all available tactics of extermination were used. What inadequate intervention emerged arrived much too late to save the lives of thousands of people. Those responsible for protecting the Muslims failed in their mission. It was indeed true that an unsafe "Safe Area" was worse than none at all.

10. DENIAL: This is the final stage of genocide. It is present throughout and also follows genocide for as long as it is allowed to prosper. Crucially, it is one of the surest predictors of future violence. The perpetrators attempt to cover up the evidence and intimidate the witnesses. They deny that they committed any crimes. Victims are blamed and are often accused of being perpetrators. International tribunals or national courts must be established where evidence can be heard, and the perpetrators punished. Even this, however, may not be enough to deter future genocides.

As has been discussed throughout this book, the genocide denial that exists today, in the RS and across the region, is one of the most significant obstacles to peace and reconciliation in post-war Bosnia.

These are ten formally agreed upon stages of genocide. There is some discussion in policy and academic circles, however, of an additional 11th stage which should be added to the model: the glorification of war criminals. This phenomenon is unfolding with ever-increasing frequency and intensity in Bosnia. There is a new literary category of books written by or about war criminals, which not only denies their participation in genocide but glorifies their violent campaigns as a struggle for national liberation. Nedžad Avdić described the evening when he attended such a book launch at the Cultural Center in Srebrenica. That is just one example. There are at least three publishers that participate in the prestigious Belgrade Book Fair who publish books that promote war criminals. When these books are published, there are often book launches and book reviews written in the mainstream press which spread information that has been judicially proven to be untrue.[15]

In addition to developing the ten stages of genocide, Dr. Stanton has established an organization called Genocide Watch, whose purpose is to build an international movement for intervention and prevention against genocide. Their website includes an interactive world map that contains past and current data about genocide and other mass atrocities by country or nation. It also includes current articles about vulnerable people around the world who are at risk for or are experiencing genocide.[16] Genocide Watch issues three levels of Genocide Alerts, based on the 10 Stages:

A Genocide Watch is declared when there are signs of the early stages of the genocidal process.
A Genocide Warning is called when the genocidal process has reached the stages of preparation by perpetrators and persecution of a targeted group.
A Genocide Emergency is declared when the genocidal process has reached the stage of genocidal massacres and other acts of genocide.[17]

At the time of this writing, there are numerous Genocide Watches and Genocide Warnings in place. There are also eight designated Genocide Emergencies. This means that there are at least eight places in the world that have reached the stage of genocidal massacres and other acts of genocide. In some of these places, more than one group have been designated as victims.[18] It is up to all of us to make sure that the world knows this is happening.

Genocide Watch issues statements about matters of concern for the long-term prevention of genocide and other mass atrocities. On July 1, 2018, Genocide Watch issued a statement on Forced Family Separation, Detention and Deportation in the United States: "Genocide Watch expresses alarm over the accelerated practice of family separation…. The cruelty of taking children, including infants, from their parents at the border cannot be justified by any laws or policy agendas."[19]

As the situation in the United States grows more and more concerning, right wing nationalism is also increasing in Poland and Hungary among other places in Europe. Never have hate groups felt so free to pronounce their beliefs or to act upon them. Mass deportation is occurring among identified groups of people and there is now a "Muslim ban" in place in the U.S. In many countries, there are organized efforts to suppress free press by banning certain news agencies from events or press conferences. Language equating people with animals is frequently used in an attempt to dehumanize specific groups. This language is called "eliminationist rhetoric," which is a policy or belief that a certain group should be expelled or eliminated. It is always dangerous.

> The existence of eliminationist beliefs and desires, conversations and ideologies, and acts and policies has been a central feature of all eras of human history and all sorts of societies. Eliminationism's many forms are better known by their particular and spectacularly horrible consequences and names, such as genocide, the desire to *eliminate* peoples or groups[20]

On the stages of genocide, the United States is currently listed at stage six, Polarization.[21]

One lesson learned from Bosnia is the importance of countering dangerous labeling and rhetoric. There are positive steps being taken in this direction from several parts of society in the U.S.

> Encouraging responses have come from the electorate, business leaders, government officials and the international community. Individuals and groups are following the recommendations for action presented in the Southern Poverty Law Center's guide to combating hate in supporting victims, speaking up, pressuring leaders and staying engaged. Business leaders have also expressed their discontent with Trump's polarizing statements. Local governments are declaring themselves sanctuary cities or cities of resistance. At the national level, strong statements have been made by leaders of all of the military branches.[22]

Resistance to dehumanization, hate speech, othering, genocide denial and the formation of hate groups are the first steps toward ending human rights violations and mass atrocities. Bosnia has taught us the dire consequences of failing to resist radical hatred. The fight against genocide begins with each individual who confronts prejudice, discrimination, and hatred in their community, wherever they find it. The prevention of genocide is a collective responsibility shared by all.

Conclusion: Moving Forward

In order to really understand Bosnian culture at its best, you need to ride in Džona's van from Sarajevo to Srebrenica and then back again. Džona drives in both directions each day. You meet him in Sarajevo usually around 6:30 a.m.; sometimes the van is already full and other times you are the first one in. Either way, the journey is almost always the same. Some people get in the van from a conveniently accessed pick-up site like a hotel or taxi stand. Many people, however, are found while driving down narrow winding roads in the city and the outskirts. I have seen more backroads in both Sarajevo and Srebrenica because of Džona's van. Sometimes people recognize each other in the van but often it is only on the ride to Srebrenica that people get acquainted in true Bosnian fashion. Food is always shared and, without exception, at some point every single person in the van will be talking at the same time, sometimes with escalating volume.

There are always traditionally dressed older women, sometimes a man or two, or perhaps a young child. Women who board the van almost always have several heavy plastic bags, whose contents remain a mystery, at least for a while. Out of those bags inevitably comes bread, cheese, candy, sometimes knitted slippers or maybe a tomato. All of this is shared with everyone in the van.

It took me a while to realize that nobody is ever yelling at each other in the van; the conversation is just loud and animated, even among strangers. Lots of advice is given, along with smiles, pats on the arm and offers to help. When we stop at the store half-way to our destination, people in the van often assume that I don't know what to do or that I don't have any Bosnian currency, so they offer to help me. It's rare that I don't end up with a gift of a pear or bag of cookies or even an onion to bring home.

By the end of the trip, and particularly coming back from Srebrenica, tomatoes, strawberries or potatoes have usually found their way into the van for delivery to someone in the city. Sometimes these fruits and vegetables are picked up in a tiny village filled with fields of crops, greenhouses, row after row of raspberries, chickens running amuck, and a large friendly dog. It is like a secret garden, a place of charm and beauty in the midst of fields where genocide took place.

Riding with Džona is one of my favorite experiences in Bosnia. The van is hot when you wish it wouldn't be and cold when you hope it will be warm. It's sometimes crowded and uncomfortable but none of that matters because the community that lives inside that van is a gift every single time.

It was only fitting that I took Džona's van to the funeral of Hatidža Mehmedović, a human rights activist and survivor of the Srebrenica genocide. Any other kind of transportation would not have seemed right. Getting dropped off at Hasan's office at the Memorial brought news that Saliha Osmanović wasn't going to be able to come to Hatidža's service because she had no way to get from her village into Srebrenica. Hasan quickly found a taxi driver to pick her up from home and bring her to the Cultural Center where the memorial service was being held.

I had only been in the Srebrenica Cultural Center one other time. During the 20th anniversary of the genocide, there was a program featuring several *hafiz*, someone who has completely memorized, word for word, the entire Koran. They took turns reciting parts of the Koran and chanting spiritual songs. I remember that evening as mystical and incredibly moving. The funeral was equally moving, and although the room was filled with sorrow, it was a wonderful tribute to an amazing woman. By the time Saliha arrived, the service had already started. When she entered the hot room, it was clear she had already been crying for some time. We were standing in the back because there were no seats. Hasan asked a small boy to move so that Saliha could take his seat, but this required her crawling over the back of the chair, which was not easy for her. I'm not sure I've ever seen her so sad. Without Hasan, she would have been forgotten and would not have been able to come to this memorial of her friend. She feels alone because she is.

Hundreds of people gathered for Hatidža's memorial service and funeral. People who spoke talked about how she had started the Mothers of Srebrenica association after losing her husband, two sons, two brothers and other family members in the genocide. When talking about her achievements, speakers described Hatidža as "the mother of all children, regardless of their national identity, race or heritage, who fought for justice until the last day."[1]

Hatidža's death was covered by media from around the world, including the *Washington Post*, *New York Times*, ABC News, and the *Irish Independent*.[2] The tributes to Hatidža at her memorial service in Srebrenica were echoed in numerous articles that praised her benevolence and her tireless advocacy.

Closer to home, unfortunately, the vice president of the Serbian parliament, Vjerica Radeta, sent out this tweet, mocking Hatidža's death:

> I've just read that Hatidža Mehmetovic from the "Businesswomen of Srebrenica" [sic] organization has died. I wonder who will bury her. Her husband or her sons?[3]

These vile words sparked outrage, including from Sonja Biserko of the Helsinki Committee for Human Rights in Serbia, who we met earlier in this book. In reference to Radeta's tweet, Sonja said: "That is an image of the state of the spirit of Serbia and its society today or, at least, one part of its political elite which, actually not only questions all the sufferings on the territory of former Yugoslavia which relate to other people, but mocks and ridicules them."[4] This is the world in which the Bosnian Muslims live. Even people who are respected and praised around the world are met with ridicule and disdain in the RS and in Serbia. They are assaulted sometimes daily with genocide denial and mockery of their experiences. They are saddled with a political system that allows this to happen. How they remain such good, kind, generous people amid such relentless abuse and indignity, will forever be a mystery to me.

Hatidža's memorial was organized by ordinary citizens. It was not an official Srebrenica commemoration. It was attended by ambassadors and others from the international community but was boycotted by the Srebrenica mayor and the RS authorities. It was held in the Cultural Center, the same place where Nedžad attended the book launch written by the genocide denier. Officials did attend that event, not to protect Nedžad, but to support the author. Nedžad was back in the Cultural Center for Hatidža's memorial service as were several other people in this book, including Staša from Belgrade, Saliha, Hajra, Nura, and Haso.

It was an intense two weeks before Hatidža's funeral for the Bosnian Muslims in Srebrenica. The coffins arrived in Potočari and the July 11 commemoration and burial took place the following day. A few days after that were the visits to the execution sites. Then came the news of Hatidža's death which was a jolt to everyone who knew her. When Hasan heard the news about Hatidža's death, he wrote the loveliest tribute:

> My heart broke and my soul crashed when I heard that our dearest Hatidža Mehmedović passed away last night. I have spent years with her at the Memorial and she always called me "son." She was the head of the Mothers of Srebrenica Association and a genuine advocate for victims of the Srebrenica genocide, both in the country and abroad. You will always be my hero and my ultimate inspiration. I already miss you my dearest Hatidža. We will never forget you and will keep on doing all you have fought for all these years.

Anyone who believes the world to be a just place has not spent time in Bosnia, particularly in Srebrenica. Yet, in spite of their tremendous suffering, people's resilience moves them forward. The community is strong and continues to work together to support each other and to fight for justice. On the day of the funeral, Srebrenica was overflowing with people. Seeing how they cared for each other, how they laughed and talked after the service, I was reminded as I am always reminded, of Bosnia's true essence. It is a place of beauty and sorrow, unspeakable tragedy and horror, solidarity and generosity, graciousness of spirit and a resilience that allows so many people to somehow continue moving forward day after day.

Survivors are on the front line of fighting for justice on a daily basis and they will never stop. This is Srebrenica winning.

Chapter Notes

Preface

1. Wertheimer.
2. Popular "name explain": Why Bosnia and Herzegovina has two names.
3. https://www.icty.org/en/about.
4. Klein.
5. Traynor & O'Kane.
6. Lakic, Sararjevo remembers children killed during siege.
7. Cuhara, Bonny, Efendic, & Hodzic.

Introduction

1. Malcolm, N.R., Lampe, J.R., Pickering, P., Bosnia and Herzegovina.
2. Clayfield.
3. Ebener.
4. Malcolm, N. *Bosnia: A short history*. This is a good source for those interested in the history of Yugoslavia and Bosnia.
5. The Iron Curtain was the virtual boundary line dividing Europe in two different political areas from 1945 to 1991: Western Europe had political freedom; Eastern Europe was under communist Soviet rule. The term also symbolized the way the Soviet Union blocked its territories from open contact with the West.
6. Morgan.
7. Traynor & O'Kane.
8. Lakic.
9. Bell.
10. TRT World.
11. Constitution.net.
12. Facing History and Ourselves, Raphael Lemkin and the Genocide Convention.
13. *Ibid*.
14. *Ibid*.
15. Winter.
16. International Criminal Court, The ICC Rome Statute is 20.
17. Human Rights Watch, The International Criminal Court and the United States.
18. *Ibid*.
19. It should be noted that the Republika Srpska authorities dispute the methodology and refuse to recognize these results.
20. Central Intelligence Agency.
21. World Jewish Congress.
22. *Ibid*.
23. *Ibid*.
24. *Ibid*.
25. UNESCO.
26. Sijarić.
27. BBC News.

Chapter 1

1. Osat is an area of many villages about 15 miles from the town of Srebrenica.
2. Sase, a village that contains a lead and zinc mine. Fatima's father worked there. Originally it was a silver mine which is how Srebrenica got its name. Srebro means silver in Bosnian.
3. Zeleni Jadar is a valley, village and secondary mass grave site 30 miles [50 kilometers] from Kravica.
4. Zvijezda is about a mile from Bratunac on the way to Srebrenica.
5. Čauš is a high hill behind the battery factory.
6. Ibro Nuhanović is the father of Hasan Nuhanović.
7. Rhode, 10 years on, tormenting memories of Srebrenica.
8. Vuk Karadžić is still a primary school in Bratunac where people were killed in 1992 and again in July 1995.
9. These were the people on the Death March.
10. Karakaj is a small village six miles outside of Zvornik on the way to Bijeljina.
11. Jugo & Wastell.
12. The Hague, Milenko Zivanovic in the Hague for the first time.
13. In 2013, Hasan Hasanović, Hasan Nuhanović, Saliha Osmanović and Hakija Huseinović traveled to London to mark anniversary of the genocide. They met with prime minister David Cameron, visited the House of Lords and spoke at Lancaster House.
14. Sobelman.
15. International Criminal Tribunal for the former Yugoslavia (2010, April 26) [Court transcript].
16. Nino is Hajra Ćatić's son.
17. Mladic present during the Orahovac massacre.
18. Execution site at Petkovici Dam.

Chapter 2

1. A small UN base on the outskirts of Srebrenica, located in a former embroidery plant. Occupied by the Canadian Peacekeepers followed by the Dutch.
2. Human Rights Watch, Chemical warfare in Bosnia? The strange experiences of the Srebrenica survivors.
3. Bajram marks the end of the holy month of Ramadan.
4. Grbavci School is where prisoners were brought from Bratunac and other detention sites and later killed at Orahovac.
5. Ako bog da is a term meaning "God willing."
6. Dražen Erdemović was a Bosnian Serb soldier. He participated in the executions of hundreds of men at Branjevo. He was the first person to enter a guilty plea at the Tribunal in exchange for a lighter sentence. He received 5 years' imprisonment.
7. Srebrenica's Hasan Hasanovic is among the celebrities who marked 2014.
8. Castle.
9. Srebrenica mass grave uncovered 20 years after massacre.
10. Balias is a derogatory term for Muslims.
11. Vozuća is a town in Tuzla canton, 22 miles from Tuzla.
12. "Destiny."

Chapter 3

1. Bajina Bašta is also the birthplace of Hasan Hasanović, co-author of this book and Saliha Osmanović's home is across the river.
2. Hasanović, H.
3. International Criminal Tribunal for the Former Yugoslavia (2000, March 22) [Court transcript]. Nesib's complete testimony can be found here.
4. Zivstepa, *Ratko Mladic, Srebrenica Fontana Hotel 2—July 11, 1995.*
5. Zivstepa, *Ratko Mladic, Srebrenica Fontana Hotel—July 12, 1995.*
6. Ibro was the father of Hasan Nuhanović.
7. Sito-Sucic, ICJ rejects request for revision of Bosnia genocide ruling.

Chapter 4

1. Initially, graves are marked with green, temporary tombstones. Within a year each green tombstone is replaced with a permanent one made of white marble.
2. Misirlije is a popular guest house and restaurant serving traditional Bosnian food. It is located up a hill in Srebrenica.
3. Željko Ražnatović, known as Arkan, commanded a paramilitary group known as Arkan's tigers. They were known as brutal killers and perpetrators of sexual violence.
4. Ljubovija, Serbia is a 25-minute drive from Srebrenica.
5. The post office was the same building where Philippe Morillon, UN Commander for Bosnia and Herzegovina gave his famous speech assuring residents of Srebrenica that they were under the protection of the United Nations.
6. Srebrenica-Potočari Memorial Center.
7. Kazani is a place on the outskirts of the town of Srebrenia where many people said goodbye to their families on July 11. It is also where the men and boys started to gather for the Death March. Additionally it is the site of the cemetery where Saliha's youngest son Edin is buried.
8. The white house sits across the road from the entrance to the UN Dutch base. When men and boys were separated from women they were taken to this white house. They were subsequently transported and killed. The documentary that is shown every day at the Memorial contains footage of men and boys sitting on the balcony of this house with a huge pile of their personal belongings in front of the house.
9. Staša Zajović who is featured in this book, is the Director of Women in Black Belgrade.
10. Kirsch.
11. Bočin Potok is located underneath Kamenice Hill near Kravica.
12. Dragana Vučetić is the Chief Forensic Anthropologist at the ICMP in Tuzla.
13. SIPA, The State Investigation and Protection Agency, is the official state police agency of Bosnia and Herzegovina.
14. Midžic, List gradjana Bosne i Hercegovine u Holandiji. Nasa Bosna.
15. Bajina Bašta is also near where Nesib was born and where Hasan Hasnović, co-author of this book, was born. It is in Serbia right across the River Drina.
16. Osat is an area of many villages about 15 miles from the town of Srebrenica.

Chapter 5

1. Praljak: Bosnian Croat war criminal dies after taking poison in court.
2. Bacic.
3. Radio Free Europe Radio Liberty, Croatian ceremony honors convicted war criminal Praljak.
4. Al Jazeera, Bombed Bosnian bridge reopened.
5. Eckardt & Banic.
6. Topham.
7. *Ibid.*
8. Milorad Dodik is a Serb nationalist and a voracious genocide denier. He was the President of the RS and is now the Serb member of the Presidency of Bosnia.
9. Rudic.
10. International Residual Mechanism for Criminal Tribunals, Radislav Krstic becomes the first person to be convicted of genocide at the ICTY and is sentenced to 46 years imprisonment.
11. International Residual Mechanisms for Criminal Tribunals, ICTY convicts Ratko Mladić for genocide, war crimes, and crimes against humanity.
12. International Criminal Tribunal for the Former Yugoslavia, ICTY convicts Ratko Mladić for genocide, war crimes and crimes against humanity [Press release].
13. International Criminal Tribunal for the For-

mer Yugoslavia, Tribunal convicts Radovan Kardžić for crimes in Bosnia and Herzegovina [Press release].
  14. BIRN.
  15. Jovanović.
  16. Ozturk & Besic.
  17. International Residual Mechanism for Criminal Tribunals, Keraterm camp [Drawing].
  18. Ozturk & Besic.
  19. Post-Conflict Research Center.
  20. Bowcott, Serb nationalist Vojislav Šešelj acquitted of war crimes at The Hague.
  21. Gadzo.
  22. Center for Women's Studies Belgrade.
  23. CodePink.
  24. Kern.
  25. Braun, Pfeil, & Visevic.
  26. Partos.
  27. Women in Black.
  28. Munira Subašić is the President of an Association called Movement of Mothers of Srebrenica and Žepa Enclaves. Her husband and son were killed in the genocide. She is a powerful activist for truth and justice who has won many national and international awards for her work.
  29. Jovanović.
  30. Fisk, Europe has a troublingly short memory over Serbia's Aleksander.
  31. Lawyers' Committee for Human Rights.
  32. Foreign Affairs.
  33. Amnesty International.
  34. Yanev, Cupido, van Sliedregt, Ventura, Roth, & de Hemptinne, Modes of liability in International Criminal Law.
  35. Mr. Klarin is the founder and Editor-in-Chief of SENSE-Tribunal, a specialized media service that regularly covers the work of the ICTY and other international courts in The Hague.
  36. Humanitarian Law Center.
  37. *Ibid.*
  38. Fisk, Bosnia War Crimes: 'The rapes went on day and night': Robert Fisk, in Mostar, gathers detailed evidence of the systematic sexual assaults on Muslim women by Serbian 'White Eagle' gunmen.
  39. International Residual Mechanism for Criminal Tribunals, Development of the local judiciaries.
  40. Trnovo Execution (Srebrenica).
  41. The State Security Service is explained in further detail in Milutinovic.
  42. RECOM, What is RECOM?
  43. Personal communication, January 7, 2019.

Chapter 6

  1. Sorguc, Srebrenica cover-up: The search for secret graves continues.
  2. Amnesty International.
  3. International Criminal Tribunal for the former Yugoslavia, The Tribunal-Establishment.
  4. International Criminal Tribunal for the Former Yugoslavia, Key figures of the cases.
  5. NPR.
  6. International Criminal Tribunal for the Former Yugoslavia, Judgement List. Information about all cases and verdicts can be found here.
  7. International Residual Mechanism for Criminal Tribunals, About.
  8. International Commission on Missing Persons.
  9. Personal communication, Bomberger.
  10. Srebrenica: Remembering for the future, Heinrich Böll Foundation, Sarajevo, December 2010.
  11. Kladanj is a town where the refugees from Potočari were deported. It is 21 miles (35 kilometers) from Tuzla.
  12. Remembering Srebrenica.
  13. Office of the High Representative, Decision establishing and registering the Foundation of the Srebrenica-Potočari Memorial and Cemetery.
  14. Office of the High Representative, Decision ordering the transfer of ownership of the Battery Factory "AS"-Srebrenica to the Foundation of the Srebrenica-Potočari Memorial and Cemetery and establishing an ad hoc Battery Factory "AS" a.d.-Srebrenica compensation commission.
  15. Leydesdorff, S. Surviving the Bosnian Genocide: The women of Srebrenica speak.

Chapter 7

  1. Center for Complicated Grief.
  2. *Ibid.*
  3. *Ibid.*
  4. *Ibid.*
  5. *Ibid.*
  6. Personal communication, Bomberger.
  7. Rudic, Mejdini, Grebo, Haxhiaj, & Milekic.
  8. O'Malley.
  9. Zastrow, Chasing the shadow grief [PDF].
  10. Basoglu, Livanou, Crnobarić, Francisković, Suljić, Durić, Vranesić.
  11. Layne, Olsen, Baker, Legerski, Isakson, Pašalić, Duraković-Belko, Dapo, Campara, Arslanagić, Saltzman, Paynoos.
  12. Hasanović, Psychological consequences of war-traumatized children and adolescents in Bosnia and Herzegovina.
  13. Paulsen, Emotional experiences of post-war youth from Bosnia-Herzegovina: A systematic review.
  14. Boss, Ambiguous loss research, theory, and practice: Reflections after 9/11.
  15. Prigerson, Shear, Jacobs, Reynolds, Maciejewski, Davidson, Rosenheck, Piklonis, Wortman, Williams, Widiger, Frank, Kupfer, Zisook.
  16. Nartova-Bochaver, Donat, & Rüprich.
  17. Joseph.
  18. Mayo Clinic.
  19. National Institute of Mental Health.
  20. Prager.
  21. Auerhahn.
  22. Ryan, Chaudieu, Ancelin, & Saffery.
  23. American Psychological Association, What is cognitive behavioral therapy?
  24. American Psychological Association, Eye movement desensitization and reprocessing (EMDR) therapy.

25. Shapiro.
26. Hasanović, Morgan, Oakley, Richman, Šabanovic, Pajević.
27. Socolovsky.
28. Lončar, Medved, Jovanović, Hotujac.
29. *Ibid.*
30. Fisk, Bosnia War crimes: 'The rapes went on day and night': Robert Fisk, in Mostar, gathers detailed evidence of the systematic sexual assaults on Muslim women by Serbian 'White Eagle' gunmen.
31. International Criminal Court, The ICC Rome Statute is 20.
32. International Residual Mechanism for Criminal Tribunals, Crimes of sexual violence.
33. Black.
34. Buss.
35. Sorguc, Bosnian Serb Hague convict faces new war crime trial.
36. United Nations Human Rights Officer of the High Commissioner, Rape: weapon of war.
37. Office of the Special Representative of the Secretary-General on Sexual Violence in Conflict, About the Office.
38. Blackburn.
39. United Nations Security Council, Security council adopts resolution calling upon Belligerents Worldwide to adopt concrete commitments on ending sexual violence in conflict.
40. Medica Zenica.

Chapter 8

1. Sarajevo Times Team.
2. Posters of General Ratko Mladic all over Srebrenica.
3. United Nations Office on Genocide Prevention and the Responsibility to Protect, Responsibility to Protect.
4. Sito-Sucic, Women force French former general from Srebrenica.
5. BuddenBrook.
6. PUCE.
7. United Nations Security Council, Security Council resolution 819 (1993) [Bosnia and Herzegovina].
8. Dobbs, Why Srebrenica?
9. Srebrenica grave exhumed at former UN base.
10. Ryngaert.
11. Agence France-Presse in The Hague.
12. *Ibid.*
13. Sablijakovic.
14. Daugirdas.
15. United Nations, May we all learn and act on the lessons of Srebrenica, says Secretary-General, in message to anniversary ceremony.
16. United Nations, At meeting commemorating twentieth anniversary of Srebrenica killings, security council fails to adopt resolution.
17. *Ibid.*
18. *Ibid.*
19. Hatidža Mehmedović was president of the Mothers of Srebrenica Association headquartered in Srebrenica. She lost her husband and two sons in the genocide.
20. Stewart.
21. Sito-Sucic, Women force French former general from Srebrenica.
22. *Ibid.*
23. Dobbs, Why Srebrenica?
24. Ryngaert & Schrijver.
25. Organization for Security and Co-operation in Europe.
26. Borger.
27. Nardelli, Dzidic, & Jukic.
28. Radio Free Europe/Radio Liberty.
29. TRT World.
30. International Institute for Middle East and Balkan Studies.
31. Borger.
32. Office of the High Representative, Mandate.
33. *Ibid.*
34. Paddy Ashdown: British marine who led Bosnia with an iron fist.
35. N1 Sarajevo, Bosnia's international administrator could impose ban on genocide denial.

Chapter 9

1. Professor Stanton is the founding president and legal director of Genocide Watch.
2. Miller.
3. Druckman.
4. Pickel.
5. Southern Poverty Law Center, New hate map helps users explore landscape of hate.
6. Cai & Landon.
7. Graham-McLay.
8. Al Jazeera, Mosque shooter brandished material glorifying Serb nationalism.
9. International Criminal Tribunal for the Former Yugoslavia, Court transcript Slobodan Milosevic.
10. Armatta.
11. Southern Poverty Law Center, White nationalist.
12. Southern Poverty Law Center, New hate map helps users explore landscape of hate.
13. *Ibid.*
14. Stanton, The ten stages of genocide.
15. Lakic, Vladisavljevic, & Rudic.
16. Genocide Watch.
17. *Ibid.*
18. *Ibid.*
19. Joeden-Forgey.
20. Worse than War.
21. Genocide Watch, Genocide Watch statement on forced family separation, detention, and deportation.
22. *Ibid.*

Conclusion

1. N1 Sarajevo, Srebrenica activist Hatidza Mehmedovic laid to rest.
2. N1 Sarajevo, World media mark the death of Hatidza Mehmedovic.
3. Wesolowsky.
4. *Ibid.*

Bibliography

Agence France-Presse in The Hague (2019, July 19). Dutch court reduces state liability for Srebrenica massacre. *The Guardian*. Retrieved from https://www.theguardian.com/world/2019/jul/19/dutch-supreme-court-reduces-responsibility-for-srebrenica-massacre.

Al Jazeera. Bombed Bosnian bridge reopened (2004, July 4). *AlJazeera*. Retrieved from https://www.aljazeera.com/archive/2004/07/200849145414987728.html.

Al Jazeera (2019, March 15). Mosque shooter brandished material glorifying Serb nationalism. *AlJazeera*. Retrieved from https://www.aljazeera.com/news/2019/03/zealand-mosque-gunman-inspired-serb-nationalism-190315141305756.html.

American Psychological Association (n.d.). What is cognitive behavioral therapy? Retrieved from https://www.apa.org/ptsd-guideline/patients-and-families/cognitive-behavioral.

American Psychological Association (2020). Eye movement desensitization and reprocessing (EMDR) therapy. Retrieved from https://www.apa.org/ptsd-guideline/treatments/eye-movement-reprocessing.

Amnesty International (n.d.). The International Criminal Court [Fact sheet]. Retrieved from https://www.amnestyusa.org/pdfs/IJA_Factsheet_1_International_Criminal_Court.pdf.

Armatta, J. (2003). Milosevic's propaganda war. Retrieved from https://classroom.synonym.com/what-are-the-seven-techniques-of-propaganda-12080912.html.

Auerhahn, N., & Laub, D. (1998). Intergenerational memory of the Holocaust. In Y. Danieli (Ed.), *International handbook of multigenerational legacies of trauma* (pp. 21–42). New York: Plenum Press.

Bacic, M. (2017, January 12). War criminal in the Hague but still a war hero in Croatia. *EuroNews*. Retrieved from https://www.euronews.com/2017/12/01/war-criminal-in-the-hague-but-still-a-war-hero-in-croatia.

Balkan Investigative Reporting Network in Bosnia and Herzegovina (2010, November 18). Jevic et al.: Fleeing Srebrenica. *Justice Report*. Retrieved from http://www.justice-report.com/en/articles/jevic-et-al-fleeing-srebrenica.

Balkan Investigative Reporting Network in Bosnia and Herzegovina (2011, May 27). Comrade General's "words of encouragement." *Detektor*. Retrieved from http://detektor.ba/en/comrade-generals-words-of-encouragement/.

Başoglu, M., Livanou, M., Crnobarić, C., Francisković, T., Suljić, E., Durić, D., & Vranesić, M. (2005). Psychiatric and cognitive effects of war in former Yugoslavia: Association of lack of redress for trauma and posttraumatic stress reactions. *JAMA.294*(5), 580–590. doi: https://doi.org/10.1001/jama.294.5.580.

BBC News (2016, January 29). A point of view: Why survivors' stories matter. [Podcast transcript]. *BBC News*. Retrieved from https://www.bbc.com/news/magazine-35418124.

Belew, K. (2018). *Bring the war home: The white power movement and paramilitary America*. Cambridge, MA: Harvard University Press.

Belgrade district court found four "Scorpions" guilty (2007). Retrieved from https://humanrightshouse.org/articles/belgrade-district-court-found-four-scorpions-guilty/?fbclid=IwAR3Xa-o4rVaizGvPWLiaPvfZ8CBHqWEWUKxNarnxCO_8pg6_pFg2sRhzkX4.

Bell, M. (2012 April). Sarajevo: Another market massacre. Retrieved from https://www.bbc.com/news/av/uk-17402772/sarajevo-another-market-massacre.

Berry, M.E. (2018). *War, women, and power: From violence to mobilization in Rwanda and Bosnia-Herzegovina*. Cambridge, UK: Cambridge University Press.

BIRN (2010 March 31). Serbia adopts resolution condemning Srebrenica massacre. Retrieved from https://balkaninsight.com/2010/03/31/serbia-adopts-resolution-condemning-srebrenica-massacre/.

Biserko, S. (2010). *Srebrenica: Remembrance for the future* (2nd ed.). Sarajevo, Bosnia and Herzegovina: Heinrich Boll Foundation.

Biserko, S. (2017). *Yugoslavia from a historical perspective*. Serbia: Helsinki Committee for Human Rights.

Black, I. (2000, March 21). Serbs "enslaved Muslim women at rape camps." *The Guardian*. Retrieved from https://www.theguardian.com/world/2000/mar/21/warcrimes.balkans.

Blackburn, Y. (2016, August 25). Rape in conflict is a war crime, no matter how you spin it. *Huffpost*. Retrieved from https://www.huffpost.com/entry/rape-in-conflict-is-a-war_b_8018366.

Blitzer, J. (2019, December 6). A new report on family separations shows the depths of Trump's negligence. *The New Yorker*. Retrieved from https://www.newyorker.com/news/news-desk/a-new-report-on-family-separations-shows-the-depths-of-trumps-negligence.

Bob Stewart: Genocide in Srebrenica as a big stain on the conscience of international community (2014, December 3). *Sarajevo Times*. Retrieved from https://www.sarajevotimes.com/bob-stewart-genocide-srebrenica-big-stain-conscience-international-community/.

Borger, J. (2015, November 10). Bosnia's bitter, flawed peace deal, 20 years on. *The Guardian*. Retrieved from https://www.theguardian.com/global/2015/nov/10/bosnia-bitter-flawed-peace-deal-dayton-agreement-20-years-on.

Bosnia and Herzegovina population (2020). Retrieved March 8th, 2020, from http://worldpopulationreview.com/countries/bosnia-and-herzegovina-population/.

Bosnian Serb jailed for massacre (2009, June 12). *BBC News*. Retrieved from http://news.bbc.co.uk/2/hi/europe/8097918.stm.

Bosnia's international administrator could impose ban on genocide denial (2019, December 12). Retrieved from http://rs.n1info.com/English/NEWS/a551960/Valentin-Inzko-s-office-working-on-a-law-banning-genocide-denial.html?fbclid=IwAR2L88Mwxdw2FhmkPsaW2NzPEsZBGqabspBttzasvoUOKXo3ca0oXeA5OQo.

Boss, P.G. (1980). The relationship of psychological father presence, wife's personal qualities and wife/family dysfunction in families of missing fathers. *Journal of Marriage and Family, 42*(3), 541–549. doi: 10.2307/351898.

Boss, P.G. (2004). Ambiguous loss research, theory, and practice: reflections after 9/11. *Journal of Marriage and Family, 66*(3), 551–566.

Bowcott, O. (2016, March 31). Serb nationalist Vojislav Šešelj acquitted of war crimes at The Hague. *The Guardian*. Retrieved from https://www.theguardian.com/law/2016/mar/31/serb-nationalist-vojislav-seselj-acquitted-war-crimes-crimes-against-humanity-icty-the-hague.

Bowcott, O. (2017, November 29). Bosnian Croat war criminal dies after taking poison in UN courtroom. *The Guardian*. Retrieved from https://balkaninsight.com/2017/11/29/slobodan-praljak-hague-tribunal-poison-11-29-2017/.

Bowcott, O. (2017, December 20). Yugoslavia tribunal closes, leaving a powerful legacy of war crimes justice. *The Guardian*. Retrieved from https://www.theguardian.com/law/2017/dec/20/former-yugoslavia-war-crimes-tribunal-leaves-powerful-legacy-milosevic-karadzic-mladic.

Braun, C., Pfeil, M., & Visevic, D. (2016, July 4). Yugoslavia 1991: How can a war start if nobody wants it? *Spiegal Online International*. Retrieved from https://www.spiegel.de/international/tomorrow/war-in-yugoslavia-and-the-peace-movement-that-preceded-it-a-1100626.html.

Brennen, T., Hasanović, M., Zotović, M., Blix, I., Skar, A.M., Prelić, N.K., Mehmedović, I., Pajević, I., Popović, N., & Gavrilov-Jerković, V. (2010). Trauma exposure in childhood impairs the ability to recall specific autobiographical memories in late adolescence. *Journal of Traumatic Stress, 23*(2), 240–247. doi: 10.1002/jts.20513.

BuddenBrook Xx (2015 July 22). Phillion Morillon. [Youtube]. Retrieved from https://www.youtube.com/watch?v=jz54fqS7S2Q.

Buss, D. (n.d.). Prosecuting mass rape prosecutor v. Dragoljub Kunarac, Radomir Kovac an Zoran Vukovic. Retrieved from https://eige.europa.eu/library/resource/IAV_ADL225277.

Cai, W., & Landon, S. (2019, April 3). Attacks by white supremacists are growing. So are their connections. *New York Times*. Retrieved from https://www.nytimes.com/interactive/2019/04/03/world/white-extremist-terrorism-christchurch.html?mtrref=www.google.com&gwh=61329590843879081EA018125A6C571A&gwt=pay&assetType=REGIWALL.

Carey, B. (2018, December 10). Can we really inherit trauma? *New York Times*. Retrieved from https://www.nytimes.com/2018/12/10/health/mind-epigenetics-genes.html.

Castle, S. (2000, March 16). Srebrenica: "The wounded begged to be killed." *Independent*. Retrieved from https://www.independent.co.uk/news/world/europe/srebrenica-the-wounded-begged-to-be-killed-282584.html.

Center for Complicated Grief (2017). *Overview*. Retrieved from https://complicatedgrief.columbia.edu/professionals/complicated-grief-professionals/overview/.

Center for Women's Studies Belgrade (2019). *Lecturers*. Retrieved January 2, 2020 from https://www.zenskestudie.edu.rs/en/about-us/lecturers?fbclid=IwAR1aHV_YS_-tmOpUX-T0vF5JrPMQ4EeruKbPQYb3Qi-sD9g4zAFP3kyNf9Q.

Central Intelligence Agency (2020). Europe: Bosnia and Herzegovina. Retrieved from https://www.cia.gov/library/publications/the-world-factbook/geos/print_bk.html.

Charny, I.W. Templates for gross denial of a known genocide: A manual. In Charny, I.W. (Ed.), *Encyclopedia of genocide* (vol. 1), Santa Barbara, CA: ABC-Clio.

Chetnik (n.d.). *In Encyclopedia Britannica online*. Retrieved from https://www.britannica.com/topic/Chetnik.

Clayfield, M. (2017 October 14). Bosnia and Herzgovina may never be clear of landmines. Retrieved from https://www.abc.net.au/news/2017-10-15/bosnia-may-never-be-clear-of-land-mines/9029692.

Coalition for International Justice (2005, May 31). Chilling video footage shown of purported execution of Srebrenica Muslims by "Scorpions" paramilitary unit-allegedly under Serbian MUP command. *Institute for War and Peace Reporting*. Retrieved from https://iwpr.net/global-voices/chilling-video-footage-shown-purported-execution-srebrenica-muslims-scorpions.

Coalition for the International Criminal Court (2019, March 11). Kathryne Bomberger, Director-General,

International Commission on Missing Person on International Women's Day. Retrieved from: http://www.coalitionfortheicc.org/document/kathryne-bomberger-directorgeneral-international-commission-missing-person-international.

CodePink (2019). *Issues & campaigns*. Retrieved from https://www.codepink.org/issues_campaigns.

Constitution Net (2016). Constitutional history of Bosnia and Herzegovina. Retrieved from http://constitutionnet.org/country/bosnia-and-herzegovina.

Crouch, M. (2018). What are the seven techniques of propaganda? Retrieved from https://classroom.synonym.com/what-are-the-seven-techniques-of-propaganda-12080912.html.

Cuhara, A., Bonny, T., Efendic, R., & Hodzic, T. (2017). *Scream for Me Sarajevo*. [Motion Picture]. Bosnia and Herzegovina: Eagle Rock Entertainment.

Daugirdas, K. (2018). Can you sue international organizations? The Supreme Court decides to weigh in. Retrieved from https://www.justsecurity.org/57265/sue-international-organizations-supreme-court-decides-weigh/.

Delić, A., Hasanović, M., Avdibegović, E., Dimitrijević, A., Hancheva, C., Scher, C., Stefanović-Stanojević, T., Streeck-Fischer, A., & Hamburger, A. (2014). Academic model of trauma healing in post-war societies. *Acta Medica Academica, 43*(1). doi: http://dx.doi.org/10.5644/ama2006-124.103.

Dickerson, C., & Nixon, R. (2017, December 21). Trump administration considers separating families to combat illegal immigration. *New York Times*. Retrieved from https://www.nytimes.com/2017/12/21/us/trump-immigrant-families-separate.html.

Dobbs, M. (2012, February 17). *Srebrenica executions—Trnovo*. [Video file]. Retrieved from https://www.youtube.com/watch?v=Gk5xOM7ECwI.

Dobbs, M. (2012, March 13). Why Srebrenica? *Foreign Policy*. Retrieved from https://foreignpolicy.com/2012/03/13/why-srebrenica/.

Dobbs, M. (2012 April). The "feel good response" to mass atrocity: From Srebrenica to Homs. Retrieved from https://foreignpolicy.com/2012/04/12/the-feel-good-response-to-mass-atrocity-from-srebrenica-to-homs/.

Druckman, D. (1994). Nationalism, patriotism, and group loyalty: A social psychological perspective. *Mershon International Studies Review, 38*(1), 43. doi:10.2307/222610.

DW Staff (2006, November 3). The charges against Slobodan Milosevic. *Deutsche Welle*. Retrieved from https://www.dw.com/en/the-charges-against-slobodan-milosevic/a-1931386.

Džidić, D., Dzidic, D., Ristic, M., Domanovic, M., Çollaku, P., & Milekic, S. (2014, December 8). Arkan's paramilitaries: Tigers who escaped justice. *Balkan Transitional Justice*. Retrieved from https://balkaninsight.com/2014/12/08/arkan-s-paramilitaries-tigers-who-escaped-justice/.

Ebener, D. (2014, July 17). Being Catholic in Croatia is more nationality than religion. *The Catholic Messenger*. Retrieved from http://www.catholicmessenger.net/2014/07/being-catholic-in-croatia-is-more-nationality-than-religion/.

Eckardt, A., & Banic, V. (2017, March 19). Bosnian war, 25 years later: Mostar Bridge illustrates lingering divide. *NBC News*. Retrieved from https://www.nbcnews.com/news/world/bosnian-war-25-years-later-mostar-bridge-illustrates-lingering-divide-n731066.

Edwards, M. (2019 January 2). The president who wants to break up his own country. *The Atlantic*. Retrieved from https://www.theatlantic.com/international/archive/2019/01/serb-president-dodik-bosnia/579199/.

Execution site at Petkovici Dam (2013). Retrieved from http://www.sense-agency.com/icty/execution-site-at-petkovci-dam.29.html?news_id=15045&fbclid=IwAR0Lda0ehcOKOgkPwCvYKrIzJuYz42G9AFJON_QtusMOWuKZUdgS7ezOho4.

Facing History and Ourselves (n.d.). Explainer: White nationalism [Handout]. Retrieved from https://www.facinghistory.org/chunk/explainer-white-nationalism.

Facing History and Ourselves (n.d.). Raphael Lemkin and the Genocide Convention. Retrieved from https://www.facinghistory.org/holocaust-and-human-behavior/chapter-11/raphael-lemkin-and-genocide-convention.

Fink, S.L. (2004). *War hospital: A true story of surgery and survival*. United States: Public Affairs.

Fisk, R. (1993, February 8). Bosnia War crimes: "The rapes went on day and night": Robert Fisk, in Mostar, gathers detailed evidence of the systematic sexual assaults on Muslim women by Serbian "White Eagle" gunmen. *Independent*. Retrieved from https://www.independent.co.uk/news/world/europe/bosnia-war-crimes-the-rapes-went-on-day-and-night-robert-fisk-in-mostar-gathers-detailed-evidence-of-1471656.html.

Fisk, R. (2016, May 14). Europe has a troublingly short memory over Serbia's Aleksander Vucic. *Independent*. Retrieved from https://www.independent.co.uk/voices/europe-has-a-troublingly-short-memory-over-serbia-s-aleksander-vucic-a7029221.html.

Foreign Affairs (2008, Spring). Interview with David Owen on the Balkans. *Foreign Affairs*. Retrieved from https://www.foreignaffairs.com/articles/1993-03-01/interview-david-owen-balkans.

Friedman, U. (2011, May 26). Where was Ratko Mladic hiding? *The Atlantic*. Retrieved from https://www.theatlantic.com/international/archive/2011/05/where-was-ratko-mladic-hiding/351131/.

Gadzo, M. (2018, April 11). Serbian "radical" Vojislav Seselj convicted of war crimes. *AlJazeera*. Retrieved from https://www.aljazeera.com/news/europe/2018/04/serbian-radical-vojislav-seselj-convicted-war-crimes-180411124256468.html.

Genocide Watch (n.d.). Retrieved from https://www.genocidewatch.com/.

Genocide Watch (n.d.). United States of America. Retrieved from https://www.genocidewatch.com/united-states-of-america.

Genocide Watch (2018). Genocide Watch statement on forced family separation, detention and deportation. (2018). Retrieved from https://www.genocidewatch.com/copy-of-current-genocide-watch-aler-1.

Graham-McLay, C. (2019, May 2). Death toll in New Zealand mosque attacks rises to 51. *New York Times*. Retrieved from https://www.nytimes.com/2019/05/02/world/asia/new-zealand-attack-death-toll.html.

The Hague (2013, October 31). Milenko Zivanovic in The Hague for the first time. *Sense Tribunal*. Retrieved from http://www.sense-agency.com/icty/milenko-zivanovic-in-the-hague-for-the-first-time.29.html?news_id=15442.

Hasanović, H. (2016). *Surviving Srebrenica*. Tarland, Aberdeenshire: The Lumphanan Press.

Hasanović, M. (2011). *Psychological consequences of war-traumatized children and adolescents in Bosnia and Herzegovina*. Acta Medica Academica. 40. 45–66. 10.5644/ama2006-124.8.

Hasanović, M., Morgan, S., Oakley, S., Richman, S., Šabanovic, & Š. Pajević, I. (2018). Development of EMDR in Bosnia and Herzegovina—From an idea to the first EMDR conference. *Psychiatria Danubina, 30*(5), 243–248.

Hearst, D., Walker, M., & Norton-Taylor, R. (1999, May 27). Milosevic indicted for war crimes. *The Guardian*. Retrieved from https://www.theguardian.com/world/1999/may/27/warcrimes.davidhearst.

Helsinki Committee for Human Rights in Serbia (2019). Helsinki committee for human rights in Serbia in 2019. Retrieved from https://www.helsinki.org.rs/about.html.

Herman, J.L. (1992). *Trauma and recovery: The aftermath of violence-from domestic abuse to political terror*. New York: Basic Books.

Hill, C.R. (2014). *Outpost: A diplomat at work*. New York: Simon & Schuster.

History. (n.d.). Retrieved from https://www.history.com/.

Hohmann, J. (2017, August 16). The daily 202: False moral equivalency is not a bug of Trumpism. It's a feature. *The Washington Post*. Retrieved from https://www.washingtonpost.com/news/powerpost/paloma/daily-202/2017/08/16/daily-202-false-moral-equivalency-is-not-a-bug-of-trumpism-it-s-a-feature/5993b25930fb0433811d6965/.

Hren, H., & Begović, N. (1998). *The Srebrenica deadly summer*. Tuzla, Bosnia and Herzegovina: Srebrenica Women's Citizen Association.

Human Rights Watch (1998). Chemical warfare in Bosnia? The strange experiences of the Srebrenica survivors. Retrieved from https://www.hrw.org/legacy/reports98/bosniacw/index.html.

Human Rights Watch (2019 March 15). The International Criminal Court and the United States. Retrieved from https://www.hrw.org/news/2019/03/15/qa-international-criminal-court-and-united-states#2.

Human Rights Watch (2020). Justice at risk: War crimes trials in Croatia, Bosnia and Herzegovina, and Serbia and Montenegro. Retrieved from https://www.hrw.org/report/2004/10/13/justice-risk/war-crimes-trials-croatia-bosnia-and-herzegovina-and-serbia-and.

Humanitarian Law Center (n.d.). About us. Retrieved from http://www.hlc-rdc.org/?page_id=14390&lang=de.

Hundreds attend funeral for mothers of Srebrenica leader (2018, July 25). *Voice of America*. Retrieved from https://www.voanews.com/europe/hundreds-attend-funeral-mothers-srebrenica-leader.

Illic, I. (2017, November 29). Croatian PM Plenkovic regrets Praljak's death in The Hague. *Reuters*. Retrieved from https://www.reuters.com/article/us-warcrimes-bosnia-croatia/croatian-pm-plenkovic-regrets-praljaks-death-in-the-hague-idUSKBN1DT2HW.

Infoplease (n.d.). Bosnia and Herzegovina. Retrieved from https://www.infoplease.com/world/countries/bosnia-and-herzegovina.

International Commission on Missing Persons (n.d). Retrieved from https://www.icmp.int/.

International Court of Justice (n.d.). Retrieved from https://www.icj-cij.org/en.

International Criminal Court (n.d.). The ICC Rome Statute is 20. Retrieved from https://www.icc-cpi.int/romestatute20.

International Criminal Court (2011). Rome statute of the International Criminal Court. Retrieved from https://www.icc-cpi.int/resourcelibrary/official-journal/rome-statute.aspx.

International Criminal Tribunal for the Former Yugoslavia (n.d.). About the ICTY. Retrieved from https://www.icty.org/en/about.

International Criminal Tribunal for the former Yugoslavia (n.d.). ICTY remembers: The Srebrenica genocide 1995–2015. Retrieved from https://www.irmct.org/specials/srebrenica20/.

International Criminal Tribunal for the Former Yugoslavia (n.d.). Judgement list. Retrieved from https://www.icty.org/en/cases/judgement-list.

International Criminal Tribunal for the Former Yugoslavia (n.d.). Lord David Owen. Retrieved from https://www.icty.org/en/content/lord-david-owen.

International Criminal Tribunal for the Former Yugoslavia (n.d.). The Tribunal-Establishment. Retrieved from https://www.icty.org/en/about/tribunal/establishment.

International Criminal Tribunal for the Former Yugoslavia (1995, November 16). Radovan Karadzic and Ratko Mladic accused of genocide following the take-over of Srebrenica [Press release]. Retrieved from https://www.icty.org/en/press/radovan-karadzic-and-ratko-mladic-accused-genocide-following-take-over-srebrenica.

International Criminal Tribunal for the Former Yugoslavia (2000, March 22). [Court transcript]. Retrieved from https://www.icty.org/x/cases/krstic/trans/en/000322it.htm?fbclid=-IwAR0bDK_udxyvlzf7fr3icY06g5do-o613eFNZIhEgIBvsD59fxUkm16CwPo.

International Criminal Tribunal for the former Yugoslavia (2003, May 20). [Court transcript]. Retrieved from https://urldefense. com/v3/__https://www.icty.org/x/cases/ slobodan_milosevic/trans/en/030520ED. htm__;!!NCZxaNi9jForCP_SxBKJCA!BoGB4H WWdvpAr3s0gXz31mLIvGWX3kN4Pt8gf5Em VRp-7tR9m8oHdS3w7QzK6lQL$.

International Criminal Tribunal for the former Yugoslavia (2010, April 26). [Court transcript]. Retrieved from https://www.icty.org/x/cases/ tolimir/trans/en/100426ED.htm?fbclid=IwAR 2VYO71OEYwflH1TSlqDhAYpEd4LoZmnZ_ d10T1caeYj8Br-u00jSWZvsQ.

International Criminal Tribunal for the Former Yugoslavia (2016, March 24). Tribunal convicts Radovan Karadžić for crimes in Bosnia and Herzegovina [Press release]. Retrieved from https:// www.icty.org/en/press/tribunal-convicts-radovan-karadzic-for-crimes-in-bosnia-and-herzegovina.

International Criminal Tribunal for the Former Yugoslavia (2017, November). ICTY convicts Ratko Mladić for genocide, war crimes and crimes against humanity [Press release]. Retrieved from: https://www.icty.org/en/press/icty-convicts-ratko-mladi%C4%87-for-genocide-war-crimes-andcrimes-against-humanity.

International Criminal Tribunal for the Former Yugoslavia (2019, August). Key figures of the cases. Retrieved from https://www.icty.org/en/cases/key-figures-cases.

International IDEA (2016). Constitutional history of Bosnia and Herzegovina. Retrieved from http://constitutionnet.org/country/bosnia-and-herzegovina.

International Institute for Middle East and Balkan Studies (2015). Bosnia and Herzegovina: The final phase of genocide? Retrieved from https://www. ifimes.org/en/9009.

International Residual Mechanism for Criminal Tribunals (n.d.). About. Retrieved from https://www. irmct.org/en/about.

International Residual Mechanism for Criminal Tribunals (n.d.). Crimes of sexual violence. Retrieved from https://www.icty.org/en/features/crimes-sexual-violence.

International Residual Mechanism for Criminal Tribunals (n.d.). Development of the local judiciaries. Retrieved from https://www.icty.org/en/outreach/capacity-building/development-local-judiciaries.

International Residual Mechanism for Criminal Tribunals (n.d.). Dražen Erdemović. Retrieved from https://www.icty.org/en/content/dra%C5%BEen-erdemovi%C4%87.

International Residual Mechanism for Criminal Tribunals (1995, November 16). Radovan Karadzic and Ratko Mladic accused of genocide following the take-over of Srebrenica [Press release]. Retrieved from https://www.icty.org/en/press/radovan-karadzic-and-ratko-mladic-accused-genocide-following-take-over-srebrenica.

International Residual Mechanism for Criminal Tribunals (2001, August 2). Radislav Krstic becomes the first person to be convicted of genocide at the ICTY and is sentenced to 46 yeas imprisonment [Press release]. Retrieved from https:// www.icty.org/en/press/radislav-krstic-becomes-first-person-be-convicted-genocide-icty-and-sentenced-46-years.

International Residual Mechanism for Criminal Tribunals (2002, August 28). Keraterm camp [Drawing]. Retrieved from https://www.irmct. org/specials/1000words/item-5-keraterm-camp. html.

International Residual Mechanism for Criminal Tribunals (2016, March 24). Tribunal convicts Radovan Karadžić for crimes in Bosnia and Herzegovina [Press release]. Retrieved from https:// www.icty.org/en/press/tribunal-convicts-radovan-karadzic-for-crimes-in-bosnia-and-herzegovina.

International Residual Mechanisms for Criminal Tribunals (2017, November 22). ICTY convicts Ratko Mladić for genocide, war crimes and crimes against humanity [Press release]. Retrieved from https://www.icty.org/en/press/icty-convicts-ratko-mladić-for-genocide-war-crimes-and-crimes-against-humanity.

Joeden-Forgey, E.V. (2018). Genocide watch issues statement on forced family separation, detention & deportation in the United States. Retrieved from https://www.genocidewatch. com/single-post/2018/07/02/Genocide-Watch-Issues-Statement-on-Forced-Family-Separation-Detention-Deportation-in-the-United-States.

Joseph, S. (2011). Post-traumatic stress disorder: Is shell shock the same as PTSD? Retrieved from https://www.psychologytoday.com/us/blog/what-doesnt-kill-us/201111/is-shell-shock-the-same-ptsd.

Jovanović, S. M. (2019). Confronting recent history: Media in Serbia during Aleksandar Vučić's Ministry of Information in the Milošević era (1998–1999). *Hiperboreea, 6*(1), 61–74. Retrieved from https://du.idm.oclc.org/login?url=https://search-proquest-com.du.idm.oclc.org/docview/22576701 37?accountid=14608.

Jugo, A., & Wastell, S. (2015). Disassembling the pieces, reassembling the social: The forensic and political lives of secondary mass graves in Bosnia and Herzegovina. In Anstett, É., & Dreyfus, J. (Eds.), *Human remains and identification: Mass violence, genocide, and the "forensic turn"* (pp. 142–174). Manchester: Manchester University Press.

Kaufman, M.T. (1999, March 28). Milosevic: For Serbs, Apparatchik as nationalist hero. *New York Times*. Retrieved from https://archive.nytimes. com/www.nytimes.com/library/world/europe/ 032899kosovo-slobodan.html.

Kern, R. (2016, July 29). The Zetra project: Remembering the concert that tried to save Yugoslavia. *Balkanist*. Retrieved from https://balkanist.net/ the-zetra-project-remembering-the-concert-that-tried-to-save-yugoslavia/.

Kirmayer, L. J., Gone, J. P., & Moses, J. (2014). Rethinking historical trauma. *Transcultural Psychiatry, 51*(3), 299–319. https://doi.org/10.1177/ 1363461514536358.

Kirsch, M. (2009, August 13). Revisiting the Tuzla massacre. *AlJazeera*. Retrieved from https://www.

aljazeera.com/news/europe/2009/08/200981018 1813969925.html.

Klarin, M. (2016). Srebrenica: Genocide in eight acts. Retrieved from https://srebrenica.sense-agency.com/en/.

Klein, J.M. (2017, February 22). In pursuit of justice. *The Pennsylvania Gazette*. Retrieved from https://thepenngazette.com/in-pursuit-of-justice/.

Kolk, B.V.D. (2016). *The body keeps the score: Brain, mind, and body in the healing of trauma*. New York: Penguin.

Kuwert, P., Glaesmer, H., Eichhorn, S., Grundke, E., Pietrzak, R.H., Freyberger, H.J., & Klauer, T. (2014). Long-term effects of conflict-related sexual violence compared with non-sexual war trauma in female World War II survivors: A matched pairs study. *Archives of Sexual Behavior, 43*(6), 1059–1064.

Lakic, M. (2018, April 3). Sarajevo remembers children killed during siege. *Balkan Transitional Justice*. Retrieved from https://balkaninsight.com/2018/04/03/sarajevo-remembers-children-killed-during-siege-04-03-2018/.

Lakic, M., Vladisavljevic, A., & Rudic, F. (2019 October 19). State of denial: The books rewriting the Bosnian War. Retrieved from https://balkaninsight.com/2018/10/19/state-of-denial-the-books-rewriting-the-bosnian-war-10-18-2018/.

Lawyers' Committee for Human Rights (2010, January 4). Declaration on Srebrenica. *Peščanik*. Retrieved from https://pescanik.net/declaration-on-srebrenica/.

Layne, C.M., Olsen, J.A. Baker, A. Legerski, J.P., Isakson, B., Pašalić, A., Duraković-Belko, E., Đapo, N., Ćampara, N., Arslanagić, B., Saltzman, W.R., & Pynoos, R.S. (2010). Unpacking trauma exposure risk factors and differential pathways of influence: predicting postwar mental distress in Bosnian adolescents. *Child Development, 81*(4), 1053–1076. doi: https://doi-org.du.idm.oclc.org/10.1111/j.1467-8624.2010.01454.x.

Leydesdorff, S. (2011). *Surviving the Bosnian genocide: The women of Srebrenica speak*. Bloomington: Indiana University Press.

Locke, B. (2018, February 22). Amnesty international just officially declared Trump a human rights violator. *Washington Press*. Retrieved from https://washingtonpress.com/2018/02/22/amnesty-international-just-officially-declared-trump-human-rights-violater/.

Lončar, M., Medved, V., Jovanović, N., & Hotujac, L. (2006). Psychological consequences of rape on women in 1991–1995 war in Croatia and Bosnia and Herzegovina. *Croatian Medical Journal, 47*(1), 67–75.

Malcolm, N. (1996). *Bosnia: A short history*. United Kingdom: NYU Press.

Malcolm, N.R., Lampe, J.R., & Pickering, P. (n.d.). Bosnia and Herzegovina. In *Encyclopedia Britannica*. Retrieved from https://www.britannica.com/place/Bosnia-and-Herzegovina.

Mayo Clinic (n.d.). Post-traumatic stress disorder (PTSD). Retrieved from https://www.mayoclinic.org/diseases-conditions/post-traumatic-stress-disorder/symptoms-causes/syc-20355967.

Medica Zenica (2018). *About us*. Retrieved from http://medicazenica.org/en/about-us/.

Midžic, M. (2013, April 4). List gradjana Bosne i Hercegovine u Holandiji. *Nasa Bosna*. Retrieved from https://platformbih.nl/Nasa%20Bosna/Nasa%20Bosna%2027.pdf.

Miller, P.D. (2018, January 3). Trump's nationalism is arbitrary, dangerous, incoherent and silly. *Foreign Policy*. Retrieved from https://foreignpolicy.com/2018/01/03/trumps-nationalism-is-arbitrary-dangerous-incoherent-and-silly/.

Milutinovic, R. (2018, May 18). Serbian state security "controlled Scorpions paramilitary unit." Retrieved from https://balkaninsight.com/2017/11/08/serbian-state-security-controlled-scorpions-paramilitary-unit-11-08-2017/.

Mirceva, S. (2004). Why the International Criminal Court is different. Retrieved from https://www.globalpolicy.org/component/content/article/164/28450.html.

Mirsad, T. (n.d.). [LinkedIn page]. Retrieved January 2, 2020, from https://ba.linkedin.com/in/tokaca-mirsad-4a832774?fbclid=-IwAR2xKPCq9ecxQaHzwrj9f9VV0A-Lo71wz-ld-aZ8vfvXmtIlS3TK2FIMYzY.

Mladic present during the Orahovac massacre (2011). Retrieved from https://srebrenica-genocide.blogspot.com/2011/11/mladic-present-during-orahovac-massacre.html?m=1&fbclid=IwAR3_aOgZ9LhhIAjIXrHdd_l3UGQMudibRBmTPRToDqX-Pu6_Mso7VrkqUhs.

Momartin, S., Silove, D., Manicavasagar, V., & Steel, Z. (2004). Complicated grief in Bosnian refugees: Associations with posttraumatic stress disorder and depression. *Comprehensive Psychiatry, 45*(6), 475–482. doi: https://doi.org/10.1016/j.comppsych.2004.07.013.

Morgan, D. Yugoslavia's multi-ethnic make up could lead to its unraveling. Retrieved from https://www.washingtonpost.com/wp-srv/inatl/longterm/bosvote/1989.htm.

N1 Sarajevo (2018, July 23). World media mark the death of Hatidza Mehmedovic. *N1*. Retrieved from http://ba.n1info.com/English/NEWS/a274721/World-media-mark-the-death-of-Hatidza-Mehmedovic.html.

N1 Sarajevo (2018, July 25). Srebrenica activist Hatidza Mehmedovic laid to rest. Retrieved from http://ba.n1info.com/English/NEWS/a275225/Srebrenica-activist-Hatidza-Mehmedovic-laid-to-rest.html.

N1 Sarajevo (2019 May). High Representative: I will use the Bonn powers when the time is right. Retrieved from http://ba.n1info.com/English/NEWS/a344646/Inzko-Dodik-is-playing-with-fire.html.

N1 Sarajevo (2019, December 12). Bosnia's international administrator could impose ban on genocide denial. Retrieved from http://rs.n1info.com/English/NEWS/a551960/Valentin-Inzko-s-office-working-on-a-law-banning-genocide-denial.html?fbclid=IwAR2L88Mwxdw2FhmkPsaW2NzPEsZBGqabspBttzasvoUOKXo3ca0oXeA5OQo.

Nardelli, A., Dzidic, D., & Jukic, E. (2014, October 8).

Bosnia and Herzegovina: The world's most complicated system of government? *The Guardian.* Retrieved from https://www.theguardian.com/news/datablog/2014/oct/08/bosnia-herzegovina-elections-the-worlds-most-complicated-system-of-government.

Nartova-Bochaver, S., Donat, M., & Rüprich, C. (2019). Subjective well-being from a just-world perspective: A multi-dimensional approach in a student sample. *Frontiers in Psychology.* doi: https://doi.org/10.3389/fpsyg.2019.01739.

National Institute of Mental Health (n.d.). Post-traumatic stress disorder [Fact sheet]. Retrieved from https://www.nimh.nih.gov/health/publications/post-traumatic-stress-disorder-ptsd/index.shtml.

Nelson, J. (n.d.). Enclaves & exclaves [Story map]. Retrieved from http://storymaps.esri.com/stories/2017/enclaves-exclaves/index.html.

News and Guts (2019 December 10). Donald Trump's lies prompt a new level of fact checking from *The Washington Post.* Retrieved from https://www.newsandguts.com/video/donald-trumps-lies-prompt-a-new-level-of-fact-checking-from-the-washington-post/.

NPR (2016 October 18). Last Nuremberg prosecutor has 3 words of advice: "Law not war." [Audio file]. *NPR.* Retrieved from https://www.npr.org/sections/parallels/2016/10/18/497938049/the-last-nuremberg-prosecutor-has-3-words-of-advice-law-not-war.

Nuhanović, H. (2007). *Under the UN flag: The international community and the Srebrenica Genocide.* Bosnia and Herzegovina: DES.

Nuremberg prosecutor still haunted by Nazi defendants (2017, May 4). Retrieved from https://www.cbsnews.com/news/nuremberg-prosecutor-still-haunted-by-nazi-defendants/.

Office of the High Representative (2000, May 10). Decision establishing and registering the Foundation of the Srebrenica-Potočari Memorial and cemetery. Retrieved from http://www.ohr.int/?p=67761.

Office of the High Representative (2000, October 25). Decision on the location of a cemetery and a monument for the victims of Srebrenica. Retrieved from http://www.ohr.int/?p=67588.

Office of the High Representative (2003, March 25). Decision ordering the transfer of ownership of the of the Battery Factory "AS"—Srebrenica to the Foundation of the Srebrenica-Potočari Memorial and Cemetery and establishing an ad hoc Battery Factory "AS" a.d.—Srebrenica Compensation Commission. Retrieved from http://www.ohr.int/?p=65883.

Office of the High Representative (2007, June 25). Decision enacting the law on the Center for the Srebrenica-Potočari Memorial and cemetery for the victims of the 1995 genocide. Retrieved from http://www.ohr.int/?p=64715.

Office of the High Representative (2015). Retrieved from http://www.ohr.int/?lang=en.

Office of the High Representative (2015). Mandate. Retrieved from http://www.ohr.int/?page_id=1161.

Office of the Special Representative of the Secretary-General on Sexual Violence in Conflict (n.d.). About the office. Retrieved from https://www.un.org/sexualviolenceinconflict/about-us/about-the-office/.

Office of the Spokesman (1995, November 30). Summary of the Dayton Peace Agreement on Bosnia-Herzegovina [Fact sheet]. Retrieved from http://hrlibrary.umn.edu/icty/dayton/daytonsum.html.

Oldest.org (n.d.). 8 Oldest cemeteries in the world. Retrieved from https://www.oldest.org/culture/cemeteries/.

O'Malley, P. (2017). Shadow grief. Retrieved from http://drpatrickomalley.com/shadow-grief/.

Organization for Security and Co-operation in Europe. (1995, December 14). Dayton Peace Agreement. Retrieved from https://www.osce.org/bih/126173.

Ozturk, T., & Besic, V. (2019). Bosnia: 3,176 white ribbons mark Prijedor massacre. Retrieved from https://www.aa.com.tr/en/europe/bosnia-3-176-white-ribbons-mark-prijedor-massacre/1494419.

Paddy Ashdown: British marine who led Bosnia with an iron fist (2018, December 2013). *Bangkok Post.* Retrieved from https://www.bangkokpost.com/.

Panić, K. (2015). The proud soldiers from the Balkans. Retrieved from https://www.fairplanet.org/story/the-proud-soldiers-from-the-balkans/.

Partos, G. (2003, June 13). Vukovar massacre: What happened. *BBC News.* Retrieved from http://news.bbc.co.uk/2/hi/europe/2988304.stm.

Paulsen, Natalya (2016). Emotional experiences of post-war youth from Bosnia-Herzegovina: A systematic review. Retrieved from Sophia, the St. Catherine University repository website: https://sophia.stkate.edu/msw_papers/649.

PeaceWomen (2010). International: UN-wartime rape no more inevitable, acceptable than mass murder. Retrieved from https://www.peacewomen.org/content/international-un-wartime-rape-no-more-inevitable-acceptable-mass-murder.

Pensky, M., & Rubaii, N. (2017, August 21). Warning signs of mass violence—in the US? *The Conversation.* Retrieved from https://theconversation.com/warning-signs-of-mass-violence-in-the-us-82546.

Perlez, J. (1997, August 10). Serbian media is a one-man show. *New York Times.* Retrieved from https://www.nytimes.com/1997/08/10/weekinreview/serbian-media-is-a-one-man-show.html.

Petrila, A. (2018, May 27). Trump's dangerous language. *Denver Post.* Guest Commentary. http://digital.olivesoftware.com/Olive/ODN/DenverPost/shared/ShowArticle.aspx?doc=TDP%2F2018%2F05%2F27&entity=Ar06101&sk=54E7A711&mode=text.

Pfaff, W. (1999, November 24). In frank account, U.N. admits failure at Srebrenica. *The Baltimore Sun.* Retrieved from https://www.baltimoresun.com/news/bs-xpm-1999-11-24-9911240265-story.html.

Pickel, A. (2014). Nationalism and violence: A mechanismic explanation.(pp. 1–30, Working paper No. CSGP 07/1). Ontario, Canada: Trent University.

PLBIH [Screen name] (2019, February 21). *Sre-*

brenica Genocide—Skorpioni Execution (Trnovo '95-full video) [Video file]. Retrieved from https://www.youtube.com/watch?v=nuddfY00kKo&feature=share&fbclid=IwAR1uFY0j-gkXnJiHQ0S-MAP0sYGPiyfDyHc-pPbNUfkimdgfLNoRXsxkq8.

Pollack, M.S.C.E. (2010). Intentions of burial: Mourning politics, and memorials following the massacre at Srebrenica. *Journal of Death Studies, 27*(2), 125–142. doi: https://doi.org/10.1080/07481180302893.

Popular "name explain": Why Bosnia and Herzegovina has two names (2018, February 4). *Sarajevo Times.* Retrieved from https://www.sarajevotimes.com/popular-name-explain-bosnia-herzegovina-two-names/.

Post-Conflict Research Center (2017, May 31). 31 May 1992—Remembering Prijedor. Retrieved from https://p-crc.org/2017/05/31/31-may-1992-remembering-prijedor/.

Posters of General Ratko Mladic all over Srebrenica (2020, January 11). *Sarajevo Times.* Retrieved from https://www.sarajevotimes.com/posters-of-general-ratko-mladic-all-over-srebrenica/.

Powell, S., Butollo, W., & Hagl, M. (2010). Missing or killed: The differential effect on mental health in women in Bosnia and Herzegovina of the confirmed or unconfirmed loss of their husbands. *European Psychologist, 15*(3), 185–192. https://doi.org/10.1027/1016-9040/a000018.

Prager, J. (2003). Lost childhood, lost generations: The intergenerational transmission of trauma. *Journal of Human Rights, 2*(2), 173–181. doi: 10.1080/1475483032000078161.

Praljak: Bosnian Croat war criminal dies after taking poison in court (2017, November 29). *BBC World News.* Retrieved from: https://www.bbc.com/news/world-europe-42163613.

Prigerson, H.G., Shear, M.K., Jacobs, S.C., Reynolds, C.F., Maciejewski, P.K., Davidson, J.R.T., Rosenheck, R., Piklonis, P.A., Wortman, C.B., Williams, J.B.W., Widiger, T. A., Frank, E., Kupfer, D.J., & Zisook, S. (1999). Consensus criteria for traumatic grief: a preliminary empirical test. *The British Journal of Psychiatry, 174*(1), 67–73. doi: https://doi-org.du.idm.oclc.org/10.1192/bjp.174.1.67.

Prosecutor v. Radislav Krstić, Case No. IT-98-33-T, Judgement, 2 August 2001 ("*Krstić* Trial Judgement" or "Trial Judgement").

Prosecutor v. Radislav Krstić, Case No. IT-98-33-A, Judgement, 19 April 2004 ("*Krstić* Appeals Judgement" or "Appeals Judgement").

PUCE, I. (2016 July 11). General Morillon promises to protect people of Srebrenica. Retrieved from https://www.youtube.com/watch?v=PNSjidJNdeQ.

Radio Free Europe Radio Liberty (2017). The siege of Sarajevo. Retrieved from https://www.rferl.org/a/twenty-five-years-on-from-the-siege-of-sarajevo/28407397.html.

Radio Free Europe Radio Liberty (2017, December 11). Croatian ceremony honors convicted war criminal Praljak. Retrieved from https://www.rferl.org/a/croatia-bosnian-croat-war-criminal-praljak-honored/28910360.html.

Radio Free Europe/Radio Liberty [Screen name] (2019, October 18). *Is the World's Most Complicated Government in Bosnia-Herzegovina* [Video file]. Retrieved from https://www.youtube.com/watch?v=yN8fwVypbPE.

Rank, S.M. (2020 March). What was the iron curtain? Retrieved from https://www.historyonthenet.com/what-was-the-iron-curtain.

RECOM (2018). What is RECOM? Retrieved from https://www.recom.link/about-recom/what-is-recom/.

RECOM (2019). Remember Stupni do crimes. Retrieved from http://www.recom.link/.

Remembering Srebrenica (2014 December). Srebrenica-Potoçari Memorial and Cemetery. Retrieved from https://www.srebrenica.org.uk/lessons-from-srebrenica/srebrenica-potocari-memorial/.

Reuters (2018 December 18). United States added to list of most dangerous countries for journalists for first time. Retrieved from https://www.nbcnews.com/news/world/united-states-added-list-most-dangerous-countries-journalists-first-time-n949676.

Rhode, D. (2005, July 10). 10 years on, tormenting memories of Srebrenica. *New York Times.* Retrieved from https://www.nytimes.com/2005/07/10/world/europe/10-years-on-tormenting-memories-of-srebrenica.html.

Rhode, D. (2012). *Endgame: The betrayal and fall of Srebrenica, Europe's worst massacre since World War II.* New York: Penguin Books.

Rubin, A.J. (2005, June 13). Video alters Serbs' view of Bosnian War. *Los Angeles Times.* Retrieved from https://www.latimes.com/archives/la-xpm-2005-jun-13-fg-bosnia13-story.html.

Rudic, F. (2018, June 15). Serbia "used Yugoslav army for war goals": Report. *Balkan Transitional Justice.* Retrieved from https://balkaninsight.com/2018/06/15/report-details-serbian-1990s-takeover-of-yugoslav-army-06-15-2018/.

Rudic, F., Mejdini, F., Grebo, L., Haxhiaj, S., & Milekic, S. (2018, August 30). Missing persons: Balkan families suffer as search goes on. *Balkan Transitional Justice.* Retrieved from https://balkaninsight.com/2018/08/30/missing-persons-balkan-families-suffer-as-search-goes-on-08-29-2018/.

Ryan, J., Chaudieu, I., Ancelin, M.L., & Saffery, R. (2016). Biological underpinnings of trauma and post-traumatic stress disorder: Focusing on genetics and epigenetics. *Epigenomics, 8*(11), 1553–1569. doi: 10.2217/epi-2016-0083.

Ryngaert, C., & Schrijver, N. (2015). Lessons learned from the Srebrenica massacre: From UN peacekeeping reform to legal responsibility. *Netherlands International Law Review, 62*(2), 219–227. doi: 10.1007/s40802-015-0034-x.

Sablijakovic, D. (2001). REPORT: French Srebrenica Inquiry. Retrieved from https://iwpr.net/global-voices/report-french-srebrenica-inquiry.

Sarajevo Times Team (n.d.). About us. Retrieved from https://www.sarajevotimes.com/about-us/.

Sargent, G. (2019 February 1). In remarkable exchange, Trump offers startling view of role of free press. Retrieved from https://www.washingtonpost.

Bibliography

- com/opinions/2019/02/01/remarkable-exchange-trump-offers-startling-view-role-free-press/?utm_term=.97a977898ff1.
- Saric, V., & Herman, E.D. (2014). Why Bosnia has the world's highest youth unemployment rate. Retrieved from https://www.pri.org/stories/2014-10-09/why-bosnia-has-worlds-highest-youth-unemployment-rate.
- Serb paramilitaries found guilty in war crimes trial (2007, April 10). *The Guardian*. Retrieved from https://www.theguardian.com/world/2007/apr/10/balkans.warcrimes.
- Shapiro F. (2014). The role of eye movement desensitization and reprocessing (EMDR) therapy in medicine: Addressing the psychological and physical symptoms stemming from adverse life experiences. *The Permanente journal*, *18*(1), 71–77. doi:10.7812/TPP/13-098.
- Sijarić, M. (n.d.). Sarajevo Haggadah. Retrieved from https://www.zemaljskimuzej.ba/en/archaeology/middle-ages/sarajevo-haggadah.
- Simon, D. (2018, January 14). President Trump's other insensitive comments on race and ethnicity. *CNN*. Retrieved from https://www.cnn.com/2018/01/11/politics/president-trump-racial-comments-tweets/index.html.
- Sito-Sucic, D. (2010, September 3). Women force French former general from Srebrenica. *Reuters*. Retrieved from https://www.reuters.com/article/uk-bosnia-srebrenica-general/women-force-french-former-general-from-srebrenica-idUKTRE6823BD20100903.
- Sito-Sucic, D., & Katana, G. (2017, March 9). ICJ rejects request for revision of Bosnia genocide ruling. *Reuters*. Retrieved from https://www.reuters.com/article/us-bosnia-icj-revision/icj-rejects-request-for-revision-of-bosnia-genocide-ruling-idUSKBN16G25X.
- Slobodan Praljak suicide: War criminal "took cyanide" in Hague court (2017, December 1). *BBC World News*. Retrieved from https://www.bbc.com/news/world-europe-42204587.
- Smith-Spark, L., & Borcak, M. (2017, November 30). Dutch authorities probe Bosnian war criminal's courtroom suicide. *CNN*. Retrieved from https://www.cnn.com/2017/11/30/europe/slobodan-praljak-hague-death/index.html.
- Sobelman, B. (2011, January 18). Israel: Israeli citizen suspected of involvement in Bosnia war crimes arrested. *Los Angeles Times*. Retrieved from https://latimesblogs.latimes.com/babylonbeyond/2011/01/israel-israeli-citizen-suspected-of-involvement-in-bosnia-war-crimes-arrested.html?fbclid=IwAR2Q7Tieyfw3H1n1_-gIIvsgYUtaWOKY6kp_1Tkqo6kNB020XPEkht2kSU.
- Socolovsky, J. (2000, March 20). Foca trial to begin in The Hague. *Associated Press News*. Retrieved from https://apnews.com/85ff88aeadd41f973fcc1d9ead641e3b.
- Sorguc, A. (2019, January). Bosnian Serb Hague convict faces new war crime trial. Retrieved from https://balkaninsight.com/2019/01/11/bosnian-serb-hague-convict-faces-new-war-crime-trial-01-11-2019/.
- Sorguc, A. (2019, July 9). Srebrenica cover-up: The search for secret graves continues. *Balkan Transitional Justice*. Retrieved from https://balkaninsight.com/2019/07/09/srebrenica-cover-up-the-search-for-secret-graves-continues/.
- Southern Poverty Law Center (n.d.). White nationalist. Retrieved from https://www.splcenter.org/fighting-hate/extremist-files/ideology/white-nationalist.
- Southern Poverty Law Center (2019). New hate map helps users explore landscape of hate. Retrieved from https://www.splcenter.org/fighting-hate/intelligence-report/2019/new-hate-map.
- Srebrenica grave exhumed at former UN base (2012, August 2). *The Journal.ie*. Retrieved from https://www.thejournal.ie/srebrenica-grave-exhumed-at-former-un-base-543243-Aug2012/.
- Srebrenica mass grave uncovered 20 years after massacre (2015, December 9). *I24 News*. Retrieved from https://www.i24news.tv/en/news/international/europe/95111-151209-srebrenica-mass-grave-uncovered-20-years-after-massacre.
- Srebrenica-Potocari Memorial Center (n.d.). Retrieved from https://www.potocarimc.org/index.php/memorijalni-centar.
- Srebrenica's Hasan Hasanovic is among the celebrities who marked 2014 (2015, January 96). Retrieved from http://prosvjetitelj-muallim.org/timovi/timovi-u-dijaspori/item/525-srebrenicanin-hasan-hasanovic-medu-licnostima-koje-su-obiljezile-2014-godinu.html.
- Stanton, G.H. (1996). The ten stages of genocide. Retrieved from https://www.genocidewatch.com/ten-stages-of-genocide.
- Stojanovic, D. (2017, November 29). Croat general performs ultimate act at war crimes trial. *Associated Press News*. Retrieved from https://apnews.com/6a5ae2972f6541e290aa25cac9401155/Croat-general-performs-ultimate-act-at-war-crimes-trial.
- Subotic, J. (2020, January 24). Why the Yugoslav Memorial Pavilion at Auschwitz stands empty. *Balkan Transitional Justice*. Retrieved from https://balkaninsight.com/2020/01/24/why-the-yugoslav-memorial-pavilion-at-auschwitz-stands-empty/.
- Sudetic, C. (1999). *Blood and vengeance: One family's story of the war in Bosnia*. New York: Penguin Books.
- Suljagic, E. (2019, October 3). Memory of Srebrenica. *The News*. Retrieved from https://www.thenews.com.pk/print/535470-memory-of-srebrenica.
- Sunter, D. (2005, August 2). Serbia: Mladic "recruited" infamous Scorpions. *Institute for War and Peace Reporting*. Retrieved from https://iwpr.net/global-voices/serbia-mladic-%E2%80%9Crecruited%E2%80%9D-infamous-scorpions.
- Tingler, J. (2016). Holocaust denial and holocaust memory: The case of Ernst Zündel. *Genocide Studies International*, *10*(2), pp. 210–229.
- Topham, K. (2016, September 9). The danger of false equivalence. *Huffpost*. Retrieved from https://www.huffpost.com/entry/the-danger-of-false-equivalence_b_57db909ae4b04fa361d99724?g

uccounter=1&guce_referrer=aHR0cHM6Ly93 d3cuZ29vZ2xlLmNvbS8&guce_referrer_sig=- AQAAAMtvYWzfErDPq4Zn9ZA_958GO30- xmyYg-pOGas1oqWOZG3jdwHILZuFBiB- j4VrDl0tFaRsJwgaOzTG36vi_GFXJb49lp9b X0RIGr8A3-y7btyeHjIxr3onRNP2rh1WHBn 0qtaymxu81KAv39MRuyJVC3s_TmEoYZg_ AjG2EQ1G.

Traynor, I. (2003, July 10). Ian Traynor on the survivors of a Serbian death squad. Retrieved December 28, 2019, from https://www.theguardian.com/world/2003/jul/10/warcrimes.balkans.

Traynor, I. (2007, April 11). Serbia jails death squad men for Srebrenica killings. *The Guardian*. Retrieved from https://www.theguardian.com/world/2007/apr/11/balkans.

Traynor, I., & O'Kane, M. (2018, July 13). The siege of Sarajevo—Archive, 1993. *The Guardian*. Retrieved from https://www.theguardian.com/world/from-the-archive-blog/2018/jul/13/siege-of-sarajevo-ian-traynor-maggie-okane-1993.

Trnovo Execution (Srebrenica) (n.d.). Retrieved from http://www.bosniafacts.info/history/serbian-aggression/trnovo-execution-video-srebrenica.

TRT World [Screen name] (2018, April 17). *Does Bosnia have the most complicated political system in Europe?* [Video file]. Retrieved from https://www.youtube.com/watch?v=sCEYDdMue-8.

Truck carrying 35 Srebrenica victims passes through Sarajevo (2018, September 09). Retrieved from http://ba.n1info.com/English/NEWS/a271692/Truck-carrying-35-Srebrenica-victims-passes-through-Sarajevo.html.

2019 Index of Economic Freedom (2019). *Bosnia and Herzegovina* [Data set]. Retrieved from https://www.heritage.org/index/country/bosniaherzegovina.

UNESCO (2018 March). Jewish cemetery in Sarajevo. Retrieved from https://whc.unesco.org/en/tentativelists/6334/.

United Nations (2005, July 11). "May we all learn and act on the lessons of Srebrenica," says Secretary-General, in message to anniversary ceremony [Press release]. Retrieved from https://www.un.org/press/en/2005/sgsm9993.doc.htm.

United Nations (2015, July 8). At meeting commemorating twentieth anniversary of Srebrenica killings, security council fails to adopt resolution [Press release]. Retrieved from https://www.un.org/press/en/2015/sc11961.doc.htm.

United Nations (2019). UN documentation: International Court of Justice. Retrieved from http://research.un.org/en/docs/icj.

United Nations (2019). UN documentation: International law. Retrieved from https://research.un.org/en/docs/law/courts.

United Nations Educational, Scientific and Cultural Organization (2018). Jewish cemetery in Sarajevo. Retrieved from https://whc.unesco.org/en/tentativelists/6334/.

United Nations Human Right Office of the High Commissioner (n.d.). Rape: Weapon of war. Retrieved from https://www.ohchr.org/en/newsevents/pages/rapeweaponwar.aspx.

United Nations Human Rights Office of the High Commissioner (2018). Genocide: "Never again" has become "time and again." Retrieved from https://www.ohchr.org/EN/NewsEvents/Pages/Genocide0918-7808.aspx/.

United Nations Office on Genocide Prevention and the Responsibility to Protect (n.d.). Responsibility to protect. Retrieved from https://www.un.org/en/genocideprevention/about-responsibility-to-protect.shtml.

The United Nations on the Srebrenica's pillar of shame (2007). Tuzla, Bosnia and Herzegovina: Harfo-graf, d.o.o.

United Nations Peacekeeping (1996). United Nations protection force. Retrieved from https://peacekeeping.un.org/en/mission/past/unprof_b.htm.

United Nations Security Council (1993 April). Security Council Resolution 819 (1993) [Bosnia and Herzegovina]. Retrieved from https://www.refworld.org/docid/3b00f2bc28.html.

United Nations Security Council (2019). Security council adopts resolution calling upon Belligerents Worldwide to adopt concrete commitments on ending sexual violence in conflict [Meetings coverage]. Retrieved from https://www.un.org/press/en/2019/sc13790.doc.htm.

United States Holocaust Memorial Museum (n.d.). The UN designates the city a "safe area." Retrieved from https://www.ushmm.org/genocide-prevention/countries/bosnia-herzegovina/srebrenica/background/safe-area.

United to End Genocide (2016). What is Genocide? The origins and naming of genocide. Retrieved from http://endgenocide.org/learn/what-is-genocide/.

US to deny visas for ICC members investigating alleged war crimes (2019, March 15). *The Guardian*. Retrieved from https://www.theguardian.com/us-news/2019/mar/15/mike-pompeo-us-war-crimes-investigation-international-criminal-court.

US withdraws from UN Human Rights Council (2018, June 20). *AlJazeera*. Retrieved from https://www.aljazeera.com/news/2018/06/withdraws-human-rights-council-180619173311272.html.

Video Alters Serbs' View of Bosnian War (2005, June 13). Retrieved from https://www.latimes.com/archives/la-xpm-2005-jun-13-fg-bosnia13-story.html.

Vukušić, I. (2018). Nineteen minutes of horror: Insights from the Scorpions execution video. *Genocide Studies and Prevention: An International Journal, 12*(2), 33–53. Retrieved from https://scholarcommons.usf.edu/cgi/viewcontent.cgi?article=1527&context=gsp.

Wertheimer, L. (Host) (1995, July 13). Events in Srebrenica repeating 1992–1993 history [Podcast episode transcript]. In *All Things Considered*. Retrieved from http://pd.npr.org/anon.npr-mp3/npr/atc/1995/07/19950713_atc_02.mp3.

Wesolowsky, T. (2018, July 25). Death of outspoken Srebrenica mother mocked by top Serbian official. *Radio Free Europe Radio Liberty*. Retrieved from https://www.rferl.org/a/serbian-parliament-deputy-speaker-mocks-srebrenica-mother-s-death/29390764.html.

Winter, J. (2013, June 3). Prophet without honors. Retrieved from https://www.chronicle.com/article/Raphael-Lemkin-a-Prophet/139515.

Wolf, R. (2018, April 24). Travel ban lexicon: From candidate Donald Trump's campaign promises to President Trump's tweets. *USA Today*. Retrieved from https://www.usatoday.com/story/news/politics/2018/04/24/travel-ban-donald-trump-campaign-promises-president-tweets/542504002/.

Wolfelt, A.D. (2007). *Living in the shadow of the ghosts of grief: Step into the light*. Fort Collins, CO: Companion Press.

Wolfgang Petritsch (n.d.). Retrieved from https://www.huffpost.com/author/wolfgang-petritsch?guccounter=1.

Women in Black (2019). Retrieved from http://womeninblack.org.

World Jewish Congress (2018). Bosnia and Herzegovina. Retrieved from https://www.worldjewishcongress.org/en/about/communities/BA.

World Population Review (2020). Bosnia and Herzegovina population 2020. Retrieved from http://worldpopulationreview.com/countries/bosnia-and-herzegovina-population/.

Worse Than War (n.d.). Understanding genocides eliminationism. Retrieved from https://www.pbs.org/wnet/worse-than-war/featured/understanding-genocide-eliminationism/26/.

Yanev, L. (2019). Joint criminal enterprise. In T. Gal, D. Roseen, & T. Van Poecke (Authors) & J. De Hemptinne, R. Roth, E. Van Sliedregt, M. Cupido, M. Ventura, & L. Yanev (Eds.), *Modes of liability in international criminal law* (pp. 121–170). Cambridge: Cambridge University Press. doi:10.1017/9781108678957.006.

Yanev, L. D., Cupido, M., van Sliedregt, E., Ventura, M., Roth, R., & de Hemptinne, J. (Eds.) (2019). *Modes of liability in international criminal law*. Cambridge University Press. https://doi.org/10.1017/9781108678957.

Yehuda, R., & Lehrner, A. (2018). Intergenerational transmission of trauma effects: Putative role of epigenetic mechanisms. *World Psychiatry, 17*(3), 243–257. doi: 10.1002/wps.20568.

Youth unemployment rate for Bosnia and Herzegovina (2019, November 15). Retrieved from https://fred.stlouisfed.org/series/SLUEM1524ZSBIH#.

Zastrow, N. (2011). Chasing the shadow of grief [PDF]. Retrieved from http://www.wingsgrief.org/wp-content/uploads/2011/10/ChasingShadowofGrief.pdf.

Zivstepa [Screen name] (2013, February 21). *Ratko Mladic, Srebrenica Fontana Hotel—July 12, 1995*. [Video file]. Retrieved from https://www.youtube.com/watch?v=urpbonh7kj8.

Zivstepa [Screen name] (2013, February 22). *Ratko Mladic, Srebrenica Fontana Hotel 2—July 11, 1995* [Video file]. Retrieved from https://www.youtube.com/watch?v=b3XSmDYV6BM.

Interviews

Avdić, Nedžad. March 2015.
Avdić, Nedžad. September 2019.
Biserko, Sonja. November 2017.
Ćatić, Hajra. March 2015.
Dautbašić-Klempić, Fatima. March 2015.
Hasanović, Hasan Aziz. December 2017.
Hasanović, Hasan Aziz. September 2019.
Hasanović, Hasan Sejfo. March 2015.
Hasanović, Haso. March 2015.
Hasić, Ahmo. March 2015.
Hasić, Ahmo. August 2017.
Huseinović, Hakija. August 2017.
Husić, Sabiha. December 2017.
Kandić, Nataša. November 2017.
Korač, Žarko. November 2017.
Mandžić, Nesib. March 2015.
Mustafić, Nura. March 2015.
Nukić, Ramiz. March 2015.
Orić, Mevludin. March 2015.
Osmanović, Saliha. March 2015.
Zajović, Staša. November 2017.

Index

Numbers in ***bold italics*** indicate pages with illustrations

Ahmić, Zekira Kira 142
Amanpour, Christiane 188
APC 1, 56, 71, 105, 136, 204
Arkan's Tigers 133-134
Army of BiH *see* Bosnian Army
Ashdown, Paddy 189, 211
Avdić, Nedžad 5, 21-22, 62-79, 146, 190, 218, 221-222

Batković Concentration Camp 7, 41, 57
Battery Factory *see* Memorial Center *see* Potočari
Belgrade 6, 8, 15, 23, 28-29, 61, 63, 89-91, 125-126, 133, 137, 141, 143-145, 151, 158-160, 164-172, 174-179, 181, 186, 218, 222
Bihać 4, 8, 205
Bijeljina 7-8, 32, 41, 71, 91
Biserko, Sonja 5, 172-177, 221
Bosniak 2, 8, 27-33, 91, 128, 135, 160-164, 184, 205, 209, 212, 217; Bosnian Muslims 2, 6-7, 27-28, 116, 126, 128, 161, 215, 221-222
Bosnian Army 2, 52, 92-93, 126, 162, 191-192
Bosnian Muslims *see* Bosniak
Bosnian Serb Army *see* BSA
Branjevo 5, 8, 38-39, 41, ***43***, 184
Bratunac 6, 8-10, 19, 37-38, 48, 55-56, 70-71, 81-82, 90, 103, 106, 115-116, 120, 126, 128, 137, 144, 153, 203
BSA 1-4, 6-10, 16, 25, 29-30, 104, 138, 163, 175, 201, 205-206, 211, 217
Buljim 8, 10, 46, 52-53, 61, 113, 115, 146
Burnice 8, 97, 114-115

Canadian Battalion *see* Peacekeepers
Canadian Peacekeepers *see* Peacekeepers
CANBAT *see* Peacekeepers
Ćatić, Hajra 5, 70, 132-143, 188, 222
Ćatić, Junuz 133, 135-136
Ćatić, Nermin 133-134, 142
Ćatić Nino 5, 56, 132-136, 139, 141-143, 204

cemetery *see* Memorial; Potočari
Chetnik 2, 54-56, 59, 61, 82-83, 85-87, 116, 134, 136
Clinton, Pres. Bill 32, 106, 186, 189
column *see* Death March
concentration camps 31, 163, 203, 210, 217; Keraterm 163; Omarska 163; Trnopolje 163
crimes against humanity 4, 6, 31-32, 173, 185, 199-200, 204, 208
Croatia *see* Yugoslavia

Dautbašić-Klempić, Fatima, M.D. 5, 81-90, 94-95, 98, 204
Dayton Accords *see* Dayton Peace Agreement
Dayton Agreement *see* Dayton Peace Agreement
Dayton-Paris Agreement *see* Dayton Peace Agreement
Dayton Peace Accords *see* Dayton Peace Agreement
Dayton Peace Agreement 2-3, 16, 26, 168, 203, 209-211, 213; Dayton Accords 2, 17, 26, 209; Dayton Agreement 2, 26, 30-31, 209, 212; Dayton-Paris Agreement 209; Dayton Peace Accords 2, 26; The General Framework Agreement for Peace in Bosnia and Herzegovina 2, 26, 30, 209; Paris Protocol 209
Death March 2-3, 5, 7-10, ***14***, 16, 23, 30, 81, 86-87, 89-90, 95, 98-99, 101, 103, 106-107, 121-123, 136-137, 150, 167, 187, 191-192; column 2, 46, 53-54, 68-70, 96, 100, 114-115, 122, 135
denial 17, 20, 21, 22-23, 32, 79, 80, 109-110, 149, 155, 158, 161-162, 170-171, 173-174, 186, 203, 206-208, 210-213, 216-219, 221, 222
Djindjić, Zoran 6, 159
Doctors Without Borders *see* MSF
Dodik, Milorad 160
Drina river 8, 40, 67, 71, 151, 162
Dubrave 8, 11, 86, 99, 117, 136, 147
DUTCHBAT *see* Peacekeepers

Erdemović, Dražen 100, 110
EU 1, 2, 61, 109, 164, 170-171, 174, 176, 188
European Union *see* EU
execution sites, primary *see* Branjevo; Kozluk; Kravica Warehouse; Orahovac; Petkovci Dam; Pilica Cultural Center

Federation of BiH 8, 10, 30, 189, 202, 209-211
Foča 8, 61, 179, 200-201

General Framework Agreement for Peace in Bosnia and Herzegovina *see* Dayton Peace Agreement
genocide: definition 31; stages 216-18
Genocide Memorial *see* Memorial; Potočari
Goražde 4, 8, 29, 205

Hadžibulić, Mafija 149, 192
The Hague *see* ICTY
Hasanović, Hajro 96, 99-100
Hasanović, Hasan Aziz 5, 17, 19-25, 28, 43-44, 62, 82, 84, 90, 103-112, 126, 132, 139, 158, 165, 184, 187, 190-192, 204-205, 221-222
Hasanović, Hasan Sejfo 5, 25, 90-103, 167
Hasanović, Hasib 90, 96, 98-101
Hasanović, Haso 5, 25, 57, 113-119, 146, 222
Hasanović, Husein 82, 103, 106
Hasanović, Mevludin 199
Hasanović, Omer 82, 139, 187
Hasić, Ahmo 5, 23, 36-43
Helsinki Committee for Human Rights of Serbia *see* Biserko, Sonja
High Representative *see* HR
Hodžić, Refik 41
Hotel Fontana 6, 8, 128
HR 1, 3, 142, 189, 211, 213
Humanitarian Law Center *see* Kandić, Nataša

Index

Huseinović, Hakija 6, 43–50, 146, 190
Husić, Sabiha 6, 23, 201–202

ICC 1, 4, 31–32, 173, 185
ICJ 1, 31, 109, 130, 173, 180, 185, 210
ICMP 1, 3. 7, 99, 100, 121, 138, 140, 148, 184, 186–188, 190
ICTY 1, 3, 5, 6, 7, 18, 22–26, 31–32, 38, 48–49, 109, 111, 118, 125, 128, 142, 154–155, 157–158, 162–163, 165, 169, 172–179, 181–182, 184–186, 188, 200, 203, 210–211
IFOR 1, 3, 141
International Commission on Missing Persons *see* ICMP
International Court of Justice *see* ICJ
International Criminal Court *see* ICC
International Criminal Tribunal for the former Yugoslavia *see* ICTY
Inzko, Valentin 213
Islamophobia 161, 164, 215
Izetbegović, Alija 6, 39, 209

Jadar river 9, 97, 123
JNA 1, 3–4, 10, 29, 55, 63, 90–92, 95, 146, 160, 166–167, 178
joint criminal enterprise 173–174, 180, 208

Kamenice Hill 7, 9, 46, 54, 86, 96–98, 120–121
Kandić, Nataša 6, 168, 177–182
Karadžić, Radovan 2, 6, 16, 42, 49, 79–80, 109, 157, 162–163, 172, 186, 211–212, 215
Karremans, Thomas 6, 128
Keraterm *see* concentration camps
Kladanj 9, 46, 48, 56–57, 66, 137, 147, 189
Konjević Polje 9, 38, 52, 55–56, 64, 70–71, 114–115, 123, 136
Korač, Žarko 6, 159–165
Kosovo *see* Yugoslavia
Kozluk 9, *112*, 138–139, 150, 184
Kravica Warehouse 5, 6, 8–10, 46, 48–*50*, 54, 56, 97, 114, 161–162, 184
Krstić, Radislav 49
Kulaglić, Amir 182

Lolići 9, 47, 115

Macedonia *see* Yugoslavia
Mandžić, Nesib 6, 38, 125–130
Mašović, Amor 99, 179
medical care in Srebrenica *see* Doctors Without Borders; MSF
Mehmedović, Hatidža 208, 220–222
Memorial *see* Memorial Center; Potočari
Memorial Center 25–26, 189–190; Battery Factory 7–8, 10, 19, 28, 30, 86, *127*, 189–190; Cemetery 19, 26, 63, 78, 102, 106–107, 110, 118, 132, 149, 189–192, 208; Genocide Memorial 3, 5, 19, 26, 44, 103, 141, 177; Memorial 3, 19, 26, 108, 110, 177, 208; Srebrenica-Potočari Genocide Memorial 5, 18, 184, *191*; Srebrenica-Potočari Memorial Center and Cemetery 184, 189; *see also* Potočari
Milići 9, 63, 140, 203
Milošević, Slobodan 6, 15, 17, 25, 28–29, 126, 157–160, 167–172, 174–175, 178, 181–182, 186, 206, 209–212, 215–216
Mladić, Ratko 2, 6–8, 37–38, 42, 46, 49, 57, 63, 79, 109–110, 118–119, 125, 128–129, 153–155, 157, 161–163, 172, 181, 186, 203, 211–212
Montenegro *see* Yugoslavia
Morillon, Philippe 7, 53, 66, 93–94, 104–105, 204, 208
Mostar 32, 157, 164, 182
mother's associations 5, 20, 100, 132, 137, 141, 206, 208, 221–222; women's associations 20, 137–138, 140, 142, 184, 188–189
MSF (Médecins Sans Frontières; Doctors Without Borders) 1, 3–4, 52, 83–84, 86, 95, 129
Mustafić, Alija 144, 146–149
Mustafić, Fuad 146, 148
Mustafić, Hasan 143–144, 146–147
Mustafić, Mirsad 144, 146–147
Mustafić, Nura 7, 87, 143–150, 169, 192, 222

NATO 1, 3, 30, 129, 145, 164, 174
Nezuk 3, 9, 16, 59, 90, 99, 101–102, 191
NGO 1, 3, 137, 141, 148, 182, 201
Nova Kasaba 9, 55, 60, 63–64, 75–76, 114
Nuhanović, Hasan 7, 44, 49, 129, 141–142
Nuhanović, Ibro 28, 38, 128–129
Nukić, Ramiz 7, 9–10, 46–48, 119–124

Office of the High Representative *see* OHR
OHR 1, 3, 31, 189, 211, 213
Omanović, Ćamila 7, 38, 128–129
Omarska *see* concentration camps
Orahovac 7, 9, 48–49, *62*, 184
Orić, Mevludin 7, 48, 50–61, 117
Orić, Naser 7, 46, 52, 116–117
OSCE 1, 3, 130
Osmanović, Edin 150, 152
Osmanović, Nermin 150–154
Osmanović, Ramo 7, 146, 150–154
Osmanović, Saliha 7, 23–24, 44, 140, 146, 148, 150–156, 169, 189–191, 221–222

Paris Protocol *see* Dayton Peace Agreement

Pavlović, Dušan 79
Peace March 3, 63, 97, 101, 191–192
Peacekeepers 1, 2, 4, 30, 205, 208; Canadian Battalion 1, 2, 8, 15, 30, 94, 205; Canadian Peacekeepers 94, 205; CANBAT 1, 30, 94; Dutch Battalion 1, 2, 15–16, 30, 68, 85, 94–96, 127–129, 189, 190, 205–207; DUTCHBAT 1, 2, 6, 15, 30, 128, 206; Dutch Peacekeepers 8, 38, 205–206
Petkovci dam 5, 9, 62, 75, *80*, 184
Petkovci School 9, *21*–22, 62, 78, 80
Pilica 38, 40; Cultural Center 10, 110–*112*, 184; School 38
playground massacre 3, 15, 66, 84, 93, 104–105, 152, 204
Potočari 3, 16, 18–20, 26, 28, 30, 37–38, 41, 44, 46, 52, 54–55, 60, 63, 67–68, 70–71, 76, 78, 85–86, 89, 92, 96, 99–102, 106, 110, 112–113, 117–118, 120, 124–125, *127*–129, 132, 135–136, 141–142, 145–148, 152–153, 155, 181, 184, 188–192, 204, 206, 208, 222; *see also* Memorial Center
Praljak, Slobodan 157–158, 165, 172–174, 182
Prijedor 163, 210, 217
psychological issues 17, 25, 93, 193; PTSD (post-traumatic stress disorder) 196–198, 200; trauma 17, 23–25, 87, 95, 100, 102–105, 108, 112, 117, 119, 121, 136, 194, 196–199, 200, 202; treatment providers 6, 78, 137, 159, 199
PTSD (post-traumatic stress disorder) *see* psychological issues

RECOM/REKOM 1, 20, 181–182
"Remembering Srebrenica" 44
Republika Srpska *see* RS
Residual Mechanism for Criminal Tribunals 186
RS 1, 6, 8–10, 15–17, 20, 27–28, 30, 32, 60–61, 106, 109–110, 128, 142, 160, 163–164, 181, 185, 189, 202–203, 209–210, 212, 218, 221

Safe Area 4, 8, 10, 15, 19, 30, 52, 66, 93–94, 145, 188, 204–205, 208, 217–218
Sandići meadow 10, 46, 49, 62, 70, 115, 136, 146, 147, 192
Sarajevo 4, 10, 15, 18, 20, 24–25, 28–30, 32–33, 38, 44–45, 49–50, 108, 119, 125, 130, 133, 141, 143, 153, 158, 162, 166–167, 169, 172, 181, 186, 188, 190, 196, 201, 203, 205, 207, 210, 220
Scorpions 6, 168–169, 177, 179–181
Scream for Me Sarajevo 25
Serbia *see* Yugoslavia
Šešelj 165, 174–175
Slovenia *see* Yugoslavia
Srebrenica-Potočari Genocide

Index

Memorial *see* Memorial Center; Potočari
Srebrenica-Potočari Memorial Center and Cemetery *see* Memorial Center; Potočari
Stewart, Colonel Bob 208
Sućeska 10, 45–49, 118
Suljić, Šefik 41–43, 158
Šušnjari 10, 53, 68, 96, 113, 121

Tito 4, 15, 28, 49, 166, 178
Tolimir, Zdrako 49
trauma *see* psychological issues
Tribunal *see* ICTY
Trnopolje *see* concentration camps
Tuzla 4, 10–11, 16, 30, 32, 37–38, 46, 48, 52–53, 59, 64–66, 68, 70–71, 77, 83–84, 86–88, 93, 97, 99–100, 102, 106, 113–114, 116–118, 121–123, 125, 135–138, 140–142, 146–148, 154–155, 158, 165, 179, 182, 186–189, 199, 205, 208

Udrč mountain 10, 54, 97–98
UNDP (United Nations Development Program) 1, 143
UNESCO 1, 33, 157
UNHCR (United Nations High Commissioner for Refugees) 1, 4, 8, 10, 83, 126
United Nations 1–4, 7–8, 10, 15–16, 19, 22–23, 25, 30–32, 37–38, 52–53, 56, 64, 66,-68, 71, 84–86, 93–96, 102, 105, 109, 113, 116, 124–125, 127–128, 137, 145, 162, 185, 188, 189, 201, 203–208, 211, 217–218
United Nations Protection Force *see* UNPROFOR
UNPF (United Nations Peacekeeping Force) 1
UNPROFOR 1, 4, 7, 14, 52, 93, 203, 206, 208
USAID 1, 4

verdicts 25, 31, 130, 157, 162, 173–177, 180, 203
Vojvodina *see* Yugoslavia
Vučić, Aleksandar 168, 170–171, 182
Vuk Karadžić school 38, 115
Vukovar 10, 90–91, 95, 167, 171

war crimes 3–4, 6, 25, 32, 108, 110, 142, 157–158, 172–174, 179–181, 185–186, 188, 199, 201, 204, 208, 211
WIB 1, 7, 137–138, 165–171, 175, 177–178
Women in Black *see* WIB
women's associations *see* mother's associations

Yugoslav People's Army *see* JNA
Yugoslavia: Croatia 4, 6, 10, 15, 27–29, 51, 55, 63, 90, 92, 102, 130, 144, 157, 159, 160–161, 164–165, 167, 172–174, 178–179, 181, 209, 212; history 3, 4, 6, 12, 15–17, 25, 27–29, 32–33, 91, 138, 143, 151, 157–161, 164, 166–168, 172, 176–179, 181–183, 185–186, 188, 199, 207, 215–217, 221; Kosovo 6, 15, 28, 55, 170, 172, 175–176, 179, 215; Macedonia 15, 28, 133–134, 160; Montenegro 15, 27–29, 144; Serbia 2, 5–8, 15, 22–23, 27–29, 36, 38, 40, 42, 45, 55–56, 63–64, 70–72, 74, 89–90, 92, 109–110, 115–116, 125–126, 129–130, 133, 144, 146, 151, 154–155, 157–182, 188, 200, 205–210, 212, 215, 217, 221; Slovenia 15, 28–29, 45, 102, 160; Vojvodina 15, 28, 165

Zagreb 10, 51–52, 118, 133, 144–145, 157, 164, 186
Zajović, Staša 7, 165–171, 177–178, 222
Žepa 4, 10, 29, 44, 48, 67, 126, 188, 205
Živinice 8, 11, 46, 48, 103, 154
Zvornik 11, 41, 63, 71, 92, 94, 116, 137

CPSIA information can be obtained
at www.ICGtesting.com
Printed in the USA
LVHW051402100423
743966LV00011B/962

9 781476 683348